W9-DCW-687

# PRINCIPLES AND PRIVILEGE

# PRINCIPLES
## AND
# PRIVILEGE

———

*Two Women's Lives on a
Georgia Plantation*

FRANCES A. KEMBLE
*and*
FRANCES A. BUTLER LEIGH

With a New Introduction by Dana D. Nelson

*Ann Arbor Paperbacks*

THE UNIVERSITY OF MICHIGAN PRESS

F
290
K315
1995

1998   1997   1996   1995     4  3  2  1


A CIP catalogue record for this book is available from the British Library.


**Library of Congress Cataloging-in-Publication Data**

Kemble, Fanny, 1809–1893.
   Principles and privilege : two women's lives on a Georgia
plantation / Frances A. Kemble and Frances A. Butler Leigh ; with a
new introduction by Dana D. Nelson.
      p.   cm. — (Ann Arbor paperbacks)
   ISBN 0-472-09522-6 (alk. paper). — ISBN 0-472-06522-X (pbk. :
alk. paper)
   1. Plantation life—Georgia—History—19th century.  2. Slavery—
Georgia.  3. Slaves—Georgia—Social conditions.  4. Georgia—
History—1775–1865.  5. Reconstruction—Georgia.  6. Kemble, Fanny,
1809–1893—Diaries.  7. Leigh, Frances Butler, 1838–1910.
I. Leigh, Frances Butler, 1838–1910.  II. Title.
F290.K315   1994
975.8'03—dc20                                              94-29442
                                                              CIP

# INTRODUCTION

In 1832, British actress Fanny Kemble (1809–93) came to the United States for a two-year acting tour with her father, Charles Kemble, the renowned Shakespearian actor. There she would meet and marry a wealthy young Philadelphian, Pierce (Mease) Butler (1810–67), a man who was in line to inherit huge plantations and hundreds of slaves in Georgia. Fanny and Pierce had two daughters, Sarah (1835–1908) and Frances (1838–1910). Delving into Butler family history before and after Fanny Kemble yields a rich story—one that mixes Britain and the United States, North and South, slave and free, Yankee and Confederate, and abolitionists and proslavery apologists, legislators, thespians, novelists, planters, and sharecroppers. The Butler/Kemble legacy is fascinating and well documented. Of special interest for this volume are the voices of two women, Fanny Kemble and her namesake daughter, Frances Butler Leigh.

In 1863, Fanny Kemble published a book she had composed during her residence on her husband's Georgia plantations in the winter of 1838–39. Her *Journal of a Residence on a Georgian Plantation* (1863) chronicles her dismay at the conditions of the slaves there along with her observations on the manners and customs of the free

Southerners. Her daughter Frances Butler Leigh's *Ten Years on a Georgia Plantation*, published in London in 1883, registers her radically different impressions of Southern culture along with the record of her struggles and successes at running the plantations single-handedly after her father's death in the 1860s. The daughter's memoir at no point mentions the mother's, yet her scrupulous silence itself encodes a response to her mother.[1]

These two texts, read together, provide an important record in the history of Anglo-American women during the nineteenth-century (offering as well some measure of insight into the lives of African American women during the antebellum and Reconstruction periods). Contradicting stereotyped notions that well-to-do women in Victorian America lived in political naïveté, both Fanny Kemble and Frances Butler Leigh strongly assert their political awareness, personal ambitions, intellectual and moral accountability, financial acumen, and physical abilities. What makes the two texts compelling as a pair is the pronounced difference in political sympathy between mother and daughter that exists alongside the many congruences in their personalities and literary styles. The two books weave a rich—and not always harmonious—dialogue between a mother and daughter in the nineteenth-century United States.

## Family Histories

Fanny Kemble became a sensation on the United States theatrical scene in 1832. She was the third of five children born to Charles Kemble and Maria-Therese DeCamp Kemble, a family three generations strong in theatrical careers (including actress Sarah Siddons, Charles's sister) when Fanny was born in 1809. Fanny began her own

acting career at the age of nineteen as part of an attempt
to save her father's Theatre Royal Covent Garden from
sale by creditors. A great success in her leading roles,
Fanny attracted crowds that temporarily saved the the-
ater from insolvency. Soon after, Charles talked her into a
two-year American tour. She agreed to help raise money
for the still faltering Covent Garden, despite her lack of
fondness for either acting or the thought of visiting
America.

Despite her reluctance, Fanny was an even bigger success at acting in the United States Her vibrancy and energy attracted many admirers even while it garnered her
criticism. However unorthodox her behavior, people flocked
by the droves to see her perform in Boston, New York,
Philadelphia, and Baltimore. There were men who followed
her from city to city; the most devoted was Pierce Butler,
who even joined the theatrical music ensemble traveling
with the Kembles to remain near Fanny.

If acting was the legacy of the British Kembles, the
American Butlers had a notable legacy of their own. Major Pierce Butler (1744–1822), the grandfather of Fanny's
suitor, was born as the third son of Irish nobility. With no
prospects for inheritance, he accepted a regimental commission in the British army at the age of twelve; by the
age of twenty-two, he had been promoted to Major and
was serving in the American colonies. He married the
daughter of a well-to-do merchant and slave trader in
South Carolina. Within in year of their marriage, Polly
Middleton Butler inherited a vast estate and hundreds of
slaves from her maternal grandmother, providing her husband with the opportunity for a new career as a planter.
Butler apparently liked it, for in 1773, in the midst of colonial rumblings and discontent, Major Butler sold his
regimental commission and used the money to begin pur-

chasing lands in Georgia, where he planned to raise cotton and rice.

Major Butler, like many American colonists, had divided allegiances during the Revolution. He contributed to the patriot militia, but refused to sign the Declaration of Independence. By the beginning of the war, Major Butler had become a political figure in South Carolina, serving as their delegate to the Constitutional Congress and eventually as their first United States Senator. In Philadelphia, Butler's most enduring claim to fame might be the fugitive slave clause to the Constitution, which was unanimously adopted by the Congress as the second paragraph of section 2, article 4.

By the late 1800s, having continued to purchase lands in Georgia, Butler commanded some of the most potentially productive tracts of land and largest communities of slaves in the Southern states, thereby garnering influence that was social, economic, political, and legislative. A strong-willed man, Butler aimed to control the legacy he had built from beyond the grave, refusing his patrimony to his only surviving son (Thomas, whom he felt was weak-willed), and bestowing it instead on the sons of his eldest daughter, Sarah Butler Mease. The condition for the sons' inheritance was that they abandon their own patronym and legally replace it with "Butler" by their sixteenth birthday. The first two sons, Thomas and John, refused to do so, but the youngest, Major Butler's namesake, did, ensuring the continuance of the Butler lands in the Butler name, under "Butlers" of whom the Major approved.[2]

So, when Pierce wooed and won the heart of the vocally abolitionist Fanny Kemble in 1834 (he was twenty-four; she was twenty-five), he was in line to own some of the largest and most productive plantations in the United

States.[3] Fanny either did not know this, or she did not see this potentially explosive issue as an immediate concern.[4] Other factors may have had larger, more immediate weight; the circumstances surrounding her decision to marry were emotionally tumultuous. Accepting Pierce's proposal meant enduring continued separation from her family as well as breaking her promise to her father to tour yet another year in England. And, in the midst of Pierce's courtship, her beloved aunt and traveling companion, Adelaide De Camp, or "Dall," was injured in a carriage accident and died after a protracted illness. Perhaps it was mourning the loss of Aunt Dall's affection that made Fanny so suddenly determined to marry Pierce, a choice Fanny's family and friends and biographers have puzzled over. Whether she questioned their compatibility, it is clear that Fanny did speculate at the cost to her sense of self that nineteenth-century norms of marriage would entail. In a letter she wrote to Catherine Sedgwick on May 31, she postscripted to her signature, "Fanny Kemble," this interesting remark: "I don't think I shall ever make out to sign anything but that!"[5]

But marry she did, signing over the Kemble name and the proceeds from her share of the Kemble tour to her father before his return to England. Shortly thereafter, Fanny decided to publish the journal she had kept recording her impressions of America during her acting tour. She had arranged the book contract before her marriage, thinking that the money could provide additional support for Aunt Dall. Deciding to give the money to Dall's sister, Victoire, Fanny resolved to go ahead with publication, despite Pierce's admonitions.

*Journal of Frances Anne Butler* (1835) was a scandal for the Butler family. Packed with satirical quips about leading American citizens, and often derisive of United

States culture, the book was widely scorned by reviewers both in the United States and in Britain.[6] Appearing as it did in an era when ridiculing American culture as "provincial" was a favorite sport in British presses, the *Journal* hit a sore spot in her newly adopted country.[7] If cultural anxiety was America's, *gender* anxiety apparently was transatlantic: Fanny was chided as "un-sexed" and "unlady-like" for her outspokenness both in England and the United States.[8] Embarrassed by the public stir, all coming as a result of the very forwardness and confidence of opinion he had earlier admired, Pierce was not at all receptive to the notion of Fanny's keeping a journal when, several years later, he decided the family should spend a winter in Georgia overseeing the management of his newly inherited plantations.

Fanny and Pierce Butler arrived at the plantations in late December, 1838, with their two young daughters— Sarah, aged three, and Frances Ann, newly born. The two girls would grow up on opposite sides of the slave issue. Sarah, or Sally, as she was called, certainly the more impressionable of the two on this trip and constantly worried over by her mother for the way she seemed to enjoy being catered to by the slaves, would grow up opposed to slavery, marry an avowed abolitionist, and work on behalf of the Union during the Civil War. Frances—or Fan—after only a brief visit back to the South in 1861, would become an ardent supporter of the Confederate cause and a proslavery apologist. Several years after returning to run the Georgia plantations after the war, Fan would marry a British proslavery sympathizer.

Apparently Fanny did look forward to the trip to Georgia in 1838. Shunning publicly activist abolitionism, she believed she could do more good privately by ameliorating slave conditions and by convincing her husband through example of the humanity of slaves and the inhumanity of slavery. Fanny, as nineteenth-century women often did, kept a journal addressed as a series of letters to her close friend Elizabeth Dwight Sedgwick (an educator who ran a girl's school and sister-in-law of the famous novelist, Catherine Maria Sedgwick).[9] When the Butler family discovered this, they mounted steady and vociferous pressure against her publishing the journal. Having several years earlier dropped plans to publish an antislavery tract at Pierce's entreaty, Fanny once again bowed to family pressure, even refusing a request for it from the prominent abolitionist Lydia Maria Child.[10] Not until years after her divorce, fearing her native England would back the Confederacy rather than the Union, did Fanny decide to publish the *Journal of a Residence on a Georgian Plantation*.

While her *Journal* had much to say on the condition of slaves and on Fanny's feelings about slavery, it is largely silent about her marriage's escalating conflicts. The discord between Fanny and Pierce over their opposing attitudes toward slavery was henceforward to be an issue, each believing the other would change if importuned frequently and passionately enough.[11] Their disagreement on this volatile issue was coupled with a temperamental incompatibility that had always distressed Fanny. According to Pierce himself, she was frequently threatening to leave him from the first year of their marriage. Pierce seems to have fueled the fires, although family papers are more circumspect on this topic. One of Fanny's biographers, Fanny Kemble Wister, hints broadly that Pierce was living with a slave woman during his visits to Georgia when unattended by Fanny. It seems also that he had affairs with numerous other women (in fact, he engaged in a duel with a business partner, James Schott, who alleged that he caught Pierce in bed with Mrs. Schott),[12] and he was later suspected by Fanny of improper relations with their children's nurse in England.

Whatever the causes for dissension, their life together was undoubtedly stormy and unhappy, although, like many couples, they had an extraordinarily difficult time separating. There was a series of estrangements in the United States and Britain, each followed by intense negotiations between the two. Finally, Pierce made Fanny sign a contract that required her to give up her close friendship with Elizabeth and Charles Sedgwick on condition of being able to have access to her daughters. Fanny "broke" the contract according to Pierce, when he conveyed to her a letter from the Sedgwicks, which she opened it, assuming that he wished her to do so. It was a trap he used as a rationale to kick her out of the house for the last time.

Clearly it is reasonable to ask: why did Fanny choose to marry a man like Pierce? The two were not compatible temperamentally or intellectually. Fanny Kemble Wister, Sarah's granddaughter, wryly observes that Pierce's attendance at the Pennsylvania Constitutional Convention in October, 1837, was "the only time that he is known to have participated in anything but his own pleasure" until the years after the war.[13] Fanny, in contrast, took a definite joy in her ability to work and to earn money. A union of minds never seemed possible: Pierce, as Fanny at one point generously described him, was "mathematical" and factual, while Fanny was a lover of fiction and philosophy.[14] And they had radically different opinions as to a woman's "place": Pierce expected unquestioning and silent submission, and Fanny firmly believed in maintaining her own moral agency, arguing that her accountability was only to God, and certainly not to Pierce.

Speculating that each was blinded by physical attraction during their courtship, most commentators have been unable to find other ways to explain what could initially have bound the two together in what was to be such a spectacularly unhappy union. Most note that while Fanny's life with Pierce was filled with alternating scenes of anguish, anger, and affection, her life after the divorce was placid, and she never chose to remarry. What seems better worth analyzing than their initial infatuation is the intensity of their married relationship, paradoxically growing stronger as the love apparently soured. We could call that "fatal attraction." From a less romanticized angle, however, we might usefully consider the toxic quality of the cement that held them so strongly after their courtship progressed into marriage. One of the deadliest dynamics a relationship can enter is for each to try to change the other into an ideal rather than accepting the partner as she or he is. Throughout their marriage Fanny and Pierce held fiercely to their respective ideals—Fanny wanting Pierce to live up to her ethical and artistic passions, Pierce wanting a famous woman made docile and acquiescent wife.[15] In each case, the image did real damage to the *actual* person. As a consequence, their interaction was grounded in manipulation, force, and entreaty as neither was willing to surrender to the mold the other had created.

In the divorce suit that he filed in Philadelphia in 1848, Pierce contended that Fanny had "willfully, maliciously, and without due cause, deserted him" in 1845. Divorce had become steadily more accepted in United States courts during the years after the Revolution—in fact, the idea of divorce was based on the same theoretical appeals by which the Puritans left England and the American colonies declared their independence over a hundred years later.[16] No matter how much more easily accepted by the legal community, the Kemble divorce was a spectacle for the Philadelphia social scene. Pierce employed among his legal counsel Daniel Webster and George Mifflin Dallas, who then was serving as the vice president of the United States under James Polk. Fanny herself had an impressive array of lawyers, including Elizabeth Sedgwick's husband, Charles, and Massachusetts senator Rufus Choate. She initially planned to contest the divorce and requested a jury trial. But when it became clear that Pierce was to be awarded custody of the daughters, she backed down on the condition that she be given the mortgage to the Butler property in what is now Germantown, Pennsylvania; $1500 per year in support; and the right to visit her daughters for two months each summer.

After the divorce became final in 1849, Fanny immediately resumed her maiden name and continued supporting herself in the United States and England by giving dramatic readings and by publishing a number of memoirs as well as some of her poetry. Single life for Fanny was productive, intellectually satisfying, and much happier. She lived for a time in a cottage next to her friends Elizabeth and Charles Sedgwick in Massachusetts. After her daughters were married, she lived periodically with each of them.

Pierce, meanwhile, fared less well, and he did so with a flair that made it clear that drama was not only Fanny's forte but his as well. Shortly after the divorce, he published an account of *why* he divorced Fanny, a red leatherbound volume entitled *Mr. Butler's Statement* (1850), which he presented to friends and acquaintances. His penchant for gambling, both at the card table and in the stock market, finally got him into trouble. In 1859, he was forced to sell much of his Philadelphia property and, finally, his share of the Georgia slaves, to make good on his debts. A sensational event for the public, Pierce's auction was one of the largest single-plantation slave auctions in U. S. history; even the New York *Tribune* sent a reporter to cover it. It was a devastating event for the slaves, most of whose families had worked on the various Butler plantations for generations. The auction made some effort to preserve nuclear families, small comfort to members of extended kin networks that composed Butler's "holdings." Four hundred thirty-six slaves were auctioned, netting Pierce over three hundred thousand dollars. Four hundred thirty-six dollars of that was returned to the slaves in the form of a silver dollar piece that Pierce personally gave each departing slave, providing a tableau for newspaper cartoonists to lampoon nationwide. From a cynical point of view, selling the slaves was a stroke of financial wizardry: since the Emancipation Proclamation was to free those same slaves only a few years later, Pierce was able to profit rather than losing his inheritance with their freedom.

Since reaching her majority in 1856, Sarah had refused to travel to the South out of opposition to slavery, despite her great affection for her father. Less emotionally close to her mother, Sarah nonetheless had in common with Fanny a love of writing. Sarah contributed a number of historical, travel, and nature essays, to the *Atlantic Monthly*, as well as keeping a Civil War diary that was printed for the first time in 1978[17] In the same year as the famous auction, Sarah married Dr. Owen Jones Wister (1825–96). They had one child, named after his father. Dan, as they called their son, would grow up a writer too, producing one of the paradigmatic western novels of the United States, *The Virginian* (1902). He was also to preface his aunt's *Ten Years on a Georgia Plantation* with a poem about the end of the Civil War, "Brothers Again." Interestingly enough, his attitudes about race and region probably ran in closer sympathy with his grandfather, aunt, and uncle—views that are evidenced in his 1906 novel *Lady Baltimore*. Whatever his political leanings, he was always very close emotionally to his grandmother Fanny.

In his last trip to the Georgia plantations before the outbreak of the Civil War, Pierce was accompanied by Fan. Daughter and father were together in Charleston when war was declared on April 12, 1862. Although many friends and even Sarah expected Pierce to join the Confederate army, he returned with Fan to Philadelphia. Shortly after, he was arrested by the U. S. marshal under suspicion of gunrunning for the Confederacy. His imprisonment was brief, but it embittered Pierce. He gained his release by promising not to betray Union interests, and for the remainder of the war, he kept quiet about his opinions, as did Fan. But when Lincoln died in 1865, Pierce refused to drape his windows in black, the customary sign in Philadelphia of respect for deceased dignitaries. An attack against his house for this outrage was narrowly averted by the influence of a generous local abolitionist, Morris Davis. Pierce departed Philadelphia for Georgia shortly thereafter, followed by Fan.

Pierce expected his former slaves to return to the Butler properties to find their families. His plan was to be there ready to offer them sharecropping deals that would allow him to continue to profit from their labor. His arrival disappointed the many who had already returned hoping that the land would belong to them as part of the Confederacy's defeat. Disillusionment ran both ways. When Pierce and Fan arrived, the plantation houses had been gutted and stripped. The project was going to be a new one for the father-daughter team. They faced strikingly altered relations with the freed slaves. No matter how much they appealed to the imperious status of their former relationship and their continuing economic clout, the men and women now enjoying a sense of freedom found ways to resist by leaving the fields early, buying their own land with earned proceeds from the Butlers, purchasing their supplies off the plantation, or dressing in ways that defied their former slave status.

Fan returned to Philadelphia for the hot summers of 1866–67, but Pierce chose to stay, working hard to salvage a profit from the plantations. He apparently contracted malaria in mid-August of 1867 and died shortly thereafter. Fanny Kemble, who was residing in England at the time, immediately returned to the United States to be with her daughters. Sarah was so affected by her father's death that she suffered from a temporary loss of memory, but Fan translated her grief into determination. She single-handedly overtook the management of the plantations, plunging in with grit and intelligence.

Unlike her mother before her, Fan had little patience with the complaints from the people who worked the plantations. Her concern was "rice, rice, rice" (303), and the freed slaves were, in her estimation, too often an impediment to her crop goals. She considered bringing in Chinese laborers and worked to update and purchase new machinery to aid with the crop effort. Like her mother, she strove to improve the hospital on Butler's Island and to provide a school for the children. In the midst of her efforts, she was visited by a party of British and Philadelphians. One of the group was the Reverend James Wentworth Leigh, known affectionately as "Jimbo" among his friends for his blackface part in a Cambridge minstrel show. Just months later, Fan returned his visit in Stoneleigh, England, chaperoned by Sarah. Before she left, they became engaged, and they married the following year in London.

After a year in England, hearing troublesome reports from Georgia, James and Frances Leigh returned in 1873 to the plantations, with new plans for improved profits, including the replacement of African American labor with British workers (it failed dismally). James Leigh was enthusiastic about the plantations, and was apparently well liked by the workers. One of his projects was to oversee the construction of an Episcopal church at Darien for the African American parishioners, which he named St. Cyprian's. As in years before, the family traveled north for the summer to avoid the malaria season. Fan gave birth to their first child, Alice Dudley Leigh, in Philadelphia in 1874 and their second, Pierce Butler Leigh, on the plantation, in 1876. Their son lived only twenty-four hours. That trauma, combined with falling crop prices, flooding, and constant difficulties procuring the quality of labor that they felt necessary, influenced their decision to leave the plantations for good.

They sailed to England in 1877 with Fanny. From this point, Fanny occasionally resided with the Leighs. Publicly, mother and daughter managed a good relationship, despite occasional strains—for instance, when Fanny refused to attend the christening ceremony for a second son, again named Pierce Butler Leigh, in 1879. Instead, she prayed "to avert . . . the evil omen of such a name."[18] Mother's and daughter's differences seem to have reached two distinct crisis points, the first during the Civil War, due to the heightened tensions and raised stakes of wartime and, of course, to Fanny's publication of the *Journal*. The second came some twenty years later, in the 1880s, when Fanny was preparing another memoir, *Records of a Later Life* (1882). One scholar has speculated that Frances Leigh composed *Ten Years on a Georgia Plantation* in reaction both to her mother's beginning work on the new memoirs and to the death of that second Pierce in 1880.[19] We do know, certainly, that on May 1, 1881, Fan wrote her mother, threatening that she would never forgive her if she printed "stories" about Pierce (she apparently forgave or overlooked the fact that these stories were in circulation largely thanks to her father's publishing them in *Mr. Butler's Statement*). She revealed that the "bitterness" she had always felt about her mother's publication of the Georgian *Journal* had prevented her from ever allowing a copy in her own household. Fan ended the letter by "imploring" her mother "not to alienate my affection from you entirely" by publishing such stories.[20] Fanny apparently respected her daughter's ultimatum, although it seems doubtful that she would have been any more explicit than she had been in the Georgian *Journal* or her 1847 memoir, *A Year of Consolation*. However thankful Fan may have felt at her mother's continuing discretion about Pierce, her own publication of *Ten Years on a Georgia Plantation* in effect drew another, political, line over which she forbade her mother to cross. They apparently negotiated a quiescent relationship in the years following by avoiding controversial topics—politics or Pierce—entirely.

Fan seems to have made a good choice of a partner in James Leigh. Her affection for her husband helped compensate for the fact that she did not particularly like residing in England. An American counterpoint to her mother, who got into so much trouble for her criticisms of the United States, Fan frequently complained of British citizens and culture. But James took it all with apparently good nature, having always regarded her as a "fair queen." Fanny approved of her daughter's choice of a husband despite their political differences and became very fond of James. Fanny passed away in 1893 at the Leigh home on Gloucester Place, while Fan was in the United States visiting Sarah. The two sisters sold off the Georgia properties in 1908. Sarah died that year at Butler place in Philadelphia; Fan passed away two years later in England. Her bereaved husband, who lived on thirteen years longer, had a memorial stained-glass window erected in the Hereford Cathedral. And Fan was remembered by a forty-two-day mourning period by the people at St. Cyprian's Church in Darien, Georgia, who draped in black the Mann School, which Fan had contributed much to funding.

## The Butler Plantations

The Georgia that Fanny visited in 1838 was a state firmly committed to plantation and slave culture. It was organized as a freeholding colony in 1733 by General James Oglethorpe. Despite an act in 1735 that forbade the importation or sale of Africans, settlers constantly found ways to circumvent the law. By 1750, it was repealed: Georgia officially embraced slavery. Wealthy aristocrats, hoping to duplicate the fantastic profits enjoyed by rice and indigo planters in South Carolina, began clearing the coast. At the same time, the newly discovered tidal-flow method made rice culture more feasible and profitable. The lucrative end of new technologies typically depending on cheap labor, this technological advance like later innovations, such as the steam engine and the cotton gin, led to an explosion in the importation and sale of slaves. In the following years, European settlers imported thousands of enslaved Africans: by the early 1800s, African and African-descended peoples formed anywhere from 70 to 80 percent of the total population of the tidewater counties of Camden, Glynn, McIntosh, and Liberty, where the Butler plantations were located.[21]

The statistically representative slave lived her or his life on a plantation with more than twenty slaves. But, as James Oakes has carefully observed, the statistically representative slaveholder had not hundreds but five or fewer.[22] Thus, the experience of the Butlers was *not* representative of the majority of free "white" Georgians, as Julia Smith points out: "during the nineteenth century the rice magnates of coastal Georgia, like their forebears and relatives along the Carolina coast, constituted the elite of the planter aristocracy."[23] Their wealth grew to even larger proportions because Georgia fields proved even more productive than South Carolinian lands. Thanks to that abundance, the planter aristocracy lived a comfortable life, predominantly away from the plantations where they made their profit. Most practiced local absentee management, residing mainly in inland Georgia cities and visiting the plantations usually only during the cooler, winter months. Preferring the cultural benefits of city life and having associated what was actually malaria with the "miasmatic air" of the warm, swampy coast, the planter elite argued that it was imperative to their lives and lifestyle to live inland.

If the sickle cell of African-descended peoples gave them some protection against malaria (and hence gave rise to the popular myth that only African slaves were suited for working along coastal Georgia), it provided them no protection against other hazards of being overworked and badly treated in an already taxing environment. As Smith observes, "it was an error to think that black laborers could withstand the humid summer climate in the South and that white laborers could not. Blacks suffered and died from the depleting effects of humidity and disease caused by unsanitary conditions, while white laborers refused to work in such an environment."[24] Contemporaries noticed that conditions were devastating the slaves. Basil Hall, a British officer traveling through the South felt the conclusion was unavoidable: these people were dying from the work combined with the climate on the rice plantations. He observes:

the most unhealthy work in which the slaves were employed, and in spite of every care, that they sank under
it in great numbers. The causes of this dreadful mortality, are constant moisture and heat of the atmosphere, together with the alternate floodings and drying
of the fields, on which the negroes are perpetually at
work, often ankle deep in mud, with their bare heads
exposed to the fierce rays of the sun.[25]

The belief that only people of African descent could work
the fields survived, then, in the face of contradictory evidence.

We see how powerful the mythology is in Fanny's observations on this subject. Trapped in ambivalence between
what she sees and what she has been told to be true, she
notes in one sentence that the slaves have "much *less* power
of resistance to disease" than "we" do, but noting in the
next that it is "impossible" for the "whites" to stay during
the summer (108). Fan also notices the poor health of the
freed African Americans, although with apparently less
ambivalence. She comments at one point that the freed
African Americans "seem to be dying out so fast" (308) This
note contradicts her repeated assertions that people of
African descent can endure work in the rice fields; as her
other observations document, the reverse seems more true.
But her point is strategic to a different agenda, coming as
it does in the context of arguments about African-descended peoples being debilitated by freedom, actually
degenerating, which was a popular scientific argument of
the period. Thus, for Fan, the fact that freed slaves died
in the field had to do with surrounding political, rather
than physical, conditions.

Many of the people who worked on the Butler plantations had come from areas in Africa where rice cultivation

was practiced.[26] Euro-Americans prized and adopted the cultural and technical expertise that the various Africans brought with them to America.[27] They devalued African cultures, languages, and religious traditions, but the Butler slaves were able to preserve all three to an unusual extent, according to Malcolm Bell, Jr., because of Major Butler's militaristic discipline on the plantations. The slaves were strictly prohibited from visiting other plantations or local towns. In their isolation, the slaves shared their home cultures with each other, creating a distinctly Africanized community—including their own peculiar dialect of English—that was remarked upon by local people.[28] Because the enforced social seclusion led to such a highly developed, close-knit community, the auction of half that community in 1859 was calamitous for *all* the Butler slaves. Of course, the policy that forged that community worked to the advantage of the Butlers, as Fan noted approvingly of Hampton Point (the name of one of the Butler's two Georgia plantations) in 1868. Further away from the "demoralizing effect" of the "Yankees" than Butler's Island, "here, everything moves on steadily and quietly, as it used to do in the old times" (288).

## Genre, Politics, and Truth

Mother and daughter share an intense love for the Georgia lands, and each balances narrative with sketches of the natural surroundings. Fanny clearly bequeathed to Fan her fine eye for detail: Fan's book frequently echoes her mother's lyrical descriptions of slow-moving rivers, of woods draped with mysterious Spanish moss and graced with magnolias. She also shares her mother's concerns to improve the beauty of the property by planting oranges, myrtles, and magnolias.

Despite their common tie to the lands, their narratives partake of distinct literary traditions and genres. Fanny's *Journal of a Residence on a Georgian Plantation* most immediately is a journal. Fanny wrote it, in a series of letters, as a record of her experiences for Elizabeth Sedgwick. But she also clearly aimed it for a larger audience from the start. Though she long refrained from publishing her journal, she circulated it through a close circle of friends and performed parts of it in private readings. Given the subject of Fanny's book, we can see that she positions herself within a burgeoning field of abolitionist literature. Lydia Maria Child, an eminent novelist, journalist, and historian, and a prominent abolitionist who edited the *National Anti-Slavery Standard* from 1832 to 1834, certainly recognized it as such. Abolitionist literature was situated within a larger field of didactic, or sentimental, fiction, a diverse body of literature that is finally receiving the close attention it deserves for the huge impact it had in nineteenth-century American culture.[29] Thus, Fanny's *Journal* stands in the nineteenth-century tradition of social critiques by women that includes Child's *Hobomok* (1824), Harriet Beecher Stowe's *Uncle Tom's Cabin* (1852), Rebecca Harding Davis's *Life in the Iron Mills* (1861), and Helen Hunt Jackson's *A Century of Dishonor* (1881).

We might also argue that Frances Butler Leigh's memoir, *Ten Years on a Georgia Plantation* takes a position within moral or didactic literature, trying to "teach" the postwar North (and pro-North sympathizers in England) a more favorable view of Anglo-Southerners. Because it relies less on sympathy than on ironic examples of Southern goodness and Northern ineptitude, it would be more accurate to connect Leigh's work to the body of apologist literature that came from the Reconstruction South—lit-

erature that would alternately elevate Southern values
over Northern ones and try to reestablish brotherly bonds
among whites across regional lines, such as Thomas Nelson
Page's *Red Rock* (1898), Thomas Dixon's *The Clansman*
(1905), as well as an ongoing body of defense and regional
literature by Southern women. This genre includes writ-
ers who use a diary format to depict the Civil War, such as
Phoebe Yates Pember's *A Southern Woman's Story* (1879),
Mary Boykin Chestnutt's *Civil War Diary* (1905), and Eliza
Frances Andrew's *The War-Time Journal of a Georgia Girl,
1864–1865* (1908), and women who write about postwar
life either through autobiographical formats or through
fiction, such as Susan Dabney Smeder's *Memories of a
Southern Planter* (1889), Patience Pennington's *A Woman
Rice Planter* (1913), Grace King's *Tales of a Time and Place*
(1892) and *Balcony Stories* (1893), and Kate Chopin's
*Bayou Folks* (1894) and *A Night in Acadie* (1897). All these
texts, with their sensitive portrayals of Anglo-American
Southern cultures, looked toward and took part in the re-
gionalist and local color literary movements.

The *Journal* and *Ten Years* have in common an appeal
to local color's predecessor: travel literature. This is a genre
that usually is characterized by some kind of objective
voice—usually belonging to an outsider—that describes the
countryside and the manners and customs of local people
for an audience who has not been there. Fanny is clearly
such an outsider—she was never again allowed back onto
the Georgia plantations after her visit. But Fan, too, is at
least at first a stranger to the culture she returns to after
the war. As Karen Sanchez-Eppler points out, she encounters there a radically different place, one where identities
and relationships must be forged anew. The strangeness
she experiences is clear in her frequent references to herself other former planters feeling like "aliens and foreign-

ers" (303).[30] She was in fact consulting travel literature
about Africa during this period, which provided support,
and perhaps direction, for her ethnological observations,
"finding how exactly the same characteristics show themselves among the negroes there" (262).[31]

Fanny composed her journal in a rough form while on
the plantations, revising it later and hoping to add to it
still further in subsequent visits down South. While Fan
wrote her book years later in retrospect, she managed to
duplicate the contemporary quality of her mother's journal by including letters that she had sent to family members from the plantation. Clearly, each woman is aware
that her firm stake in a particular political allegiance could
open her to charges of bias (in Fanny's case this became
precisely true). Each is motivated, however, by the urge to
tell a particular and pressing truth: for Fanny the truth
of slavery from the perspective of the suffering slaves, and
for Fan the truth of degraded Anglo-Southerners and their
valiant struggles at redeeming their war-trampled land.
Now that we can read these texts together, we can begin
to see more clearly the selective and partial quality of any
particular person's truth, whatever their ethical, moral,
or political stance. Both women believed passionately the
"truth" of their account, yet each conflicts with the other
at many points. What we might learn here is that "truths"
of history can only be recovered in the dynamics of dialogue—as a *multivalent* truth such as that we can begin
to see in the coded addresses of Fan to her mother and in
each woman's literary response to a larger and ongoing
cultural debate over region, race, and gender.

We should also learn, as Fanny notes of slave women
and as Fan notes of Anglo-Southern perspectives, that
dominant culture often refuses to give voice to the "truths"
of dominated and conquered peoples. We might say that

the "truth" of Butler plantation, then, was always contingent, depending to a large extent on the social position and the belief system held by any particular person. It is worth thinking about how, if we had, say, the journal of a female field-worker who was deeply Christian or the reminiscences of a "mulatto" house slave embittered by being forced to give sexual services to an overseer, we would have still more radically different versions of Butler plantation "truth."

## Fanny Kemble on the Butler Plantations

Fanny Kemble's *Journal of a Residence on a Georgian Plantation*, published in 1863 in London and the United States (appearing there the week after the Union victory at Gettysburg), remains one of the most useful accounts students of United States, African American, Southern, and women's history and literature have of plantation life in the South before the Civil War. Rich in detail and lyrical in style, the text might well be considered an American "classic" of the status of *Uncle Tom's Cabin* (1852), Harriet Beecher Stowe's famous novel, or the more recently rediscovered *Incidents in the Life of a Slave Girl* (1861), Harriet Jacobs's pseudonymous account of slave life. Like Jacobs's narrative, Kemble's account fell into long oblivion after the war. The *Journal* was castigated by Southern apologists for bias, exaggeration, and inaccuracy. Since the plantation fell into disrepair even before the war, some of the landmarks referred to by Fanny could not be seen by casual observers. Fanny does make sweeping generalizations about slavery on the basis of her limited experience in Georgia that simply did not hold true for other regions of the South. More particularly, she fudges—apparently intentionally—the date of the duel that she recounts between two Georgia men. As legal historian John Anthony Scott recounts in his authoritative edition of Kemble's journal in 1961, the geographical details of the *Journal* have been corroborated a century later by careful archeological digs and surveys. Her portrayals of the slave system in coastal Georgia have been substantially confirmed for that region by historians. As for the duel, as Scott notes, dueling was a fact not only of Georgian life but of Fanny's own experience with Pierce. Moving the date of the Hazzard/Wylly duel some six months to make it seem as though she had been there at the time allows her discreetly to convey some of the personal agony she experienced out of this social practice.[32] For whatever Fanny may not have known about slave conditions throughout the rest of the South, she paid particular attention to the people she met there and the voices she heard—enough to be able to record an instance of "signifying" among the slaves, when she notes the humorous slippage between pronunciations of "expect" and "suspect," guessing that the pun might well be intended (112).[33]

If post–Civil War commentators and historians managed for a time to bury Fanny's *Journal* in disapprobation, many contemporary reviewers admired it, noting its focus on the intense difficulties faced by slave women.[34] One of the particular achievements of Fanny's volume was to give voice to slave women who, in effect, had none. She not only recounts the day-to-day complaints of the Butler slave women but is fascinated with their personal voices and histories, weaving their names and words into a journal that becomes both theirs and hers. "I give you the woman's words" (153), she declares to Elizabeth, later agonizing that she cannot "write down the voice and look of abject misery" with which these women so often gave Fanny their narratives (167).

In telling their stories, Fanny grows in awareness of how the particular, gender-based oppression of slave women corresponds to her own subjugation in the legal and social systems of the nineteenth-century United States. This recognition comes exactly when she tries the hardest to lend her voice to the plight of the slave women, interceding on their behalf with Pierce. He at first refuses to treat her stories seriously, asserting that they are exaggerations and lies. Later, forbidding her to tell them, he exercises the prerogative not just of master as owner but of master as man. He calls for the silence of women—both the concerns of the slave women and Fanny's right to speak about them and her own.

Pierce's exercise of masculine authority leads Fanny more consciously to identify *as a woman* with the slave women. She experiences that identification at some points as a sympathetic collapse—"I had to cry out for them, for *us*." She does not, however, let her sympathetically imagined connection with the enslaved women override her consciousness of privilege, as when she guiltily wonders what those women must think of her, "a woman, a creature like themselves, who has borne children too, what sort of feeling they have toward me. I wonder it is not one of murderous hate—that they should lie here almost dying with unpaid labor for me" (169). She became acutely conscious of the oppressive roles slaveholding women could play in the "disgusting stories" she daily heard from the plantation women (167).

Her experiences with slave women bring Fanny to a more complex view of her own status within her marriage and within patriarchal culture both North and South. We might consider how the enslaved Psyche serves not only as Fanny's "racial" and social counterpoint but a metonymical figure for Fanny's own sense of mental distress and of entrapment. Fanny suddenly confronts in the passage on Psyche her ironically willing acceptance of the status of *feme covert* [sic] in marriage,[35] made all the more poignant because she had previously been financially independent: "For the last four years of my life that preceded my marriage I literally coined money, and never until this moment, I think, did I reflect on the great means of good, to myself and others, that I so gladly agreed to give up forever" (105). Fanny recognizes that it is only by her relationship with Pierce's economic "power and privilege" that she is differentiated practically from the slave Psyche. The mode of her life with Pierce may be *actually* dependent on slaves, but both the slaves and Fanny are *legally* dependent upon the whim of the master, as this entry on Psyche makes clear.

## Frances Butler Leigh on the Georgia Plantations

Mother and daughter would each arrive at a fundamentally new sense of self on the plantations. If what the twenty-nine-year-old Fanny encountered there was a recognition of her lack of agency as a married woman—her *subjugation to* the master in a social system that ranked people based on both race and gender—she used her sense of injustice as a backbone for personal fortitude throughout the rest of her life. Fan encountered something very different in her twenty-ninth year on the plantations. She was to establish her own ability as a woman working alongside men, discovering her ability to *be* the "master."

Fanny Kemble journeyed to a prosperous and confident Georgia in 1838. Fan's return in 1865 with her father was a much grimmer trip. They left Philadelphia, where they were untouched by the war except for Pierce's brief prison sojourn, for the war-ravaged South, encountering what Fan described as a "conquered country" and a "crushed" people (228, 233). Arriving finally at the plantation, unlike her mother years before, Fan is steeled for what she will find— a gutted house and missing possessions. She is equipped, both practically—with her chairs, washstands, bedsteads, tubs, tables, and china—and ideologically, as we see when one of her first actions is to prominently hang her portrait of General Robert E. Lee. The latter gesture is complex, embodying as it must have an emotional release for Fan, who in Philadelphia had to suppress demonstrations of her allegiance to the Confederate cause. But it serves another, defensive strategy, giving the newly freed African Americans notice as to where the sympathies of their former owners lie. Fan is applauded here by her father and the overseer for what is framed as a classically feminine gesture—quickly putting the house in order, practically, politically, and symbolically.

Within a couple of years, Fan's concerns extended beyond household management, and her readers received fewer details of rain pouring through the roof and more of its effects on the crops. The measure of difference between leaky roofs and flooding fields parallels a striking dissimilarity between Fan's expression of emotion in her memoir and her mother's in her *Journal*. Fanny Kemble's text is overtly emotive, configured around a sympathetic response to the slaves, which is documented by outbursts of tears: Fanny's identification with the slaves, especially the women, makes her so continually unhappy that she cries. The fact that Pierce does not understand Fanny's tears is, in the sympathetic conceptual realm, the greatest indictment of his character, as well as an explanation that nineteenth-century audiences would have accepted as a sign of Fanny and Pierce's basic incompatibility.

Fan, in contrast, has no such tears to shed, even among

her Southern compatriots, perhaps reflecting the decline
in popularity of sentimentalism. Instead of weeping over
what she finds herself unable to change, Fan's tears mark
her sheer determination to succeed. When the household
goods arrive after a long delay, soaked through by rain,
Fan cracks, only briefly before carrying on.  Unlike her
mother, who cries for the suffering of the slaves, Fan indulges in a "violent attack of hysterics from fatigue and
excitement" *after* she conquers the difficulties the freed
slaves are causing *her* (see 242, 271). Thus, where her
mother weeps at her failure to ameliorate conditions for
the slaves, Fan's tears counterpoint her successes in an
environment where the social rules about gender said she
would fail.

   The episode that is closed by Fan's "attack of hysterics"
is a key one in her text. Fan is negotiating for a new identity here, stepping practically—and perhaps emotionally—
into her father's place. The ground she stakes for that
negotiation is her relation with the freed slaves—men and
women who are themselves struggling to articulate a new
identity, one that would ideally replace their former ge-
neric enslaved status with individual agency and freedom.
They must, like Fan, shape this identity both personally
and for their larger community. We see in this episode how
the men practice their entitlement to freedom by exercis-
ing the voice that had so long been denied them, trying to
make Fan listen to *them* before they agree to her sharecropping conditions. Fan consents to hear them, but as
her actions evince, in the new legal code of the South, it is
only the letter, and not the spirit, that changes: "I was"
she concludes, "immovable" (271). Her personal triumph
here lies in her ability to dominate the *freed* slaves. To
that extent, she not only steps into her father's "mastery";
she surpasses it.

At the height of the Victorian social doctrine of "separate spheres," Fan works as both "master" and "mistress" of the plantation. She does not surrender her stereotypical "feminine" interests, attending to philanthropic concerns on the plantation like hospital conditions, schooling, and religion, and taking sentimental pleasure in providing a Christmas tree for the plantation children. She also takes on, with a degree of success as high as (and sometimes higher than) her "gentlemen" colleagues the duties of finance, labor, and crop management. She works to find new technology and different labor methods to make her fields more efficient and her crops more lucrative. She negotiates her contracts with her employees personally. And she does battle when necessary with the "Yankees" who to some degree were charged with regulating her operations, particularly in respect to the freed men and women on her plantation. She portrays herself in these efforts as decisive, distinguished from her "timid, and irresolute" agents and overseers (295). In opposition to her African American employees, and in contrast to her Anglo-American *male* employees and colleagues, Fan defines her success. It is certain that she sees her struggle for identity as a brand of warfare. The language she uses to describe her relations with those around her is aggressive, strategic, and occasionally violent—she breaks the "backbone of the opposition," keeps the "upper hand," and "triumphs" over the Yankee captain only to feel "checkmated" later on (272, 279–82). And she calmly keeps a pistol by her bed, her defense against potential conspiracies of freed slaves, from which, she decides, the "Yankee" soldiers will not protect her.

It is interesting to speculate that Fan might have been more comfortable behaving with stereotypical "masculine" assertiveness because her mother had set her such a precedent. Local Philadelphians like Sydney George Fisher often commented on Fanny Kemble's preference of men's clothing for horse riding.[36] And the "manly" independence that by turns offended and fascinated Fisher served as Pierce's "fundamental" grounds for divorce.[37] It does seem that Fan saw her work on the plantations as a "manly" adventure from the start, when she recounts feeling "like Robinson Crusoe with three hundred men Fridays" (237).

As the two letters she includes addressed to her mother suggest, Fan somewhat defensively hoped her mother would sympathize with her struggles against the odds. These two letters are fascinating moments in a text that in every other way refuses to acknowledge Fanny or her politics. The first letter is remarkable for the simple fact that unlike all other "addressed" letters included in the text, this one has no "end." A suggestive slip, it symbolically offers the rest of the text as a letter to her mother. Her second letter is a testimonial to her success, the news of which, she relates, "has spread far and wide" (324). Fan has not just lived up to the reputation of her father, she has made her own reputation among her father's fellow planters. Fanny assumes that her mother is not sympathetic to her project,[38] but her appeal aims for praise in terms that she must know her mother will identify with: "Dear M[other]—don't laugh at my boasting. I have worked so hard and cared so much about it, that it is more to me than I can express to know that I have succeeded" (324).

## Race and Class

The pride that Fan feels in her ability to dominate her difficulties also underwrites her use of "my people" in references to the ex-slaves. As her narrative progresses, her use of the term becomes more and more obviously paternalistic in its proprietary, as opposed to benevolent, sense. Fan takes active part in the redefinition of social and labor relations of the Reconstruction South, where the old racial hierarchies had been leveled in theory by the Emancipation Proclamation. Reconstruction thus presented an arena of struggle between those who imagined new ways to order society and those who sought to reassert the old. Notably, Fan's tones of ownership ("my people") predominate later in the text, after she has put into effect a new ideological appropriation of the exslaves' labor. It is clear that Fan could never have described the plantations as "successful" (i.e., lucrative) if the workers were as singularly unproductive as she is constantly asking her various readers to believe. To justify her exploitation of their labor—the fact that Fanny Kemble faced very squarely when she affirmed that "by their unpaid labor I live" (89)—in the new South, Fan must believe that it is actually *she* who does the work, and therefore she who deserves the majority of profit. For this reason, it is necessary that she would believe "that if I wanted a thing done I first had to tell the negroes to do it, then show them how, and finally do it myself" (255). Constant assertions about their ineffectuality, coupled with repeated assertions that only people of African descent can raise rice, provide the imaginative apparatus that allows Fan to see as just profit what actually amounts to modified exploitation.

From this angle of analysis, we begin to see the intertwining of race and class, both practically and ideologically. Fan's memoir gives us glimpses into how the Reconstruction South began to bring African Americans into the very class system from which they had earlier been barred. Fan, for instance, complains that freed slaves do not make good employees. They are satisfied with subsistence living, "not yet having learned to want the things money alone can give" (289). Not wanting more than they need, they are not willing to work harder than necessary—i.e., as hard as Fan needs them to make a profit herself. Yet when the freed men and women *do* begin evidencing desire for those "things money alone can give," such as land, and hats, she complains about that, too. The fact that she contradicts herself, though, is less about sloppy thinking than about the fundamental contradictions of the class system, which requires social stratification even as it encourages people to move out of their level and into another.

There are bridges between Fan and her mother on this issue of class. Both Fan and her mother bring their own "white" personal servant on their trip with them. Both of them have certain ideas about social place and are comfortable moving in a stratified social system. They are, perhaps, at ease in that system because they believe themselves to be at or close to the top of it: both mother and daughter see themselves as a social model for those whom they are trying to uplift, even though the fact that they each have servants indicates that they do not expect everyone to rise to their station.

In Fanny's attitudes toward poor "whites" we can begin to see common patterns of thought between racism and class elitism, and in this pattern we discover a similarity between the attitudes of mother and daughter. Fan does not talk about Anglo-Southerners outside the planters' stratum. Her mother, by contrast, pays a good deal of attention to the poorer "white" Georgians in letters recounting her journey to the plantation, which were published a couple years after the visit in *Bentley's Miscellaney*,[39] and in the *Journal* letter that discusses her trip into the pine barren. Fanny cannot find sympathy for their conditions and freely records the disgust she experiences when she must board with the farmers and backwoods folk, or pinelander people she encounters. Over and over she complains against their "dirty" habits. "Filth" is the vice she attacks immediately upon her arrival at the plantations among the slaves. While she does not evidence much hope that the pinelanders will overcome the "sinister" deficiencies of character that keep them so filthy, she seems to believe that the African slaves can. Whenever Fanny finds the slaves deprecating their "race," she responds with a little lesson, explaining "the question is one of moral and mental culture—not the color of an integument," assuring them that "white people are as dirty and dishonest as colored folks, when they have suffered the same lack of decent training" (181).

Still, conceptually, the problem of racism might reside a little deeper for Fanny than what she consciously understood. The preceding passage is introduced by her expression of surprise at the clean condition of a slave cabin, to which a slave woman responds, "Missis no 'spect to find colored folks' house clean as white folks'" (180). Clearly, Fanny *wanted* to find them that way, believing cleanliness was evidence of moral enterprise. But the fact that she repeatedly describes the skin color of African-descended slaves in terms of dirt and filth raises an issue worth thinking hard about and begins to suggest why she could not expect to see them "clean," that is, the epistemological seductiveness of "black/white" thinking in Western conceptual systems. In Western metaphysics and theology, "black" has always been about filth, moral degradation, and evil. "White" has always represented purity, moral worth, and positive good. It is curious to stop occasionally and realize the conceptual grip this system has on thinking about race in the United States both historically and contemporarily. "Whites" are not white; "blacks" are a panoply of browns and are sometimes so "light" that they "pass" for "white." That Fanny (and many who get to class themselves as "whites") are lured by this unconscious tow is not surprising—that is what makes the system so effective. But not being conscious of it can compromise even the best of commitments to confronting racism. As Fanny repeatedly describes the colors of slaves as "sooty," "dirt-colored," and "dingy," and the "mulatto" children as having more "regular features"—that is, more like "whites"— she is subscribing to a mental standard that regularizes and privileges the appearance of "white" over "black." This, combined with her attitudes about class, may begin to explain what often seems like surprising insensitivity in her dealings with her "peculiar slave," Jack. And conversely, we can see how the implicit racism in Fanny's attitudes about "filth" might have been what kept her from feeling any compassion for the impoverished conditions of the pinelanders.

Both Fanny's text and Fan's use appeals to "beauty" and "aesthetics" to make natural certain social systems and social relationships seem invisible or as if they had no alternative. Fanny's project of "uplift"—which depended for its logic on the beauty of middle-class lifestyles and European features—had much in common with the stances of abolitionist reformers. We can find similarities in even the most courageous and strong-minded, like Lydia Maria Child, whose 1867 novel *Romance of the Republic* models a utopian postwar project of racial uplift and intermarriage, and whose very similar agenda translates thus: if "we" help "them" look and behave like "us," the "problem" will be solved. If this way of thinking is culturally solipsistic, at least it holds out the *promise* of shared benefits, something that France Butler Leigh's mind-set did not do.

Fan shares her mother's aversion to the "coarse wooly" hair of the African Americans, as we see when she chides the freed women for their "strong inclination to give up wearing their pretty picturesque head handkerchiefs" (274). But Fan's appeals to aesthetics are not concerned with homogenizing society either educationally or physically. Her concern here is that by abandoning their scarves, the freed women are aspiring to the status of their "white sisters." In the same way that she ideologically appropriates her workers' labor by imagining she does it, she also seeks to remove the actual evidence of their performed labor from her field of vision, noting how much more pleasant another plantation is for the fact that neither the quarters *nor* the fields can be seen from the mansion. All evidences of what supports the wealth enjoyed by the household are made invisible. She imagines carrying out the same project on her plantation, moving the workers to "where I can neither see, hear, nor smell them" and expanding her garden accordingly (285). Each "aesthetic," then, removes "blacks" from the picture; Fanny's by assimilating them into "whiteness," and Fan's by keeping them "black" but keeping them out of her sight.

This reading should not encourage us to miss seeing the complexity of Fan's relationship with the people who worked the Butler plantations. The general expressions of her affection ("my dear people") are perhaps less telling than the particular mentions she makes of people—curiously unnamed—toward whom she expresses kindness and who return that kindness to her, like the woman weeping on the church steps for whom Fan intercedes, the "old woman" who comforts Fan when she is crying, and the blind woman who blesses Fan by telling her that in heaven "I shall look for your works, as I shall know dem" (266, 325–26). By and large, though, her attitudes toward the people who work for her demonstrate the key insight her mother had into the operations of racism, that "blacks"

"are always prejudged on their supposed general characteristics, and never judged after the fact on the merit of
any special instance" (120). While Fanny herself often gen-
eralizes about how "blacks" are as a group, she is also at
pains to relate the particular stories of slave women.[40] Fan,
by contrast, is almost exclusively interested in presenting
a generalized, ethnologized "Negro" to her reader. This may
explain her apparent unwillingness to give names to the
individual women with whom she would seem to have more
personal relationships.

Therein lies the differing political aims of the two works.
Fanny Kemble is appealing to her reader to realize that
the slaves are individual human beings and therefore
should not be treated differently from other human beings by being forced into slavery. Frances Butler Leigh is
trying to establish that people of African descent are different as a group from people of European descent—less
civilized, less worthy—and therefore more available for
different standards of treatment both in the past and the
present.

## Gender and Region

If ideas about class fed nineteenth-century thinking about
race, so too did ideas about gender provided metaphors
for regional politics. At one point, Fanny explains to Elizabeth that "another instance of the horrible injustice of this
system of slavery" is that it robs men of the right to be the
sole supporter of both himself and his wife. "He would be
able to procure for her comfort in sickness or health, and
beyond the necessary household work, which the wives of
most artisans are inured to, she would have no labor to
encounter" (128–29). Fanny here defines the "maleness"
of a husband through a classed relationship toward his

wife—he earns and dispenses the money; the wife lives in leisure as evidence of his earning ability. Notably, this is a relationship that Fanny has earlier despaired of in her own case. In fact, her dissatisfaction with the way the social structure of marriage asked women to surrender their independence might well be one of the reasons she never remarried.

We should also note the unconscious force of this second cultural binary, male/female, where "male" connotes activity and ability and "female" connotes its opposite, passivity and dependence. Fanny's acquiescence to this cultural definition affected both her relationship with Pierce and her reading of the South. The more unhappy Fanny becomes with Pierce's response to slavery, the more she begins to suggest that he is "unmanly." Noting with disgusted irony that the practice of task labor in the field demonstrates a "noble admission of female equality," she complains frequently of slavery's unfairness toward women. In this regard, she worries that her trip to the plantations will "lessen her respect" for Pierce, since "the details of slaveholding are so unmanly . . . I know not how anyone with the spirit of a man can condescend to them" (180). It is clear that Fanny did not keep such sentiments to herself when she later relates having said to him that "I thought female labor of the sort exacted from these slaves, and corporal chastisement such as they endure, must be abhorrent to any manly or humane man" (115). Her collapse of the two adjectives *manly* and *humane* constitutes an insult that cuts to the core of Pierce's deepest social conditioning and acquired identity. It appeals specifically to a reversal of the power relationship that constructs the male/female binary: strength/dependence. By suggesting that Pierce is "unmanly," Fanny mocks him by implying that he is weak and dependent—womanly—instead of the "master" he sees himself as being. She also uses this conceptual grid to characterize the politics of the South, implied in her descriptions of the Anglo-Southern population as passive and indolent. Her characterization of the South, for instance, as being dependent on "Yankee enterprise and funds" for any civil improvements depends for its imaginative appeal on the male/female binary, as do her observations on the generally "declining prosperity" of the plantation system for want of industry and financial acumen (135). The victorious Union would deploy the same salvo at the end of the Civil War, when, for instance, Northern cartoonists depicted the defeated president of the Confederacy, Jefferson Davis, as trying to flee surrender disguised in a lady's hoopskirts. Political allegiances notwithstanding, it is important to understand the misogyny embedded in such metaphors that castigate failed or compromised men as (regular) women. We should also consider how acquiescing to a worldview that makes entire groups of people available for different treatment based on gender can metaphorically provide a justification for doing so based on region or race.

*Ten Years on a Georgia Plantation* responds defensively to the terms used by her mother and the general culture in describing the region Fan loved. While Fan is incommoded in her journey south much as her mother was years before, she explains the causes not as pinelander slovenliness but as a result of the pillaging of the South planned by Sherman and conducted by Union troops. What Fanny described as the indolent and lazy habits of Southern culture in general and Southern "ladies" in particular, Fan is careful to reappropriate in her description of the summer she spends in the pinelands of South Carolina, where she describes a disheartened and impoverished, but courageous and hard working, "commonwealth" of planters who live in conditions, she emphasizes, that were "very healthy and the sanitary laws very strict" (297–98). Where Fanny described the Anglo-American South as unchristian for their involvement in slavery, Fan suggests that it is the Northerners who are unchristian for their ruthless devastation of Southern population and property. In fact, she suggestively compares the "Yankees" to Satan when she describes them as deceiving the freed slaves by offering them a "taste . . . of the tree of knowledge" (243). These tacit dialogues between mother and daughter and between North and South provide us with an insights into how cultures exist, as Hazel Carby has recently observed, by and through their relationship with other cultures.[41] We can see here, for instance, how "Southern pride" could serve as a defensive response (then as, perhaps, now) to the postwar arrogance of Northern culture, who portrayed the South in derogatory terms meant to repeatedly humiliate them and remind them of their loss.

## Conclusion

We often fail to read texts such as Fan's *Ten Years on a Georgia Plantation* that we presently designate ethically naive or politically compromised. But to do that is to risk three kinds of ignorance. First, we risk not fully understanding the terms by which arguments for and against slavery and racism have been formulated in the past. By reading both *Journal of a Residence on a Georgian Plantation* and *Ten Years on a Georgia Plantation*, we can learn much more about racism, its interactions with gender and class, and its subtle historical permutations than we ever could by reading Fanny Kemble's text alone. Second, we risk stereotyping Confederate sympathizers in ignorance. By listening to Fan's voice, we can begin to develop a more complex and realistic view of people as individuals—even those whom we may not be finally able to fully understand or agree with. Fan's story is fascinating—a "white" woman who claims her independence in a culture that would deny it, mainly by posing it against that of her "black" exslaves. As such, stands as an important historical record in a moment in U. S. legal history when our country's Anglo-American male legislature gave themselves the choice between offering the vote to Anglo-American women or African American men. Third, we risk believing that there is ever one authoritative version of "the story," "reality," or "history." All of these are contingent on lived experiences; all are bound to social conditioning and limitations. Reading Fan's memoir of her experiences with sensitivity to the ways in which it is responding to both family and national politics can make us more sensitive to the complexity of social and political dialogue. The two texts together point toward other voices that did not have access to publication, like the enslaved, and later freed, African American women on the Butler plantations.

Thus, *Journal of a Residence on a Georgian Plantation* and *Ten Years on a Georgia Plantation* complicate our understanding of issues of power and empowerment for women. They give us the opportunity to reflect on the rich, and often painful, complexities of relationships between mothers and daughters and the coded ways in which these dialogues can take place. Out of the fascination each woman had with language, nature, and peoples' behavior, we have textured portrayals of pre- and postwar Southern culture and everyday life. Fanny Kemble and Frances Butler Leigh provide two very different and valuable narratives about the ways that women have found to forge strong personal identities and literary voices. We are fortunate to have each and to have the opportunity to read them together.

## Note on Names

Both Kemble and Leigh follow nineteenth-century convention in dashing out "genteel names." The names of close members of the family, and identifiable, frequently mentioned neighbors, employees, and visitors are provided for the reader's convenience.

*Journal of a Residence on a Georgian Plantation*

E——: Elizabeth Sedgwick

Mr. ——; Mr. B——; ——: Pierce Butler

Major ——: Major Butler, Pierce's maternal grandfather

Mr. O——: plantation overseer during Fanny's stay

Mr. K——: interchangeably Roswell King, Sr., or his son, Roswell King, Jr., the latter of which is also referred to as "Massa R——" or "Mr. R—— K——", both of whom worked as Butler plantation overseers

Dr. H——: James Holmes, M.D., (note: in the section on the Hazard/Wylly duel, "Dr. H——" refers to Thomas Hazard, son of Colonel William Hazard)

Mr. J— C——: James Hamilton Couper, a neighboring planter (also "Mr. C——," "old Mr. C——"

Captain F——: John Fraser, manager of Hamilton plantation

M——: Margery O'Brien, Fanny's (Irish) personal maid.

S——: Daughter Sarah (Sally)

Baby: Daughter Frances (Fan)

*Ten Years on a Georgia Plantation*

O.W.: Owen Wister, Sarah Butler Wister's son

S——: Sarah, Fan's Sister

Brother-in-law: Owen Wister, Sr., Sarah's husband

M——: Fanny Kemble, Fan's mother (NB: p. 297 "M——" is probably Fan's personal servant, not Fanny)

Mr. J——: plantation manager hired after the Civil War
Mr. N——: John Nightingale, plantation manager hired
to replace Mr. J——

NOTES

I owe thanks to Phil Lapsansky, Research Librarian at the Library Company of Philadelphia, for his endless expertise on Philadelphia history and his help on Kemble/Butler history in particular. Thanks also to my colleagues at Louisiana State University, Professor Peggy Prenshaw and especially Professor John Lowe, who commented in numerous helpful ways on the introduction. Finally, I want to dedicate this project to *my* mother, Delana Dawn Nelson.

1. Fanny, for her own part, does not mention the daughter's publication in any of her subsequently published memoirs.

2. Pierce Butler (Mease) shortly thereafter agreed to split his inheritance with the middle brother when John changed his mind and, consequently, his name, past his sixteenth-birthday deadline.

3. Pierce would not acquire his inheritance until his Aunt Frances, who was holding the land in trust, died.

4. Fanny herself suggests this ambiguity, asserting in her letter on Psyche that she was unaware of Pierce's holdings when she married him, but then countering that "even if [she] had," she would not have understood the implications.

5. Fanny Kemble Wister, *Fanny, The American Kemble: Her Journals and Unpublished Letters* (Tallahassee, Fl.: South Pass Press, 1972), 139.

6. Various reviews scolded Fanny for "vulgarity, " for lacking "the finer and higher qualities which adorn the female character," and for having "unsexed" herself. See Malcolm Bell, Jr., *Major Butler's Legacy: Five Generations of a Slaveholding Family* (Athens: University of Georgia Press, 1987), 263, for a survey of the reviews. See also J. C. Furnas, *Fanny Kemble: Leading*

*Lady of the Nineteenth-Century Stage* (New York: Dial Press, 1982), 160–65. Fanny's first journal has recently been reprinted. See *Fanny Kemble: Journal of a Young Actress*, ed. Monica Gaugh (New York: Columbia University Press, 1990).

7. In 1820, Sidney Smith published a scathing review of American culture in the *Edinburgh Review* (33:78–80), observing that "considering their [i.e., American] numbers, indeed, and the favourable circumstances in which they have been placed, they have yet done marvelously little to assert the honour of such a descent, or to show that their English blood has been exalted or refined by their republican training." He goes on to query, "In the four quarters of the globe, who reads an American book? or goes to an American play? or looks at an American picture or statue?" Such criticisms were smarting in the public consciousness of the early Republic, and this defensive discomfort provided the context for Fanny's first publication. See Furnas's discussion of the social and literary issues surrounding Kemble's American *Journal* (*Fanny Kemble*, 151–58).

8. The *Journal* was spoofed in various ways, including an amusingly titled pamphlet, *My Conscience! Fanny Thimble Cutler's Journal of a Residence in America. Whilst Performing a Profitable Theatre Engagement. Beating the Nonsensical Fanny Kemble Journal—All Hollow!* wherein Pierce is renamed "Fierce Cutler." Despite the indignant uproar on both sides of the Atlantic, many readers who criticized the *Journal* also admitted to liking it very much. See Furnas, *Fanny Kemble*, 164.

9. For an excellent history of women's traditions of diary and journal writing in the United States, see Margo Culley, *A Day at a Time: The Diary Literature of American Women from 1764 to the Present* (New York: Feminist Press, 1985).

10. For Kemble's own mentions of Child's solicitations, see Fanny Kemble, *Records of a Later Life* (New York: Holt, 1882), 324, 328, 355.

11. Lydia Maria Child recorded a public scene between Fanny and Pierce in 1838 in a letter to a friend:

It seems she keeps tugging at her husband's conscience all the time, about his slaves. One day he begged her to spare him—

saying "You know, Fanny, we don't feel alike on that subject. If I objected to it in my conscience, as you do, I would emancipate them all." "Pierce," exclaimed she, "look me full in the face, and say that in your conscience you think it is right to hold slaves, and I will never again speak to you on the subject." He met her penetrating glance for a moment—lowered his eyes—and between a blush and a smile, said, "Fanny, I cannot do it." (Quoted in Bell, *Major Butler's Legacy*, 266.)

12. See [James Schott], *A Statement by James Schott* (Baltimore, 1844).

13. Wister, *The American Kemble*, 157.

14. Quoted in Bell, *Major Butler's Legacy*, 290.

15. Henry James, a friend to Fanny Kemble and Sarah Kemble Wister, would depict a man with impulses very similar to Pierce's in the character of Basil Ransom, from *The Bostonians*.

16. For a history of divorce in America, see Glenda Riley, *Divorce: An American Tradition* (New York: Oxford University Press, 1991), especially her introduction, 3–9.

17. Fanny Kemble Wister, ed., "Sarah Butler Wister's Civil War Diary," *Pennsylvania Magazine of History and Biography* 52 (1978): 271–327. The original diary is housed at the Historical Society of Pennsylvania in the Wister Family Papers.

18. Quoted in Furnas, *Fanny Kemble*, 414.

19. See Bell, *Major Butler's Legacy*, 439. He, perhaps unfairly, describes Fan's impulse as "paranoid."

20. Letter in Wister Family Papers, Historical Society of Pennsylvania. It is quoted at length by Furnas, *Fanny Kemble*, 413.

21. For a useful history of rice plantation culture, see Julia Floyd Smith, *Slavery and Rice Culture in Low Country Georgia* (Knoxville: University of Tennessee, 1985).

22. James Oakes, *The Ruling Race: A History of American Slaveholders* (New York: Vintage, 1983), x.

23. Smith, *Slavery and Rice Culture*, 5.

24. Smith, *Slavery and Rice Culture*, 59.

25. Quoted in Bell, *Major Butler's Legacy*, 127.

26. See Bell, *Major Butler's Legacy*, 130.

27. See Dan Littlefield, *Rice and Slaves: Ethnicity and the Slave Trade in South Carolina* (Baton Rouge: Louisiana State University Press, 1981), 74–114, who carefully compares African rice-culture techniques with Portuguese and colonial American to conclude that while the Portuguese "may have introduced Asian rice . . . the agricultural techniques appear to be purely African" (96).

28. See Bell, *Major Butler's Legacy*, 134, and Charles Joyner, *Down by the Riverside: A South Carolina Slave Community* (Urbana: University of Illinois Press, 1984).

29. See for instance, Jane Tompkins, *Sensational Designs: The Cultural Work of American Fiction, 1790–1860* (New York: Oxford University Press, 1985), and Shirley Samuels, ed., *The Culture of Sentiment: Race, Gender and Sentimentality in Nineteenth-Century America* (New York: Oxford University Press, 1992).

30. Karen Sanchez-Eppler, correspondence with University of Michigan Press, March 11, 1991, 4.

31. For a useful and important discussion of travel writing as a genre in the context of postcolonial theory, see Mary Louise Pratt, *Imperial Eyes* (New York: Routledge, 1992). See also Dorothy Hammond and Alta Jablow, *The Africa That Never Was: Four Centuries of British Writing about Africa* (New York: Twayne, 1970).

32. John A. Scott, "Editor's Introduction," *Journal of a Residence on a Georgian Plantation in 1838–1839* (Athens: University of Georgia Press, 1984), lvii. See also Furnas, *Fanny Kemble*, 397–99. For a thorough, general background of dueling in Southern culture, see Bertram Wyatt-Brown, *Honor and Violence in the Old South* (New York: Oxford University Press, 1986), 142–53.

33. For a discussion of the Black English practice of "signifying" see Geneva Smitherman, *Talkin' and Testifyin': The Language of Black America* (Boston: Houghton Mifflen, 1977), 101–67, and Henry Louis Gates, *The Signifying Monkey: A Theory of Afro-American Literary Criticism* (New York: Oxford University Press, 1988), 44–88.

34. See Scott's "Editor's Introduction," lii-liv, for a discussion of the reviews.

35. *Feme covert* [*sic*], based in English common law, dictated that at the point of marriage, a woman lost her legal identity, which was subsumed to that of her husband. For a fuller discussion, consult Carol Himowitz and Michaele Weissman, *A History of Women in America* (New York: Bantam, 1978), 22–25, and Linda Kerber, *Women of the Republic: Intellect and Ideology in Revolutionary America* (New York: Norton, 1986), 119–21.

36. Sydney George Fisher, *A Philadelphia Perspective: The Diary of Sydney George Fisher Covering the Years 1834–1871*, ed. Nicholas B. Wainwright (Philadelphia: Historical Society of Pennsylvania, 1967). See, for example, his entry for April 19, 1840, 100, where he describes meeting Fanny

on horseback, and alone. She is very independent and rides about constantly unattended . . . Her costume was becoming and peculiar. A green cloth riding habit, with rolling collar & open in front, under it, a *man's* waistcoat with rolling collar, yellow & gilt buttons, a calico shirt collar & breast, blue striped & turned over & a black silk cravat tied sailor fashion, with a man's hat & a veil.

37. In *Mr. Butler's Statement* (Philadelphia: J. C. Clarke, 1850), Pierce solemnly records as evidence on his behalf that Fanny unreasonably "held that marriage should be companionship on equal terms—partnership, in which, if both partners agree with it is well; but if they do not, neither is bound to yield —and that at no time has one partner a right to control the other."

38. In fact, in a letter to a friend in 1869, Fanny makes it clear that while she supported the endeavors of her daughter, in general, she did not think the enterprise of reopening plantations in the South praiseworthy. She comments with sympathy on a letter she has just received from Fan and then observes:

For my own part, the result seems to me the only one to have been rationally expected, and I have no hope whatever that as long as one man, once a planter, and one man, once a slave, survives, any successful cultivation of the southern estates will be achieved . . . It is unlucky, no doubt, for the present holders of southern property, but then the world has laws, and I do not know that the planters of the southern states were sufficiently meritorious folk to have earned a miracle, especially a very immoral one, for their heirs. (*Further Records, 1848–1883* [New York, 1891], 349–50)

39. *Bentley's Miscellaney*, 1841. Fanny later included the letters in *Records of a Later Life* (New York, 1882), 1:170–217.

40. The same generosity is not evidenced in Fanny's depictions of either the elite or the poor Anglo-Southerners, who she characterizes as evincing "stupid sameness," detailing exceptions without altering her overall condemnation.

41. Hazel Carby, "The Canon: Civil War and Reconstruction," *Michigan Quarterly Review* 28 (1989): 42–43.

JOURNAL

OF

A RESIDENCE ON A

# GEORGIAN PLANTATION

IN 1838—1839.

By FRANCES ANNE KEMBLE.

SLAVERY THE CHIEF CORNER STONE.

'This stone (Slavery), which was rejected by the first builders, is become the chief stone of the corner in our new edifice.'—*Speech of* ALEXANDER H. STEPHENS, *Vice-President of the Confederate States: delivered March* 21, 1861.

TO

# ELIZABETH DWIGHT SEDGWICK,

THIS JOURNAL,

ORIGINALLY KEPT FOR HER,

IS

MOST AFFECTIONATELY

𝔇𝔢𝔡𝔦𝔠𝔞𝔱𝔢𝔡.

# PREFACE.

THE following diary was kept in the winter and spring of 1838–9, on an estate consisting of rice and cotton plantations, in the islands at the entrance of the Altamaha, on the coast of Georgia.

The slaves in whom I then had an unfortunate interest were sold some years ago. The islands themselves are at present in the power of the Northern troops. The record contained in the following pages is a picture of conditions of human existence which I hope and believe have passed away.

LONDON, *January* 16, 1863.

# JOURNAL.

Philadelphia, December, 1838.

My DEAR E——,—I return you Mr. ——'s letter. I do not think it answers any of the questions debated in our last conversation at all satisfactorily: the *right* one man has to enslave another, he has not the hardihood to assert; but in the reasons he adduces to defend that act of injustice, the contradictory statements he makes appear to me to refute each other. He says, that to the Continental European protesting against the abstract iniquity of slavery, his answer would be, "The slaves are infinitely better off than half the Continental peasantry." To the Englishman, "They are happy compared with the miserable Irish." But supposing that this answered the question of original injustice, which it does not, it is not a true reply. Though the negroes are fed, clothed, and housed, and though the Irish peasant is starved, naked, and roofless, the bare name of freemen—the lordship over his own person, the power to choose and will—are blessings beyond food, raiment, or shelter; possessing which, the want of every comfort of life is yet more tolerable than their fullest enjoyment without them. Ask the thousands of ragged destitutes who yearly land upon these shores to seek the means of existence — ask the friendless, penniless foreign emigrant if he will give up his present misery, his future uncertainty, his doubtful and difficult struggle for life at once, for the secure, and, as it is called, fortunate dependence of the slave: the indignation with which he would spurn the offer will prove that he possesses one good beyond all others, and that his birthright as a man is more precious to him yet than the mess of pottage for which he is told to exchange it because he is starving.

Of course the reverse alternative can not be offered to the slaves, for at the very word the riches of those who own them would make themselves wings and flee away. But I do not admit the comparison between your slaves and even the lowest class of European free laborers, for the former are *allowed* the exercise of no faculties but those which they enjoy in common with the brutes that perish. The just comparison is between the slaves and the useful animals to whose level your laws reduce them; and I will acknowledge that the slaves of a kind owner may be as well cared for, and as happy, as the dogs and horses of a merciful master; but the latter condition—*i. e.*, that of happiness—must again depend upon the complete perfection of their moral and mental degradation. Mr. ——, in his letter, maintains that they *are* an inferior race, and, compared with the whites, "*animals*, incapable of mental culture and moral improvement:" to this I can only reply, that if they are incapable of profiting by instruction, I do not see the necessity for laws inflicting heavy penalties on those who offer it to them. If they really are brutish, witless, dull, and devoid of capacity for progress, where lies the *danger* which is constantly insisted upon of offering them that of which they are incapable. We have no laws forbidding us to teach our dogs and horses as much as they can comprehend; nobody is fined or imprisoned for reasoning upon knowledge and liberty to the beasts of the field, for they are incapable of such truths. But these themes are forbidden to slaves, not because they can not, but because they can and would seize on them with avidity — receive them gladly, comprehend them quickly; and the masters' power over them would be annihilated at once and forever. But I have more frequently heard not that they were incapable of receiving instruction, but something much nearer the truth —that knowledge only makes them miserable: the moment they are in any degree enlightened, they become unhappy. In the letter I return to you Mr. —— says that the very slightest amount of education, merely teaching them to read, "impairs their value as slaves, for it instantly destroys their contentedness, and, since you do not contemplate changing their condition, it is surely doing them an ill service to destroy their acquiescence in it;" but this is a very different ground of argument from the other. The discontent they evince upon the mere dawn of an advance in intelligence proves not only that they can acquire, but combine ideas, a process to which it is very difficult to assign a limit; and there indeed the whole question lies, and there and nowhere else the shoe really pinches. A slave is ignorant; he eats, drinks, sleeps, labors, and is happy. He learns to read; he feels, thinks, reflects, and becomes miserable. He discovers himself to be one of a debased and degraded race, deprived of the elementary rights which God has granted to all men alike; every action is controlled, every word noted; he may not stir beyond his appointed bounds, to the right hand or to the left, at his own will, but at the will of another he may be sent miles and miles of weary journeying—tethered, yoked, collared, and fettered—away from whatever he may know as home, severed from all those ties of blood and affection which he alone of all human, of all living creatures on the face of the earth, may neither enjoy in peace nor defend when they are outraged. If he is well treated, if his master be tolerably humane or even understand his own interest tolerably, this is probably *all* he may have to endure: it is only to the consciousness of these evils that knowledge and reflection awaken him. But how is it if

his master be severe, harsh, cruel—or even only careless
—leaving his creatures to the delegated dominion of some
overseer or agent, whose love of power, or other evil dispositions, are checked by no considerations of personal
interest? Imagination shrinks from the possible result
of such a state of things; nor must you, or Mr. ——, tell
me that the horrors thus suggested exist only in imagination. The Southern newspapers, with their advertisements of negro sales and personal descriptions of fugitive
slaves, supply details of misery that it would be difficult
for imagination to exceed. Scorn, derision, insult, menace
—the handcuff, the lash—the tearing away of children
from parents, of husbands from wives—the weary trudg-
ing in droves along the common highways, the labor of
body, the despair of mind, the sickness of heart—these
are the realities which belong to the system, and form the
rule, rather than the exception, in the slave's experience.
And this system exists here in this country of yours,
which boasts itself the asylum of the oppressed, the home
of freedom, the one place in all the world where all men
may find enfranchisement from all thraldoms of mind, soul,
or body—the land elect of liberty.

Mr. —— lays great stress, as a proof of the natural inferiority of the blacks, on the little comparative progress
they have made in those states where they enjoy their
freedom, and the fact that, whatever quickness of parts
they may exhibit while very young, on attaining maturity
they invariably sink again into inferiority, or at least me-
diocrity, and indolence. But surely there are other causes
to account for this besides natural deficiency, which must,
I think, be obvious to any unprejudiced person observing
the condition of the free blacks in your Northern communities. If, in the early portion of their life, they escape
the contempt and derision of their white associates—if
the blessed unconsciousness and ignorance of childhood

keeps them for a few years unaware of the conventional proscription under which their whole race is placed (and it is difficult to walk your streets, and mark the tone of insolent superiority assumed by even the gutter-urchins over their dusky contemporaries, and imagine this possible)—as soon as they acquire the first rudiments of knowledge, as soon as they begin to grow up and pass from infancy to youth, as soon as they cast the first observing glance upon the world by which they are surrounded, and the society of which they are members, they must become conscious that they are marked as the Hebrew lepers of old, and are condemned to sit, like those unfortunates, without the gates of every human and social sympathy. From their own sable color, a pall falls over the whole of God's universe to them, and they find themselves stamped with a badge of infamy of Nature's own devising, at sight of which all natural kindliness of man to man seems to recoil from them. They are not slaves indeed, but they are pariahs; debarred from all fellowship save with their own despised race—scorned by the lowest white ruffian in your streets, not tolerated as companions even by the foreign menials in your kitchen. They are free certainly, but they are also degraded, rejected, the offscum and the offscouring of the very dregs of your society; they are free from the chain, the whip, the enforced task and unpaid toil of slavery; but they are not the less under a ban. Their kinship with slaves forever bars them from a full share of the freeman's inheritance of equal rights, and equal consideration and respect. All hands are extended to thrust them out, all fingers point at their dusky skin, all tongues—the most vulgar, as well as the self-styled most refined—have learned to turn the very name of their race into an insult and a reproach. How, in the name of all that is natural, probable, possible, should the spirit and energy of any human creature support itself under such an accumulation of injustice and obloquy? Where shall any mass of men be found with power of character and mind sufficient to bear up against such a weight of prejudice? Why, if one individual rarely gifted by heaven were to raise himself out of such a slough of despond, he would be a miracle; and what would be his reward? Would he be admitted to an equal share in your political rights? would he ever be allowed to cross the threshold of your doors? would any of you give your daughter to his son, or your son to his daughter? would you, in any one particular, admit him to the footing of equality which any man with a white skin would claim, whose ability and worth had so raised him from the lower degrees of the social scale? You would turn from such propositions with abhorrence, and the servants in your kitchen and stable— the ignorant and boorish refuse of foreign populations, in whose countries no such prejudice exists, imbibing it with the very air they breathe here—would shrink from eating at the same table with such a man, or holding out the hand of common fellowship to him. Under the species of social proscription in which the blacks in your Northern cities exist, if they preserved energy of mind, enterprise of spirit, or any of the best attributes and powers of free men, they would prove themselves, instead of the lowest and least of human races, the highest and first, not only of all that do exist, but of all that ever have existed; for they alone would seek and cultivate knowledge, goodness, truth, science, art, refinement, and all improvement, purely for the sake of their own excellence, and without one of those incentives of honor, power, and fortune, which are found to be the chief, too often the only, inducements which lead white men to the pursuit of the same objects.

You know very well, dear E——, that in speaking of the free blacks of the North I here state nothing but what is true, and of daily experience. Only last week I heard in this very town of Philadelphia of a family of strict probity and honor, highly principled, intelligent, well-educated, and accomplished, and (to speak in the world's language) respectable in every way—i. e., *rich.* Upon an English lady's stating it to be her intention to visit these persons when she came to Philadelphia, she was told that if she did nobody else would visit *her;* and she probably would excite a malevolent feeling, which might find vent in some violent demonstration against this family. All that I have now said of course bears only upon the condition of the free colored population of the North, with which I am familiar enough to speak confidently of it. As for the slaves, and their capacity for progress, I can say nothing, for I have never been among them to judge what faculties their unhappy social position leaves to them unimpaired. But it seems to me that no experiment on a sufficiently large scale can have been tried for a sufficient length of time to determine the question of their incurable inferiority. Physiologists say that three successive generations appear to be necessary to produce an effectual change of constitution (bodily and mental), be it for health or disease. There are positive physical defects which produce positive mental ones; the diseases of the muscular and nervous systems descend from father to son. Upon the agency of one corporal power how much that is not corporal depends; from generation to generation internal disease and external deformity, vices, virtues, talents, and deficiencies are transmitted, and by the action of the same law it must be long indeed before the offspring of slaves —creatures begotten of a race debased and degraded to the lowest degree, themselves born in slavery, and whose progenitors have eaten the bread and drawn the breath of slavery for years—can be measured, with any show of justice, by even the least favored descendants of European nations, whose qualities have been for centuries devel-

oping themselves under the beneficent influences of freedom, and the progress it inspires.

I am rather surprised at the outbreak of violent disgust
which Mr. —— indulges in on the subject of amalgamation, as that formed no part of our discussion, and seems
to me a curious subject for abstract argument. I should
think the intermarrying between blacks and whites a matter to be as little insisted upon if repugnant, as prevented
if agreeable to the majority of the two races. At the
same time, I can not help being astonished at the furious
and ungoverned execration which all reference to the possibility of a fusion of the races draws down upon those
who suggest it, because nobody pretends to deny that,
throughout the South, a large proportion of the population
is the offspring of white men and colored women. In
New Orleans, a class of unhappy females exists whose
mingled blood does not prevent their being remarkable
for their beauty, and with whom no man, no *gentleman*,
in that city shrinks from associating; and while the slaveowners of the Southern States insist vehemently upon the
mental and physical inferiority of the blacks, they are be-
nevolently doing their best, in one way at least, to raise
and improve the degraded race, and the bastard population which forms so ominous an element in the social safety of their cities certainly exhibit in their forms and features the benefit they derive from their white progenitors.
It is hard to conceive that some mental improvement does
not accompany this physical change. Already the finer
forms of the European races are cast in these dusky
moulds: the outward configuration can hardly thus improve without corresponding progress in the inward capacities. The white man's blood and bones have begotten this bronze race, and bequeathed to it, in some degree,
qualities, tendencies, capabilities, such as are the inheritance of the highest order of human animals. Mr. ——

(and many others) speaks as if there were a natural repugnance in all whites to any alliance with the black race;
and yet it is notorious, that almost every Southern planter
has a family more or less numerous of illegitimate colored
children. Most certainly, few people would like to assert
that such connections are formed because it is the *interest*
of these planters to increase the number of their human
property, and that they add to their revenue by the closest intimacy with creatures that they loathe, in order to
reckon among their wealth the children of their body.
Surely that is a monstrous and unnatural supposition, and
utterly unworthy of belief. That such connections exist
commonly is a sufficient proof that they are not abhorrent
to nature; but it seems, indeed, as if marriage (and not
concubinage) was the horrible enormity which can not be
tolerated, and against which, moreover, it has been deemed
expedient to enact laws. Now it appears very evident
that there is no law in the white man's nature which prevents him from making a colored woman the mother of
his children, but there *is* a law on his statute-books forbidding him to make her his wife; and if we are to admit
the theory that the mixing of the races is a monstrosity,
it seems almost as curious that laws should be enacted to
prevent men marrying women toward whom they have an
invincible natural repugnance, as that education should by
law be prohibited to creatures incapable of receiving it.
As for the exhortation with which Mr. —— closes his letter, that I will not "go down to my husband's plantation
prejudiced against what I am to find there," I know not
well how to answer it. Assuredly I *am* going prejudiced
against slavery, for I am an Englishwoman, in whom the
absence of such a prejudice would be disgraceful. Nevertheless, I go prepared to find many mitigations in the
practice to the general injustice and cruelty of the system
—much kindness on the part of the masters, much content

on that of the slaves; and I feel very sure that you may rely upon the carefulness of my observation, and the accuracy of my report, of every detail of the working of the thing that comes under my notice; and certainly, on the plantation to which I am going, it will be more likely that I should some things extenuate, than set down aught in malice.                    Yours ever faithfully.

---

Darien, Georgia.

DEAR E——,—Minuteness of detail, and fidelity in the account of my daily doings, will hardly, I fear, render my letters very interesting to you now; but, cut off as I am here from all the usual resources and amusements of civilized existence, I shall find but little to communicate to you that is not furnished by my observations on the novel appearance of external nature, and the moral and physical condition of Mr. ——'s people. The latter subject is, I know, one sufficiently interesting in itself to you, and I shall not scruple to impart all the reflections which may occur to me relative to their state during my stay here, where inquiry into their mode of existence will form my chief occupation, and, necessarily also, the staple commodity of my letters. I purpose, while I reside here, keeping a sort of journal, such as Monk Lewis wrote during his visit to his West India plantations. I wish I had any prospect of rendering my diary as interesting and amusing to you as his was to me.

In taking my first walk on the island, I directed my steps toward the rice mill, a large building on the banks of the river, within a few yards of the house we occupy. Is it not rather curious that Miss Martineau should have mentioned the erection of a steam mill for threshing rice somewhere in the vicinity of Charleston as a singular novelty, likely to form an era in Southern agriculture, and to produce the most desirable changes in the system of labor by which it is carried on? Now on this estate alone there are three threshing mills—one worked by steam, one by the tide, and one by horses; there are two private steam mills on plantations adjacent to ours, and a public one at Savannah, where the planters who have none on their own estates are in the habit of sending their rice to be threshed at a certain percentage; these have all been in operation for some years, and I therefore am at a loss to understand what made her hail the erection of the one at Charleston as likely to produce such immediate and happy results. By-the-by — of the misstatements, or rather mistakes, for they are such, in her books, with regard to certain facts — her only disadvantage in acquiring information was not by any means that natural infirmity on which the periodical press, both here and in England, has commented with so much brutality. She had the misfortune to possess, too, that unsuspecting reliance upon the truth of others which they are apt to feel who themselves hold truth most sacred; and this was a sore disadvantage to her in a country where I have heard it myself repeatedly asserted—and, what is more, much gloried in —that she was purposely misled by the persons to whom she addressed her inquiries, who did not scruple to disgrace themselves by imposing in the grossest manner upon her credulity and anxiety to obtain information. It is a knowledge of this very shameful proceeding which has made me most especially anxious to avoid *fact hunting*. I might fill my letters to you with accounts received from others, but, as I am aware of the risk which I run in so doing, I shall furnish you with no details but those which come under my own immediate observation. To return to the rice mill: it is worked by a steam-engine of thirty horse power, and, besides threshing great part of our own rice, is kept constantly employed by the neighboring planters, who send their grain to it in preference to the more distant mill at Savannah, paying, of course, the same percentage, which makes it a very profitable addition to the estate. Immediately opposite to this building is a small shed, which they call the cook's shop, and where the daily allowance of rice and corn grits of the people is boiled and distributed to them by an old woman, whose special business this is. There are four settlements or villages (or, as the negroes call them, camps) on the island, consisting of from ten to twenty houses, and to each settlement is annexed a cook's shop with capacious caldrons, and the oldest wife of the settlement for officiating priestess. Pursuing my walk along the river's bank, upon an artificial dike, sufficiently high and broad to protect the fields from inundation by the ordinary rising of the tide—for the whole island is below high-water mark—I passed the blacksmith's and cooper's shops. At the first all the common iron implements of husbandry or household use for the estate are made, and at the latter all the rice barrels necessary for the crop, besides tubs and buckets, large and small, for the use of the people, and cedar tubs, of noble dimensions and exceedingly neat workmanship, for our own household purposes. The fragrance of these when they are first made, as well as their ample size, renders them preferable as dressing-room furniture, in my opinion, to all the china foot-tubs that ever came out of Staffordshire. After this I got out of the vicinity of the settlement, and pursued my way along a narrow dike—the river on the one hand, and, on the other, a slimy, poisonous-looking swamp, all rattling with sedges of enormous height, in which one might lose one's way as effectually as in a forest of oaks. Beyond this, the low rice-fields, all clothed in their rugged stubble, divided by dikes into monotonous squares, a species of prospect by no means beautiful to the mere lover of the picturesque. The only thing that I met with to attract my attention was a most beautiful species of ivy, the leaf longer and more graceful than that of the common English creeper, glittering with the highest varnish, delicately veined, and of a rich brown-green, growing in profuse garlands from branch to branch of some stunted evergreen bushes which border the dike, and which the people call salt-water bush. My walks are rather circumscribed, inasmuch as the dikes are the only promenades. On all sides of these lie either the marshy rice-fields, the brimming river, or the swampy patches of yet unreclaimed forest, where the hugh cypress-trees and exquisite evergreen undergrowth spring up from a stagnant sweltering pool, that effectually forbids the foot of the explorer.

As I skirted one of these thickets to-day, I stood still to admire the beauty of the shrubbery. Every shade of green, every variety of form, every degree of varnish, and all in full leaf and beauty in the very depth of winter. The stunted dark-colored oak; the magnolia bay (like our own culinary and fragrant bay), which grows to a very great size; the wild myrtle, a beautiful and profuse shrub, rising to a height of six, eight, and ten feet, and branching on all sides in luxuriant tufted fullness; most beautiful of all, that pride of the South, the magnolia grandiflora, whose lustrous dark green perfect foliage would alone render it an object of admiration, without the queenly blossom whose color, size, and perfume are unrivaled in the whole vegetable kingdom. This last magnificent creature grows to the size of a forest tree in these swamps, but seldom adorns a high or dry soil, or suffers itself to be successfully transplanted. Under all these the spiked palmetto forms an impenetrable covert, and from glittering graceful branch to branch hang garlands of evergreen creepers, on which the mocking-birds are swinging and singing even now; while I, bethinking me of the pinching cold that is at this hour tyrannizing over your region, look round on this strange scene—on these green woods, this unfettered river, and sunny sky—and feel very much like one in another planet from yourself.

The profusion of birds here is one thing that strikes me as curious, coming from the vicinity of Philadelphia, where even the robin redbreast, held sacred by the humanity of all other Christian people, is not safe from the *gunning* prowess of the unlicensed sportsmen of your free country. The negroes (of course) are not allowed the use of fire-arms, and their very simply constructed traps do not do much havoc among the feathered hordes that haunt their rice-fields. Their case is rather a hard one, as partridges, snipes, and the most delicious wild ducks abound here, and their allowance of rice and Indian meal would not be the worse for such additions. No day passes that I do not, in the course of my walk, put up a number of the land birds, and startle from among the gigantic sedges the long-necked water-fowl by dozens. It arouses the kill-ing propensity in me most dreadfully, and I really enter-tain serious thoughts of learning to use a gun, for the mere pleasure of destroying these pretty birds as they whirr from their secret coverts close beside my path. How strong an instinct of animal *humanity* this is, and how strange if one be more strange than another. Reflection rebukes it almost instantaneously, and yet for the life of me I can not help wishing I had a fowling-piece whenev-er I put up a covey of these creatures; though I suppose, if one were brought bleeding and maimed to me, I should begin to cry, and be very pathetic, after the fashion of Jacques. However, one must live, you know; and here our living consists very mainly of wild ducks, wild geese, wild turkeys, and venison. Now, perhaps, can one imag-ine the universal doom overtaking a creature with less misery than in the case of the bird who, in the very mo-ment of his triumphant soaring, is brought dead to the ground. I should like to bargain for such a finis myself amazingly, I know, and have always thought that the death I should prefer would be to break my neck off the back of my horse at a full gallop on a fine day. Of course a bad shot should be hung—a man who shatters his birds' wings and legs; if I undertook the trade, I would learn of some Southern duelist, and always shoot my bird through the head or heart—as an expert murderer knows how. Besides these birds of which we make our prey, there are others that prey upon their own fraternity. Hawks of every sort and size wheel their steady rounds above the rice-fields; and the great turkey-buzzards—those most unsightly carrion birds—spread their broad black wings, and soar over the river like so many mock eagles. I do not know that I ever saw any winged creature of so forbidding an aspect as these same turkey-buzzards; their heavy flight, their awkward gait, their bald-looking head and neck, and their devotion to every species of foul and detestable food, render them almost abhorrent to me. They abound in the South, and in Charleston are held in especial veneration for their scavenger-like propensities, killing one of them being, I believe, a finable offense by the city police regulations. Among the Brobdignagian sedges that in some parts of the island fringe the Altamaha, the nightshade (apparently the same as the European creeper) weaves a perfect matting of its poisonous garlands, and my remembrance of its prevalence in the woods and hedges of England did not reconcile me to its appearance here. How much of this is mere association I can not tell; but, whether the wild duck makes its nest under its green arches, or the alligators and snakes of the Altamaha have their secret bowers there, it is an evil-looking weed, and I shall have every leaf of it cleared away.

I must inform you of a curious conversation which took place between my little girl and the woman who performs for us the offices of chambermaid here—of course one of Mr. ——'s slaves. What suggested it to the child, or whence indeed she gathered her information, I know not; but children are made of eyes and ears, and nothing; however minute, escapes their microscopic observation. She suddenly began addressing this woman. "Mary, some persons are free and some are not (the woman made no reply). I am a free person (of a little more than three years old). I say, I am a free person, Mary—do you know that?" "Yes, missis." "Some persons are free and some are not—do you know that, Mary?" "Yes, missis, *here*," was the reply; "I know it is so here, in this world." Here my child's white nurse, my dear Margery, who had hitherto been silent, interfered, saying, "Oh, then you think it will not always be so?" "Me hope not, missis." I am afraid, E——, this woman actually imagines that there will be no slaves in heaven; isn't that preposterous, now, when, by the account of most of the Southerners, slavery itself must be heaven, or something uncommonly like it? Oh, if you could imagine how this title "Missis," addressed to me and to my children, shocks all my feelings! Several times I have exclaimed, "For God's sake do not call me that!" and only been awakened, by the stupid amazement of the poor creatures I was addressing, to the perfect uselessness of my thus expostulating with them; once or twice, indeed, I have done more—I have explained to them, and they appeared to comprehend me well, that I had no ownership over them, for that I held such ownership sinful, and that, though I was the wife of the man who pretends to own them, I was, in truth, no more their mistress than they were mine. Some of them I know understood me, more of them did not.

Our servants—those who have been selected to wait upon us in the house—consist of a man, who is quite a tolerable cook (I believe this is a natural gift with them, as with Frenchmen); a dairy-woman, who churns for us; a laundry-woman; her daughter, our housemaid, the aforesaid Mary; and two young lads of from fifteen to twenty, who wait upon us in the capacity of footmen. As, however, the latter are perfectly filthy in their persons and clothes—their faces, hands, and naked feet being literally incrusted with dirt—their attendance at our meals is not, as you may suppose, particularly agreeable to me, and I dispense with it as often as possible. Mary, too, is so intolerably offensive in her person that it is impossible to endure her proximity, and the consequence is that, among Mr. ——'s slaves, I wait upon myself more than I have ever done in my life before. About this same personal offensiveness, the Southerners, you know, insist that it is inherent with the race, and it is one of their most cogent reasons for keeping them as slaves. But, as this very disagreeable peculiarity does not prevent Southern women from hanging their infants at the breasts of negresses, nor almost every planter's wife and daughter from having one or more little pet blacks sleeping like puppy-dogs in their very bedchamber, nor almost every planter from admitting one or several of his female slaves to the still closer intimacy of his bed, it seems to me that this objection to doing them right is not very valid. I can not imagine that they would smell much worse if they were free, or come in much closer contact with the delicate organs of their white fellow-countrymen; indeed, inasmuch as good deeds are spoken of as having a sweet savor before God, it might be supposed that the freeing of the blacks might prove rather an odoriferous process than the contrary. However this may be, I must tell you that this potent reason for enslaving a whole race of people is no more potent with me than most of the others adduced to support the system, inasmuch as, from observation and some experience, I am strongly inclined to believe that peculiar igno-

rance of the laws of health and the habits of decent cleanliness are the real and only causes of this disagreeable
characteristic of the race, thorough ablutions and change
of linen, when tried, having been perfectly successful in
removing all such objections; and if ever you have come
into any thing like neighborly proximity with a low Irishman or woman, I think you will allow that the same causes
produce very nearly the same effects. The stench in an
Irish, Scotch, Italian, or French hovel are quite as intolerable as any I ever found in our negro houses, and the filth
and vermin which abound about the clothes and persons
of the lower peasantry of any of those countries as abominable as the same conditions in the black population of
the United States. A total absence of self-respect begets
these hateful physical results, and in proportion as moral
influences are remote, physical evils will abound. Well-
being, freedom, and industry induce self-respect, self-respect induces cleanliness and personal attention, so that
slavery is answerable for all the evils that exhibit themselves where it exists—from lying, thieving, and adultery,
to dirty houses, ragged clothes, and foul smells.

But to return to our Ganymedes. One of them—the
eldest son of our laundry-woman, and Mary's brother, a
boy of the name of Aleck (Alexander)—is uncommonly
bright and intelligent; he performs all the offices of a
well-instructed waiter with great efficiency, and any where
out of slave land would be able to earn fourteen or fifteen
dollars a month for himself; he is remarkably good tem-
pered and well disposed. The other poor boy is so stupid
that he appears sullen from absolute darkness of intellect;
instead of being a little lower than the angels, he is scarcely a little higher than the brutes, and to this condition are
reduced the majority of his kind by the institutions under
which they live. I should tell you that Aleck's parents
and kindred have always been about the house of the

overseer, and in daily habits of intercourse with him and his wife; and wherever this is the case the effect of involuntary education is evident in the improved intelligence of the degraded race. In a conversation which Mr. —— had this evening with Mr. O——, the overseer, the latter mentioned that two of our carpenters had in their leisure time made a boat, which they had disposed of to some neighboring planter for sixty dollars.

Now, E——, I have no intention of telling you a one-sided story, or concealing from you what are cited as the advantages which these poor people possess; you, who know that no indulgence is worth simple justice, either to him who gives or him who receives, will not thence conclude that their situation thus mitigated is, therefore, what it should be. On this matter of the sixty dollars earned by Mr. ——'s two men much stress was laid by him and his overseer. I look at it thus: If these men were industrious enough, out of their scanty leisure, to earn sixty dollars, how much more of remuneration, of comfort, of improvement might they not have achieved were the price of their daily labor duly paid them, instead of being unjustly withheld to support an idle young man and his idle family—i. e., myself and my children.

And here it may be well to inform you that the slaves on this plantation are divided into field-hands and mechanics or artisans. The former, the great majority, are the more stupid and brutish of the tribe; the others, who are regularly taught their trades, are not only exceedingly expert at them, but exhibit a greater general activity of intellect, which must necessarily result from even a partial degree of cultivation. There are here a gang (for that is the honorable term) of coopers, of blacksmiths, of bricklayers, of carpenters, all well acquainted with their peculiar trades. The latter constructed the wash-hand stands, clothes-presses, sofas, tables, etc., with which our house is furnished, and they are very neat pieces of workmanship —neither veneered or polished indeed, nor of very costly materials, but of the white pine wood planed as smooth as marble—a species of furniture not very luxurious perhaps, but all the better adapted therefore to the house itself, which is certainly rather more devoid of the conveniences and adornments of modern existence than any thing I ever took up my abode in before. It consists of three small rooms, and three still smaller, which would be more appropriately designated as closets, a wooden recess by way of pantry, and a kitchen detached from the dwelling —a mere wooden out-house, with no floor but the bare earth, and for furniture a congregation of filthy negroes, who lounge in and out of it like hungry hounds at all hours of the day and night, picking up such scraps of food as they can find about, which they discuss squatting down upon their hams, in which interesting position and occupation I generally find a number of them whenever I have sufficient hardihood to venture within those precincts, the sight of which and its tenants is enough to slacken the appetite of the hungriest hunter that ever lost all nice regards in the mere animal desire for food. Of our three apartments, one is our sitting, eating, and *living* room, and is sixteen feet by fifteen. The walls are plastered indeed, but neither painted nor papered; it is divided from our bedroom (a similarly elegant and comfortable chamber) by a dingy wooden partition covered all over with hooks, pegs, and nails, to which hats, caps, keys, etc., etc., are suspended in graceful irregularity. The doors open by wooden latches, raised by means of small bits of packthread—I imagine, the same primitive order of fastening celebrated in the touching chronicle of Red Riding Hood; how they shut I will not attempt to describe, as the shutting of a door is a process of extremely rare occurrence throughout the whole Southern country. The third room,

a chamber with sloping ceiling, immediately over our sitting-room and under the roof, is appropriated to the nurse
and my two babies.  Of the closets, one is Mr.——, the
overseer's, bedroom, the other his office or place of business; and the third, adjoining our bedroom, and opening
immediately out of doors, is Mr.——'s dressing-room and
cabinet d'affaires, where he gives audiences to the negroes,
redresses grievances, distributes red woolen caps (a singular gratification to a slave), shaves himself, and performs the other offices of his toilet.  Such being our abode,
I think you will allow there is little danger of my being
dazzled by the luxurious splendors of a Southern slave
residence.  Our sole mode of summoning our attendants
is by a pack-thread bell-rope suspended in the sitting-
room.  From the bedrooms we have to raise the windows
and our voices, and bring them by power of lungs, or help
ourselves—which, I thank God, was never yet a hardship
to me.

I mentioned to you just now that two of the carpenters
had made a boat in their leisure time.  I must explain
this to you, and this will involve the mention of another
of Miss Martineau's mistakes with regard to slave labor,
at least in many parts of the Southern States.  She mentions that on one estate of which she knew, the proprietor
had made the experiment, and very successfully, of ap-
pointing to each of his slaves a certain task to be performed in the day, which once accomplished, no matter
how early, the rest of the four-and-twenty hours were allowed to the laborer to employ as he pleased.  She mentions this as a single experiment, and rejoices over it as
a decided amelioration in the condition of the slave, and
one deserving of general adoption.  But in the part of
Georgia where this estate is situated, the custom of task
labor is universal, and it prevails, I believe, throughout
Georgia, South Carolina, and parts of North Carolina; in

other parts of the latter state, however—as I was informed by our overseer, who is a native of that state—the estates are small, rather deserving the name of farms, and
the laborers are much upon the same footing as the laboring men at the North, working from sunrise to sunset in
the fields with the farmer and his sons, and coming in with
them to their meals, which they take immediately after
the rest of the family.   In Louisiana and the new southwestern slave states, I believe, task labor does not prevail;
but it is in those that the condition of the poor human
cattle is most deplorable, as you know it was there that
the humane calculation was not only made, but openly and
unhesitatingly avowed, that the planters found it, upon
the whole, their most profitable plan to work off (kill with
labor) their whole number of slaves about once in seven
years, and renew the whole stock.   By-the-by, the Jewish institution of slavery is much insisted upon by the
Southern upholders of the system; perhaps this is their
notion of the Jewish jubilee, when the slaves were by Mo-
ses's strict enactment to be all set free.   Well, this task
system is pursued on this estate; and thus it is that the
two carpenters were enabled to make the boat they sold
for sixty dollars.   These tasks, of course, profess to be
graduated according to the sex, age, and strength of the
laborer; but in many instances this is not the case, as I
think you will agree when I tell you that on Mr. ——'s
first visit to his estates he found that the men and the
women who labored in the fields had the same task to
perform.   This was a noble admission of female equality,
was it not?—and thus it had been on the estate for many
years past.   Mr. ——, of course, altered the distribution
of the work, diminishing the quantity done by the women.

I had a most ludicrous visit this morning from the
midwife of the estate—rather an important personage
both to master and slave, as to her unassisted skill and

science the ushering of all the young negroes into their existence of bondage is intrusted. I heard a great deal of conversation in the dressing-room adjoining mine while performing my own toilet, and presently Mr. —— opened my room door, ushering in a dirty, fat, good-humored looking old negress, saying, "The midwife, Rose, wants to make your acquaintance." "Oh massa!" shrieked out the old creature, in a paroxysm of admiration, "where you get this lilly alabaster baby!" For a moment I looked round to see if she was speaking of my baby; but no, my dear, this superlative apostrophe was elicited by the fairness of *my skin:* so much for degrees of comparison. Now I suppose that if I chose to walk arm in arm with the dingiest mulatto through the streets of Philadelphia, nobody could possibly tell by my complexion that I was not his sister, so that the mere quality of mistress must have had a most miraculous effect upon my skin in the eyes of poor Rose. But this species of outrageous flattery is as usual with these people as with the low Irish, and arises from the ignorant desire, common to both the races, of propitiating at all costs the fellow-creature who is to them as a Providence — or rather, I should say, a fate — for 'tis a heathen and no Christian relationship. Soon after this visit, I was summoned into the wooden porch or piazza of the house, to see a poor woman who desired to speak to me. This was none other than the tall, emaciated-looking negress who, on the day of our arrival, had embraced me and my nurse with such irresistible zeal. She appeared very ill to-day, and presently unfolded to me a most distressing history of bodily afflictions. She was the mother of a very large family, and complained to me that, what with childbearing and hard field labor, her back was almost broken in two. With an almost savage vehemence of gesticulation, she suddenly tore up her scanty clothing, and exhibited a spectacle with which I was inconceivably shocked and sickened. The facts, without any of her corroborating statements, bore tolerable witness to the hardships of her existence. I promised to attend to her ailments and give her proper remedies; but these are natural results, inevitable and irremediable ones, of improper treatment of the female frame; and, though there may be alleviation, there can not be any cure when once the beautiful and wonderful structure has been thus made the victim of ignorance, folly, and wickedness.

After the departure of this poor woman, I walked down the settlement toward the Infirmary or hospital, calling in at one or two of the houses along the row. These cabins consist of one room, about twelve feet by fifteen, with a couple of closets smaller and closer than the state-rooms of a ship, divided off from the main room and each other by rough wooden partitions, in which the inhabitants sleep. They have almost all of them a rude bedstead, with the gray moss of the forests for mattress, and filthy, pestilential-looking blankets for covering. Two families (sometimes eight and ten in number) reside in one of these huts, which are mere wooden frames pinned, as it were, to the earth by a brick chimney outside, whose enormous aperture within pours down a flood of air, but little counteracted by the miserable spark of fire, which hardly sends an attenuated thread of lingering smoke up its huge throat. A wide ditch runs immediately at the back of these dwellings, which is filled and emptied daily by the tide. Attached to each hovel is a small scrap of ground for a garden, which, however, is for the most part untended and uncultivated. Such of these dwellings as I visited to-day were filthy and wretched in the extreme, and exhibited that most deplorable consequence of ignorance and an abject condition, the inability of the inhabitants to secure and improve even such pitiful comfort as might yet be achieved by them. Instead of

the order, neatness, and ingenuity which might convert
even these miserable hovels into tolerable residences,
there was the careless, reckless, filthy indolence which
even the brutes do not exhibit in their lairs and nests,
and which seemed incapable of applying to the uses of
existence the few miserable means of comfort yet within
their reach. Firewood and shavings lay littered about
the floors, while the half-naked children were cowering
round two or three smouldering cinders. The moss with
which the chinks and crannies of their ill-protecting
dwellings might have been stuffed was trailing in dirt
and dust about the ground, while the back door of the
huts, opening upon a most unsightly ditch, was left wide
open for the fowls and ducks, which they are allowed to
raise, to travel in and out, increasing the filth of the
cabin by what they brought and left in every direction.
In the midst of the floor, or squatting round the cold
hearth, would be four or five little children from four to
ten years old, the latter all with babies in their arms, the
care of the infants being taken from the mothers (who
are driven afield as soon as they recover from child labor),
and devolved upon these poor little nurses, as they are
called, whose business it is to watch the infant, and carry
it to its mother whenever it may require nourishment.
To these hardly human little beings I addressed my remonstrances about the filth, cold, and unnecessary wretchedness of their room, bidding the elder boys and girls
kindle up the fire, sweep the floor, and expel the poultry.
For a long time my very words seemed unintelligible to
them, till, when I began to sweep and make up the fire,
etc., they first fell to laughing, and then imitating me.
The incrustations of dirt on their hands, feet, and faces
were my next object of attack, and the stupid negro practice (by-the-by, but a short time since nearly universal in
enlightened Europe) of keeping the babies with their feet

bare, and their heads, already well capped by nature with
their woolly hair, wrapped in half a dozen hot, filthy
coverings.  Thus I traveled down the " street," in every
dwelling endeavoring to awaken a new perception, that
of cleanliness, sighing, as I went, over the futility of my
own exertions, for how can slaves be improved?  Nathless, thought I, let what can be done; for it may be that,
the two being incompatible, improvement may yet expel
slavery ; and so it might, and surely would, if, instead of
beginning at the end, I could but begin at the beginning
of my task.  If the mind and soul were awakened, instead
of mere physical good attempted, the physical good would
result, and the great curse vanish away ; but my hands
are tied fast, and this corner of the work is all that I may
do.  Yet it can not be but, from my words and actions,
some revelations should reach these poor people ; and
going in and out among them perpetually, I shall teach,
and they learn involuntarily a thousand things of deepest
import.  They must learn, and who can tell the fruit of
that knowledge alone, that there are beings in the world,
even with skins of a different color from their own, who
have sympathy for their misfortunes, love for their virtues, and respect for their common nature—but oh! my
heart is full almost to bursting as I walk among these
most poor creatures.

The Infirmary is a large two-story building, termina-
ting the broad orange-planted space between the two
rows of houses which form the first settlement ; it is
built of whitewashed wood, and contains four large-sized
rooms.  But how shall I describe to you the spectacle
which was presented to me on entering the first of
these?  But half the casements, of which there were six,
were glazed, and these were obscured with dirt, almost as
much as the other windowless ones were darkened by the
dingy shutters, which the shivering inmates had fastened

to in order to protect themselves from the cold. In the enormous chimney glimmered the powerless embers of a few sticks of wood, round which, however, as many of the sick women as could approach were cowering, some on wooden settles, most of them on the ground, excluding those who were too ill to rise; and these last poor wretches lay prostrate on the floor, without bed, mattress, or pillow, buried in tattered and filthy blankets, which, huddled round them as they lay strewed about, left hardly space to move upon the floor. And here, in their hour of sickness and suffering, lay those whose health and strength are spent in unrequited labor for us—those who, perhaps even yesterday, were being urged on to their unpaid task—those whose husbands, fathers, brothers, and sons were even at that hour sweating over the earth, whose produce was to buy for us all the luxuries which health can revel in, all the comforts which can alleviate sickness. I stood in the midst of them, perfectly unable to speak, the tears pouring from my eyes at this sad spectacle of their misery, myself and my emotion alike strange and incomprehensible to them. Here lay women expecting every hour the terrors and agonies of childbirth, others who had just brought their doomed offspring into the world, others who were groaning over the anguish and bitter disappointment of miscarriages— here lay some burning with fever, others chilled with cold and aching with rheumatism, upon the hard cold ground, the draughts and dampness of the atmosphere increasing their sufferings, and dirt, noise, and stench, and every aggravation of which sickness is capable, combined in their condition—here they lay like brute beasts, absorbed in physical suffering; unvisited by any of those Divine influences which may ennoble the dispensations of pain and illness, forsaken, as it seemed to me, of all good; and yet, O God, Thou surely hadst not forsaken them! Now pray take notice that this is the hospital of an estate where the

owners are supposed to be humane, the overseer efficient
and kind, and the negroes remarkably well cared for and
comfortable. As soon as I recovered from my dismay, I
addressed old Rose the midwife, who had charge of this
room, bidding her open the shutters of such windows as
were glazed, and let in the light. I next proceeded to
make up the fire; but, upon my lifting a log for that purpose, there was one universal outcry of horror, and old
Rose, attempting to snatch it from me, exclaimed, "Let
alone, missis—let be; what for you lift wood? you have
nigger enough, missis, to do it!" I hereupon had to explain to them my view of the purposes for which hands
and arms were appended to our bodies, and forthwith began making Rose tidy up the miserable apartment, removing all the filth and rubbish from the floor that could be
removed, folding up in piles the blankets of the patients
who were not using them, and placing, in rather more
sheltered and comfortable positions, those who were unable to rise. It was all that I could do, and having enforced upon them all my earnest desire that they should
keep their room swept, and as tidy as possible, I passed
on to the other room on the ground floor, and to the two
above, one of which is appropriated to the use of the men
who are ill. They were all in the same deplorable condition, the upper rooms being rather the more miserable, inasmuch as none of the windows were glazed at all, and
they had, therefore, only the alternative of utter darkness,
or killing draughts of air from the unsheltered casements.
In all, filth, disorder, and misery abounded; the floor was
the only bed, and scanty begrimed rags of blankets the
only covering. I left this refuge for Mr. ——'s sick dependents with my clothes covered with dust, and full of
vermin, and with a heart heavy enough, as you will well
believe. My morning's work had fatigued me not a little,
and I was glad to return to the house, where I gave vent

to my indignation and regret at the scene I had just witnessed to Mr. —— and his overseer, who, here, is a member of our family. The latter told me that the condition of the hospital had appeared to him, from his first entering upon his situation (only within the last year), to require a reform, and that he had proposed it to the former manager, Mr. K——, and Mr. ——'s brother, who is part proprietor of the estate, but, receiving no encouragement from them, had supposed that it was a matter of indifference to the owners, and had left it in the condition in which he had found it, in which condition it has been for the last nineteen years and upward.

This new overseer of ours has lived fourteen years with an old Scotch gentleman, who owns an estate adjoining Mr. ——'s, on the island of St. Simon's, upon which estate, from every thing I can gather, and from what I know of the proprietor's character, the slaves are probably treated with as much humanity as is consistent with slavery at all, and where the management and comfort of the hospital in particular had been most carefully and judiciously attended to. With regard to the indifference of our former manager upon the subject of the accommodation for the sick, he was an excellent overseer, *videlicet* the estate returned a full income under his management, and such men have nothing to do with sick slaves: they are tools, to be mended only if they can be made available again; if not, to be flung by as useless, without farther expense of money, time, or trouble.

I am learning to row here, for circumscribed, as my walks necessarily are, impossible as it is to resort to my favorite exercise on horseback upon these narrow dikes, I must do something to prevent my blood from stagnating; and this broad brimming river, and the beautiful light canoes which lie moored at the steps, are very inviting persuaders to this species of exercise. My first attempt was confined to pulling an oar across the stream, for which I rejoiced in sundry aches and pains altogether novel, letting alone a delightful row of blisters on each of my hands.

I forgot to tell you that in the hospital were several sick babies, whose mothers were permitted to suspend their field labor in order to nurse them. Upon addressing some remonstrances to one of these, who, besides having a sick child, was ill herself, about the horribly dirty condition of her baby, she assured me that it was impossible for them to keep their children clean; that they went out to work at daybreak, and did not get their tasks done till evening, and that then they were too tired and worn out to do any thing but throw themselves down and sleep. This statement of hers I mentioned on my return from the hospital, and the overseer appeared extremely annoyed by it, and assured me repeatedly that it was not true.

In the evening Mr. ——, who had been over to Darien, mentioned that one of the storekeepers there had told him that, in the course of a few years, he had paid the negroes of this estate several thousand dollars for moss, which is a very profitable article of traffic with them: they collect it from the trees, dry and pick it, and then sell it to the people in Darien for mattresses, sofas, and all sorts of stuffing purposes, which, in my opinion, it answers better than any other material whatever that I am acquainted with, being as light as horse-hair, as springy and elastic, and a great deal less harsh and rigid. It is now bedtime, dear E——, and I doubt not it has been sleepy time with you over this letter long ere you came thus far. There is a preliminary to my repose, however, in this agreeable residence, which I rather dread, namely, the hunting for, or discovering without hunting, in fine relief upon the whitewashed walls of my bedroom, a most hideous and detestable species of *reptile* called centipedes, which come out of the cracks and crevices of the walls, and fill my very heart with dismay. They are from an inch to two inches long, and appear to have not a hundred, but a thousand legs. I can not ascertain very certainly from the negroes whether they sting or not, but they look exceedingly as if they might, and I visit my babies every night in fear and trembling, lest I should find one or more of these hateful creatures mounting guard over them. Good-night; you are well to be free from centipedes—better to be free from slaves.

----

Dear E——, —This morning I paid my second visit to the Infirmary, and found there had been some faint attempt at sweeping and cleaning, in compliance with my entreaties. The poor woman Harriet, however, whose statement with regard to the impossibility of their attending properly to their children had been so vehemently denied by the overseer, was crying bitterly. I asked her what ailed her, when, more by signs and dumb show than words, she and old Rose informed me that Mr. O—— had flogged her that morning for having told me that the women had not time to keep their children clean. It is part of the regular duty of every overseer to visit the Infirmary at least once a day, which he generally does in the morning, and Mr. O——'s visit had preceded mine but a short time only, or I might have been edified by seeing a man horsewhip a woman. I again and again made her repeat her story, and she again and again affirmed that she had been flogged for what she told me, none of the whole company in the room denying it or contradicting her. I left the room because I was so disgusted and indignant that I could hardly restrain my feelings, and to express them could have produced no single good result. In the next ward, stretched upon the ground, apparently either asleep or so overcome with sickness as to be incapable of moving, lay an immense woman; her stature, as she cumbered the earth, must have been, I should think, five feet seven or eight, and her bulk enormous. She was wrapped in filthy rags, and lay with her face on the floor. As I approached, and stooped to see what ailed her, she suddenly threw out her arms, and, seized with violent convulsions, rolled over and over upon the floor, beating her head violently upon the ground, and throwing her enormous limbs about in a horrible manner. Immediately upon the occurrence of this fit, four or five women threw themselves literally upon her, and held her down by main force; they even proceeded to bind her legs and arms together, to prevent her dashing herself about; but this violent coercion and tight bandaging seemed to me, in my profound ignorance, more likely to increase her illness by impeding her breathing and the circulation of her blood, and I bade them desist, and unfasten all the strings and ligatures not only that they had put round her limbs, but which, by tightening her clothes round her body, caused any obstruction. How much I wished that, instead of music, and dancing, and such stuff, I had learned something of sickness and health, of the conditions and liabilities of the human body, that I might have known how to assist this poor creature, and to direct her ignorant and helpless nurses! The fit presently subsided, and was succeeded by the most deplorable prostration and weakness of nerves, the tears streaming down the poor woman's cheeks in showers, without, however, her uttering a single word, though she moaned incessantly. After bathing her forehead, hands, and chest with vinegar, we raised her up, and I sent to the house for a chair with a back (there was no such thing in the hospital), and we contrived to place her in it. I have seldom seen finer women than this poor creature and her younger sister, an immense strapping lass called Chloe — tall, straight, and extremely well made—who was assisting her sister, and whom I had remarked, for the extreme delight and merriment which my cleansing propensities seemed to give her, on my last visit to the hospital. She was here taking care of a sick baby, and helping to nurse her sister Molly, who, it seems, is subject to those fits, about which I spoke to our physician here—an intelligent man residing in Darien, who visits the estate whenever medical assistance is required. He seemed to attribute them to nervous disorder, brought on by frequent childbearing. This woman is young, I suppose at the outside not thirty, and her sister informed me that she had had ten children—ten children, E——! Fits and hard labor in the fields, unpaid labor, labor exacted with stripes—how do you fancy that? I wonder if my mere narration can make your blood boil as the facts did mine? Among the patients in this room was a young girl, apparently from fourteen to fifteen, whose hands and feet were literally rotting away piecemeal, from the effect of a horrible disease, to which the negroes are subject here, and I believe in the West Indies, and when it attacks the joints of the toes and fingers, the pieces absolutely decay and come off, leaving the limb a maimed and horrible stump! I believe no cure is known for this disgusting malady, which seems confined to these poor creatures. Another disease, of which they complained much, and which, of course, I was utterly incapable of accounting for, was a species of lock-jaw, to which their babies very frequently fall victims in the first or second week after their birth, refusing the breast, and the mouth gradually losing the power of opening itself. The horrible diseased state of head, common among their babies, is a mere result of filth and confinement, and therefore, though

I never any where saw such distressing and disgusting objects as some of these poor little woolly skulls presented, the cause was sufficiently obvious.( Pleurisy, or a tendency to it, seems very common among them; also peripneumonia, or inflammation of the lungs, which is terribly prevalent, and generally fatal. Rheumatism is almost universal; and as it proceeds from exposure, and want of knowledge and care, attacks indiscriminately the young and old. A great number of the women are victims to falling of the womb and weakness in the spine; but these are necessary results of their laborious existence, and do not belong either to climate or constitution.)

I have ingeniously contrived to introduce bribery, corruption, and pauperism, all in a breath, upon this island, which, until my advent, was as innocent of these pollutions, I suppose, as Prospero's isle of refuge. Wishing, however, to appeal to some perception, perhaps a little less dim in their minds than the abstract loveliness of cleanliness, I have proclaimed to all the little baby nurses that I will give a cent to every little boy or girl whose baby's face shall be clean, and one to every individual with clean face and hands of their own. My appeal was fully comprehended by the majority, it seems, for this morning I was surrounded, as soon as I came out, by a swarm of children carrying their little charges on their backs and in their arms, the shining, and, in many instances, wet faces and hands of the latter bearing ample testimony to the ablutions which had been inflicted upon them. How they will curse me and the copper cause of all their woes in their baby bosoms! Do you know that, little as grown negroes are admirable for their personal beauty (in my opinion, at least), the black babies of a year or two old are very pretty; they have, for the most part, beautiful eyes and eyelashes, the pearly perfect teeth, which they retain after their other juvenile graces have left them;

their skins are all (I mean of blacks generally) infinitely finer and softer than the skins of white people. Perhaps you are not aware that among the white race the *finest grained* skins generally belong to persons of dark complexion. This, as a characteristic of the black race, I think might be accepted as some compensation for the coarse woolly hair. The nose and mouth, which are so peculiarly displeasing in their conformation in the face of a negro man or woman, being the features least developed in a baby's countenance, do not at first present the ugliness which they assume as they become more marked; and when the very unusual operation of washing has been performed, the blood shines through the fine texture of the skin, giving life and richness to the dingy color, and displaying a species of beauty which I think scarcely any body who observed it would fail to acknowledge. I have seen many babies on this plantation who were quite as pretty as white children, and this very day stooped to kiss a little sleeping creature that lay on its mother's knees in the Infirmary—as beautiful a specimen of a sleeping infant as I ever saw. The caress excited the irrepressible delight of all the women present—poor creatures! who seemed to forget that I was a woman, and had children myself, and bore a woman's and a mother's heart toward them and theirs; but, indeed, the Honorable Mr. Slumkey could not have achieved more popularity by his performances in that line than I by this exhibition of feeling; and, had the question been my election, I am very sure nobody else would have had a chance of a vote through the island. But wisely is it said that use is second nature, and the contempt and neglect to which these poor people are used make the commonest expression of human sympathy appear a boon and gracious condescension. While I am speaking of the negro countenance, there is another beauty which is not at all unfrequent among those I see here

—a finely-shaped oval face—and those who know (as all painters and sculptors, all who understand beauty do) how much expression there is in the outline of the head, and how very rare it is to see a well-formed face, will be apt to consider this a higher matter than any coloring, of which, indeed, the red and white one so often admired is by no means the most rich, picturesque, or expressive. At first the dark color confounded all features to my eye, and I could hardly tell one face from another.  Becoming, however, accustomed to the complexion, I now perceive all the variety among these black countenances that there is among our own race, and as much difference in features and in expression as among the same number of whites.  There is another peculiarity which I have remarked among the women here—very considerable beauty in the make of the hands ; their feet are very generally ill made, which must be a natural, and not an acquired defect, as they seldom injure their feet by wearing shoes. The figures of some of the women are handsome, and their carriage, from the absence of any confining or tightening clothing, and the habit they have of balancing great weights on their heads, erect and good.

At the upper end of the row of houses, and nearest to our overseer's residence, is the hut of the head driver. Let me explain, by the way, his office.   The negroes, as I before told you, are divided into troops or gangs, as they are called ; at the head of each gang is a driver, who stands over them, whip in hand, while they perform their daily task, who renders an account of each individual slave and his work every evening to the overseer, and receives from him directions for their next day's tasks.   Each driver is allowed to inflict a dozen lashes upon any refractory slave in the field, and at the time of the offense ; they may not, however, extend the chastisement, and if it is found ineffectual, their remedy lies in reporting the unmanageable individual either to the head driver or the overseer, the former of whom has power to inflict three dozen lashes at his own discretion, and the latter as many as he himself sees fit, within the number of fifty; which limit, however, I must tell you, is an arbitrary one on this plantation, appointed by the founder of the estate, Major ——, Mr. ——'s grandfather, many of whose regulations, indeed I believe most of them, are still observed in the government of the plantation. Limits of this sort, however, to the power of either driver, head driver, or overseer, may or may not exist elsewhere; they are, to a certain degree, a check upon the power of these individuals; but in the absence of the master, the overseer may confine himself within the limit or not, as he chooses; and as for the master himself, where is his limit? He may, if he likes, flog a slave to death, for the laws which pretend that he may not are a mere pretense, inasmuch as the testimony of a black is never taken against a white; and upon this plantation of ours, and a thousand more, the overseer is the *only* white man, so whence should come the testimony to any crime of his? With regard to the oft-repeated statement that it is not the owner's interest to destroy his human property, it answers nothing; the instances in which men, to gratify the immediate impulse of passion, sacrifice not only their eternal, but their evident, palpable, positive worldly interest, are infinite. Nothing is commoner than for a man under the transient influence of anger to disregard his worldly advantage; and the black slave, whose preservation is indeed supposed to be his owner's interest, may be, will be, and is occasionally sacrificed to the blind impulse of passion.

To return to our head driver, or, as he is familiarly called, head man, Frank—he is second in authority only to the overseer, and exercises rule alike over the drivers and the gangs in the absence of the sovereign white man from the estate, which happens whenever Mr. O—— visits the other two plantations at Woodville and St. Simon's. He is sole master and governor of the island, appoints the work, pronounces punishments, gives permission to the men to leave the island (without it they never may do so), and exercises all functions of undisputed mastery over his fellow-slaves, for you will observe that all this while he is just as much a slave as any of the rest. Trustworthy, upright, intelligent, he may be flogged to-morrow if Mr. O—— or Mr. —— so please it, and sold the next day, like a cart-horse, at the will of the latter. Besides his various other responsibilities, he has the key of all the stores, and gives out the people's rations weekly; nor is it only the people's provisions that are put under his charge—meat, which is only given out to them occasionally, and provisions for the use of the family, are also intrusted to his care. Thus you see, among these *inferior* creatures, their own masters yet look to find, surviving all their best efforts to destroy them, good sense, honesty, self-denial, and all the qualities, mental and moral, that make one man worthy to be trusted by another. From the imperceptible but inevitable effect of the sympathies and influences of human creatures toward and over each other, Frank's intelligence has become uncommonly developed by intimate communion in the discharge of his duty with the former overseer, a very intelligent man, who has only just left the estate, after managing it for nineteen years; the effect of this intercourse, and of the trust and responsibility laid upon the man, are that he is clear-headed, well judging, active, intelligent, extremely well mannered, and, being respected, he respects himself. He is as ignorant as the rest of the slaves; but he is always clean and tidy in his person, with a courteousness of demeanor far removed from servility, and exhibits a strong instance of the intolerable and wicked injustice of the system under

which he lives, having advanced thus far toward improvement, in spite of all the bars it puts to progress; and here
being arrested, not by want of energy, want of sense, or
any want of his own, but by being held as another man's
property, who can only thus hold him by forbidding him
farther improvement. When I see that man, who keeps
himself a good deal aloof from the rest, in his leisure hours
looking, with a countenance of deep thought, as I did to-
day, over the broad river, which is to him as a prison wall,
to the fields and forest beyond, not one inch or branch of
which his utmost industry can conquer as his own, or acquire and leave an independent heritage to his children, I
marvel what the thoughts of such a man may be. I was
in his house to-day, and the same superiority in cleanliness, comfort, and propriety exhibited itself in his dwelling as in his own personal appearance and that of his wife
—a most active, trustworthy, excellent woman, daughter
of the oldest, and probably most highly respected of all
Mr. ——'s slaves. To the excellent conduct of this woman, and, indeed, every member of her family, both the present and the last overseer bear unqualified testimony.

As I was returning toward the house after my long
morning's lounge, a man rushed out of the blacksmith's
shop, and, catching me by the skirt of my gown, poured
forth a torrent of self-gratulations on having at length
found the "right missis." They have no idea, of course,
of a white person performing any of the offices of a servant, and as throughout the whole Southern country the
owner's children are nursed and tended, and sometimes
*suckled* by their slaves (I wonder how this inferior milk
agrees with the lordly *white* babies?), the appearance of
M—— with my two children had immediately suggested
the idea that she must be the missis. Many of the poor
negroes flocked to her, paying their profound homage
under this impression; and when she explained to them

that she was not their owner's wife, the confusion in their minds seemed very great—Heaven only knows whether they did not conclude that they had two mistresses, and Mr. —— two wives; for the privileged race must seem, in their eyes, to have such absolute masterdom on earth, that perhaps they thought polygamy might be one of the sovereign white men's numerous indulgences. The ecstasy of the blacksmith on discovering the "right missis" at last was very funny, and was expressed with such extraordinary grimaces, contortions, and gesticulations, that I thought I should have died of laughing at this rapturous identification of my most melancholy relation to the poor fellow.

Having at length extricated myself from the group which forms round me whenever I stop but for a few minutes, I pursued my voyage of discovery by peeping into the kitchen garden. I dared do no more; the aspect of the place would have rejoiced the very soul of Solomon's sluggard of old—a few cabbages and weeds innumerable filled the neglected-looking inclosure, and I ventured no farther than the entrance into its most uninviting precincts. You are to understand that upon this swamp island of ours we have quite a large stock of cattle, cows, sheep, pigs, and poultry in the most enormous and inconvenient abundance. The cows are pretty miserably off for pasture, the banks and pathways of the dikes being their only grazing ground, which the sheep perambulate also, in earnest search of a nibble of fresh herbage; both the cows and sheep are fed with rice flour in great abundance, and are pretty often carried down for change of air and more sufficient grazing to Hampton, Mr. ——'s estate, on the island of St. Simon's, fifteen miles from this place, farther down the river—or rather, indeed, I should say in the sea, for 'tis salt water all round, and one end of the island has a noble beach open to the vast Atlantic.

The pigs thrive admirably here, and attain very great perfection of size and flavor, the rice flour upon which they are chiefly fed tending to make them very delicate. As for the poultry, it being one of the few privileges of the poor blacks to raise as many as they can, their abundance is literally a nuisance—ducks, fowls, pigeons, turkeys (the two latter species, by-the-by, are exclusively the master's property), cluck, scream, gabble, gobble, crow, cackle, fight, fly, and flutter in all directions, and to their immense concourse, and the perfect freedom with which they intrude themselves even into the piazza of the house, the pantry, and kitchen, I partly attribute the swarms of fleas, and other still less agreeable vermin, with which we are most horribly pestered.

My walk lay to-day along the bank of a canal, which has been dug through nearly the whole length of the island, to render more direct and easy the transportation of the rice from one end of the estate to another, or from the various distant fields to the principal mill at Settlement No. 1. It is of considerable width and depth, and opens by various locks into the river. It has, unfortunately, no trees on its banks, but a good foot-path renders it, in spite of that deficiency, about the best walk on the island. I passed again to-day one of those beautiful evergreen thickets, which I described to you in my last letter; it is called a reserve, and is kept uncleared and uncultivated in its natural swampy condition, to allow of the people's procuring their firewood from it. I can not get accustomed, so as to be indifferent to this exquisite natural ornamental growth, and think, as I contemplate the various and beautiful foliage of these watery woods, how many of our finest English parks and gardens owe their chiefest adornments to plantations of these shrubs, procured at immense cost, reared with infinite pains and care, which are here basking in the winter's sunshine, waiting to be cut down for firewood! These little groves are peopled with wild pigeons and birds, which they designate here as blackbirds. These sometimes rise from the rice fields with a whirr of multitudinous wings that is almost startling, and positively overshadow the ground beneath like a cloud.

I had a conversation that interested me a good deal, during my walk to-day, with my peculiar slave Jack. This lad, whom Mr. —— has appointed to attend me in my roamings about the island, and rowing expeditions on the river, is the son of the last head driver, a man of very extraordinary intelligence and faithfulness—such, at least, is the account given of him by his employers (in the burial-ground of the negroes is a stone dedicated to his memory, a mark of distinction accorded by his masters, which his son never failed to point out to me when we passed that way). Jack appears to inherit his quickness of apprehension; his questions, like those of an intelligent child, are absolutely inexhaustible; his curiosity about all things beyond this island, the prison-house of his existence, is perfectly intense; his countenance is very pleasing, mild, and not otherwise than thoughtful; he is, in common with the rest of them, a stupendous flatterer, and, like the rest of them, also seems devoid of physical and moral courage. To-day, in the midst of his torrent of inquiries about places and things, I suddenly asked him if he would like to be free. A gleam of light absolutely shot over his whole countenance, like the vivid and instantaneous lightning; he stammered, hesitated, became excessively confused, and at length replied, " Free, missis! what for me wish to be free? Oh no, missis, me no wish to be free, if massa only let we keep pig!" The fear of offending by uttering that forbidden wish—the dread of admitting, by its expression, the slightest discontent with his present situation—the desire to conciliate my favor, even at the expense of strangling the intense natural longing that absolutely glowed in his every feature—it was a sad spectacle, and I repented my question. As for the pitiful request, which he reiterated several times, adding, "No, missis, me no want to be free; me work till me die for missis and massa," with increased emphasis; it amounted only to this, that negroes once were, but no longer are, permitted to keep pigs. The increase of filth and foul smells consequent upon their being raised is, of course, very great; and, moreover, Mr. —— told me, when I preferred poor Jack's request to him, that their allowance was no more than would suffice their own necessity, and that they had not the means of feeding the animals. With a little good management they might very easily obtain them, however; their little "kail-yard" alone would suffice to it, and the pork and bacon would prove a most welcome addition to their farinaceous diet. You perceive at once (or, if you could have seen the boy's face, you would have perceived at once) that his situation was no mystery to him; that his value to Mr. ——, and, as he supposed, to me, was perfectly well known to him, and that he comprehended immediately that his expressing even the desire to be free might be construed by me into an offense, and sought, by eager protestations of his delighted acquiescence in slavery, to conceal his soul's natural yearning, lest I should resent it. 'Twas a sad passage between us, and sent me home full of the most painful thoughts. I told Mr. ——, with much indignation, of poor Harriet's flogging, and represented that if the people were to be chastised for any thing they said to me, I must leave the place, as I could not but hear their complaints, and endeavor, by all my miserable limited means, to better their condition while I was here. He said he would ask Mr. O—— about it, assuring me, at the same time, that it was impossible to believe a single word any of these people said. At dinner, accordingly, the inquiry

was made as to the cause of her punishment, and Mr.
O—— then said it was not at all for what she had told
me that he had flogged her, but for having answered him
impertinently; that he had ordered her into the field,
whereupon she had said she was ill and could not work;
that he retorted he knew better, and bade her get up and
go to work; she replied, " Very well, I'll go, but I shall
just come back again!" meaning that when in the field
she would be unable to work, and obliged to return to the
hospital. " For this reply," Mr. O—— said, " I gave her
a good lashing; it was her business to have gone into the
field without answering me, and then we should have
soon seen whether she could work or not; I gave it to
Chloe too for some such impudence." I give you the
words of the conversation, which was prolonged to a great
length, the overseer complaining of the sham sicknesses
of the slaves, and detailing the most disgusting struggle
which is going on the whole time, on the one hand to inflict, and on the other to evade oppression and injustice.
With this sauce I ate my dinner, and truly it tasted bitter.

Toward sunset I went on the river to take my rowing
lesson. A darling little canoe, which carries two oars and
a steersman, and rejoices in the appropriate title of the
" Dolphin," is my especial vessel; and with Jack's help
and instructions, I contrived this evening to row upward
of half a mile, coasting the reed-crowned edge of the isl-
and to another very large rice mill, the enormous wheel
of which is turned by the tide. A small bank of mud and
sand, covered with reedy coarse grass, divides the river
into two arms on this side of the island; the deep channel is on the outside of this bank, and as we rowed home
this evening, the tide having fallen, we scraped sand almost the whole way. Mr. ——'s domain, it seems to me,
will presently fill up this shallow stream, and join itself to

the above-mentioned mud-bank. The whole course of this most noble river is full of shoals, banks, mud, and sand-bars, and the navigation, which is difficult to those who know it well, is utterly baffling to the inexperienced. The fact is, that the two elements are so fused hereabouts that there are hardly such things as earth or water proper; that which styles itself the former is a fat, muddy, slimy sponge, that, floating half under the turbid river, looks yet saturated with the thick waves which every now and then reclaim their late dominion, and cover it almost entirely; the water, again, cloudy and yellow, like pea-soup, seems but a solution of such islands, rolling turbid and thick with alluvium, which it both gathers and deposits as it sweeps along with a swollen, smooth rapidity, that almost deceives the eye. Amphibious creatures, alligators, serpents, and wild-fowl haunt these yet but half-formed regions, where land and water are of the consistency of hasty-pudding—the one seeming too unstable to walk on, the other almost too thick to float in. But then the sky —if no human chisel ever yet cut breath, neither did any human pen ever write light; if it did, mine should spread out before you the unspeakable glories of these Southern heavens, the saffron brightness of morning, the blue intense brilliancy of noon, the golden splendor and the rosy softness of sunset. Italy and Claude Lorraine may go hang themselves together! Heaven itself does not seem brighter or more beautiful to the imagination than these surpassing pageants of fiery rays, and piled-up beds of orange, golden clouds, with edges too bright to look on, scattered wreaths of faintest rosy bloom, amber streaks and pale green lakes between, and amid sky all mingled blue and rose tints, a spectacle to make one fall over the side of the boat, with one's head broken off with looking adoringly upward, but which, on paper, means nothing.

At six o'clock our little canoe grazed the steps at the

landing. These were covered with young women, and
boys, and girls, drawing water for their various household
purposes. A very small cedar pail—a piggin as they
termed it—serves to scoop up the river water; and having, by this means, filled a large bucket, they transfer this
to their heads, and, thus laden, march home with the purifying element—what to do with it I can not imagine, for
evidence of its ever having been introduced into their
dwellings I saw none. As I ascended the stairs, they surrounded me with shrieks and yells of joy, uttering exclamations of delight and amazement at my rowing. Considering that they dig, delve, carry burdens, and perform
many more athletic exercises than pulling a light oar, I
was rather amused at this; but it was the singular fact
of seeing a white woman stretch her sinews in any toil-
some exercise which astounded them, accustomed as they
are to see both men and women of the privileged skin es-
chew the slightest shadow of labor as a thing not only
painful, but degrading. They will learn another lesson
from me, however, whose idea of heaven was pronounced
by a friend of mine, to whom I once communicated it, to
be "devilish hard work!" It was only just six o'clock,
and these women had all done their tasks. I exhorted
them to go home and wash their children, and clean their
houses and themselves, which they professed themselves
ready to do, but said they had no soap. Then began a
chorus of mingled requests for soap, for summer clothing,
and a variety of things, which, if "Missis only give we,
we be so clean forever!"

This request for summer clothing, by-the-by, I think a
very reasonable one. The allowance of clothes made yearly to each slave by the present regulations of the estate is
a certain number of yards of flannel, and as much more
of what they call plains—an extremely stout, thick, heavy
woolen cloth, of a dark gray or blue color, which resem-

bles the species of carpet we call drugget. This, and two pair of shoes, is the regular ration of clothing; but these plains would be intolerable to any but negroes, even in winter, in this climate, and are intolerable to them in the summer. A far better arrangement, in my opinion, would be to increase their allowance of flannel and under clothing, and to give them dark chintzes instead of these thick carpets, which are very often the only covering they wear at all. I did not impart all this to my petitioners, but, disengaging myself from them, for they held my hands and clothes, I conjured them to offer us some encouragement to better their condition by bettering it as much as they could themselves—enforced the virtue of washing themselves and all belonging to them, and at length made good my retreat. As there is no particular reason why such a letter as this should ever come to an end, I had better spare you for the present. You shall have a faithful journal, I promise you, henceforward, as hitherto, from yours ever.

---

DEAR E——,—We had a species of fish this morning for our breakfast which deserves more glory than I can bestow upon it. Had I been the ingenious man who wrote a poem upon fish, the white mullet of the Altamaha should have been at least my heroine's cousin. 'Tis the heavenliest creature that goes upon fins. I took a long walk this morning to Settlement No. 3, the third village on the island. My way lay along the side of the canal, beyond which, and only divided from it by a raised narrow causeway, rolled the brimming river, with its girdle of glittering evergreens, while on my other hand a deep trench marked the line of the rice fields. It really seemed as if the increase of merely a shower of rain might join all these waters together, and lay the island under its original cov-

ering again. I visited the people and houses here. I
found nothing in any respect different from what I have
described to you at Settlement No. 1. During the course
of my walk, I startled from its repose in one of the rice
fields a huge blue heron. You must have seen, as I often
have, these creatures stuffed in museums; but 'tis another
matter, and far more curious, to see them stalking on their
stilts of legs over a rice field, and then, on your near approach, see them spread their wide heavy wings, and throw
themselves upon the air, with their long shanks flying
after them in a most grotesque and laughable manner.
They fly as if.they did not know how to do it very well;
but standing still, their height (between four and five feet)
and peculiar color, a dusky, grayish blue, with black about
the head, render their appearance very beautiful and striking.

In the afternoon I and Jack rowed ourselves over to
Darien. It is Saturday—the day of the week on which
the slaves from the island are permitted to come over to
the town to purchase such things as they may require and
can afford, and to dispose, to the best advantage, of their
poultry, moss, and eggs. I met many of them paddling
themselves singly in their slight canoes, scooped out of
the trunk of a tree, and parties of three and four rowing
boats of their own building, laden with their purchases,
singing, laughing, talking, and apparently enjoying their
holiday to the utmost. They all hailed me with shouts
of delight as I pulled past them, and many were the in-
junctions bawled after Jack to "mind and take good care
of missis!" We returned home through the glory of a
sunset all amber-colored and rosy, and found that one of
the slaves, a young lad for whom Mr.—— has a particular
regard, was dangerously ill. Dr. H—— was sent for; and
there is every probability that he, Mr.——, and Mr. O——
will be up all night with the poor fellow. I shall write

more to-morrow. To-day being Sunday, dear E——, a large boat full of Mr. ——'s people from Hampton came up, to go to church at Darien, and to pay their respects to their master, and see their new "missis." The same scene was acted over again that occurred on our first arrival. A crowd clustered round the house door, to whom I and my babies were produced, and with every individual of whom we had to shake hands some half a dozen times. They brought us up presents of eggs (their only wealth), beseeching us to take them; and one young lad, the son of head man Frank, had a beautiful pair of chickens, which he offered most earnestly to S——. We took one of them, not to mortify the poor fellow, and a green ribbon being tied round its leg, it became a sacred fowl, "little missis's chicken." By-the-by, this young man had so light a complexion, and such regular straight features, that, had I seen him any where else, I should have taken him for a southern European, or, perhaps, in favor of his tatters, a gipsy; but certainly it never would have occurred to me that he was the son of negro parents. I observed this to Mr. ——, who merely replied, "He is the son of head man Frank and his wife Betty, and they are both black enough, as you see." The expressions of devotion and delight of these poor people are the most fervent you can imagine. One of them, speaking to me of Mr. ——, and saying that they had heard that he had not been well, added, "Oh! we hear so, missis, and we not know what to do. Oh! missis, massa sick, all him people *broken!*"

Dr. H—— came again to-day to see the poor sick boy, who is doing much better, and bidding fair to recover. He entertained me with an account of the Darien society, its aristocracies and democracies, its little grandeurs and smaller pettinesses, its circles higher and lower, its social jealousies, fine invisible lines of demarkation, imperceptible shades of different respectability, and delicate divisions of genteel, genteeler, genteelest. "For me," added the worthy doctor, "I can not well enter into the spirit of these nice distinctions; it suits neither my taste nor my interest, and my house is, perhaps, the only one in Darien where you would find all these opposite and contending elements combined." The doctor is connected with the aristocracy of the place, and, like a wise man, remembers, notwithstanding, that those who are not are quite as liable to be ill, and call in medical assistance, as those who are. He is a shrewd, intelligent man, with an excellent knowledge of his profession, much kindness of heart, and apparent cheerful good temper. I have already severely tried the latter by the unequivocal expression of my opinions on the subject of slavery, and, though I perceived that it required all his self-command to listen with any thing like patience to my highly incendiary and inflammatory doctrines, he yet did so, and though he was, I have no doubt, perfectly horror-stricken at the discovery, lost nothing of his courtesy or good-humor. By-the-by, I must tell you that, at an early period of the conversation, upon my saying, "I put all other considerations out of the question, and first propose to you the injustice of the system alone," "Oh," replied my friend the doctor, "if you put it upon that ground, you *stump* the question at once; I have nothing to say to that whatever, but," and then followed the usual train of pleadings—happiness, tenderness, care, indulgence, etc., etc., etc.—all the substitutes that may or may not be put in the place of *justice*, and which these slaveholders attempt to persuade others, and perhaps themselves, effectually supply its want. After church hours the people came back from Darien. They are only permitted to go to Darien to church once a month. On the intermediate Sundays they assemble in the house of London, Mr. ——'s head cooper, an excellent and pious man, who, Heaven alone knows how, has obtained some little knowledge of reading, and who reads prayers and the Bible to his fellow-slaves, and addresses them with extemporaneous exhortations. I have the greatest desire to attend one of these religious meetings, but fear to put the people under any, the slightest restraint. However, I shall see by-and-by how they feel about it themselves.

You have heard, of course, many and contradictory statements as to the degree of religious instruction afforded to the negroes of the South, and their opportunities of worship, etc. Until the late abolition movement, the spiritual interests of the slaves were about as little regarded as their physical necessities. The outcry which has been raised with threefold force within the last few years against the whole system has induced its upholders and defenders to adopt, as measures of personal extenuation, some appearance of religious instruction (such as it is), and some pretense at physical indulgences (such as they are), bestowed apparently voluntarily upon their dependents. At Darien a church is appropriated to the especial use of the slaves, who are almost all of them Baptists here; and a gentleman officiates in it (of course white), who, I understand, is very zealous in the cause of their spiritual well-being. He, like most Southern men, clergy or others, jump the present life in their charities to the slaves, and go on to furnish them with all requisite conveniences for the next. There were a short time ago two free black preachers in this neighborhood, but they have lately been ejected from the place. I could not clearly learn, but one may possibly imagine, upon what grounds.

I do not think that a residence on a slave plantation is likely to be peculiarly advantageous to a child like my eldest. I was observing her to-day among her swarthy worshipers, for they follow her as such, and saw, with dismay, the universal eagerness with which they sprang to obey her little gestures of command. She said something about a swing, and in less than five minutes head man Frank had erected it for her, and a dozen young slaves were ready to swing little "missis." ——, think of learning to rule despotically your fellow-creatures before the first lesson of self-government has been well spelt over! It makes me tremble; but I shall find a remedy, or remove myself and the child from this misery and ruin.

ᵥ You can not conceive any thing more grotesque than the Sunday trim of the poor people, their ideality, as Mr. Combe would say, being, I should think, twice as big as any rational bump in their head. Their Sabbath toilet really presents the most ludicrous combination of incongruities that you can conceive—frills, flounces, ribbons; combs stuck in their woolly heads, as if they held up any portion of the stiff and ungovernable hair; filthy finery, every color in the rainbow, and the deepest possible shades blended in fierce companionship round one dusky visage; head-handkerchiefs, that put one's very eyes out from a mile off; chintzes with sprawling patterns, that might be seen if the clouds were printed with them; beads, bugles, flaring sashes, and, above all, little fanciful aprons, which finish these incongruous toilets with a sort of airy grace, which I assure you is perfectly indescribable. One young man, the eldest son and heir of our washerwoman Hannah, came to pay his respects to me in a magnificent black satin waistcoat, shirt gills which absolutely ingulfed his black visage, and neither shoes nor stockings on his feet.

Among our visitors from St. Simon's to-day was Hannah's mother (it seems to me that there is not a girl of sixteen on the plantations but has children, nor a woman of thirty but has grandchildren). Old House Molly, as she is called, from the circumstance of her having been one of the slaves employed in domestic offices during Ma-

jor ——'s residence on the island, is one of the oldest and
most respected slaves on the estate, and was introduced
to me by Mr. —— with especial marks of attention and
regard; she absolutely embraced him, and seemed unable
sufficiently to express her ecstasy at seeing him again.
Her dress, like that of her daughter, and all the servants
who have at any time been employed about the family,
bore witness to a far more improved taste than the half
savage adornment of the other poor blacks, and upon my
observing to her how agreeable her neat and cleanly appearance was to me, she replied that her old master (Major ——) was extremely particular in this respect, and
that in his time all the house servants were obliged to be
very nice and careful about their persons.

She named to me all her children, an immense tribe;
and, by-the-by, E——, it has occurred to me that whereas
the increase of this ill-fated race is frequently adduced as
a proof of their good treatment and well being, it really
and truly is no such thing, and springs from quite other
causes than the peace and plenty which a rapidly increasing population are supposed to indicate.  If you will reflect for a moment upon the overgrown families of the
half-starved Irish peasantry and English manufacturers,
you will agree with me that these prolific shoots by no
means necessarily spring from a rich or healthy soil.
Peace and plenty are certainly causes of human increase,
and so is recklessness; and this, I take it, is the impulse
in the instance of the English manufacturer, the Irish peasant, and the negro slave.  Indeed here it is more than
recklessness, for there are certain indirect premiums held
out to obey the early commandment of replenishing the
earth which do not fail to have their full effect.  In the
first place, none of the cares—those noble cares, that holy
thoughtfulness which lifts the human above the brute
parent, are ever incurred here by either father or mother.

The relation indeed resembles, as far as circumstances can
possibly make it do so, the short-lived connection between
the animal and its young.  The father, having neither authority, power, responsibility, or charge in his children, is
of course, as among brutes, the least attached to his offspring; the mother, by the natural law which renders the
infant dependent on her for its first year's nourishment, is
more so; but as neither of them is bound to educate or
to support their children, all the unspeakable tenderness
and solemnity, all the rational, and all the spiritual grace
and glory of the connection, is lost, and it becomes mere
breeding, bearing, suckling, and there an end.  But it is
not only the absence of the conditions which God has af-
fixed to the relation which tends to encourage the reckless
increase of the race; they enjoy, by means of numerous
children, certain positive advantages.  In the first place,
every woman who is pregnant, as soon as she chooses to
make the fact known to the overseer, is relieved of a certain portion of her work in the field, which lightening of
labor continues, of course, as long as she is so burdened.
On the birth of a child certain additions of clothing and
an additional weekly ration are bestowed on the family;
and these matters, small as they may seem, act as powerful inducements to creatures who have none of the restrain-
ing influences actuating them which belong to the parent-
al relation among all other people, whether civilized or
savage.  Moreover, they have all of them a most distinct
and perfect knowledge of their value to their owners as
property; and a woman thinks, and not much amiss, that
the more frequently she adds to the number of her master's live-stock by bringing new slaves into the world, the
more claims she will have upon his consideration and
good-will.  This was perfectly evident to me from the
meritorious air with which the women always made haste
to inform me of the number of children they had borne,

and the frequent occasions on which the older slaves would direct my attention to their children, exclaiming, "Look, missis! little niggers for you and massa; plenty little niggers for you and little missis!" A very agreeable apostrophe to me indeed, as you will believe.

I have let this letter lie for a day or two, dear E——, from press of more immediate avocations. I have nothing very particular to add to it. On Monday evening I rowed over to Darien with Mr. —— to fetch over the doctor, who was coming to visit some of our people. As I sat waiting in the boat for the return of the gentlemen, the sun went down, or rather seemed to dissolve bodily into the glowing clouds, which appeared but a fusion of the great orb of light; the stars twinkled out in the rose-colored sky, and the evening air, as it fanned the earth to sleep, was as soft as a summer's evening breeze in the north. A sort of dreamy stillness seemed creeping over the world and into my spirit as the canoe just tilted against the steps that led to the wharf, raised by the scarce perceptible heaving of the water. A melancholy, monotonous boat-horn sounded from a distance up the stream, and presently, floating slowly down with the current, huge, shapeless, black, relieved against the sky, came one of those rough barges piled with cotton, called, hereabouts, Ocone boxes. The vessel itself is really nothing but a monstrous square box, made of rough planks, put together in the roughest manner possible to attain the necessary object of keeping the cotton dry. Upon this great tray are piled the swollen, apoplectic-looking cotton-bags, to the height of ten, twelve, and fourteen feet. This huge water-wagon floats lazily down the river, from the upper country to Darien. They are flat-bottomed, and, of course, draw little water. The stream from whence they are named is an up-country river, which, by its junction with the Ocmulgee, forms the Altamaha. Here at least,

you perceive, the Indian names remain, and long may they
do so, for they seem to me to become the very character
of the streams and mountains they indicate, and are indeed significant to the learned in savage tongues, which
is more than can be said of such titles as Jones's Creek,
Onion Creek, etc.   These Ocone boxes are broken up at
Darien, where the cotton is shipped either for the Savannah, Charleston, or Liverpool markets, and the timber of
which they are constructed sold.

We rowed the doctor over to see some of his patients
on the island, and before his departure a most animated
discussion took place upon the subject of the President of
the United States, his talents, qualifications, opinions—
above all, his views with regard to the slave system.   Mr.
——, who you know is no abolitionist, and is a very devoted Van Buren man, maintained with great warmth the
President's straightforwardness, and his evident and expressed intention of protecting the rights of the South.
The doctor, on the other hand, quoted a certain speech of
the President's upon the question of abolishing slavery in
the District of Columbia, which his fears interpreted into
a mere evasion of the matter, and an indication that at
some future period he (Mr. Van Buren) might take a different view of the subject.   I confess, for my own part,
that if the doctor quoted the speech right, and if the President is not an honest man, and if I were a Southern slaveholder, I should not feel altogether secure of Mr. Van Buren's present opinions or future conduct upon this subject.
These three *ifs*, however, are material points of consideration.   Our friend the doctor inclined vehemently to Mr.
Clay as one on whom the slaveholders could depend.
Georgia, however, as a state, is perhaps the most democratic in the Union; though here, as well as in other places
that you and I know of, a certain class, calling themselves
the first, and honestly believing themselves the best, set

their faces against the modern fashioned republicanism, professing, and, I have no doubt, with great sincerity, that their ideas of democracy are altogether of a different kind.

I went again to-day to the Infirmary, and was happy to perceive that there really was an evident desire to conform to my instructions, and keep the place in a better condition than formerly. Among the sick I found a poor woman suffering dreadfully from the earache. She had done nothing to alleviate her pain but apply some leaves, of what tree or plant I could not ascertain, and tie up her head in a variety of dirty cloths, till it was as large as her whole body. I removed all these, and found one side. of her face and neck very much swollen, but so begrimed with filth that it was really no very agreeable task to examine it. The first process, of course, was washing, which, however, appeared to her so very unusual an operation, that I had to perform it for her myself. Sweet oil and laudanum, and raw cotton, being then applied to her ear and neck, she professed herself much relieved, but I believe in my heart that the warm water sponging had done her more good than any thing else. I was sorry not to ascertain what leaves she had applied to her ear. These simple remedies resorted to by savages, and people as ignorant, are generally approved by experience, and sometimes condescendingly adopted by science. I remember once, when Mr. —— was suffering from a severe attack of inflammatory rheumatism, Dr. C—— desired him to bind round his knee the leaves of the tulip-tree—poplar I believe you call it—saying that he had learned that remedy from the negroes in Virginia, and found it a most effectual one. My next agreeable office in the Infirmary this morning was superintending the washing of two little babies, whose mothers were nursing them with quite as much ignorance as zeal. Having ordered a large tub of water, I desired Rose to undress the little creatures and give them a warm bath; the mothers looked on in unutterable dismay; and one of them, just as her child was going to be put into the tub, threw into it all the clothes she had just taken off it, as she said, to break the unusual shock of the warm water. I immediately rescued them; not but what they were quite as much in want of washing as the baby, but it appeared, upon inquiry, that the woman had none others to dress the child in when it should have taken its bath; they were immediately wrung and hung by the fire to dry; and the poor little patients, having undergone this novel operation, were taken out and given to their mothers. Any thing, however, much more helpless and inefficient than these poor ignorant creatures you can not conceive; they actually seemed incapable of drying or dressing their own babies, and I had to finish their toilet myself. As it is only a very few years since the most absurd and disgusting customs have become exploded among ourselves, you will not, of course, wonder that these poor people pin up the lower part of their infants, bodies, legs, and all, in red flannel as soon as they are born, and keep them in the self-same envelope till it literally falls off.

In the next room I found a woman lying on the floor in a fit of epilepsy, barking most violently. She seemed to excite no particular attention or compassion; the women said she was subject to these fits, and took little or no notice of her, as she lay barking like some enraged animal on the ground. Again I stood in profound ignorance, sickening with the sight of suffering which I knew not how to alleviate, and which seemed to excite no commiseration merely from the sad fact of its frequent occurrence. Returning to the house, I passed up the "street." It was between eleven o'clock and noon, and the people were taking their first meal in the day. By-the-by, E——, how do you think Berkshire county farmers would relish laboring hard all day upon *two meals* of Indian corn or hominy? Such is the regulation on this plantation, however, and I beg you to bear in mind that the negroes on Mr.——'s estate are generally considered well off. They go to the fields at daybreak, carrying with them their allowance of food for the day, which toward noon, *and not till then*, they eat, cooking it over a fire, which they kindle as best they can, where they are working. Their second meal in the day is at night, after their labor is over, having worked, at the *very least*, six hours without intermission of rest or refreshment since their noonday meal (properly so called, for 'tis meal, and nothing else). Those that I passed to-day, sitting on their door-steps, or on the ground round them eating, were the people employed at the mill and threshing-floor. As these are near to the settlement, they had time to get their food from the cookshop. Chairs, tables, plates, knives, forks, they had none; they sat, as I before said, on the earth or door-steps, and ate either out of their little cedar tubs or an iron pot, some few with broken iron spoons, more with pieces of wood, and all the children with their fingers. A more complete sample of savage feeding I never beheld. At one of the doors I saw three young girls standing, who might be between sixteen and seventeen years old; they had evidently done eating, and were rudely playing and romping with each other, laughing and shouting like wild things. I went into the house, and such another spectacle of filthy disorder I never beheld. I then addressed the girls most solemnly, showing them that they were wasting in idle riot the time in which they might be rendering their abode decent, and told them that it was a shame for any woman to live in so dirty a place and so beastly a condition. They said they had seen buckree (white) women's houses just as dirty, and they could not be expected to be cleaner than white women. I then told them that the only difference between themselves and buckree women was, that the latter were generally better informed, and, for that reason alone, it was more disgraceful to them to be disorderly and dirty. They seemed to listen to me attentively, and one of them exclaimed, with great satisfaction, that they saw I made no difference between them and white girls, and that they never had been so treated before. I do not know any thing which strikes me as a more melancholy illustration of the degradation of these people than the animal nature of their recreations in their short seasons of respite from labor. You see them, boys and girls, from the youngest age to seventeen and eighteen, rolling, tumbling, kicking, and wallowing in the dust, regardless alike of decency, and incapable of any more rational amusement; or lolling, with half-closed eyes, like so many cats and dogs, against a wall, or upon a bank in the sun, dozing away their short leisure hour, until called to resume their labors in the field or the mill. After this description of the meals of our laborers, you will, perhaps, be curious to know how it fares with our house servants in this respect. Precisely in the same manner, as far as regards allowance, with the exception of what is left from our table, but, if possible, with even less comfort, in one respect, inasmuch as no time whatever is set apart for their meals, which they snatch at any hour, and in any way that they can—generally, however, standing, or squatting on their hams round the kitchen fire. They have no sleeping-rooms in the house, but when their work is over, retire, like the rest, to their hovels, the discomfort of which has to them all the addition of comparison with our mode of living. Now, in all establishments whatever, of course some disparity exists between the comforts of the drawing-room and best bedrooms, and the servants' hall and attics, but here it is no longer a matter of degree. The young woman who performs the office of lady's-maid, and the lads who wait upon us at table, have neither table to feed at nor chair to sit down upon themselves. The boys sleep at night on the hearth by the kitchen fire, and the women upon a rough board bedstead, strewed with a little tree moss. All this shows how very torpid the sense of justice is apt to lie in the breasts of those who have it not awakened by the peremptory demands of others.

In the North we could not hope to keep the worst and poorest servant for a single day in the wretched discomfort in which our negro servants are forced habitually to live. I received a visit this morning from some of the Darien people. Among them was a most interesting young person, from whose acquaintance, if I have any opportunity of cultivating it, I promise myself much pleasure. The ladies that I have seen since I crossed the Southern line have all seemed to me extremely sickly in their appearance—delicate in the refined term, but unfortunately sickly in the truer one. They are languid in their deportment and speech, and seem to give themselves up, without an effort to counteract it, to the enervating effect of their warm climate. It is undoubtedly a most relaxing and unhealthy one, and therefore requires the more imperatively to be met by energetic and invigorating habits both of body and mind. Of these, however, the Southern ladies appear to have, at present, no very positive idea. Doctor —— told us to-day of a comical application which his negro man had made to him for the coat he was then wearing. I forget whether the fellow wanted the loan, or the absolute gift of it, but his argument was (it might have been an Irishman's) that he knew his master intended to give it to him by-and-by, and that he thought he might as well let him have it at once as keep him waiting any longer for it. This story the doctor related with great glee, and it furnishes a very good sample of what the Southerners are fond of exhibiting, the degree of license to which they capriciously permit their favorite slaves occasionally to carry their familiarity. They seem to consider it as an undeniable proof of the general kindness with which their dependents are treated. It is as good a proof of it as the maudlin tenderness of a fine lady to her lapdog is of her humane treatment of animals in general. Servants whose claims to respect are properly understood by themselves and their employers, are not made pets, playthings, jesters, or companions of, and it is only the degradation of the many that admits of this favoritism to the few—a system of favoritism which, as it is perfectly consistent with the profoundest contempt and injustice, degrades the object of it quite as much, though it oppresses him less, than the cruelty practiced upon his fellows. I had several of these favorite slaves presented to me, and one or two little negro children, who their owners assured me were quite pets. The only real service which this arbitrary good-will did to the objects of it was quite involuntary and unconscious on the part of their kind masters—I mean the inevitable improvement in intelligence which resulted to them from being more constantly admitted to the intercourse of the favored white race.

I must not forget to tell you of a magnificent bald-headed eagle which Mr. —— called me to look at early this morning. I had never before seen alive one of these national types of yours, and stood entranced as the noble creature swept, like a black cloud, over the river, his bald white head bent forward and shining in the sun, and his fierce eyes and beak directed toward one of the beautiful wild ducks on the water, which he had evidently marked for his prey. The poor little duck, who was not ambitious of such a glorification, dived, and the eagle hovered above the spot. After a short interval, its victim rose to the surface several yards nearer shore. The great king of

birds stooped nearer, and again the watery shield was interposed. This went on until the poor water-fowl, driven
by excess of fear into unwonted boldness, rose, after repeatedly diving, within a short distance of where we
stood. The eagle, who, I presume, had read how we were
to have dominion over the fowls of the air (bald-headed
eagles included), hovered sulkily a while over the river,
and then, sailing slowly toward the woods on the opposite
shore, alighted and furled his great wings on a huge cypress limb, that stretched itself out against the blue sky,
like the arm of a giant, for the giant bird to perch upon.

I am amusing myself by attempting to beautify, in some
sort, this residence of ours. Immediately at the back of
it runs a ditch, about three feet wide, which empties and
fills twice a day with the tide. This lies like a moat on
two sides of the house. The opposite bank is a steep
dike, with a footpath along the top. One or two willows
droop over this very interesting ditch, and I thought I
would add to their company some magnolias and myrtles,
so as to make a little evergreen plantation round the house.
I went to the swamp reserves I have before mentioned to
you, and chose some beautiful bushes—among others, a
very fine young pine, at which our overseer and all the negroes expressed much contemptuous surprise; for, though
the tree is beautiful, it is also common, and with them, as
with wiser folk, 'tis "nothing pleases but rare accidents."
In spite of their disparaging remarks, however, I persisted
in having my pine-tree planted, and I assure you it formed
a very pleasing variety among the broad, smooth-leaved
evergreens about it. While forming my plantation, I had
a brand thrown into a bed of tall yellow sedges which
screen the brimming waters of the noble river from our
parlor window, and which I therefore wished removed.
The small sample of a Southern conflagration which en-
sued was very picturesque, the flames devouring the light

growth, absolutely licking it off the ground, while the
curling smoke drew off in misty wreaths across the river.
The heat was intense, and I thought how exceedingly and
unpleasantly warm one must feel in the midst of such a
forest burning as Cooper describes. Having worked my
appointed task in the garden, I rowed over to Darien and
back, the rosy sunset changing mean time to starry evening, as beautiful as the first the sky ever was arrayed in.

I saw an advertisement this morning in the paper which
occasioned me much thought. Mr. J—— C—— and a Mr.
N——, two planters of this neighborhood, have contracted to dig a canal, called the Brunswick Canal, and, not
having hands enough for the work, advertise at the same
time for negroes on hire and for Irish laborers. Now the
Irishmen are to have twenty dollars a month wages, and
to be "found" (to use the technical phrase), which finding
means abundant food, and the best accommodations which
can be procured for them. The negroes are hired from
their masters, who will be paid, of course, as high a price
as they can obtain for them—probably a very high one, as
the demand for them is urgent—they, in the mean time,
receiving no wages, and nothing more than the miserable
negro fare of rice and corn grits. Of course the Irishmen
and these slaves are not allowed to work together, but are
kept at separate stations on the canal. This is every way
politic, for the low Irish seem to have the same sort of
hatred of negroes which sects, differing but little in their
tenets, have for each other. The fact is, that a condition
in their own country nearly similar has made the poor
Irish almost as degraded a class of beings as the negroes
are here, and their insolence toward them, and hatred of
them, are precisely in proportion to the resemblance between them. This hiring out of negroes is a horrid aggravation of the miseries of their condition; for if, on the
plantations, and under the masters to whom they belong,

their labor is severe and their food inadequate, think what it must be when they are hired out for a stipulated sum to a temporary employer, who has not even the interest which it is pretended an owner may feel in the welfare of his slaves, but whose chief aim it must necessarily be to get as much out of them, and expend as little on them, as possible. Ponder this new form of iniquity, and believe me ever your most sincerely attached.

---

DEAREST E——,—After finishing my last letter to you, I went out into the clear starlight to breathe the delicious mildness of the air, and was surprised to hear rising from one of the houses of the settlement a hymn sung apparently by a number of voices. The next morning I inquired the meaning of this, and was informed that those negroes on the plantation who were members of the Church were holding a prayer-meeting. There is an immensely strong devotional feeling among these poor people. The worst of it is, that it is zeal without understanding, and profits them but little; yet light is light, even that poor portion that may stream through a keyhole, and I welcome this most ignorant profession of religion in Mr. ——'s dependents as the herald of better and brighter things for them. Some of the planters are entirely inimical to any such proceedings, and neither allow their negroes to attend worship, or to congregate together for religious purposes, and truly I think they are wise in their own generation. On other plantations, again, the same rigid discipline is not observed; and some planters and overseers go even farther than toleration, and encourage these devotional exercises and professions of religion, having actually discovered that a man may become more faithful and trustworthy, even as a slave, who acknowledges the higher influences of Christianity, no matter in how small a de-

gree. Slaveholding clergymen, and certain piously inclined planters, undertake, accordingly, to enlighten these
poor creatures upon these matters, with a safe understanding, however, of what truth is to be given to them,
and what is not; how much they may learn to become
better slaves, and how much they may not learn, lest they
cease to be slaves at all. The process is a very ticklish
one, and but for the Northern public opinion, which is
now pressing the slaveholders close, I dare say would not
be attempted at all. As it is, they are putting their own
throats and their own souls in jeopardy by this very endeavor to serve God and Mammon. The light that they
are letting in between their fingers will presently strike
them blind, and the mighty flood of truth which they are
straining through a sieve to the thirsty lips of their slaves
sweep them away like straws from their cautious moor-
ings, and overwhelm them in its great deeps, to the waters of which man may in nowise say, thus far shall ye
come and no farther. The community I now speak of,
the white population of Darien, should be a religious one,
to judge by the number of churches it maintains. However, we know the old proverb, and, at that rate, it may
not be so godly after all. Mr. —— and his brother have
been called upon at various times to subscribe to them
all; and I saw this morning a most fervent appeal, extremely ill spelled, from a gentleman living in the neighborhood of the town, and whose slaves are notoriously
ill treated, reminding Mr. —— of the precious souls of his
human cattle, and requesting a farther donation for the
Baptist Church, of which most of the people here are
members. Now this man is known to be a hard master;
his negro houses are sheds not fit to stable beasts in; his
slaves are ragged, half naked, and miserable; yet he is
urgent for their religious comforts, and writes to Mr.
—— about "their souls—their precious souls." He was

over here a few days ago, and pressed me very much to attend his church. I told him I would not go to a church where the people who worked for us were parted off from us as if they had the pest, and we should catch it of them. I asked him, for I was curious to know, how they managed to administer the sacrament to a mixed congregation? He replied, Oh, very easily; that the white portion of the assembly received it first, and the blacks afterward. "A new commandment I give unto you, that ye love one another, even as I have loved you." Oh, what a shocking mockery! However, they show their faith, at all events, in the declaration that God is no respecter of persons, since they do not pretend to exclude from His table those whom they most certainly would not admit to their own.

I have, as usual, allowed this letter to lie by, dear E——, not in the hope of the occurrence of any event—for that is hopeless—but until my daily avocations allowed me leisure to resume it, and afforded me, at the same time, matter wherewith to do so. I really never was so busy in all my life as I am here. I sit at the receipt of custom (involuntarily enough) from morning till night—no time, no place, affords me a respite from my innumerable petitioners; and whether I be asleep or awake, reading, eating, or walking—in the kitchen, my bedroom, or the parlor, they flock in with urgent entreaties and pitiful stories, and my conscience forbids my ever postponing their business for any other matter; for, with shame and grief of heart I say it, by their unpaid labor I live—their nakedness clothes me, and their heavy toil maintains me in luxurious idleness. (Surely the least I can do is to hear these, my most injured benefactors; and, indeed, so intense in me is the sense of the injury they receive from me and mine, that I should scarce dare refuse them the very clothes from my back, or food from my plate, if they asked me for it. In taking my daily walk round the banks yesterday, I found that I was walking over violet roots. The season is too little advanced for them to be in bloom, and I could not find out whether they were the fragrant violet or not.

Mr. —— has been much gratified to-day by the arrival of Mr. K——, who, with his father, for nineteen years was the sole manager of these estates, and discharged his laborious task with great ability and fidelity toward his employers. How far he understood his duties to the slaves, or whether, indeed, an overseer can, in the nature of things, acknowledge any duty to them, is another question. He is a remarkable man, and is much respected for his integrity and honorable dealing by every body here. His activity and energy are wonderful; and the mere fact of his having charge of for nineteen years, and personally governing, without any assistance whatever, seven hundred people scattered over three large tracts of land, at a considerable distance from each other, certainly bespeaks efficiency and energy of a very uncommon order. The character I had heard of him from Mr. —— had excited a great deal of interest in me, and I was very glad of this opportunity of seeing a man who for so many years had been sovereign over the poor people here. I met him walking on the banks with Mr. —— as I returned from my own ramble, during which nothing occurred or appeared to interest me, except, by-the-by, my unexpectedly coming quite close to one of those magnificent scarlet birds which abound here, and which dart across your path like a winged flame. Nothing can surpass the beauty of their plumage, and their voice is excellently melodious—they are lovely.

My companions, when I do not request the attendance of my friend Jack, are a couple of little terriers, who are endowed to perfection with the ugliness and the intelligence of their race; they are of infinite service on the plantation, as, owing to the immense quantity of grain, and chaff, and such matters, rats and mice abound in the mills and store-houses. I crossed the threshing-floor to-day—a very large square, perfectly level, raised by artificial means about half a foot from the ground, and covered equally all over, so as to lie quite smooth, with some preparation of tar. It lies immediately between the house and the steam mill, and on it much of the negroes' work is done—the first threshing is given to the rice, and other labors are carried on. As I walked across it to-day, passing through the busy groups, chiefly of women, that covered it, I came opposite to one of the drivers, who held in his hand his whip, the odious insignia of his office. I took it from him; it was a short stick of moderate size, with a thick square leather thong attached to it. As I held it in my hand, I did not utter a word; but I conclude, as is often the case, my face spoke what my tongue did not, for the driver said, "Oh, missis, me use it for measure; me seldom strike nigger with it." For one moment I thought I must carry the hateful implement into the house with me. An instant's reflection, however, served to show me how useless such a proceeding would be. The people are not mine, nor their drivers, nor their whips. I should but have impeded, for a few hours, the man's customary office, and a new scourge would have been easily provided, and I should have done nothing, perhaps worse than nothing.

After dinner I had a most interesting conversation with Mr. K——. Among other subjects, he gave me a lively and curious description of the Yeomanry of Georgia, more properly termed pine-landers. Have you visions now of well-to-do farmers with comfortable homesteads, decent habits, industrious, intelligent, cheerful, and thrifty? Such, however, is not the Yeomanry of Georgia. Labor being

here the especial portion of slaves, it is thenceforth degraded, and considered unworthy of all but slaves.   No
white man, therefore, of any class puts hand to work of
any kind soever.   This is an exceedingly dignified way of
proving their gentility for the lazy planters who prefer an
idle life of semistarvation and barbarism to the degradation of doing any thing themselves; but the effect on the
poorer whites of the country is terrible.   I speak now of
the scattered white population, who, too poor to possess
land or slaves, and having no means of living in the towns,
squat (most appropriately is it so termed) either on other
men's land or government districts—always here swamp
or pine barren—and claim masterdom over the place they
invade till ejected by the rightful proprietors.   These
wretched creatures will not, for they are whites (and labor belongs to blacks and slaves alone here), labor for
their own subsistence.   They are hardly protected from
the weather by the rude shelters they frame for themselves in the midst of these dreary woods.   Their food is
chiefly supplied by shooting the wild-fowl and venison,
and stealing from the cultivated patches of the plantations
nearest at hand.   Their clothes hang about them in filthy
tatters, and the combined squalor and fierceness of their
appearance is really frightful.

This population is the direct growth of slavery.   The
planters are loud in their execrations of these miserable
vagabonds; yet they do not see that so long as labor is
considered the disgraceful portion of slaves, these free
men will hold it nobler to starve or steal than till the
earth, with none but the despised blacks for fellow-laborers.   The blacks themselves—such is the infinite power
of custom—acquiesce in this notion, and, as I have told
you, consider it the lowest degradation in a white to use
any exertion.   I wonder, considering the burdens they
have seen me lift, the digging, the planting, the rowing,

and the walking I do, that they do not utterly contemn me, and, indeed, they seem lost in amazement at it.

Talking of these pine-landers—gipsies, without any of the romantic associations that belong to the latter people —led us to the origin of such a population, slavery; and you may be sure I listened with infinite interest to the opinions of a man of uncommon shrewdness and sagacity, who was born in the very bosom of it, and has passed his whole life among slaves. If any one is competent to judge of its effects, such a man is the one; and this was his verdict: "I hate slavery with all my heart; I consider it an absolute curse wherever it exists. It will keep those states where it does exist fifty years behind the others in improvement and prosperity." Farther on in the conversation he made this most remarkable observation: "As for its being an irremediable evil—a thing not to be helped or got rid of—that's all nonsense; for, as soon as people become convinced that it is their interest to get rid of it, they will soon find the means to do so, depend upon it." And undoubtedly this is true. This is not an age, nor yours a country, where a large mass of people will long endure what they perceive to be injurious to their fortunes and advancement. Blind as people often are to their highest and truest interests, your country folk have generally shown remarkable acuteness in finding out where their worldly progress suffered let or hinderance, and have removed it with laudable alacrity. Now the fact is not at all as we at the North are sometimes told, that the Southern slaveholders deprecate the evils of slavery quite as much as we do; that they see all its miseries; that, moreover, they are most anxious to get rid of the whole thing, but want the means to do so, and submit most unwillingly to a necessity from which they can not extricate themselves. All this I thought might be true before I went to the South, and often has the charitable supposition checked the condemnation which was indignantly rising to my lips against these murderers of their brethren's peace. A little reflection, however, even without personal observation, might have convinced me that this could not be the case. If the majority of Southerners were satisfied that slavery was contrary to their worldly fortunes, slavery would be at an end from that very moment; but the fact is—and I have it not only from observation of my own, but from the distinct statement of some of the most intelligent Southern men that I have conversed with—the only obstacle to immediate abolition throughout the South is the immense value of the human property, and, to use the words of a very distinguished Carolinian, who thus ended a long discussion we had on the subject, " I'll tell you why abolition is impossible: because every healthy negro can fetch a thousand dollars in the Charleston market at this moment." And this opinion, you see, tallies perfectly with the testimony of Mr. K——.

He went on to speak of several of the slaves on this estate as persons quite remarkable for their fidelity and intelligence, instancing old Molly, Ned the engineer, who has the superintendence of the steam-engine in the rice mill, and head man Frank, of whom, indeed, he wound up the eulogium by saying he had quite the principles of a white man, which I thought most equivocal praise, but he did not intend it as such. As I was complaining to Mr. —— of the terribly neglected condition of the dikes, which are in some parts so overgrown with gigantic briers that 'tis really impossible to walk over them, and the trench on one hand, and river on the other, afford one extremely disagreeable alternatives, Mr. K—— cautioned me to be particularly on my guard not to step on the thorns of the orange-tree. These, indeed, are formidable spikes, and, he assured me, were peculiarly poisonous to the flesh. Some of the most painful and tedious wounds he had ever seen, he said, were incurred by the negroes running these large green thorns into their feet.

This led him to speak of the glory and beauty of the orange-trees on the island before a certain uncommonly severe winter, a few years ago, destroyed them all. For five miles round the banks grew a double row of noble orange-trees, as large as our orchard apple-trees, covered with golden fruit and silver flowers. It must have been a most magnificent spectacle, and Captain F——, too, told me, in speaking of it, that he had brought Basil Hall here in the season of the trees blossoming, and he had said it was as well worth crossing the Atlantic to see that as to see the Niagara. Of all these noble trees nothing now remains but the roots, which bear witness to their size, and some young sprouts shooting up, affording some hope that, in the course of years, the island may wear its bridal garland again. One huge stump close to the door is all that remains of an enormous tree that overtopped the house, from the upper windows of which oranges have been gathered from off its branches, and which, one year, bore the incredible number of 8542 oranges. Mr. K—— assured me of this as a positive fact, of which he had at the time made the entry in his journal, considering such a crop from a single tree well worthy of record. Mr. —— was called out this evening to listen to a complaint of overwork from a gang of pregnant women. I did not stay to listen to the details of their petition, for I am unable to command myself on such occasions, and Mr. —— seemed positively degraded in my eyes as he stood enforcing upon these women the necessity of their fulfilling their appointed tasks. How honorable he would have appeared to me begrimed with the sweat and soil of the coarsest manual labor, to what he then seemed, setting forth to these wretched, ignorant women, as a duty, their unpaid exacted labor! I turned away in bitter disgust. I hope

this sojourn among Mr. ——'s slaves may not lessen my
respect for him, but I fear it; for the details of slaveholding are so unmanly, letting alone every other consideration, that I know not how any one with the spirit of a
man can condescend to them.

I have been out again on the river, rowing. I find nothing new. Swamps crowned with perfect evergreens are
the only land (that's Irish!) about here, and, of course,
turn which way I will, the natural features of river and
shore are the same. I do not weary of these most exquisite watery woods, but you will of my mention of them, I
fear. Adieu.

————————

DEAREST E——, — Since I last wrote to you I have
been actually engaged in receiving and returning visits;
for even to this *ultima thule* of all civilization do these
polite usages extend. I have been called upon by several
families residing in and about Darien, and rowed over in
due form to acknowledge the honor. How shall I describe Darien to you? The abomination of desolation is
but a poor type of its forlorn appearance, as, half buried
in sand, its straggling, tumble-down wooden houses peer
over the muddy bank of the thick slimy river. The whole
town lies in a bed of sand: side-walks, or mid-walks, there
be none distinct from each other; at every step I took my
feet were ankle deep in the soil, and I had cause to rejoice
that I was booted for the occasion. Our worthy doctor,
whose lady I was going to visit, did nothing but regret
that I had not allowed him to provide me a carriage,
though the distance between his house and the landing is
not a quarter of a mile. The magnitude of the exertion
seemed to fill him with amazement, and he over and over
again repeated how impossible it would be to prevail on
any of the ladies there to take such a walk. The houses

seemed scattered about here and there, apparently without any design, and looked, for the most part, either unfinished or ruinous. One feature of the scene alone recalled the villages of New England—the magnificent oaks, which seemed to add to the meanness and insignificance of the human dwellings they overshadowed by their enormous size and grotesque forms. They reminded me of the elms of New Haven and Stockbridge. They are quite as large, and more picturesque, from their sombre foliage and the infinite variety of their forms—a beauty wanting in the New England elm, which invariably rises and spreads in a way which, though the most graceful in the world, at length palls on the capricious human eye, which seeks, above all other beauties, variety. Our doctor's wife is a New England woman; how can she live here? She had the fair eyes and hair, and fresh complexion of your part of the country, and its dearly beloved snuffle, which seemed actually dearly beloved when I heard it down here. She gave me some violets and narcissus, already blossoming profusely—in January—and expressed, like her husband, a thousand regrets at my having walked so far.

A transaction of the most amusing nature occurred to-day with regard to the resources of the Darien Bank, and the mode of carrying on business in that liberal and en-lightened institution, the funds of which I should think quite incalculable—impalpable, certainly, they appeared by our experience this morning.

The river, as we came home, was covered with Ocone boxes. It is well for them they are so shallow-bottomed, for we rasped sand all the way home through the cut and in the shallows of the river.

I have been over the rice mill, under the guidance of the overseer and head man Frank, and have been made acquainted with the whole process of threshing the rice, which is extremely curious; and here I may again mention another statement of Miss Martineau's, which I am told is, and I should suppose, from what I see here, must be a mistake. She states that the chaff of the husks of the rice is used as a manure for the fields, whereas the people have to-day assured me that it is of so hard, stony, and untractable a nature as to be literally good for nothing. Here I know it is thrown away by cart-loads into the river, where its only use appears to be to act like ground-bait, and attract a vast quantity of small fish to its vicinity. The number of hands employed in this threshing mill is very considerable, and the whole establishment, comprising the fires, and boilers, and machinery of a powerful steam-engine, are all under negro superintendence and direction. After this survey I occupied myself with my infant plantation of evergreens round the dike, in the midst of which interesting pursuit I was interrupted by a visit from Mr. B——, a neighboring planter, who came to transact some business with Mr. —— about rice which he had sent to our mill to have threshed, and the price to be paid for such threshing. The negroes have presented a petition to-day that they may be allowed to have a ball in honor of our arrival, which demand has been acceded to, and furious preparations arè being set on foot.

On visiting the Infirmary to-day, I was extremely pleased with the increased cleanliness and order observable in all the rooms. Two little filthy children, however, seemed to be still under the *ancien régime* of non-ablution; but upon my saying to the old nurse Molly, in whose ward they were, "Why, Molly, I don't believe you have bathed those children to-day," she answered, with infinite dignity, "Missis no b'lieve me wash um pickaninny! and yet she 'tress me wid all um niggar when 'em sick." The injured innocence and lofty conscious integrity of this speech silenced and abashed me; and yet I can't help it, but I don't believe to this present hour that those children had had any experience of water, at least not washing water, since they first came into the world.

I rowed over to Darien again, to make some purchases, yesterday, and, inquiring the price of various articles, could not but wonder to find them at least three times as dear as in your Northern villages. The profits of these Southern shopkeepers (who for the most part are thoroughbred Yankees, with the true Yankee propensity to trade, no matter on how dirty a counter, or in what manner of wares) are enormous. The prices they ask for every thing, from colored calicoes for negro dresses to piano-fortes (one of which, for curiosity sake, I inquired the value of), are fabulous, and such as none but the laziest and most reckless people in the world would consent to afford. On our return we found the water in the cut so extremely low that we were obliged to push the boat through it, and did not accomplish it without difficulty. The banks of this canal, when they are thus laid bare, present a singular appearance enough — two walls of solid mud, through which matted, twisted, twined, and tangled, like the natural veins of wood, runs an everlasting net of indestructible roots, the thousand toes of huge cypress feet. The trees have been cut down long ago from the soil, but these fangs remain in the earth without decaying for an incredible space of time. This long endurance of immersion is one of the valuable properties of these cypress roots; but, though excellent binding stuff for the sides of a canal, they must be pernicious growth in any land used for cultivation that requires deep tillage. On entering the Altamaha, we found the tide so low that we were much obstructed by the sand-banks, which, but for their constant shifting, would presently take entire possession of this noble stream, and render it utterly impassable from shore to shore, as it already is in several parts of the channel at certain seasons of the tide. On landing,

I was seized hold of by a hideous old negress, named Sinda, who had come to pay me a visit, and of whom Mr.
—— told me a strange anecdote. She passed at one time
for a prophetess among her fellow-slaves on the plantation, and had acquired such an ascendency over them that,
having given out, after the fashion of Mr. Miller, that the
world was to come to an end at a certain time, and that
not a very remote one, the belief in her assertion took
such possession of the people on the estate that they refused to work, and the rice and cotton fields were threatened with an indefinite fallow in consequence of this strike
on the part of the cultivators. Mr. K——, who was then
overseer of the property, perceived the impossibility of arguing, remonstrating, or even flogging this solemn panic
out of the minds of the slaves. The great final emancipation which they believed at hand had stripped even the
lash of its prevailing authority, and the terrors of an overseer for once were as nothing, in the terrible expectation
of the advent of the universal Judge of men. They were
utterly impracticable; so, like a very shrewd man as he
was, he acquiesced in their determination not to work;
but he expressed to them his belief that Sinda was mistaken, and he warned her that if, at the appointed time, it
proved so, she would be severely punished. I do not
know whether he confided to the slaves what he thought
likely to be the result if she was in the right; but poor
Sinda was in the wrong. Her day of judgment came indeed, and a severe one it proved, for Mr. K—— had her
tremendously flogged, and her end of things ended much
like Mr. Miller's; but whereas he escaped unhanged in
spite of his atrocious practices upon the fanaticism and
credulity of his country people, the spirit of false prophecy was mercilessly scourged out of her, and the faith of
her people of course reverted from her to the omnipotent
lash again. Think what a dream that must have been

while it lasted for those infinitely oppressed people—freedom without entering it by the grim gate of death, brought down to them at once by the second coming of Christ, whose first advent has left them yet so far from it! Farewell; it makes me giddy to think of having been a slave while that delusion lasted and after it vanished.

---

DEAREST E——,—I received early this morning a visit from a young negro called Morris, who came to request permission to be baptized. The master's leave is necessary for this ceremony of acceptance into the bosom of the Christian Church; so all that can be said is, that it is to be hoped the rite itself may *not* be indispensable for salvation, as, if Mr. —— had thought proper to refuse Morris's petition, he must infallibly have been lost, in spite of his own best wishes to the contrary. I could not, in discoursing with him, perceive that he had any very distinct ideas of the advantages he expected to derive from the ceremony; but perhaps they appeared all the greater for being a little vague. I have seldom seen a more pleasing appearance than that of this young man; his figure was tall and straight, and his face, which was of a perfect oval, rejoiced in the grace, very unusual among his people, of a fine high forehead, and the much more frequent one of a remarkably gentle and sweet expression. He was, however, jet black, and certainly did not owe these personal advantages to any mixture in his blood. There is a certain African tribe from which the West Indian slave-market is chiefly recruited, who have these same characteristic features, and do not at all present the ignoble and ugly negro type, so much more commonly seen here. They are a tall, powerful people, with remarkably fine figures, regular features, and a singularly warlike and fierce disposition, in which respect they also differ

from the race of negroes existing on the American plantations. I do not think Morris, however, could have belonged to this tribe, though perhaps Othello did, which
would at once settle the difficulties of those commentators
who, abiding by Iago's very disagreeable suggestions as
to his purely African appearance, are painfully compelled
to forego the mitigation of supposing him a Moor and
not a negro. Did I ever tell you of my dining in Boston,
at the H——'s, on my first visit to that city, and sitting
by Mr. John Quincy Adams, who, talking to me about
Desdemona, assured me, with a most serious expression
of sincere disgust, that he considered all her misfortunes
as a very just judgment upon her for having married a
"nigger?" I think, if some ingenious American actor of
the present day, bent upon realizing Shakspeare's finest
conceptions, with all the advantages of modern enlightenment, could contrive to slip in that opprobrious title, with
a true South Carolinian anti-Abolitionist expression, it
might really be made quite a point for Iago, as, for instance, in his first soliloquy—"I hate the nigger," given
in proper Charleston or Savannah fashion, I am sure would
tell far better than "I hate the Moor." Only think, E——,
what a very new order of interest the whole tragedy
might receive, acted throughout from this stand-point, as
the Germans call it in this country, and called "Amalgamation, or the Black Bridal."

On their return from their walk this afternoon the children brought home some pieces of sugar-cane, of which a
small quantity grows on the island. When I am most
inclined to deplore the condition of the poor slaves on
these cotton and rice plantations, the far more intolerable
existence and harder labor of those employed on the sugar estates occurs to me, sometimes producing the effect
of a lower circle in Dante's "Hell of Horrors," opening
beneath the one where he seems to have reached the

climax of infernal punishment. You may have seen this vegetable, and must at any rate, I should think, be familiar with it by description. It is a long green reed, like the stalk of the maize, or Indian corn, only it shoots up to a much more considerable height, and has a consistent pith, which, together with the rind itself, is extremely sweet. The principal peculiarity of this growth, as perhaps you know, is that they are laid horizontally in the earth when they are planted for propagation, and from each of the notches or joints of the recumbent cane a young shoot is produced at the germinating season.

A very curious and interesting circumstance to me just now in the neighborhood is the projection of a canal, to be called the Brunswick Canal, which, by cutting through the lower part of the main land, toward the southern extremity of Great St. Simon's Island, is contemplated as a probable and powerful means of improving the prosperity of the town of Brunswick, by bringing it into immediate communication with the Atlantic. The scheme, which I think I have mentioned to you before, is, I believe, chiefly patronized by your States' folk—Yankee enterprise and funds being very essential elements, it appears to me, in all Southern projects and achievements. This speculation, however, from all I hear of the difficulties of the undertaking, from the nature of the soil, and the impossibility almost of obtaining efficient labor, is not very likely to arrive at any very satisfactory result ; and, indeed, I find it hard to conceive how this part of Georgia can possibly produce a town which can be worth the digging of a canal, even to Yankee speculators. There is one feature of the undertaking, however, which more than all the others excites my admiration, namely, that Irish laborers have been advertised for to work upon the canal, and the terms offered them are twenty dollars a month per man and their board. Now these men will have for

fellow-laborers negroes who not only will receive nothing
at all for their work, but who will be hired by the con-
tractors and directors of the works from their masters, to
whom they will hand over the price of their slaves' labor;
while it will be the interest of the person hiring them not
only to get as much work as possible out of them, but
also to provide them as economically with food, combin-
ing the two praiseworthy endeavors exactly in such judicious proportions as not to let them neutralize each other.
You will observe that this case of a master hiring out his
slaves to another employer, from whom he receives their
rightful wages, is a form of slavery which, though extremely common, is very seldom adverted to in those arguments for the system which are chiefly founded upon
the master's presumed regard for his human property.
People who have ever let a favorite house to the temporary occupation of strangers can form a tolerable idea of
the difference between one's own regard and care of one's
goods and chattels and that of the most conscientious
tenant; and whereas I have not yet observed that ownership is a very effectual protection to the slaves against
ill usage and neglect, I am quite prepared to admit that
it is a vastly better one than the temporary interest
which a lessee can feel in the live-stock he hires, out of
whom it is his manifest interest to get as much, and into
whom to put as little, as possible. Yet thousands of
slaves throughout the Southern states are thus handed
over by the masters who own them to masters who do
not; and it does not require much demonstration to prove
that their estate is not always the more gracious. Now
you must not suppose that these same Irish free laborers
and negro slaves will be permitted to work together at
this Brunswick Canal. They say that this would be utterly impossible; for why? there would be tumults, and
risings, and broken heads, and bloody bones, and all the

natural results of Irish intercommunion with their fellow-creatures, no doubt—perhaps even a little more riot and violence than merely comports with their usual habits of Milesian good fellowship; for, say the masters, the Irish hate the negroes more even than the Americans do, and there would be no bound to their murderous animosity if they were brought in contact with them on the same portion of the works of the Brunswick Canal. Doubtless there is some truth in this; the Irish laborers who might come hither would be apt enough, according to a universal moral law, to visit upon others the injuries they had received from others. They have been oppressed enough themselves to be oppressive whenever they have a chance; and the despised and degraded condition of the blacks, presenting to them a very ugly resemblance of their own home, circumstances naturally excite in them the exercise of the disgust and contempt of which they themselves are very habitually the objects; and that such circular distribution of wrongs may not only be pleasant, but have something like the air of retributive right to very ignorant folks, is not much to be wondered at. Certain is the fact, however, that the worst of all tyrants is the one who has been a slave; and, for that matter (and I wonder if the Southern slaveholders hear it with the same ear that I do, and ponder it with the same mind?), the command of one slave to another is altogether the most uncompromising utterance of insolent truculent despotism that it ever fell to my lot to witness or listen to. "You nigger—I say, you black nigger—you no hear me call you—what for you no run quick?" All this, dear E——, is certainly reasonably in favor of division of labor on the Brunswick Canal; but the Irish are not only quarrelers, and rioters, and fighters, and drinkers, and despisers of niggers—they are a passionate, impulsive, warm-hearted, generous people, much given to powerful indignations, which break out suddenly when not compelled to smoulder sullenly—pestilent sympathizers too, and with a sufficient dose of American atmospheric air in their lungs, properly mixed with a right proportion of ardent spirits, there is no saying but what they might actually take to sympathy with the slaves, and I leave you to judge of the possible consequences. You perceive, I am sure, that they can by no means be allowed to work together on the Brunswick Canal.

I have been taking my daily walk round the island, and visited the sugar mill and the threshing mill again.

Mr. —— has received another letter from Parson S—— upon the subject of more church building in Darien. It seems that there has been a very general panic in this part of the slave states lately, occasioned by some injudicious missionary preaching, which was pronounced to be of a decidedly abolitionist tendency. The offensive preachers, after sowing God only knows what seed in this tremendous soil, where one grain of knowledge may spring up a gigantic upas-tree to the prosperity of its most unfortunate possessors, were summarily and ignominiously expulsed; and now some shortsighted, uncomfortable Christians in these parts, among others this said Parson S——, are possessed with the notion that something had better be done to supply the want created by the cessation of these dangerous exhortations, to which the negroes have listened, it seems, with complacency. Parson S—— seems to think that, having driven out two preachers, it might be well to build one church, where, at any rate, the negroes might be exhorted in a safe and salutary manner, "qui ne leur donnerait point d'idées," as the French would say. Upon my word, E——, I used to pity the slaves, and I do pity them with all my soul; but, oh dear! oh dear! their case is a bed of roses to that of their owners, and I would go to the slave-block in Charleston to-morrow cheerfully to be purchased if my only option was to go thither as a purchaser. I was looking over this morning, with a most indescribable mixture of feelings, a pamphlet published in the South upon the subject of the religious instruction of the slaves, and the difficulty of the task undertaken by these reconcilers of God and Mammon really seems to me nothing short of piteous. "We must give our involuntary servants" (they seldom call them slaves, for it is an ugly word in an American mouth, you know) "Christian enlightenment," say they; and where shall they begin? "Whatsoever ye would that men should do unto you, do ye also unto them?" No; but "Servants, obey your masters;" and there, I think, they naturally come to a full stop. This pamphlet forcibly suggested to me the necessity for a slave Church Catechism, and also, indeed, if it were possible, a slave Bible. If these heaven-blinded negro enlighteners persist in their pernicious plan of making Christians of their cattle, something of the sort must be done, or they will infallibly cut their own throats with this two-edged sword of truth, to which they should in no wise have laid their hand, and would not, doubtless, but that it is now thrust at them so threateningly that they have no choice. Again and again, how much I do pity them!

I have been walking to another cluster of negro huts, known as Number Two, and here we took a boat and rowed across the broad brimming Altamaha to a place called Woodville, on a part of the estate named Hammersmith, though why that very thriving suburb of the great city of London should have been selected as the name of the lonely plank house in the midst of the pine woods which here enjoys that title I can not conceive, unless it was suggested by the contrast. This settlement is on the main land, and consists apparently merely of this house (to which the overseer retires when the poisonous malaria of the rice plantations compels him to withdraw from it), and a few deplorably miserable hovels, which appeared to me to be chiefly occupied by the most decrepid and infirm samples of humanity it was ever my melancholy lot to behold.

The air of this pine barren is salubrious compared with that of the rice islands, and here some of the oldest slaves who will not die yet, and can not work any more, are sent, to go, as it were, out of the way. Remote recollections of former dealings with civilized human beings in the shape of masters and overseers seemed to me to be the only idea not purely idiotic in the minds of the poor old tottering creatures that gathered to stare with dim and blear eyes at me and my children.

There were two very aged women, who had seen different, and, to their faded recollections, better times, who spoke to me of Mr. ——'s grandfather, and of the early days of the plantation, when they were young and strong, and worked as their children and grandchildren were now working, neither for love nor yet for money. One of these old crones, a hideous, withered, wrinkled piece of womanhood, said that she had worked as long as her strength had lasted, and that then she had still been worth her keep, for, said she, "Missus, tho' we no able to work, we make little niggers for massa." Her joy at seeing her present owner was unbounded, and she kept clapping her horny hands together and exclaiming, "While there is life there is hope; we seen massa before we die." These demonstrations of regard were followed up by piteous complaints of hunger and rheumatism, and their usual requests for pittances of food and clothing, to which we responded by promises of additions in both kinds; and I was extricating myself as well as I could from my petitioners, with the assurance that I would come by-and-by and visit them again, when I felt my dress suddenly feebly jerked, and a shrill cracked voice on the other side of me exclaimed,

"Missus, no go yet—no go away yet; you no see me, missus, when you come by-and-by; but," added the voice, in a sort of wail, which seemed to me as if the thought was full of misery, "you see many, many of my offspring." These melancholy words, particularly the rather unusual one at the end of the address, struck me very much. They were uttered by a creature which *was* a woman, but looked like a crooked, ill-built figure set up in a field to scare crows, with a face infinitely more like a mere animal's than any human countenance I ever beheld, and with that peculiar, wild, restless look of indefinite and, at the same time, intense sadness that is so remarkable in the countenance of some monkeys. It was almost with an effort that I commanded myself so as not to withdraw my dress from the yellow, crumpled, filthy claws that griped it, and it was not at last without the authoritative voice of the overseer that the poor creature released her hold of me.

We returned home certainly in the very strangest vehicle that ever civilized gentlewoman traveled in—a huge sort of cart, made only of some loose boards, on which I lay, supporting myself against one of the four posts which indicated the sides of my carriage; six horned creatures, cows or bulls, drew this singular equipage, and a yelping, howling, screaming, leaping company of half-naked negroes ran all round them, goading them with sharp sticks, frantically seizing hold of their tails, and inciting them by every conceivable and inconceivable encouragement to quick motion: thus, like one of the ancient Merovingian monarchs, I was dragged through the deep sand from the settlement back to the river, where we re-embarked for the island.

As we crossed the broad flood, whose turbid waters always look swollen as if by a series of freshets, a flight of birds sprang from the low swamp we were approaching, and literally, as it rose in the air, cast a shadow like that

of a cloud, which might be said, with but little exaggeration, to darken the sun for a few seconds. How well I
remember my poor Aunt Whitelock describing such phenomena as of frequent occurrence in America, and the
scornful incredulity with which we heard, without accepting, these legends of her Western experience! How little I then thought that I should have to cry peccavi to her
memory from the bottom of such ruts, and under the
shadow of such flights of winged creatures as she used to
describe from the muddy ways of Pennsylvania and the
muddy waters of Georgia.

The vegetation is already in an active state of demonstration, sprouting into lovely pale green and vivid red-
brown buds and leaflets, though 'tis yet early in January.

After our return home we had a visit from Mr. C——,
one of our neighbors, an intelligent and humane man, to
whose account of the qualities and characteristics of the
slaves, as he had observed and experienced them, I listened
with great interest. The Brunswick Canal was again the
subject of conversation, and again the impossibility of allowing the negroes and Irish to work in proximity was
stated, and admitted as an indisputable fact. It strikes
me with amazement to hear the hopeless doom of incapacity for progress pronounced upon these wretched slaves,
when in my own country the very same order of language
is perpetually applied to these very Irish, here spoken of
as a sort of race of demigods by negro comparison. And
it is most true that in Ireland nothing can be more savage, brutish, filthy, idle, and incorrigibly and hopelessly
helpless and incapable than the Irish appear; and yet,
transplanted to your Northern states, freed from the evil
influences which surround them at home, they and their
children become industrious, thrifty, willing to learn, able
to improve, and forming, in the course of two generations,
a most valuable accession to your laboring population.

How is it that it never occurs to these emphatical de-
nouncers of the whole negro race that the Irish at home
are esteemed much as they esteem their slaves, and that
the sentence pronounced against their whole country by
one of the greatest men of our age, an Irishman, was precisely that nothing could save, redeem, or regenerate Ireland unless, as a preparatory measure, the island were sub-
merged and all its inhabitants drowned off?

I have had several women at the house to-day asking
for advice and help for their sick children: they all came
from No. 2, as they call it, that is, the settlement or cluster of negro huts nearest to the main one, where we may
be said to reside. In the afternoon I went thither, and
found a great many of the little children ailing: there had
been an unusual mortality among them at this particular
settlement this winter. In one miserable hut I heard that
the baby was just dead; it was one of thirteen, many of
whom had been, like itself, mercifully removed from the
life of degradation and misery to which their birth appointed them; and whether it was the frequent repetition
of similar losses, or an instinctive consciousness that death
was indeed better than life for such children as theirs, I
know not, but the father and mother, and old Rose, the
nurse, who was their little baby's grandmother, all seemed
apathetic, and apparently indifferent to the event. The
mother merely repeated over and over again, "I've lost a
many; they all goes so;" and the father, without word or
comment, went out to his enforced labor.

As I left the cabin, rejoicing for them at the deliverance
out of slavery of their poor child, I found myself suddenly
surrounded by a swarm of young ragamuffins in every
stage of partial nudity, clamoring from out of their filthy
remnants of rags for donations of scarlet ribbon for the
ball, which was to take place that evening. The melancholy scene I had just witnessed, and the still sadder re-

flection it had given rise to, had quite driven all thoughts of the approaching festivity from my mind; but the sudden demand for these graceful luxuries by Mr. ——'s half-naked dependents reminded me of the grotesque mask which life wears on one of its mysterious faces; and with as much sympathy for rejoicing as my late sympathy for sorrow had left me capable of, I procured the desired ornaments. I have considerable fellow-feeling for the passion for all shades of red which prevails among these dusky fellow-creatures of mine, a savage propensity for that same color in all its modifications being a tendency of my own.

At our own settlement (No. 1) I found every thing in a high fever of preparation for the ball. A huge boat had just arrived from the cotton plantation at St. Simon's, laden with the youth and beauty of that portion of the estate who had been invited to join the party; and the greetings among the arrivers and welcomers, and the heaven-defying combinations of color in the gala attire of both, surpass all my powers of description. The ball, to which of course we went, took place in one of the rooms of the Infirmary. As the room had, fortunately, but few occupants, they were removed to another apartment, and, without any very tender consideration for their not very remote, though invisible sufferings, the dancing commenced, and was continued. Oh, my dear E——, I have seen Jim Crow — the veritable James: all the contortions, and springs, and flings, and kicks, and capers you have been beguiled into accepting as indicative of him are spurious, faint, feeble, impotent — in a word, pale Northern reproductions of that ineffable black conception. It is impossible for words to describe the things these people did with their bodies, and, above all, with their faces, the whites of their eyes, and the whites of their teeth, and certain outlines which either naturally and by the grace of heaven, or by the practice of some peculiar artistic dexterity, they bring into prominent and most ludicrous display. The languishing elegance of some—the painstaking laborious-ness of others—above all, the feats of a certain enthusias-tic banjo-player, who seemed to me to thump his instru-ment with every part of his body at once, at last so ut-terly overcame any attempt at decorous gravity on my part that I was obliged to secede; and, considering what the atmosphere was that we inhaled during the exhibi-tion, it is only wonderful to me that we were not made ill by the double effort not to laugh, and, if possible, not to breathe.

Monday, 20th.

MY DEAREST E——,—A rather longer interval than usual has elapsed since I last wrote to you, but I must beg you to excuse it. I have had more than a usual amount of small daily occupations to fill my time; and, as a mere enumeration of these would not be very interesting to you, I will tell you a story which has just formed an ad-mirable illustration for my observation of all the miseries of which this accursed system of slavery is the cause, even under the best and most humane administration of its laws and usages. Pray note it, my dear friend, for you will find, in the absence of all voluntary or even conscious cruelty on the part of the master, the best possible com-ment on a state of things which, without the slightest de-sire to injure and oppress, produces such intolerable re-sults of injury and oppression.

We have, as a sort of under nursemaid and assistant of my dear M——, whose white complexion, as I wrote you, occasioned such indignation to my Southern fellow-trav-elers, and such extreme perplexity to the poor slaves on our arrival here, a much more orthodox servant for these

parts, a young woman named Psyche, but commonly called Sack, not a very graceful abbreviation of the divine
heathen appellation : she can not be much over twenty,
has a very pretty figure, a graceful, gentle deportment,
and a face which, but for its color (she is a dingy mulatto), would be pretty, and is extremely pleasing, from the
perfect sweetness of its expression ; she is always serious,
not to say sad and silent, and has always an air of melancholy and timidity, that has frequently struck me very
much, and would have made me think some special anxiety or sorrow must occasion it, but that God knows the
whole condition of these wretched people naturally produces such a deportment, and there is no necessity to seek
for special or peculiar causes to account for it.   Just in
proportion as I have found the slaves on this plantation
intelligent and advanced beyond the general brutish level
of the majority, I have observed this pathetic expression
of countenance in them, a mixture of sadness and fear, the
involuntary exhibition of the two feelings, which I suppose must be the predominant experience of their whole
lives, regret and apprehension, not the less heavy, either
of them, for being, in some degree, vague and indefinite—
a sense of incalculable past loss and injury, and a dread
of incalculable future loss and injury.

I have never questioned Psyche as to her sadness, because, in the first place, as I tell you, it appears to me
most natural, and is observable in all the slaves whose
superior natural or acquired intelligence allows of their
filling situations of trust or service about the house and
family ; and, though I can not and will not refuse to hear
any and every tale of suffering which these unfortunates
bring to me, I am anxious to spare both myself and them
the pain of vain appeals to me for redress and help, which,
alas ! it is too often utterly out of my power to give them.
It is useless, and, indeed, worse than useless, that they

should see my impotent indignation and unavailing pity, and hear expressions of compassion for them, and horror at their condition, which might only prove incentives to a hopeless resistance on their part to a system, under the hideous weight of whose oppression any individual or partial revolt must be annihilated and ground into the dust. Therefore, as I tell you, I asked Psyche no questions; but, to my great astonishment, the other day M—— asked me if I knew to whom Psyche belonged, as the poor woman had inquired of her with much hesitation and anguish if she could tell her who owned her and her children. She has two nice little children under six years old, whom she keeps as clean and tidy, and who are sad and as silent as herself. My astonishment at this question was, as you will readily believe, not small, and I forthwith sought out Psyche for an explanation. She was thrown into extreme perturbation at finding that her question had been referred to me, and it was some time before I could sufficiently reassure her to be able to comprehend, in the midst of her reiterated entreaties for pardon, and hopes that she had not offended me, that she did not know herself who owned her. She was, at one time, the property of Mr. K——, the former overseer, of whom I have already spoken to you, and who has just been paying Mr. —— a visit. He, like several of his predecessors in the management, has contrived to make a fortune upon it (though it yearly decreases in value to the owners, but this is the inevitable course of things in the Southern states), and has purchased a plantation of his own in Alabama, I believe, or one of the Southwestern states. Whether she still belonged to Mr. K—— or not she did not know, and entreated me, if she did, to endeavor to persuade Mr. —— to buy her. Now you must know that this poor woman is the wife of one of Mr. B——'s slaves, a fine, intelligent, active, excellent young man, whose whole family are among some of the very best specimens of character and capacity on the estate. I was so astonished at the (to me) extraordinary state of things revealed by poor Sack's petition, that I could only tell her that I had supposed all the negroes on the plantation were Mr. ——'s property, but that I would certainly inquire, and find out for her, if I could, to whom she belonged, and if I could, endeavor to get Mr. —— to purchase her, if she really was not his.

Now, E——, just conceive for one moment the state of mind of this woman, believing herself to belong to a man who in a few days was going down to one of those abhorred and dreaded Southwestern states, and who would then compel her, with her poor little children, to leave her husband and the only home she had ever known, and all the ties of affection, relationship, and association of her former life, to follow him thither, in all human probability never again to behold any living creature that she had seen before; and this was so completely a matter of course that it was not even thought necessary to apprise her positively of the fact, and the only thing that interposed between her and this most miserable fate was the faint hope that Mr. —— *might have* purchased her and her children. But if he had, if this great deliverance had been vouchsafed to her, the knowledge of it was not thought necessary; and with this deadly dread at her heart she was living day after day, waiting upon me and seeing me, with my husband beside me, and my children in my arms in blessed security, safe from all separation but the one reserved in God's great providence for all His creatures. Do you think I wondered any more at the wo-begone expression of her countenance, or do you think it was easy for me to restrain within prudent and proper limits the expression of my feelings at such a state of things? And she had gone on from day to day enduring this agony, till I suppose its own intolerable pressure and

M——'s sweet countenance and gentle sympathizing voice and manner had constrained her to lay down this great burden of sorrow at our feet. I did not see Mr. —— until the evening; but, in the mean time, meeting Mr. O——, the overseer, with whom, as I believe I have already told you, we are living here, I asked him about Psyche, and who was her proprietor, when, to my infinite surprise, he told me that *he* had bought her and her children from Mr. K——, who had offered them to him, saying that they would be rather troublesome to him than otherwise down where he was going; "and so," said Mr. O——, "as I had no objection to investing a little money that way, I bought them." With a heart much lightened, I flew to tell poor Psyche the news, so that, at any rate, she might be relieved from the dread of any immediate separation from her husband. You can imagine better than I can tell you what her sensations were; but she still renewed her prayer that I would, if possible, induce Mr. —— to purchase her, and I promised to do so.

Early the next morning, while I was still dressing, I was suddenly startled by hearing voices in loud tones in Mr. ——'s dressing-room, which adjoins my bedroom, and the noise increasing until there was an absolute cry of despair uttered by some man. I could restrain myself no longer, but opened the door of communication and saw Joe, the young man, poor Psyche's husband, raving almost in a state of frenzy, and in a voice broken with sobs and almost inarticulate with passion, reiterating his determination never to leave this plantation, never to go to Alabama, never to leave his old father and mother, his poor wife and children, and dashing his hat, which he was wringing like a cloth in his hands, upon the ground, he declared he would kill himself if he was compelled to follow Mr. K——. I glanced from the poor wretch to Mr. ——, who was standing, leaning against a table with his arms folded, occasionally uttering a few words of counsel to his slave to be quiet and not fret, and not make a fuss about what there was no help for. I retreated immediately from the horrid scene, breathless with surprise and dismay, and stood for some time in my own room, with my heart and temples throbbing to such a degree that I could hardly support myself. As soon as I recovered myself I again sought Mr. O——, and inquired of him if he knew the cause of poor Joe's distress. He then told me that Mr. ——, who is highly pleased with Mr. K——'s past administration of his property, wished, on his departure for his newly-acquired slave plantation, to give him some token of his satisfaction, and *had made him a present* of the man Joe, who had just received the intelligence that he was to go down to Alabama with his new owner the next day, leaving father, mother, wife, and children behind. You will not wonder that the man required a little judicious soothing under such circumstances, and you will also, I hope, admire the humanity of the sale of his wife and children by the owner who was going to take him to Alabama, because *they* would be encumbrances rather than otherwise down there. If Mr. K—— did not do this after he knew that the man was his, then Mr. —— gave him to be carried down to the South after his wife and children were sold to remain in Georgia. I do not know which was the real transaction, for I have not had the heart to ask; but you will easily imagine which of the two cases I prefer believing.

When I saw Mr. —— after this most wretched story became known to me in all its details, I appealed to him, for his own soul's sake, not to commit so great a cruelty. Poor Joe's agony while remonstrating with his master was hardly greater than mine while arguing with him upon this bitter piece of inhumanity—how I cried, and how I adjured, and how all my sense of justice, and of

mercy, and of pity for the poor wretch, and of wretchedness at finding myself implicated in such a state of things,
broke in torrents of words from my lips and tears from
my eyes! God knows such a sorrow at seeing any one I
belonged to commit such an act was indeed a new and
terrible experience to me, and it seemed to me that I was
imploring Mr. —— to save himself more than to spare
these wretches. He gave me no answer whatever, and I
have since thought that the intemperate vehemence of my
entreaties and expostulations perhaps deserved that he
should leave me as he did without one single word of reply; and miserable enough I remained. Toward evening,
as I was sitting alone, my children having gone to bed,
Mr. O—— came into the room. I had but one subject in
my mind; I had not been able to eat for it. I could hardly sit still for the nervous distress which every thought
of these poor people filled me with. As he sat down looking over some accounts, I said to him, "Have you seen
Joe this afternoon, Mr. O——?" (I give you our conversation as it took place.) "Yes, ma'am; he is a great
deal happier than he was this morning." "Why, how is
that?" asked I, eagerly. "Oh, he is not going to Alabama. Mr. K—— heard that he had kicked up a fuss
about it (being in despair at being torn from one's wife
and children is called *kicking up a fuss;* this is a sample
of overseer appreciation of human feelings), and said that
if the fellow wasn't willing to go with him, he did not
wish to be bothered with any niggers down there who
were to be troublesome, so he might stay behind." "And
does Psyche know this?" "Yes, ma'am, I suppose so."
I drew a long breath; and whereas my needle had stum-
bled through the stuff I was sewing for an hour before, as
if my fingers could not guide it, the regularity and rapidity of its evolutions were now quite edifying. The man
was for the present safe, and I remained silently ponder-

ing his deliverance and the whole proceeding, and the conduct of every one engaged in it, and, above all, Mr. ——'s share in the transaction, and I think, for the first time, almost a sense of horrible personal responsibility and implication took hold of my mind, and I felt the weight of an unimagined guilt upon my conscience; and yet, God knows, this feeling of self-condemnation is very gratuitous on my part, since when I married Mr. —— I knew nothing of these dreadful possessions of his, and even if I had I should have been much puzzled to have formed any idea of the state of things in which I now find myself plunged, together with those whose well-doing is as vital to me almost as my own.

With these agreeable reflections I went to bed. Mr. —— said not a word to me upon the subject of these poor people all the next day, and in the mean time I became very impatient of this reserve on his part, because I was dying to prefer my request that he would purchase Psyche and her children, and so prevent any future separation between her and her husband, as I supposed he would not again attempt to make a present of Joe, at least to any one who did not wish to be *bothered* with his wife and children. In the evening I was again with Mr. O—— alone in the strange, bare, wooden-walled sort of shanty which is our sitting-room, and revolving in my mind the means of rescuing Psyche from her miserable suspense, a long chain of all my possessions, in the shape of bracelets, necklaces, brooches, earrings, etc., wound in glittering procession through my brain, with many hypothetical calculations of the value of each separate ornament, and the very doubtful probability of the amount of the whole being equal to the price of this poor creature and her children; and then the great power and privilege I had foregone of earning money by my own labor occurred to me, and I think, for the first time in my life, my past profession assumed an aspect that arrested my thoughts most seriously. For the last four years of my life that preceded my marriage I literally coined money, and never until this moment, I think, did I reflect on the great means of good, to myself and others, that I so gladly agreed to give up forever for a maintenance by the unpaid labor of slaves—people toiling not only unpaid, but under the bitter conditions the bare contemplation of which was then wringing my heart. You will not wonder that when, in the midst of such cogitations, I suddenly accosted Mr. O——, it was to this effect: "Mr. O——, I have a particular favor to beg of you. Promise me that you will never sell Psyche and her children without first letting me know of your intention to do so, and giving me the option of buying them." Mr. O—— is a remarkably deliberate man, and squints, so that, when he has taken a little time in directing his eyes to you, you are still unpleasantly unaware of any result in which you are concerned; he laid down a book he was reading, and directed his head and one of his eyes toward me and answered, "Dear me, ma'am, I am very sorry—I have sold them." My work fell down on the ground, and my mouth opened wide, but I could utter no sound, I was so dismayed and surprised; and he deliberately proceeded: "I didn't know, ma'am, you see, at all, that you entertained any idea of making an investment of that nature; for I'm sure, if I had, I would willingly have sold the woman to you; but I sold her and her children this morning to Mr. ——." My dear E——, though —— had resented my unmeasured upbraidings, you see they had not been without some good effect, and though he had, perhaps justly, punished my violent outbreak of indignation about the miserable scene I witnessed by not telling me of his humane purpose, he had bought these poor creatures, and so, I trust, secured them from any such misery in future. I jumped up and left Mr. O—— still speaking, and ran to find Mr. ——, to thank him for what he had done, and with that will now bid you good-by. Think, E——, how it fares with slaves on plantations where there is no crazy Englishwoman to weep, and entreat, and implore, and up-braid for them, and no master willing to listen to such appeals.

---

DEAR E——,—There is one privilege which I enjoy here which I think few Cockneynesses have ever had ex-perience of, that of hearing my own extemporaneous praises chanted bard-fashion by our negroes in rhymes as rude and to measures as simple as ever any illustrious fe-male of the days of King Brian Boroihme listened to. Rowing yesterday evening through a beautiful sunset into a more beautiful moonrise, my two sable boatmen en-tertained themselves and me with alternate strophe and antistrophe of poetical description of my personal at-tractions, in which my " wire waist" recurred repeatedly, to my intense amusement. This is a charm for the pos-session of which M—— (my white nursemaid) is also in-variably celebrated; and I suppose that the fine round natural proportions of the uncompressed waists of the sable beauties of these regions appear less symmetrical to eyes accustomed to them than our stay-cased figures, since " nothing pleaseth but rare accidents." Occasion-ally I am celebrated in these rowing chants as " Massa's darling," and S—— comes in for endless glorification on account of the brilliant beauty of her complexion; the other day, however, our poets made a diversion from the personal to the moral qualities of their small mistress, and after the usual tribute to her roses and lilies came the fol-lowing rather significant couplet:

"Little Missis Sally,
That's a ruling lady."

At which all the white teeth simultaneously lightened from the black visages, while the subject of this equivocal commendation sat with infantine solemnity (the profoundest, I think, that the human countenance is capable of), surveying her sable dependents with imperturbable gravity.

Yesterday morning I amused myself with an exercise of a talent I once possessed, but have so neglected that my performance might almost be called an experiment. I cut out a dress for one of the women. My education in France—where, in some important respects, I think girls are better trained than with us—had sent me home to England, at sixteen, an adept in the female mystery of needle-work. Not only owing to the Saturday's discipline of clothes-mending by all the classes—while l'Abbé Millot's history (of blessed boring memory) was being read aloud, to prevent "vain babblings," and insure wholesome mental occupation the while—was I an expert patcher and mender, darner and piecer (darning and marking were my specialties), but the white cotton embroidery of which every French woman has always a piece under her hand *pour les momens perdus*, which are thus any thing but *perdus*, was as familar to us as to the Irish cottagers of the present day, and cutting out and making my dresses was among the more advanced branches of *the* female accomplishment to which I attained.* The luxury of a lady's

* Some of our great English ladies are, I know, exquisite needle-women; but I do not think, in spite of these exceptional examples, that young English ladies of the higher classes are much skilled in this respect at the present day; and as for the democratic daughters of America, who for many reasons might be supposed likely to be well up in such housewifely lore, they are, for the most part, so ignorant of it that I have heard the most eloquent preacher of the city of New

maid of my own, indulged in ever since the days of my
"coming out," has naturally enough caused my right hand
to forget its cunning, and regret and shame at having lost
any useful lore in my life made me accede, for my own
sake, to the request of one of our multitudinous Dianas
and innumerable Chloes to cut out dresses for each of
them, especially as they (wonderful to relate) declared
themselves able to stitch them if I would do the cutting.
Since I have been on the plantation I have already spent
considerable time in what the French call "confection-
ing" baby bundles, *i. e.*, the rough and very simple tiny
habiliments of coarse cotton and scarlet flannel which form
a baby's layette here, and of which I have run up some
scores; but my present task was far more difficult.
Chloe was an ordinary mortal negress enough, but Diana
might have been the Huntress of the Woods herself, done
into the African type. Tall, large, straight, well made,
profoundly serious, she stood like a bronze statue, while I,
mounted on a stool (the only way in which I could attain
to the noble shoulders and bust of my lay figure), pinned
and measured, and cut and shaped, under the superintendence of M——, and had the satisfaction of seeing the fine
proportions of my black goddess quite becomingly clothed
in a high, tight-fitting body of the gayest chintz, which
she really contrived to put together quite creditably.

I was so elated with my own part of this performance

York advert to their incapacity in this respect as an impediment to
their assistance of the poor, and ascribe to the fact that the daughters
of his own parishioners did not know how to sew, the impossibility of
their giving the most valuable species of help to the women of the
needier classes, whose condition could hardly be more effectually improved than by acquiring such useful knowledge. I have known
young American school-girls duly instructed in the nature of the par-
allaxes of the stars, but, as a rule, they do not know how to darn their
stockings. Les Dames du Sacré Cœur do better for their high-born
and well-bred pupils than this.

that I then and there determined to put into execution a plan I had long formed of endowing the little boat in which I take what the French call my walks on the water with cushions for the back and seat of the benches usually occupied by myself and Mr. ——; so, putting on my large straw hat, and plucking up a paper of pins, scissors, and my brown holland, I walked to the steps, and, jumping into the little canoe, began piecing, and measuring, and cutting the cushions, which were to be stuffed with the tree moss by some of the people who understand making a rough kind of mattress. My inanimate subject, however, proved far more troublesome to fit than my living lay figure, for the little cockle-shell ducked, and dived, and rocked, and tipped, and courtesied, and tilted, as I knelt first on one side and then on the other, fitting her, till I was almost in despair; however, I got a sort of pattern at last, and by dint of some pertinacious efforts— which, in their incompleteness, did not escape some sarcastic remarks from Mr. —— on the capabilities of "women of genius" applied to commonplace objects—the matter was accomplished, and the little Dolphin rejoiced in very tidy back and seat cushions, covered with brown holland, and bound with green serge. My ambition then began to contemplate an awning; but the boat being of the nature of a canoe—though not a real one, inasmuch as it is not made of a single log—does not admit of supports for such an edifice.

I had rather a fright the other day in that same small craft, into which I had taken S——, with the intention of paddling myself a little way down the river and back. I used to row tolerably well, and was very fond of it, and frequently here take an oar, when the men are rowing me in the long-boat, as some sort of equivalent for my riding, of which, of course, I am entirely deprived on this little dikeland of ours; but paddling is a perfectly different process, and one that I was very anxious to achieve. My first strokes answered the purpose of sending the boat off from shore, and for a few minutes I got on pretty well; but presently I got tired of shifting the paddle from side to side, a manœuvre which I accomplished very clumsily and slowly, and yet, with all my precautions, not without making the boat tip perilously. The immense breadth and volume of the river suddenly seized my eyes and imagination as it were, and I began to fancy that if I got into the middle of the stream I should not be able to paddle myself back against it—which, indeed, might very well have proved the case. Then I became nervous, and paddled all on one side, by which means, of course, I only turned the boat round. S—— began to fidget about, getting up from where I had placed her, and terrifying me with her unsteady motions and the rocking of the canoe. I was now very much frightened, and saw that I *must* get back to shore before I became more helpless than I was beginning to feel; so, laying S—— down in the bottom of the boat as a preliminary precaution, I said to her with infinite emphasis, "Now lie still there, and don't stir, or you'll be drowned," to which, with her clear gray eyes fixed on me, and no sign whatever of emotion, she replied deliberately, "I shall lie still here, and won't stir, for I should not like to be drowned," which, for an atom not four years old, was rather philosophical. Then I looked about me, and of course having drifted, set steadily to work and paddled home, with my heart in my mouth almost till we grazed the steps, and I got my precious freight safe on shore again, since which I have taken no more paddling lessons without my slave and master, Jack.

We have had a death among the people since I last wrote to you. A very valuable slave called Shadrach was seized with a disease which is frequent, and very apt to be fatal here—peripneumonia; and, in spite of all that could be done to save him, sank rapidly, and died after an acute illness of only three days. The doctor came repeatedly from Darien, and the last night of the poor fellow's life —— himself watched with him. I suppose the general low diet of the negroes must produce some want of stamina in them; certainly, either from natural constitution or the effect of their habits of existence, or both, it is astonishing how much less power of resistance to disease they seem to possess than we do. If they are ill, the vital energy seems to sink immediately. This rice cultivation, too, although it does not affect them as it would whites—to whom, indeed, residence on the rice plantation after a certain season is impossible—is still, to a certain degree, deleterious even to the negroes. The proportion of sick is always greater here than on the cotton plantation, and the invalids of this place are not unfrequently sent down to St. Simon's to recover their strength, under the more favorable influences of the sea air and dry sandy soil of Hampton Point.

Yesterday afternoon the tepid warmth of the air and glassy stillness of the river seemed to me highly suggestive of fishing, and I determined, not having yet discovered what I could catch with what in these unknown waters, to try a little innocent paste bait—a mystery his initiation into which caused Jack much wonderment. The only hooks I had with me, however, had been bought in Darien —made, I should think, at the North expressly for this market; and so villainously bad were they, that, after trying them and my patience a reasonable time, I gave up the attempt and took a lesson in paddling instead. Among other items Jack told me of his own fishing experience was that he had more than once caught those most excellent creatures, Altamaha shad, by the fish themselves leaping out of the water and *landing*, as Jack expressed it, to

escape from the porpoises, which come in large schools up
the river to a considerable distance, occasioning, evidently,
much emotion in the bosoms of the legitimate inhabitants
of these muddy waters.  Coasting the island on our return home, we found a trap, which the last time we exam-
ined it was tenanted by a creature called a mink, now occupied by an otter.  The poor beast did not seem pleased
with his predicament; but the trap had been set by one
of the drivers, and, of course, Jack would not have meddled with it except upon my express order, which, in spite
of some pangs of pity for the otter, I did not like to give
him, as, in the extremely few resources of either profit or
pleasure possessed by the slaves, I could not tell at all
what might be the value of an otter to his captor.

Yesterday evening the burial of the poor man Shadrach
took place.  I had been applied to for a sufficient quantity
of cotton cloth to make a winding-sheet for him, and just
as the twilight was thickening into darkness I went with
Mr. —— to the cottage of one of the slaves whom I may
have mentioned to you before—a cooper of the name of
London, the head of the religious party of the inhabitants
of the island, a Methodist preacher of no small intelligence
and influence among the people—who was to perform the
burial service.  The coffin was laid on trestles in front of
the cooper's cottage, and a large assemblage of the people
had gathered round, many of the men carrying pine-wood
torches, the fitful glare of which glanced over the strange
assembly, where every pair of large white-rimmed eyes
turned upon —— and myself; we two poor creatures, on
this more solemn occasion, as well as on every other when
these people encounter us, being the objects of admiration
and wonderment, on which their gaze is immovably rivet-
ed.  Presently the whole congregation uplifted their voices
in a hymn, the first high wailing notes of which—sung all
in unison, in the midst of these unwonted surroundings—

sent a thrill through all my nerves. When the chant ceased, cooper London began a prayer, and all the people knelt down in the sand, as I did also. Mr. —— alone remained standing in the presence of the dead man and of the living God to whom his slaves were now appealing. I can not tell you how profoundly the whole ceremony, if such it could be called, affected me; and there was nothing in the simple and pathetic supplication of the poor black artisan to check or interfere with the solemn influences of the whole scene. It was a sort of conventional Methodist prayer, and probably quite as conventional as all the rest was the closing invocation of God's blessing upon their master, their mistress, and our children; but this fairly overcame my composure, and I began to cry very bitterly; for these same individuals, whose implication in the state of things in the midst of which we are living, seemed to me as legitimate a cause for tears as for prayers. When the prayer was concluded we all rose, and, the coffin being taken up, proceeded to the people's burial-ground, when London read aloud portions of the funeral service from the Prayer-book — I presume the American Episcopal version of our Church service, for what he read appeared to be merely a selection from what was perfectly familiar to me; but whether he himself extracted what he uttered I did not inquire. Indeed, I was too much absorbed in the whole scene, and the many mingled emotions it excited of awe and pity, and an indescribable sensation of wonder at finding myself on this slave soil, surrounded by MY slaves, among whom again I knelt while the words proclaiming to the living and the dead the everlasting covenant of freedom, "I am the resurrection and the life," sounded over the prostrate throng, and mingled with the heavy flowing of the vast river sweeping, not far from where we stood, through the darkness by which we were now encompassed (beyond the

immediate circle of our torch-bearers). There was something painful to me in ——'s standing while we all knelt
on the earth; for, though in any church in Philadelphia
he would have stood during the praying of any minister,
here I wished he would have knelt, to have given his
slaves some token of his belief that—at least in the sight
of that Master to whom we were addressing our worship
—all men are equal. The service ended with a short address from London upon the subject of Lazarus, and the
confirmation which the story of his resurrection afforded
our hopes. The words were simple and rustic, and of
course uttered in the peculiar sort of jargon which is the
habitual negro speech; but there was nothing in the slightest degree incongruous or grotesque in the matter or manner, and the exhortations not to steal, or lie, or neglect to
work well for massa, with which the glorious hope of im-
mortality was blended in the poor slave preacher's closing
address, was a moral adaptation, as wholesome as it was
touching, of the great Christian theory to the capacities
and consciences of his hearers. When the coffin was lowered the grave was found to be partially filled with water
—naturally enough, for the whole island is a mere swamp,
off which the Altamaha is only kept from sweeping by
the high dikes all round it. This seemed to shock and
distress the people, and for the first time during the whole
ceremony there were sounds of crying and exclamations
of grief heard among them. Their chief expression of
sorrow, however, when Mr. —— and myself bade them
good-night at the conclusion of the service, was on account
of my crying, which appeared to affect them very much,
many of them mingling with their "Farewell, good-night,
massa and missis," affectionate exclamations of "God
bless you, missis; don't cry!" "Lor, missis, don't you
cry so!" Mr. —— declined the assistance of any of the
torch-bearers home, and bade them all go quietly to their

quarters; and as soon as they had dispersed, and we had got beyond the fitful and unequal glaring of the torches, we found the shining of the stars in the deep blue lovely night sky quite sufficient to light our way along the dikes. I could not speak to ——, but continued to cry as we walked silently home; and, whatever his cogitations were, they did not take the usual form with him of wordy demonstration, and so we returned from one of the most striking religious ceremonies at which I ever assisted. Arrived at the door of the house, we perceived that we had been followed the whole way by the naked, noiseless feet of a poor half-witted creature, a female idiot, whose mental incapacity, of course, in no respect unfits her for the life of toil, little more intellectual than that of any beast of burden, which is her allotted portion here. Some small gratification was given to her, and she departed gibbering and muttering in high glee. Think, E——, of that man London, who, in spite of all the bitter barriers in his way, has learned to read, has read his Bible, teaches it to his unfortunate fellows, and is used by his owner and his owner's agents, for all these causes, as an effectual influence for good over the slaves of whom he is himself the despised and injured companion. Like them, subject to the driver's lash; like them, the helpless creature of his master's despotic will, without a right or a hope in this dreary world. But, though the light he has attained must show him the terrible aspects of his fate hidden by blessed ignorance from his companions, it reveals to him also other rights and other hopes — another world, another life — toward which he leads, according to the grace vouchsafed to him, his poor fellow-slaves. How can we keep this man in such a condition? How is such a cruel sin of injustice to be answered? Mr. ——, of course, sees and feels none of this as I do, and, I should think, must regret that he ever brought me here, to have my abhorrence of the theory of slavery deepened, and strengthened every hour of my life, by what I see of its practice.

This morning I went over to Darien upon the very female errands of returning visits and shopping. In one respect (assuredly in none other) our life here resembles existence in Venice: we can never leave home for any purpose or in any direction but by boat—not, indeed, by gondola, but the sharp-cut, well-made light craft in which we take our walks on the water is a very agreeable species of conveyance. One of my visits this morning was to a certain Miss ——, whose rather grandiloquent name and very striking style of beauty exceedingly well became the daughter of an ex-governor of Georgia. As for the residence of this princess, it was like all the planters' residences that I have seen, and such as a well-to-do English farmer would certainly not inhabit. Occasional marks of former elegance or splendor survive sometimes in the size of the rooms, sometimes in a little carved woodwork about the mantel-pieces or wainscotings of these mansions; but all things have a Castle Rackrent air of neglect, and dreary, careless untidiness, with which the dirty, barefooted negro servants are in excellent keeping. Occasionally a huge pair of dazzling shirt-gills, out of which a black visage grins as out of some vast white paper cornet, adorns the sable footman of the establishment, but unfortunately without at all necessarily indicating any downward prolongation of the garment; and the perfect tulip-bed of a head-handkerchief with which the female attendants of these "great families" love to bedizen themselves frequently stands them instead of every other most indispensable article of female attire.

As for my shopping, the goods, or rather "bads," at which I used to grumble, in your village emporium at Lenox, are what may be termed "first rate," both in excellence and elegance, compared with the vile products of every sort which we wretched Southerners are expected to accept as the conveniences of life in exchange for current coin of the realm. I regret to say, moreover, that all these infamous articles are Yankee made—expressly for this market, where every species of *thing* (to use the most general term I can think of), from list shoes to piano-fortes, is procured from the North—almost always New England, utterly worthless of its kind, and dearer than the most perfect specimens of the same articles would be any where else. The incredible variety and ludicrous combinations of goods to be met with in one of these Southern shops beats the stock of your village omnium-gatherum hollow: to be sure, one class of articles, and that probably the most in demand here, is not sold over any counter in Massachusetts—cowhides and man-traps, of which a large assortment enters necessarily into the furniture of every Southern shop.

In passing to-day along the deep sand road calling itself the street of Darien, my notice was attracted by an extremely handsome and intelligent-looking poodle, standing by a little wizen-looking knife-grinder, whose features were evidently European, though he was nearly as black as a negro, who, strange to say, was discoursing with him in very tolerable French. The impulse of curiosity led me to accost the man at the grindstone, when his companion immediately made off. The itinerant artisan was from Aix, in Provence: think of wandering thence to Darien in Georgia! I asked him about the negro who was talking to him; he said he knew nothing of him but that he was a slave belonging to somebody in the town. And upon my expressing surprise at his having left his own beautiful and pleasant country for this dreary distant region, he answered, with a shrug and a smile, "Oui, madame, c'est vrai; c'est un joli pays, mais dans ce pays-là, quand un homme n'a rien, c'est rien pour toujours." A property which many, no doubt, have come hither, like the little French knife-grinder, to increase, without succeeding in the struggle much better than he appeared to have done.

---

Dear E——,—Having made a fresh, and, as I thought, more promising purchase of fishing-tackle, Jack and I betook ourselves to the river, and succeeded in securing some immense catfish, of which, to tell you the truth, I am most horribly afraid when I have caught them. The dexterity necessary for taking them off the hook so as to avoid the spikes on their backs, and the spikes on each side of their gills, the former having to be pressed down, and the two others pressed up, before you can get any purchase on the slimy beast (for it is smooth skinned and without scales, to add to the difficulty)—these conditions, I say, make the catching of catfish questionable sport. Then, too, they hiss, and spit, and swear at one, and are altogether devilish in their aspect and demeanor; nor are they good for food, except, as Jack with much humility said this morning, for colored folks—" Good for colored folks, missis; me 'spect not good enough for white people." That 'spect, meaning *ex*pect, has sometimes a possible meaning of *su*spect, which would give the sentence in which it occurs a very humorous turn, and I always take the benefit of that interpretation. After exhausting the charms of our occupation, finding that catfish were likely to be our principal haul, I left the river and went my rounds to the hospitals. On my way I encountered two batches of small black fry, Hannah's children and poor Psyche's children, looking really as neat and tidy as children of the bettermost class of artisans among ourselves. These people are so quick and so imitative that it would be the easiest thing in the world to improve their physical condition by appealing to their emulative propensities.

Their passion for what is *genteel* might be used most advantageously in the same direction; and, indeed, I think it would be difficult to find people who offered such a fair purchase by so many of their characteristics to the hand of the reformer.

Returning from the hospital, I was accosted by poor old Teresa, the wretched negress who had complained to me so grievously of her back being broken by hard work and childbearing. She was in a dreadful state of excitement, which she partly presently communicated to me, because she said Mr. O—— had ordered her to be flogged for having complained to me as she did. It seems to me that I have come down here to be tortured, for this punishing these wretched creatures for crying out to me for help is really converting me into a source of increased misery to them. It is almost more than I can endure to hear these horrid stories of lashings inflicted because I have been invoked; and though I dare say Mr. ——, thanks to my passionate appeals to him, gives me little credit for prudence or self-command, I have some, and I exercise it, too, when I listen to such tales as these with my teeth set fast and my lips closed. Whatever I may do to the master, I hold my tongue to the slaves, and I wonder how I do it.

In the afternoon I rowed with Mr. —— to another island in the broad waters of the Altamaha, called Tunno's Island, to return the visit of a certain Dr. T——, the proprietor of the island, named after him, as our rice swamp is after Major ——. I here saw growing in the open air the most beautiful gardinias I ever beheld; the branches were as high and as thick as the largest clumps of kalmia that grow in your woods; but whereas the tough, stringy, fibrous branches of these gives them a straggling appearance, these magnificent masses of dark, shiny, glossy green leaves were quite compact, and I can not conceive any thing lovelier or more delightful than they would be

starred all over with their thick-leaved, cream-white odoriferous blossoms.

In the course of our visit a discussion arose as to the
credibility of any negro assertion, though, indeed, that
could hardly be called a discussion that was simply a
chorus of assenting opinions. No negro was to be believed on any occasion or any subject. No doubt they
are habitual liars, for they are slaves; but there are some
thrice honorable exceptions, who, being slaves, are yet not
liars; and certainly the vice results much more from the
circumstances in which they are placed than from any natural tendency to untruth in their case. The truth is that
they are always considered as false and deceitful, and it is
very seldom that any special investigation of the facts of
any particular case is resorted to in their behalf. They
are always prejudged on their supposed general characteristics, and never judged after the fact on the merit of
any special instance.

A question which was discussed in the real sense of
the term was that of plowing the land instead of having
it turned with the spade or hoe. I listened to this with
great interest, for Jack and I had had some talk upon
this subject, which began in his ardently expressed wish
that massa would allow his land to be plowed, and his
despairing conclusion that he never would, " 'cause horses
more costly to keep than colored folks," and plowing,
therefore, dearer than hoeing or digging. I had ventured
to suggest to Mr. —— the possibility of plowing some
of the fields on the island, and his reply was that the
whole land was too moist, and too much interrupted with
the huge masses of the cypress yam roots, which would
turn the share of any plow; yet there is land belonging
to our neighbor Mr. G——, on the other side of the river,
where the conditions of the soil must be precisely the
same, and yet which is being plowed before our faces.

On Mr. ——'s adjacent plantation the plow is also used extensively and successfully.

On my return to our own island I visited another of the hospitals, and the settlements to which it belonged. The condition of these places and of their inhabitants is, of course, the same all over the plantation, and if I were to describe them I should but weary you with a repetition of identical phenomena: filthy, wretched, almost naked, always barelegged and barefooted children; negligent, ignorant, wretched mothers, whose apparent indifference to the plight of their offspring, and utter incapacity to alter it, are the inevitable result of their slavery. It is hopeless to attempt to reform their habits or improve their condition while the women are condemned to field labor; nor is it possible to overestimate the bad moral effect of the system as regards the women entailing this enforced separation from their children, and neglect of all the cares and duties of mother, nurse, and even housewife, which are all merged in the mere physical toil of a human hoeing machine. It seems to me too—but upon this point I can not, of course, judge as well as the persons accustomed to and acquainted with the physical capacities of their slaves—that the labor is not judiciously distributed in many cases—at least not as far as the women are concerned. It is true that every able-bodied woman is made the most of in being driven afield as long as, under all and any circumstances, she is able to wield a hoe; but, on the other hand, stout, hale, hearty girls and boys, of from eight to twelve and older, are allowed to lounge about, filthy and idle, with no pretense of an occupation but what they call "tend baby," i. e., see to the life and limbs of the little slave infants, to whose mothers, working in distant fields, they carry them during the day to be suckled, and for the rest of the time leave them to crawl and kick in the filthy cabins or on the broiling sand

which surrounds them, in which industry, excellent enough
for the poor babies, these big lazy youths and lasses emu-
late them. Again, I find many women who have borne
from five to ten children rated as workers, precisely as
young women in the prime of their strength who have
had none; this seems a cruel carelessness. To be sure,
while the women are pregnant their task is diminished,
and this is one of the many indirect inducements held out
to reckless propagation, which has a sort of premium offered to it in the consideration of less work and more
food, counterbalanced by none of the sacred responsibilities which hallow and ennoble the relation of parent and
child; in short, as their lives are for the most part those
of mere animals, their increase is literally mere animal
breeding, to which every encouragement is given, for it
adds to the master's live-stock and the value of his estate.

----

DEAR E——,—To-day I have the pleasure of announcing to you a variety of improvements about to be made in
the Infirmary of the island. There is to be a third story
—a mere loft, indeed—added to the building; but, by affording more room for the least distressing cases of sickness to be drafted off into, it will leave the ground floor
and room above it comparatively free for the most miserable of these unfortunates. To my unspeakable satisfaction, these destitute apartments are to be furnished with
bedsteads, mattresses, pillows, and blankets; and I feel a
little comforted for the many heartaches my life here in-
flicts upon me — at least some of my twinges will have
wrought this poor alleviation of their wretchedness for
the slaves when prostrated by disease or pain.

I had hardly time to return from the hospital home this
morning before one of the most tremendous storms I ever
saw burst over the island. Your Northern hills, with their

solemn pine woods, and fresh streams and lakes, telling of a cold rather than a warm climate, always seem to me as if undergoing some strange and unnatural visitation when one of your heavy summer thunder-storms bursts over them. Snow and frost, hail and, above all, wind, trailing rain-clouds and brilliant northern lights, are your appropriate sky phenomena; here, thunder and lightning seem as if they might have been invented. Even in winter (remember, we are now in February) they appear neither astonishing nor unseasonable, and I should think in summer (but Heaven defend me from ever making good my supposition) lightning must be as familiar to these sweltering lands and slimy waters as sunlight itself.

The afternoon cleared off most beautifully, and Jack and I went out on the river to catch what might be caught. Jack's joyful excitement was extreme at my announcing to him the fact that Mr. —— had consented to try plowing on some of the driest portions of the island instead of the slow and laborious process of hoeing the fields; this is a disinterested exultation on his part, for, at any rate, as long as I am here, he will certainly be nothing but "my boy Jack," and I should think, after my departure, will never be degraded to the rank of a field-hand or common laborer. Indeed, the delicacy of his health, to which his slight, slender figure and languid face bear witness, and which was one reason of his appointment to the eminence of being "my slave," would, I should think, prevent the poor fellow's ever being a very robust or useful working animal.

On my return from the river I had a long and painful conversation with Mr. —— upon the subject of the flogging which had been inflicted on the wretched Teresa. These discussions are terrible: they throw me into perfect agonies of distress for the slaves, whose position is utterly hopeless; for myself, whose intervention in their behalf

sometimes seems to me worse than useless; for Mr. ——,
whose share in this horrible system fills me by turns with
indignation and pity. But, after all, what can he do? how
can he help it all? Moreover, born and bred in America, how should he care or wish to help it? and, of course,
he does not; and I am in despair that he does not: et
voilà, it is a happy and hopeful plight for us both. He
maintained that there had been neither hardship nor injustice in the case of Teresa's flogging; and that, moreover, she had not been flogged at all for complaining to
me, but simply because her allotted task was not done at
the appointed time. Of course this was the result of her
having come to appeal to me instead of going to her labor; and as she knew perfectly well the penalty she was
incurring, he maintained that there was neither hardship
nor injustice in the case; the whole thing was a regularly established law, with which all the slaves were perfectly well acquainted; and this case was no exception whatever. The circumstance of my being on the island could
not, of course, be allowed to overthrow the whole system
of discipline established to secure the labor and obedience
of the slaves; and if they chose to try experiments as to
that fact, they and I must take the consequences. At the
end of the day, the driver of the gang to which Teresa belongs reported her work not done, and Mr. O—— ordered him to give her the usual number of stripes, which order the driver of course obeyed, without knowing how
Teresa had employed her time instead of hoeing. But
Mr. O—— knew well enough, for the wretched woman
told me that she had herself told him she should appeal
to me about her weakness, and suffering, and inability to
do the work exacted from her.

He did not, however, think proper to exceed in her punishment the usual number of stripes allotted to the non-
performance of the appointed daily task, and Mr. ——

pronounced the whole transaction perfectly satisfactory and *en règle*. The common drivers are limited in their powers of chastisement, not being allowed to administer more than a certain number of lashes to their fellow-slaves. Head man Frank, as he is called, has alone the privilege of exceeding this limit; and the overseer's latitude of infliction is only curtailed by the necessity of avoiding injury to life or limb. The master's irresponsible power has no such bound. When I was thus silenced on the particular case under discussion, I resorted, in my distress and indignation, to the abstract question, as I never can refrain from doing; and to Mr. ——'s assertion of the justice of poor Teresa's punishment, I retorted the manifest injustice of unpaid and enforced labor; the brutal inhumanity of allowing a man to strip and lash a woman, the mother of ten children; to exact from her toil which was to maintain in luxury two idle young men, the owners of the plantation. I said I thought female labor of the sort exacted from these slaves, and corporal chastisement such as they endure, must be abhorrent to any manly or humane man. Mr. —— said he thought it was *disagreeable*, and left me to my reflections with that concession. My letter has been interrupted for the last three days—by nothing special, however. My occupations and interests here, of course, know no change; but Mr. —— has been anxious for a little while past that we should go down to St. Simon's, the cotton plantation.

We shall suffer less from the heat, which I am beginning to find oppressive on this swamp island; and he himself wished to visit that part of his property, whither he had not yet been since our arrival in Georgia; so the day before yesterday he departed to make the necessary arrangements for our removal thither; and my time in the mean while has been taken up in fitting him out for his departure.

In the morning Jack and I took our usual paddle, and, having the tackle on board, tried fishing. I was absorbed in many sad and serious considerations, and, wonderful to relate (for you know, ——, how keen an angler I am), had lost all consciousness of my occupation until, after I know not how long a time elapsing without the shadow of a nibble, I was recalled to a most ludicrous perception of my ill success by Jack's sudden observation, "Missis, fishing berry good fun when um fish bite." This settled the fishing for that morning, and I let Jack paddle me down the broad turbid stream, endeavoring to answer in the most comprehensible manner to his keen but utterly undeveloped intellects the innumerable questions with which he plied me about Philadelphia, about England, about the Atlantic, etc. He dilated much upon the charms of St. Simon's, to which he appeared very glad that we were going; and, among other items of description, mentioned what I was very glad to hear, that it was a beautiful place for riding, and that I should be able to indulge to my heart's content in my favorite exercise, from which I have, of course, been utterly debarred in this small dikeland of ours. He insinuated more than once his hope and desire that he might be allowed to accompany me, but as I knew nothing at all about his capacity for equestrian exercises, or any of the arrangements that might or might not interfere with such a plan, I was discreetly silent, and took no notice of his most comically turned hints on the subject. In our row we started a quantity of wild duck, and he told me there was a great deal of game at St. Simon's, but that the people did not contrive to catch much, though they laid traps constantly for it. Of course their possessing fire-arms is quite out of the question; but this abundance of what must be to them such especially desirable prey makes the fact a great hardship. I almost wonder they don't learn to shoot like savages with bows and arrows; but these would be weapons, and equally forbidden them.

In the afternoon I saw Mr. —— off for St. Simon's; it is fifteen miles lower down the river, and a large island at the very mouth of the Altamaha.

The boat he went in was a large, broad, rather heavy, though well-built craft, by no means as swift or elegant as the narrow eight-oared long-boat in which he generally takes his walks on the water, but well adapted for the traffic between the two plantations, where it serves the purpose of a sort of omnibus or stage-coach for the transfer of the people from one to the other, and of a baggage-wagon or cart for the conveyance of all sorts of household goods, chattels, and necessaries. Mr. —— sat in the middle of a perfect chaos of such freight; and as the boat pushed off, and the steersman took her into the stream, the men at the oars set up a chorus, which they continued to chant in unison with each other, and in time with their stroke, till the voices and oars were heard no more from the distance. I believe I have mentioned to you before the peculiar characteristics of this veritable negro minstrelsy—how they all sing in unison, having never, it appears, attempted or heard any thing like part-singing. Their voices seem oftener tenor than any other quality, and the tune and time they keep something quite wonderful; such truth of intonation and accent would make almost any music agreeable. That which I have heard these people sing is often plaintive and pretty, but almost always has some resemblance to tunes with which they must have become acquainted through the instrumentality of white men; their overseers or masters whistling Scotch or Irish airs, of which they have produced by ear these *rifacciamenti*. The note for note reproduction of "Ah! vous dirai-je, maman?" in one of the most popular of the so-called negro melodies with which all America and England are familiar, is an example of this very transparent plagiarism; and the tune with which Mr. ——'s rowers started him down the Altamaha, as I stood at the steps to see him off, was a very distinct descendant of " Coming through the Rye." The words, however, were astonishingly primitive, especially the first line, which, when it burst from their eight throats in high unison, sent me into fits of laughter.

> "Jenny shake her toe at me,
>    Jenny gone away;
> Jenny shake her toe at me,
>    Jenny gone away.
> Hurrah! Miss Susy, oh!
>    Jenny gone away;
> Hurrah! Miss Susy, oh!
>    Jenny gone away."

What the obnoxious Jenny meant by shaking her toe, whether defiance or mere departure, I never could ascertain, but her going away was an unmistakable subject of satisfaction; and the pause made on the last " oh!" before the final announcement of her departure, had really a good deal of dramatic and musical effect. Except the extemporaneous chants in our honor, of which I have written to you before, I have never heard the negroes on Mr. ——'s plantation sing any words that could be said to have any sense. To one, an extremely pretty, plaintive, and original air, there was but one line, which was repeated with a sort of wailing chorus—

> "Oh! my massa told me, there's no grass in Georgia."

Upon inquiring the meaning of which, I was told it was supposed to be the lamentation of a slave from one of the more northerly states, Virginia or Carolina, where the labor of hoeing the weeds, or grass as they call it, is not nearly so severe as here, in the rice and cotton lands of

Georgia. Another very pretty and pathetic tune began with words that seemed to promise something sentiment-al—

> "Fare you well, and good-by, oh, oh !
> I'm goin' away to leave you, oh, oh !"

but immediately went off into nonsense. verses about gentlemen in the parlor drinking wine and cordial, and ladies in the drawing-room drinking tea and coffee, etc. I have heard that many of the masters and overseers on these plantations prohibit melancholy tunes or words, and encourage nothing but cheerful music and senseless words, deprecating the effect of sadder strains upon the slaves, whose peculiar musical sensibility might be expected to make them especially excitable by any songs of a plaintive character, and having any reference to their particular hardships. If it is true, I think it a judicious precaution enough—these poor slaves are just the sort of people over whom a popular musical appeal to their feelings and passions would have an immense power.

In the evening, Mr. ——'s departure left me to the pleasures of an uninterrupted *tête-à-tête* with his cross-eyed overseer, and I endeavored, as I generally do, to atone by my conversibleness and civility for the additional trouble which, no doubt, all my outlandish ways and notions are causing the worthy man. So suggestive (to use the new-fangled jargon about books) a woman as myself is, I suspect, an intolerable nuisance in these parts; and poor Mr. O—— can not very well desire Mr. —— to send me away, however much he may wish that he would; so that figuratively, as well as literally, I fear the worthy master *me voit d'un mauvais œil*, as the French say. I asked him several questions about some of the slaves who had managed to learn to read, and by what means they had been able to do so. As teaching them is strictly prohibited by the laws, they who instructed them, and such of them as acquired the knowledge, must have been not a little determined and persevering. This was my view of the case, of course, and of course it was not the overseer's. I asked him if many of Mr. ——'s slaves could read. He said " No ; very few, he was happy to say, but those few were just so many too many." " Why, had he observed any insubordination in those who did ?" And I reminded him of Cooper London, the Methodist preacher, whose performance of the burial service had struck me so much some time ago, to whose exemplary conduct and character there is but one concurrent testimony all over the plantation. No ; he had no special complaint to bring against the lettered members of his subject community, but he spoke by anticipation. Every step they take toward intelligence and enlightenment lessens the probability of their acquiescing in their condition. Their condition is not to be changed—ergo, they had better not learn to read ; a very succinct and satisfactory argument as far as it goes, no doubt, and one to which I had not a word to reply, at any rate, to Mr. O——, as I did not feel called upon to discuss the abstract justice or equity of the matter with him ; indeed he, to a certain degree, gave up that part of the position, starting with " I don't say whether it's right or wrong ;" and in all conversations that I have had with the Southerners upon these subjects, whether out of civility to what may be supposed to be an Englishwoman's prejudices, or a forlorn respect to their own convictions, the question of the fundamental wrong of slavery is generally admitted, or, at any rate, certainly never denied. That part of the subject is summarily dismissed, and all its other aspects vindicated, excused, and even lauded, with untiring eloquence. Of course, of the abstract question I could judge before I came here, but I confess I had not the remotest idea how absolutely my observation of every detail of the system, as a practical iniquity, would go to confirm my opinion of its abomination. Mr. O—— went on to condemn and utterly denounce all the preaching, and teaching, and moral instruction upon religious subjects which people in the South, pressed upon by Northern opinion, are endeavoring to give their slaves. The kinder and the more cowardly masters are anxious to evade the charge of keeping their negroes in brutish ignorance, and so they crumble what they suppose and hope may prove a little harmless religious enlightenment, which, mixed up with much religious authority on the subject of submission and fidelity to masters, they trust their slaves may swallow without its doing them any harm—*i. e.*, that they may be better Christians and better slaves—and so, indeed, no doubt they are; but it is a very dangerous experiment, and from Mr. O——'s point of view I quite agree with him. The letting out of water, or the letting in of light, in infinitesimal quantities, is not always easy. The half-wicked of the earth are the leaks through which wickedness is eventually swamped; compromises forerun absolute surrender in most matters, and fools and cowards are, in such cases, the instruments of Providence for their own defeat. Mr. O—— stated unequivocally his opinion that free labor would be more profitable on the plantations than the work of slaves, which, being compulsory, was of the worst possible quality and the smallest possible quantity; then the charge of them before and after they are able to work is onerous, the cost of feeding and clothing them very considerable, and, upon the whole, he, a Southern overseer, pronounced himself decidedly in favor of free labor, upon grounds of expediency. Having at the beginning of our conversation declined discussing the moral aspect of slavery, evidently not thinking that position tenable, I thought I had every right to consider Mr. ——'s slave-driver a decided Abolitionist.

I had been anxious to enlist his sympathies on behalf

of my extreme desire to have some sort of garden, but did not succeed in inspiring him with my enthusiasm on the subject; he said there was but one garden that he knew of in the whole neighborhood of Darien, and that was our neighbor, old Mr. C——'s, a Scotchman on St. Simon's. I remembered the splendid gardinias on Tunno's Island, and referred to them as a proof of the material for ornamental gardening. He laughed, and said rice and cotton crops were the ornamental gardening principally admired by the planters, and that, to the best of his belief, there was not another decent kitchen or flower garden in the state but the one he had mentioned.

The next day after this conversation, I walked with my horticultural zeal much damped, and wandered along the dike by the broad river, looking at some pretty peach-trees in blossom, and thinking what a curse of utter stagnation this slavery produces, and how intolerable to me a life passed within its stifling influence would be. Think of peach-trees in blossom in the middle of February! It does seem cruel, with such a sun and soil, to be told that a garden is worth nobody's while here; however, Mr. O—— said that he believed the wife of the former overseer had made a "sort of a garden" at St. Simon's. We shall see "what sort" it turns out to be. While I was standing on the dike, ruminating above the river, I saw a beautiful white bird of the crane species alight not far from me. I do not think a little knowledge of natural history would diminish the surprise and admiration with which I regard the, to me, unwonted specimens of animal existence that I encounter every day, and of which I do not even know the names. Ignorance is an odious thing. The birds here are especially beautiful, I think. I saw one the other day, of what species of course I do not know, of a warm and rich brown, with a scarlet hood and crest—a lovely creature, about the size of your Northern robin, but more elegantly shaped.

This morning, instead of my usual visit to the Infirmary, I went to look at the work and workers in the threshing mill: all was going on actively and orderly under the superintendence of head man Frank, with whom, and a very sagacious clever fellow who manages the steam power of the mill, and is honorably distinguished as Engineer Ned, I had a small chat. There is one among various drawbacks to the comfort and pleasure of our intercourse with these colored "men and brethren," at least in their slave condition, which certainly exercises my fortitude not a little—the swarms of fleas that cohabit with these sable dependents of ours are—well—incredible; moreover, they are by no means the only or most objectionable companions one borrows from them; and I never go to the Infirmary, where I not unfrequently am requested to look at very dirty limbs and bodies in very dirty draperies, without coming away with a strong inclination to throw myself into the water, and my clothes into the fire, which last would be expensive. I do not suppose that these hateful consequences of dirt and disorder are worse here than among the poor and neglected human creatures who swarm in the lower parts of European cities; but my call to visit them has never been such as that which constrains me to go daily among these poor people, and although on one or two occasions I have penetrated into fearfully foul and filthy abodes of misery in London, I have never rendered the same personal services to their inhabitants that I do to Mr. ——'s slaves, and so have not incurred the same amount of entomological inconvenience.

After leaving the mill I prolonged my walk, and came, for the first time, upon one of the "gangs," as they are called, in full field work. Upon my appearance and approach there was a momentary suspension of labor, and the usual chorus of screams and ejaculations of welcome, affection, and infinite desires for infinite small indulgences.

I was afraid to stop their work, not feeling at all sure that urging a conversation with me would be accepted as any excuse for an uncompleted task, or avert the fatal infliction of the usual award of stripes; so I hurried off and left them to their hoeing.

On my way home I was encountered by London, our Methodist preacher, who accosted me with a request for a Prayer-book and Bible, and expressed his regret at hearing that we were so soon going to St. Simon's. I promised him his holy books, and asked him how he had learned to read, but found it impossible to get him to tell me. I wonder if he thought he should be putting his teacher, whoever he was, in danger of the penalty of the law against instructing the slaves, if he told me who he was; it was impossible to make him do so, so that, besides his other good qualities, he appears to have that most unusual one of all in an uneducated person—discretion. He certainly is a most remarkable man.

After parting with him, I was assailed by a small gang of children, clamoring for the indulgence of some meat, which they besought me to give them. Animal food is only allowed to certain of the harder working men, hedgers and ditchers, and to them only occasionally, and in very moderate rations. My small cannibals clamored round me for flesh, as if I had had a butcher's cart in my pocket, till I began to laugh, and then to run, and away they came, like a pack of little black wolves, at my heels, shrieking, "Missis, you gib me piece meat—missis, you gib me meat," till I got home. At the door I found another petitioner, a young woman named Maria, who brought a fine child in her arms, and demanded a present of a piece of flannel. Upon my asking her who her husband was, she replied, without much hesitation, that she did not possess any such appendage. I gave another look at her bonny baby, and went into the house to get the flannel for her. I afterward heard from Mr. —— that she and two other girls of her age, about seventeen, were the only instances on the island of women with illegitimate children.

After I had been in the house a little while, I was summoned out again to receive the petition of certain poor women in the family-way to have their work lightened. I was, of course, obliged to tell them that I could not interfere in the matter; that their master was away, and that, when he came back, they must present their request to him: they said they had already begged "massa," and he had refused, and they thought, perhaps, if "missis" begged "massa" for them, he would lighten their task. Poor "missis," poor "massa," poor woman, that I am to have such prayers addressed to me! I had to tell them that, if they had already spoken to their master, I was afraid my doing so would be of no use, but that when he came back I would try; so, choking with crying, I turned away from them, and re-entered the house, to the chorus of "Oh, thank you, missis! God bless you, missis!" E——, I think an improvement might be made upon that caricature published a short time ago, called the "Chivalry of the South." I think an elegant young Carolinian or Georgian gentleman, whip in hand, driving a gang of "lusty women," as they are called here, would be a pretty version of the "Chivalry of the South"—a little coarse, I am afraid you will say. Oh! quite horribly coarse, but then so true—a great matter in works of art, which nowadays appear to be thought excellent only in proportion to their lack of ideal elevation. That would be a subject, and a treatment of it, which could not be accused of imaginative exaggeration, at any rate.

In the evening I mentioned the petitions of these poor women to Mr. O——, thinking that perhaps he had the power to lessen their tasks. He seemed evidently annoyed at their having appealed to me; said that their work was

not a bit too much for them, and that constantly they
were *shamming* themselves in the family-way in order to
obtain a diminution of their labor. Poor creatures! I
suppose some of them do; but, again, it must be a hard
matter for those who do not, not to obtain the mitigation
of their toil which their condition requires; for their assertion and their evidence are never received: they can't
be believed, even if they were upon oath, say their white
taskmasters; why? because they have never been taught
the obligations of an oath, to whom made, or wherefore
binding; and they are punished both directly and indi-
rectly for their moral ignorance, as if it were a natural
and incorrigible element of their character, instead of the
inevitable result of their miserable position. The oath of
any and every scoundrelly fellow with a white skin is received, but not that of such a man as Frank, Ned, old Jacob, or Cooper London.

---

Dearest E——,—I think it right to begin this letter
with an account of a most prosperous fishing expedition
Jack and I achieved the other morning. It is true we
still occasionally drew up huge catfish, with their detestable beards and spikes, but we also captivated some magnificent perch, and the Altamaha perch are worth one's
while both to catch and to eat. On a visit I had to make
on the main land the same day, I saw a tiny strip of garden ground, rescued from the sandy road called the street,
perfectly filled with hyacinths, double jonquils, and snow-
drops, a charming nosegay for February 11. After leaving the boat on my return home, I encountered a curious
creature walking all sideways, a small cross between a
lobster and a crab. One of the negroes to whom I applied for its denomination informed me that it was a land-
crab, with which general description of this very peculiar

multipede you must be satisfied, for I can tell you no more. I went a little farther, as the nursery rhyme says, and met with a snake; and, not being able to determine, at ignorant first sight, whether it was a malignant serpent or not, I ingloriously took to my heels, and came home on the full run. It is the first of these exceedingly displeasing animals I have encountered here; but Jack, for my consolation, tells me that they abound on St. Simon's, whither we are going — "rattlesnakes, and all kinds," says he, with an affluence of promise in his tone that is quite agreeable. Rattlesnakes will be quite enough of a treat, without the vague horrors that may be comprised in the additional "all kinds." Jack's account of the game on St. Simon's is really quite tantalizing to me, who can not carry a gun any more than if I were a slave. He says that partridges, woodcocks, snipe, and wild duck abound, so that, at any rate, our table ought to be well supplied. His account of the bears that are still to be found in the woods of the main land is not so pleasant, though he says they do no harm to the people if they are not meddled with, but that they steal the corn from the fields when it is ripe, and actually swim the river to commit their depredations on the islands. It seems difficult to believe this, looking at this wide and heavy stream, though, to be sure, I did once see a young horse swim across the St. Lawrence, between Montreal and Quebec, a feat of natation which much enlarged my belief in what quadrupeds may accomplish when they have no choice between swimming and sinking.

You can not imagine how great a triumph the virtue next to godliness is making under my auspices and a judicious system of small bribery. I can hardly stir now without being assailed with cries of "Missis, missis, me mind chile, me bery clean," or the additional gratifying fact, "and chile too, him bery clean." This virtue, however, if painful to the practisers, as no doubt it is, is expensive, too, to me, and I shall have to try some moral influence equivalent in value to a cent current coin of the realm. What a poor chance, indeed, the poor abstract idea runs! however, it is really a comfort to see the poor little woolly heads now, in most instances, stripped of their additional filthy artificial envelopes.

In my afternoon's row to-day I passed a huge dead alligator, lying half in and half out of the muddy slime of the river bank—a most hideous object it was, and I was glad to turn my eyes to the beautiful surface of the mid stream, all burnished with sunset glories, and broken with the vivacious gambols of a school of porpoises. It is curious, I think, that these creatures should come fifteen miles from the sea to enliven the waters round our little rice swamp.

While rowing this evening, I was led by my conversation with Jack to some of those reflections with which my mind is naturally incessantly filled here, but which I am obliged to be very careful not to give any utterance to. The testimony of no negro is received in a Southern court of law, and the reason commonly adduced for this is, that the state of ignorance in which the negroes are necessarily kept renders them incapable of comprehending the obligations of an oath, and yet, with an inconsistency which might be said to border on effrontery, these same people are admitted to the most holy sacrament of the Church, and are certainly thereby supposed to be capable of assuming the highest Christian obligations, and the entire fulfillment of God's commandments, including, of course, the duty of speaking the truth at all times.

As we were proceeding down the river, we met the flat, as it is called, a huge sort of clumsy boat, more like a raft than any other species of craft, coming up from St. Simon's with its usual swarthy freight of Mr. ——'s dependents from that place. I made Jack turn our canoe, because the universal outcries and exclamations very distinctly intimated that I should be expected to be at home to receive the homage of this cargo of "massa's people." No sooner, indeed, had I disembarked and reached the house, than a dark cloud of black life filled the piazza and swarmed up the steps, and I had to shake hands, like a popular president, till my arm ached at the shoulder-joint.

When this tribe had dispersed itself, a very old woman, with a remarkably intelligent, nice-looking young girl, came forward and claimed my attention. The old woman, who must, I think, by her appearance, have been near seventy, had been one of the house servants on St. Simon's Island in Major ——'s time, and retained a certain dignified courtesy and respectfulness of manner which is by no means an uncommon attribute of the better class of slaves, whose intercourse with their masters, while tending to expand their intelligence, cultivates, at the same time, the natural turn for good manners which is, I think, a distinctive peculiarity of negroes, if not in the kingdom of Dahomey, certainly in the United States of America. If it can be for a moment attributed to the beneficent influence of slavery on their natures (and I think slaveowners are quite likely to imagine so), it is curious enough that there is hardly any alloy whatever of cringing servility, or even humility, in the good manners of the blacks, but a rather courtly and affable condescension which, combined with their affection for, and misapplication of, long words, produces an exceedingly comical effect. Old House Molly, after congratulating herself, with many thanks to heaven, for having spared her to see "massa's" wife and children, drew forward her young companion, and informed me she was one of her numerous grandchildren. The damsel, ycleped Louisa, made rather a shamefaced obeisance, and her old grandmother went on to inform me that she had only lately been forgiven by the overseer for an attempt to run away from the plantation. I inquired the cause of her desire to do so—a "thrashing" she had got for an unfinished task—"but lor, missis," explained the old woman, "taint no use—what use nigger run away?—de swamp all round; dey get in dar, an' dey starve to def, or de snakes eat 'em up—massa's nigger, dey don't neber run away;" and if the good lady's account of their prospects in doing so is correct (which, substituting biting for eating on the part of the snakes, it undoubtedly is), one does not see exactly what particular merit the institution of slavery as practiced on Mr. ——'s plantation derives from the fact that his "nigger don't neber run away."

After dismissing Molly and her granddaughter, I was about to re-enter the house, when I was stopped by Betty, head man Frank's wife, who came with a petition that she might be baptized. As usual with all requests involving any thing more than an immediate physical indulgence, I promised to refer the matter to Mr. ——, but expressed some surprise that Betty, now by no means a young woman, should have postponed a ceremony which the religious among the slaves are apt to attach much importance to. She told me she had more than once applied for this permission to Massa K—— (the former overseer), but had never been able to obtain it, but that now she thought she would ask " de missis."*

* Of this woman's life on the plantation I subsequently learned the following circumstances: She was the wife of head man Frank, the most intelligent and trustworthy of Mr. ——'s slaves; the head driver —second in command to the overseer, and, indeed, second to none during the pestilential season, when the rice swamps can not with impunity be inhabited by any white man, and when, therefore, the whole force employed in its cultivation on the island remains entirely under his authority and control. His wife—a tidy, trim, intelligent woman, with a pretty figure, but a decidedly negro face—was taken from him by the

Yesterday afternoon I received a visit from the wife of our neighbor, Dr. T——. As usual, she exclaimed at my good fortune in having a white woman with my children when she saw M——, and, as usual, went on to expatiate on the utter impossibility of finding a trustworthy nurse any where in the South, to whom your children could be safely confided for a day or even an hour; as usual, too, the causes of this unworthiness or incapacity for a confidential servant's occupation were ignored, and the fact laid to the natural defects of the negro race. I am sick and weary of this cruel and ignorant folly. This afternoon I went out to refresh myself with a row on the broad Altamaha and the conversation of my slave Jack, which is, I assure you, by no means devoid of interest of various kinds, pathetic and humorous. I do not know that Jack's scientific information is the most valuable in the world,

---

overseer left in charge of the plantation by the Messrs. ——, the all-efficient and all-satisfactory Mr. K——, and she had a son by him, whose straight features and diluted color, no less than his troublesome, discontented, and insubmissive disposition, bear witness to his Yankee descent. I do not know how long Mr. K——'s occupation of Frank's wife continued, or how the latter endured the wrong done to him. When I visited the island Betty was again living with her husband—a grave, sad, thoughtful-looking man, whose admirable moral and mental qualities were extolled to me by no worse a judge of such matters than Mr. K—— himself, during the few days he spent with Mr. ——, while we were on the plantation. This outrage upon this man's rights was perfectly notorious among all the slaves; and his hopeful offspring, Renty, alluding very unmistakably to his superior birth on one occasion when he applied for permission to have a gun, observed that, though the people in general on the plantation were not allowed fire-arms, he thought he might, *on account of his color*, and added that he thought Mr. K—— might have left him his. This precious sample of the mode in which the vices of the whites procure the intellectual progress of the blacks to their own endangerment was, as you will easily believe, a significant chapter to me in the black history of oppression which is laid before my eyes in this place.

and I sometimes marvel with perhaps unjust incredulity at the facts in natural history which he imparts to me; for instance, to-day he told me, as we rowed past certain mud islands, very like children's mud puddings on a rather larger scale than usual, that they were inaccessible, and that it would be quite impossible to land on one of them even for the shortest time. Not understanding why people who did not mind being up to their knees in mud should not land there if they pleased, I demurred to his assertion, when he followed it up by assuring me that there were what he called sand-sinks under the mud, and that whatever was placed on the surface would not only sink through the mud, but also into a mysterious quicksand of unknown depth and extent below it. This may be true, but sounds very strange, although I remember that the frequent occurrence of large patches of quicksand was found to be one of the principal impediments in the way of the canal speculators at Brunswick. I did not, however, hear that these sinks, as Jack called them, were found below a thick stratum of heavy mud.

In remonstrating with him upon the want of decent cleanliness generally among the people, and citing to him one among the many evils resulting from it, the intolerable quantity of fleas in all the houses, he met me full with another fact in natural history which, if it be fact and not fiction, certainly gave him the best of the argument: he declared, with the utmost vehemence, that the sand of the pine woods on the main land across the river literally swarmed with fleas; that, in the uninhabited places, the sand itself was full of them; and that, so far from being a result of human habitation, they were found in less numbers round the negro huts on the main land than in the lonely woods around them.

The plowing is at length fully inaugurated, and there is a regular jubilee among the negroes thereat. After discoursing fluently on the improvements likely to result from the measure, Jack wound up by saying he had been afraid it would not be tried on account of the greater scarcity, and consequently greater value, of horses over men in these parts—a modest and slave-like conclusion.

---

DEAREST E——,—I walked up to-day, *February* 14*th*, to see that land of promise, the plowed field: it did not look to me any thing like as heavy soil as the cold, wet, sour, stiff clay I have seen turned up in some of the swampy fields round Lenox; and as for the cypress roots which were urged as so serious an impediment, they are not much more frequent, and certainly not as resisting, as the granite knees and elbows that stick out through the scanty covering of the said clay, which mother earth allows herself as sole garment for her old bones in many a Berkshire patch of corn. After my survey, as I walked home, I came upon a gang of lusty women, as the phrase is here for women in the family-way; they were engaged in burning stubble, and I was nearly choked while receiving the multitudinous complaints and compliments with which they overwhelmed me. After leaving them, I wandered along the river side of the dike homeward, rejoicing in the buds and green things putting forth their tender shoots on every spray, in the early bees and even the less amiable wasps busy in the sunshine with flowers (weeds I suppose they should be called), already opening their sweet temptations to them, and giving the earth a spring aspect, such as it does not wear with you in Massachusetts till late in May.

In the afternoon I took my accustomed row: there had been a tremendous ebb tide, the consequence of which was to lay bare portions of the banks which I had not seen before. The cypress roots form a most extraordinary

mass of intertwined wood-work, so closely matted and
joined together that the separate roots, in spite of their
individual peculiarities, appeared only like divisions of a
continuous body; they presented the appearance in several places of jagged pieces of splintered rock, with their
huge teeth pointing downward into the water.　Their decay is so slow that the protection they afford the soft
spongy banks against the action of the water is likely to
be prolonged until the gathering and deposit of successive
layers of alluvium will remove them from the margin of
which they are now most useful supports.　On my return
home I was met by a child (as she seemed to me) carrying a baby, in whose behalf she begged me for some
clothes.　On making some inquiry, I was amazed to find
that the child was her own: she said she was married,
and fourteen years old; she looked much younger even
than that, poor creature.　Her mother, who came up while
I was talking to her, said she did not herself know the
girl's age; how horridly brutish it all did seem, to be
sure.

The spring is already here with her hands full of flowers.　I do not know who planted some straggling pyrus
japonica near the house, but it is blessing my eyes with
a hundred little flame-like buds, which will presently burst
into a blaze; there are clumps of narcissus roots sending
up sheaves of ivory blossoms, and I actually found a monthly rose in bloom on the sunny side of one of the dikes;
what a delight they are in the slovenly desolation of this
abode of mine! what a garden one might have on the
banks of these dikes, with the least amount of trouble and
care!

In the afternoon I rowed over to Darien, and there procuring the most miserable vehicle calling itself a carriage
that I had ever seen (the dirtiest and shabbiest London
hackney-coach were a chariot of splendor and ease to it),

we drove some distance into the sandy wilderness that surrounds the little town, to pay a visit to some of the resident gentry who had called upon us. The road was a deep, wearisome sandy track, stretching wearisomely into the wearisome pine forest—a species of wilderness more oppressive a thousand times to the senses and imagination than any extent of monotonous prairie, barren steppe, or boundless desert can be; for the horizon there at least invites and detains the eye, suggesting beyond its limit possible change; the lights, and shadows, and enchanting colors of the sky afford some variety in their movement and change, and the reflections of their tints; while in this hideous and apparently boundless pine barren you are deprived alike of horizon before you and heaven above you: nor sun nor star appears through the thick covert, which, in the shabby dinginess of its dark blue-green expanse, looks like a gigantic cotton umbrella stretched immeasurably over you. It is true that over that sandy soil a dark green cotton umbrella is a very welcome protection from the sun, and when the wind makes music in the tall pine-tops and refreshment in the air beneath them. The comparison may seem ungrateful enough: to-day, however, there was neither sound above nor motion below, and the heat was perfectly stifling, as we plowed our way through the resinous-smelling sand solitudes.

From time to time a thicket of exquisite evergreen shrubs broke the monotonous lines of the countless pine shafts rising round us, and still more welcome were the golden garlands of the exquisite wild jasmine, hanging, drooping, trailing, clinging, climbing through the dreary forest, joining to the warm aromatic smell of the fir-trees a delicious fragrance as of acres of heliotrope in bloom. I wonder if this delightful creature is very difficult of cultivation out of its natural region; I never remember to have seen it, at least not in blossom, in any collection of plants in the Northern states or in Europe, where it certainly deserves an honorable place for its grace, beauty, and fragrance.

On our drive we passed occasionally a tattered man or woman, whose yellow mud complexion, straight features, and singularly sinister countenance bespoke an entirely different race from the negro population in the midst of which they lived. These are the so-called pine-landers of Georgia, I suppose the most degraded race of human beings claiming an Anglo-Saxon origin that can be found on the face of the earth—filthy, lazy, ignorant, brutal, proud, penniless savages, without one of the nobler attributes which have been found occasionally allied to the vices of savage nature. They own no slaves, for they are almost without exception abjectly poor; they will not work, for that, as they conceive, would reduce them to an equality with the abhorred negroes; they squat, and steal, and starve, on the outskirts of this lowest of all civilized societies, and their countenances bear witness to the squalor of their condition and the utter degradation of their natures. To the crime of slavery, though they have no profitable part or lot in it, they are fiercely accessory, because it is the barrier that divides the black and white races, at the foot of which they lie wallowing in unspeakable degradation, but immensely proud of the base freedom which still separates them from the lash-driven tillers of the soil.*

* Of such is the white family so wonderfully described in Mrs. Stowe's "Dred," whose only slave brings up the orphaned children of his masters with such exquisitely grotesque and pathetic tenderness. From such the conscription which has fed the Southern army in the deplorable civil conflict now raging in America has drawn its rank and file. Better "food for powder" the world could scarcely supply. Fierce and idle, with hardly one of the necessities or amenities that belong to civilized existence, they are hardy endurers of hardship, and

The house at which our call was paid was set down in the midst of the Pine Barren, with half-obliterated roads and paths round it, suggesting that it might be visited and was inhabited. It was large and not unhandsome, though curiously dilapidated, considering that people were actually living in it; certain remnants of carving on the cornices and paint on the panels bore witness to some former stage of existence less neglected and deteriorated than the present. The old lady mistress of this most forlorn abode amiably inquired if so much exercise did not fatigue me; at first I thought she imagined I must have walked through the pine forest all the way from Darien, but she explained that she considered the drive quite an effort; and it is by no means uncommon to hear people in America talk of being dragged over bad roads in uneasy carriages as exercise, showing how very little they know the meaning of the word, and how completely they identify it with the idea of mere painful fatigue instead of pleasurable exertion.

Returning home, my reflections ran much on the possible future destiny of these vast tracts of sandy soil. It seems to me that the ground capable of supporting the evergreen growth, the luxuriant gardinia bushes, the bay myrtle, the beautiful magnolia grandiflora, and the powerful and gnarled live oaks, that find their sustenance in this

reckless to a savage degree of the value of life, whether their own or others. The soldier's pay, received or promised, exceeds in amount per month any thing they ever earned before per year, and the war they wage is one that enlists all their proud and ferocious instincts. It is against the Yankees—the Northern sons of free soil, free toil and intelligence, the hated Abolitionists whose success would sweep away slavery and reduce the Southern white men to work—no wonder they are ready to fight to the death against this detestable alternative, especially as they look to victory as the certain promotion of the refuse of the "poor white" population of the South, of which they are one and all members, to the coveted dignity of slaveholders.

earth and under this same sky as the fir-trees, must be
convertible into a prosperous habitation for other valuable vegetable growth that would add immensely to the
wealth of the Southern states. The orange thrives and
bears profusely along this part of the sea-board of Georgia; and I can not conceive that the olive, the mulberry,
and the vine might not be acclimated, and successfully
and profitably cultivated throughout the whole of this region, the swampy lower lands alone remaining as rice plantations. The produce of these already exceeds in value
that of the once gold-growing cotton-fields; and I can not
help believing that silk, and wine, and oil may, and will,
hereafter become, with the present solitary cotton crop,
joint possessors of all this now but half-reclaimed wilderness. The soil all round Sorrento is very nearly as light,
and dry, and sandy as this, and vineyards, and olive or-
chards, and cocooneries are part of the agricultural wealth
there. Our neighbor, Mr. C——, has successfully cultivated the date-palm in his garden on the edge of the sea
at St. Simon's, and certainly the ilex, orange, and myrtle
abounding here suggest natural affinities between the
Italian soil and climate and this.

I must tell you something funny which occurred yesterday at dinner, which will give you some idea of the strange
mode in which we live. We have now not unfrequently
had mutton at table, the flavor of which is quite excellent,
as indeed it may well be, for it is raised under all the conditions of the famous *Prè salé* that the French gourmands
especially prize, and which are reproduced on our side of
the Channel in the peculiar qualities of our best South
Down. The mutton we have here grazes on the short
sweet grass at St. Simon's within sea-salt influence, and is
some of the very best I have ever tasted, but it is invariably brought to table in lumps or chunks of no particular
shape or size, and in which it is utterly impossible to rec-

ognize any part of the quadruped creature sheep with which my eyes have hitherto become acquainted. Eat it, one may and does thankfully; name it, one could not by any possibility. Having submitted to this for some time, I at length inquired why a decent usual Christian joint of mutton—leg, shoulder, or saddle—was never brought to table: the reply was that the *carpenter* always cut up the meat, and that he did not know how to do it otherwise than by dividing it into so many thick square pieces, and proceeding to chop it up on that principle; and the consequence of this is, that *four lumps* or *chunks* are all that a whole sheep ever furnishes to our table by this artistic and economical process.

This morning I have been to the hospital to see a poor woman who has just enriched Mr. —— by *borning* him another slave. The poor little pickaninny, as they called it, was not one bit uglier than white babies under similarly novel circumstances, except in one particular, that it had a head of hair like a trunk, in spite of which I had all the pains in the world in persuading its mother not to put a cap upon it. I bribed her finally by the promise of a pair of socks instead, with which I undertook to endow her child, and, moreover, actually prevailed upon her to forego the usual swaddling and swathing process, and let her poor baby be dressed at its first entrance into life as I assured her both mine had been.

On leaving the hospital I visited the huts all along the street, confiscating sundry refractory baby caps among shrieks and outcries, partly of laughter and partly of real ignorant alarm for the consequences. I think, if this infatuation for hot head-dresses continues, I shall make shaving the children's heads the only condition upon which they shall be allowed to wear caps.

On Sunday morning I went over to Darien to church. Our people's church was closed, the minister having gone to officiate elsewhere. With laudable liberality, I walked into the opposite church of a different, not to say opposite sect: here I heard a sermon, the opening of which will probably edify you as it did me, viz., that if a man was *just in all his dealings*, he was apt to think he did all that could be required of him—and no wide mistake either, one might suppose. But is it not wonderful how such words can be spoken here, with the most absolute uncon- sciousness of their tremendous bearing upon the existence of every slaveholder who hears them? Certainly the use that is second nature has made the awful injustice in the daily practice of which these people live a thing of which they are as little aware as you or I of the atmospheric air that we inhale each time we breathe. The bulk of the congregation in this church was white. The negroes are, of course, not allowed to mix with their masters in the house of God, and there is no special place set apart for them. Occasionally one or two are to be seen in the cor- ners of the singing gallery, but any more open pollution by them of their owners' church could not be tolerated. Mr. ——'s people have petitioned very vehemently that he would build a church for them on the island. I doubt, however, his allowing them such a luxury as a place of worship all to themselves. Such a privilege might not be thought well of by the neighboring planters; indeed, it is almost what one might call a whity-brown idea, danger- ous, demoralizing, inflammatory, incendiary. I should not wonder if I should be suspected of being the chief corner- stone of it, and yet I am not: it is an old hope and en- treaty of these poor people, which I am afraid they are not destined to see fulfilled.

DEAREST E——,—Passing the rice mill this morning in my walk, I went in to look at the machinery, the large steam mortars which shell the rice, and which work under the intelligent and reliable supervision of Engineer Ned. I was much surprised, in the course of conversation with him this morning, to find how much older a man he was than he appeared. Indeed, his youthful appearance had hitherto puzzled me much in accounting for his very superior intelligence and the important duties confided to him. He is, however, a man upward of forty years old, although he looks ten years younger. He attributed his own uncommonly youthful appearance to the fact of his never having done what he called field-work, or been exposed, as the common gang negroes are, to the hardships of their all but brutish existence. He said his former master had brought him up very kindly, and he had learned to tend the engines, and had never been put to any other work, but he said this was not the case with his poor wife. He wished she was as well off as he was, but she had to work in the rice-fields, and was "most broke in two" with labor, and exposure, and hard work while with child, and hard work just directly after childbearing; he said she could hardly crawl, and he urged me very much to speak a kind word for her to massa. She was almost all the time in hospital, and he thought she could not live long.

Now, E——, here is another instance of the horrible injustice of this system of slavery. In my country or in yours, a man endowed with sufficient knowledge and capacity to be an engineer would, of course, be in the receipt of considerable wages; his wife would, together with himself, reap the advantages of his ability, and share the well-being his labor earned; he would be able to procure for her comfort in sickness or in health, and beyond the necessary household work, which the wives of most

artisans are inured to, she would have no labor to encounter; in case of sickness even these would be alle-
viated by the assistance of some stout girl of all work or
kindly neighbor, and the tidy parlor or snug bedroom
would be her retreat if unequal to the daily duties of her
own kitchen. Think of such a lot compared with that of
the head engineer of Mr. ——'s plantation, whose sole
wages are his coarse food and raiment and miserable
hovel, and whose wife, covered with one filthy garment
of ragged texture and dingy color, barefooted and bareheaded, is daily driven afield to labor with aching pain-
racked joints, under the lash of a driver, or lies languishing on the earthen floor of the dismal plantation hospital
in a condition of utter physical destitution and degradation such as the most miserable dwelling of the poorest
inhabitant of your free Northern villages never beheld
the like of. Think of the rows of tidy tiny houses in the
long suburbs of Boston and Philadelphia, inhabited by
artisans of just the same grade as this poor Ned, with
their white doors and steps, their hydrants of inexhaustible fresh flowing water, the innumerable appliances for
decent comfort of their cheerful rooms, the gay wardrobe
of the wife, her cotton prints for daily use, her silk for
Sunday church-going; the careful comfort of the children's clothing, the books and newspapers in the little
parlor, the daily district school, the weekly parish church:
imagine if you can—but you are happy that you can not
—the contrast between such an existence and that of the
best mechanic on a Southern plantation.

Did you ever read (but I am sure you never did, and
no more did I) an epic poem on fresh-water fish? Well,
such a one was once written, I have forgotten by whom,
but assuredly the heroine of it ought to have been the
Altamaha shad—a delicate creature, so superior to the
animal you Northerners devour with greedy thankfulness

when the spring sends back their finny drove to your colder waters, that one would not suppose these were of the same family, instead of being, as they really are, precisely the same fish.   Certainly the mud of the Altamaha must have some most peculiar virtues; and, by-the-by, I have never any where tasted such delicious tea as that which we make with this same turbid stream, the water of which, duly filtered of course, has some peculiar softness which affects the tea (and it is the same we always use) in a most curious and agreeable manner.

On my return to the house I found a terrible disturbance in consequence of the disappearance from under cook John's safe keeping of a ham Mr. —— had committed to his charge.   There was no doubt whatever that the unfortunate culinary slave had made away in some inscrutable manner with the joint intended for our table: the very lies he told about it were so curiously shallow, childlike, and transparent, that while they confirmed the fact of his theft quite as much, if not more, than an absolute confession would have done, they provoked at once my pity and my irrepressible mirth to a most painful degree. Mr. —— was in a state of towering anger and indignation, and, besides a flogging, sentenced the unhappy cook to degradation from his high and dignified position (and, alas! all its sweets of comparatively easy labor and good living from the remains of our table) to the hard toil, coarse scanty fare, and despised position of a common field-hand.   I suppose some punishment was inevitably necessary in such a plain case of deliberate theft as this, but, nevertheless, my whole soul revolts at the injustice of visiting upon these poor wretches a moral darkness which all possible means are taken to increase and perpetuate.

In speaking of this and the whole circumstance of John's trespass to Mr. —— in the evening, I observed that the ignorance of these poor people ought to screen them from punishment. He replied that they knew well enough what was right and wrong. I asked how they could be expected to know it? He replied, by the means of Cooper London, and the religious instruction he gave them. So that, after all, the appeal is to be made against themselves to that moral and religious instruction which is withheld from them, and which, if they obtain it at all, is the result of their own unaided and unencouraged exertion. The more I hear, and see, and learn, and ponder the whole of this system of slavery, the more impossible I find it to conceive how its practisers and upholders are to justify their deeds before the tribunal of their own conscience or God's law. It is too dreadful to have those whom we love accomplices to this wickedness; it is too intolerable to find myself an involuntary accomplice to it.

I had a conversation the next morning with Abraham, cook John's brother, upon the subject of his brother's theft; and only think of the *slave* saying that "this action had brought disgrace upon the family." Does not that sound very like the very best sort of free pride, the pride of character, the honorable pride of honesty, integrity, and fidelity? But this was not all, for this same Abraham, a clever carpenter and much valued *hand* on the estate, went on, in answer to my questions, to tell me such a story that I declare to you I felt as if I could have howled with helpless indignation and grief when he departed and went to resume his work. His grandfather had been an old slave in Darien, extremely clever as a carpenter, and so highly valued for his skill and good character that his master allowed him to purchase his liberty by money which he earned by working for himself at odd times, when his task-work was over. I asked Abraham what sum his grandfather paid for his freedom: he said he did not know, but he supposed a large one, because of his being a "skilled carpenter," and so a peculiarly valuable chattel. I presume, from what I remember Major M—— and Dr. H—— saying on the subject of the market value of negroes in Charleston and Savannah, that such a man in the prime of life would have been worth from 1500 to 2000 dollars. However, whatever the man paid for his ransom, by his grandson's account, fourteen years after he became free, when he died, he had again amassed money to the amount of 700 dollars, which he left among his wife and children, the former being a slave on Major ——'s estate, where the latter remained by virtue of that fact slaves also. So this man not only bought his own freedom at a cost of *at least* 1000 dollars, but left a little fortune of 700 more at his death; and then we are told of the universal idleness, incorrigible sloth, and brutish incapacity of this inferior race of creatures, whose only fitting and Heaven-appointed condition is that of beasts of burden to the whites. I do not believe the whole low white population of the State of Georgia could furnish such an instance of energy, industry, and thrift as the amassing of this laborious little fortune by this poor slave, who left, nevertheless, his children and grandchildren to the lot from which he had so heroically ransomed himself; and yet the white men with whom I live and talk tell me, day after day, that there is neither cruelty nor injustice in this accursed system.

About half past five I went to walk on the dikes, and met a gang of the field-hands going to the tide-mill, as the water served them for working then. I believe I have told you that besides the great steam mill there is this, which is dependent on the rise and fall of the tide in the river, and where the people are therefore obliged to work by day or night, at whatever time the water serves to impel the wheel. They greeted me with their usual profusion of exclamations, petitions, and benedictions, and I parted from them to come and oversee my slave Jack, for whom I had bought a spade, and to whom I had intrusted the task of turning up some ground for me, in which I wanted to establish some of the narcissus and other flowers I had remarked about the ground and the house. Jack, however, was a worse digger than Adam could have been when first he turned his hand to it, after his expulsion from Paradise. I think I could have managed a spade with infinitely more efficiency, or rather less incapacity, than he displayed. Upon my expressing my amazement at his performance, he said the people here never used spades, but performed all their agricultural operations with the hoe. Their soil must be very light and their agriculture very superficial, I should think. However, I was obliged to terminate Jack's spooning process, and abandon, for the present, my hopes of a flower-bed created by his industry, being called into the house to receive the return visit of old Mrs. S——. As usual, the appearance, health, vigor, and good management of the children were the theme of wondering admiration; as usual, my possession of a white nurse the theme of envious congratulation; as usual, I had to hear the habitual senseless complaints of the inefficiency of colored nurses. If you are half as tired of the sameness and stupidity of the conversation of my Southern female neighbors as I am, I pity you; but not as much as I pity them for the stupid sameness of their most vapid existence, which would deaden any amount of intelligence, obliterate any amount of instruction, and render torpid and stagnant any amount of natural energy and vivacity. I would rather die—rather a thousand times—than live the lives of these Georgia planters' wives and daughters.

Mrs. S—— had brought me some of the delicious wild. jasmine that festoons her dreary pine-wood drive, and most grateful I was for the presence of the sweet wild nosegay in my highly unornamental residence. When my visitors had left me, I took the refreshment of a row over to Darien; and as we had the tide against us coming back, the process was not so refreshing for the rowers. The evening was so extremely beautiful, and the rising of the moon so exquisite, that instead of retreating to the house when I reached the island, I got into the Dolphin, my special canoe, and made Jack paddle me down the great river to meet the Lily, which was coming back from St. Simon's with Mr. ——, who has been preparing all things for our advent thither.

My letter has been interrupted, dear E——, by the breaking up of our residence on the rice plantation, and our arrival at St. Simon's, whence I now address you. We came down yesterday afternoon, and I was thankful enough of the fifteen miles' row to rest in, from the labor of leave-taking, with which the whole morning was taken up, and which, combined with packing and preparing all our own personalities and those of the children, was no sinecure. At every moment one or other of the poor people rushed in upon me to bid me good-by; many of their farewells were grotesque enough, some were pathetic, and all of them made me very sad. Poor people! how little I have done, how little I can do for them. I had a long talk with that interesting and excellent man, Cooper London, who made an earnest petition that I would send him from the North a lot of Bibles and Prayer-books; certainly the science of reading must be much more common among the negroes than I supposed, or London must look to a marvelously increased spread of the same hereafter. There is, however, considerable reticence upon this point, or else the poor slaves must consider the mere possession of the holy books as good for salvation, and as effectual for spiritual assistance to those who can not as to those who can comprehend them. Since the news of our departure has spread, I have had repeated eager entreaties for presents of Bibles and Prayer-books, and to my demurrer of "But you can't read, can you?" have generally received for answer a reluctant acknowledgment of ignorance, which, however, did not always convince me of the fact. In my farewell conversation with London I found it impossible to get him to tell me how he had learned to read: the penalties for teaching them are very severe—heavy fines, increasing in amount for the first and second offense, and imprisonment for the third.* Such a man as London is certainly aware that to teach the slaves to read is an illegal act, and he may have been unwilling to betray whoever had been his preceptor even to my knowledge; at any rate, I got no answers from him but "Well, missis, me learn; well, missis, me try;" and finally, "Well, missis, me 'spose Heaven help me;" to which I could only reply that I knew Heaven was helpful, but very hardly to the tune of teaching folks their letters. I got no satisfaction. Old Jacob, the father of Abraham, cook John, and poor Psyche's husband, took a most solemn and sad leave of me, saying he did not expect ever to see me again. I could not exactly tell why, because, though he is aged and infirm, the fifteen miles between the rice plantation and St. Simon's do not appear so insuperable a barrier between the inhabitants of the two places, which I represented to him as a suggestion of consolation.

I have worked my fingers nearly off with making, for the last day or two, innumerable rolls of coarse little baby-clothes, layettes for the use of small new-born slaves;

---

* These laws have been greatly increased in stringency and severity since these letters were written, and *death* has not been reckoned too heavy a penalty for those who should venture to offer these unfortunate people the fruit of that forbidden tree of knowledge, their access to which has appeared to their owners the crowning danger of their own precarious existence among their terrible dependents.

M—— diligently cutting and shaping, and I as diligently stitching. We leave a good supply for the hospitals, and for the individual clients besides who have besieged me ever since my departure became imminent.

Our voyage from the rice to the cotton plantation was performed in the Lily, which looked like a soldier's baggage-wagon and an emigrant transport combined. Our crew consisted of eight men. Forward in the bow were miscellaneous live-stock, pots, pans, household furniture, kitchen utensils, and an indescribable variety of heterogeneous necessaries. Enthroned upon beds, bedding, tables, and other chattels, sat that poor pretty chattel Psyche, with her small chattel children. Midships sat the two tiny free women and myself, and in the stern Mr. —— steering. And "all in the blue unclouded weather" we rowed down the huge stream, the men keeping time and tune to their oars with extemporaneous chants of adieu to the rice-island and its denizens. Among other poetical and musical comments on our departure recurred the assertion, as a sort of burden, that we were "parted in body, but not in mind," from those we left behind. Having relieved one set of sentiments by this reflection, they very wisely betook themselves to the consideration of the blessings that remained to them, and performed a spirited chant in honor of Psyche and our bouncing black housemaid, Mary.

At the end of a fifteen miles' row we entered one among a perfect labyrinth of arms or branches, into which the broad river ravels like a fringe as it reaches the sea, a dismal navigation along a dismal tract, called "Five Pound," through a narrow cut or channel of water divided from the main stream. The conch was sounded, as at our arrival at the rice-island, and we made our descent on the famous long staple cotton island of St. Simon's, where we presently took up our abode in what had all the appearance of an old, half-decayed, rattling farm-house.

This morning, Sunday, I peeped round its immediate neighborhood, and saw, to my inexpressible delight, within hail, some noble-looking evergreen oaks, and close to the house itself a tiny would-be garden, a plot of ground with one or two peach-trees in full blossom, tufts of silver narcissus and jonquils, a quantity of violets and an exquisite myrtle bush; wherefore I said my prayers with especial gratitude.

---

DEAREST E——,—The fame of my peculiar requisitions has, I find, preceded me here, for the babies that have been presented to my admiring notice have all been without caps; also, however, without socks to their opposite little wretched extremities, but that does not signify quite so much. The people, too, that I saw yesterday were remarkably clean and tidy; to be sure, it was Sunday. The whole day, till quite late in the afternoon, the house was surrounded by a crowd of our poor dependents, waiting to catch a glimpse of Mr. ——, myself, or the children; and until, from sheer weariness, I was obliged to shut the doors, an incessant stream poured in and out, whose various modes of salutation, greeting, and welcome were more grotesque and pathetic at the same time than any thing you can imagine. In the afternoon I walked with —— to see a new house in process of erection, which, when it is finished, is to be the overseer's abode and our residence during any future visits we may pay to the estate. I was horrified at the dismal site selected, and the hideous house erected on it. It is true that the central position is the principal consideration in the overseer's location; but both position and building seemed to me to witness to an inveterate love of ugliness, or, at any rate, a deadness to every desire of beauty, nothing short of horrible; and, for my own part, I think it is intolerable to have to leave the

point where the waters meet, and where a few fine picturesque old trees are scattered about, to come to this place
even for the very short time I am ever likely to spend
here.

In every direction our view, as we returned, was bounded by thickets of the most beautiful and various evergreen
growth, which beckoned my inexperience most irresistibly. —— said, to my unutterable horror, that they were
perfectly infested with rattlesnakes, and I must on no account go "beating about the bush" in these latitudes, as
the game I should be likely to start would be any thing
but agreeable to me. We saw quantities of wild plum-
trees all silvery with blossoms, and in lovely companionship and contrast with them a beautiful shrub covered
with delicate pink bloom like flowering peach-trees. After that life in the rice-swamp, where the Altamaha kept
looking over the dike at me all the time as I sat in the
house writing or working, it is pleasant to be on *terra
firma* again, and to know that the river is at the conventional, not to say natural, depth below its banks, and under my feet instead of over my head. The two plantations are of diametrically opposite dispositions—that is all
swamp, and this all sand; or, to speak more accurately,
that is all swamp, and all of this that is not swamp is sand.

On our way home we met a most extraordinary creature of the negro kind, who, coming toward us, halted,
and caused us to halt straight in the middle of the path,
when, bending himself down till his hands almost touched
the ground, he exclaimed to Mr. ——, "Massa ——, your
most obedient;" and then, with a kick and a flourish altogether indescribable, he drew to the side of the path to
let us pass, which we did perfectly shouting with laughter, which broke out again every time we looked at each
other and stopped to take breath: so sudden, grotesque,
uncouth, and yet dexterous a gambado never came into

the brain or out of the limbs of any thing but a "nig-gar."

I observed, among the numerous groups that we passed or met, a much larger proportion of mulattoes than at the rice-island; upon asking Mr. —— why this was so, he said that there no white person could land without his or the overseer's permission, whereas on St. Simon's, which is a large island containing several plantations belonging to different owners, of course the number of whites, both re-siding on and visiting the place, was much greater, and the opportunity for intercourse between the blacks and whites much more frequent. While we were still on this subject, a horrid-looking filthy woman met us with a little child in her arms, a very light mulatto, whose extraordi-nary resemblance to Driver Bran (one of the officials who had been duly presented to me on my arrival, and who was himself a mulatto) struck me directly. I pointed it out to Mr. ——, who merely answered, "Very likely his child." "And," said I, "did you never remark that Driver Bran is the exact image of Mr. K——?" "Very likely his brother," was the reply: all which rather unpleasant state of relationships seemed accepted as such a complete matter of course, that I felt rather uncomfortable, and said no more about who was like who, but came to certain con-clusions in my own mind as to a young lad who had been among our morning visitors, and whose extremely light color and straight, handsome features and striking resem-blance to Mr. K—— had suggested suspicions of a rather unpleasant nature to me, and whose sole-acknowledged parent was a very black negress of the name of Minda. I have no doubt at all, now, that he is another son of Mr. K——, Mr. ——'s paragon overseer.

As we drew near the house again we were gradually joined by such a numerous escort of Mr. ——'s slaves that it was almost with difficulty we could walk along the path. They buzzed, and hummed, and swarmed round us like flies, and the heat and dust consequent upon this friendly companionship were a most unpleasant addition to the labor of walking in the sandy soil through which we were plowing. I was not sorry when we entered the house and left our body-guard outside. In the evening I looked over the plan of the delightful residence I had visited in the morning, and could not help suggesting to Mr. —— the advantage to be gained in point of picturesqueness by merely turning the house round. It is but a wooden frame one after all, and your folks " down East" would think no more of inviting it to face about than if it was built of cards; but the fact is, here nothing signifies except the cotton crop, and whether one's nose is in a swamp and one's eyes in a sand-heap is of no consequence whatever either to one's self (if one's self was not I) or any one else.

I find here an immense proportion of old people; the work and the climate of the rice plantation require the strongest of the able-bodied men and women of the estate. The cotton crop is no longer by any means as paramount in value as it used to be, and the climate, soil, and labor of St. Simon's are better adapted to old, young, and feeble cultivators than the swamp fields of the rice-island. I wonder if I ever told you of the enormous decrease in value of this same famous sea-island long staple cotton. When Major ——, Mr. ——'s grandfather, first sent the produce of this plantation where we now are to England, it was of so fine a quality that it used to be quoted by itself in the Liverpool cotton market, and was then worth half a guinea a pound; it is now not worth a shilling a pound. This was told me by the gentleman in Liverpool who has been factor for this estate for thirty years. Such a decrease as this in the value of one's crop, and the steady increase at the same time of a slave population, now numbering between 700 and 800 bodies to clothe and house, mouths to feed, while the land is being exhausted by the careless and wasteful nature of the agriculture itself, suggests a pretty serious prospect of declining prosperity; and, indeed, unless these Georgia cotton-planters can command more land, or lay abundant capital (which they have not, being almost all of them over head and ears in debt) upon that which has already spent its virgin vigor, it is a very obvious thing that they must all very soon be eaten up by their own property. The rice plantations are a great thing to fall back upon under these circumstances, and the rice crop is now quite as valuable, if not more so, than the cotton one on Mr. ——'s estates, once so famous and prosperous through the latter.

I find any number of all but superannuated men and women here, whose tales of the former grandeur of the estate and family are like things one reads of in novels. One old woman, who crawled to see me, and could hardly lift her poor bowed head high enough to look in my face, had been in Major ——'s establishment in Philadelphia, and told with infinite pride of having waited upon his daughters and granddaughters, Mr. ——'s sisters. Yet here she is, flung by like an old rag, crippled with age and disease, living, or rather dying by slow degrees in a miserable hovel, such as no decent household servant would at the North, I suppose, ever set their foot in. The poor old creature complained bitterly to me of all her ailments and all her wants. I can do little, alas! for either. I had a visit from another tottering old crone called Dorcas, who all but went on her knees as she wrung and kissed my hands; with her came my friend Molly, the grandmother of the poor runaway girl Louisa, whose story I wrote you some little time ago. I had to hear it all over again, it being the newest event evidently in Molly's life; and it ended as before with the highly reasonable proposition:

"Me say, missis, what for massa's niggar run away? Snake eat 'em up, or dey starve to def in a swamp. Massa's niggars dey don't neber run away." If I was "massa's niggars," I "spose" I shouldn't run away either, with only those alternatives; but when I look at these wretches and at the sea that rolls round this island, and think how near the English West Indies and freedom are, it gives me a pretty severe twinge at the heart.

---

Dearest E——,—I am afraid my letters must be becoming very wearisome to you; for if, as the copy-book runs, "Variety is charming," they certainly can not be so unless monotony is also charming, a thing not impossible to some minds, but of which the copy-book makes no mention. But what will you? as the French say; my days are no more different from one another than peas in a dish, or sands on the shore: 'tis a pleasant enough life to live for one who, like myself, has a passion for dullness, but it affords small matter for epistolary correspondence. I suppose it is the surfeit of excitement that I had in my youth that has made a life of quiet monotony so extremely agreeable to me; it is like stillness after loud noise, twilight after glare, rest after labor. There is enough strangeness, too, in every thing that surrounds me here to interest and excite me agreeably and sufficiently, and I should like the wild savage loneliness of the far away existence extremely if it were not for the one small item of "the slavery."

I had a curious visit this morning from half a dozen of the women, among whom were Driver Morris's wife and Venus (a hideous old gooddess she was, to be sure), Driver Bran's mother. They came especially to see the children, who are always eagerly asked for, and hugely admired by their sooty dependents. These poor women went into ecstasies over the little white pickaninnies, and were loud and profuse in their expressions of gratitude to Massa —— for getting married and having children, a matter of thankfulness which, though it always makes me laugh very much, is a most serious one to them; for the continuance of the family keeps the estate and slaves from the hammer, and the poor wretches, besides seeing in every new child born to their owners a security against their own banishment from the only home they know, and separation from all ties of kindred and habit, and dispersion to distant plantations, not unnaturally look for a milder rule from masters who are the children of their fathers' masters. The relation of owner and slave may be expected to lose some of its harsher features, and, no doubt, in some instances, does so, when it is on each side the inheritance of successive generations. And so ——'s slaves laud, and applaud, and thank, and bless him for having married, and endowed their children with two little future mistresses. One of these women, a Diana by name, went down on her knees, and uttered in a loud voice a sort of extemporaneous prayer of thanksgiving at our advent, in which the sacred and the profane were most ludicrously mingled: her "tanks to de good Lord God Almighty that missus had come, what give de poor niggar sugar and flannel," and dat "Massa ——, him hab brought de missis and de two little misses down among de people," were really too grotesque, and yet certainly more sincere acts of thanksgiving are not often uttered among the solemn and decorous ones that are offered up to heaven for "benefits received."

I find the people here much more inclined to talk than those on the rice-island; they have less to do and more leisure, and bestow it very liberally on me; moreover, the poor old women, of whom there are so many turned out to grass here, and of whom I have spoken to you before, though they are past work, are by no means past gossip, and the stories they have to tell of the former government of the estate under old Massa K—— are certainly pretty tremendous illustrations of the merits of slavery as a moral institution.  This man, the father of the late owner, Mr. R—— K——, was Major ——'s agent in the management of this property, and a more cruel and unscrupulous one as regards the slaves. themselves, whatever he may have been in his dealings with the master, I should think it would be difficult to find, even among the cruel and unscrupulous class to which he belonged.

In a conversation with old "House Molly," as she is called, to distinguish her from all other Mollies on the estate, she having had the honor of being a servant in Major ——'s house for many years, I asked her if the relation between men and women who are what they call married, *i. e.*, who have agreed to live together as man and wife (the only species of marriage formerly allowed on the estate, I believe now London may read the Marriage Service to them), was considered binding by the people themselves and by the overseer.  She said "not much formerly," and that the people couldn't be expected to have much regard to such an engagement, utterly ignored as it was by Mr. K——, whose invariable rule, if he heard of any disagreement between a man and woman calling themselves married, was immediately to bestow them in "marriage" on other parties, whether they chose it or not, by which summary process the slightest "incompatibility of temper" received the relief of a divorce more rapid and easy than even Germany could afford, and the estate lost nothing by any prolongation of celibacy on either side. Of course, the misery consequent upon such arbitrary destruction of voluntary and imposition of involuntary ties was nothing to Mr. K——.

I was very sorry to hear to-day that Mr. O——, the

overseer at the rice-island, of whom I have made mention
to you more than once in my letters, had had one of the
men flogged very severely for getting his wife baptizéd.
I was quite unable, from the account I received, to understand what his objection had been to the poor man's desire to make his wife at least a formal Christian; but it
does seem dreadful that such an act should be so visited.
I almost wish I was back again at the rice-island; for,
though this is every way the pleasanter residence, I hear
so much more that is intolerable of the treatment of the
slaves from those I find here, that my life is really made
wretched by it.   There is not a single natural right that
is not taken away from these unfortunate people, and the
worst of all is, that their condition does not appear to me,
upon farther observation of it, to be susceptible of even
partial alleviation as long as the fundamental evil, the slavery itself, remains.

My letter was interrupted as usual by clamors for my
presence at the door, and petitions for sugar, rice, and
baby-clothes from a group of women who had done their
tasks at three o'clock in the afternoon, and had come to
say, " Ha do, missis ?" (How do you do ?), and beg something on their way to their huts.   Observing one among
them whose hand was badly maimed, one finger being reduced to a mere stump, she told me it was in consequence
of the bite of a rattlesnake, which had attacked and bitten
her child, and then struck her as she endeavored to kill
it; her little boy had died, but one of the drivers cut off
her finger, and so she had escaped with the loss of that
member only.   It is yet too early in the season for me to
make acquaintance with these delightful animals, but the
accounts the negroes give of their abundance is full of
agreeable promise for the future.   It seems singular, considering how very common they are, that there are not
more frequent instances of the slaves being bitten by

them; to be sure, they seem to me to have a holy horror of ever setting their foot near either tree or bush, or any where but on the open road and the fields where they labor; and, of course, the snakes are not so frequent in open and frequented places as in their proper coverts. The Red Indians are said to use successfully some vegetable cure for the bite, I believe the leaves of the slippery ash or elm; the only infallible remedy, however, is suction, but of this the ignorant negroes are so afraid that they never can be induced to have recourse to it, being, of course, immovably persuaded that the poison which is so fatal to the blood must be equally so to the stomach. They tell me that the cattle wandering into the brakes and bushes are often bitten to death by these deadly creatures; the pigs, whose fat, it seems, does not accept the venom into its tissues with the same effect, escape unhurt for the most part—so much for the anti-venomous virtue of adipose matter—a consolatory consideration for such of us as are inclined to take on flesh more than we think graceful.

*Monday morning*, 25th. This letter has been long on the stocks, dear E——. I have been busy all day, and tired, and lazy in the evening latterly, and, moreover, feel as if such very dull matter was hardly worth sending all the way off to where you are happy to be. However, that is nonsense; I know well enough that you are glad to hear from me, be it what it will, and so I resume my chronicle. Some of my evenings have been spent in reading Mr. Clay's anti-abolition speech, and making notes on it, which I will show you when we meet. What a cruel pity and what a cruel shame it is that such a man should either know no better or do no better for his country than he is doing now!

Yesterday I for the first time bethought me of the riding privileges of which Jack used to make such magnificent mention when he was fishing with me at the rice-island; and desiring to visit the remoter parts of the plantation and the other end of the island, I inquired into the resources of the stable. I was told I could have a mare with foal; but I declined adding my weight to what the poor beast already carried, and my only choice then was between one who had just foaled, or a fine stallion used as a plow-horse on the plantation. I determined for the latter, and shall probably be handsomely shaken whenever I take my rides abroad.

*Tuesday, the 26th.* My dearest E——, I write to you to-day in great depression and distress. I have had a most painful conversation with Mr. ——, who has declined receiving any of the people's petitions through me. Whether he is wearied with the number of these prayers and supplications, which he would escape but for me, as they probably would not venture to come so incessantly to him, and I, of course, feel bound to bring every one confided to me to him, or whether he has been annoyed at the number of pitiful and horrible stories of misery and oppression under the former rule of Mr. K——, which have come to my knowledge since I have been here, and the grief and indignation caused, but which can not, by any means, always be done away with, though their expression may be silenced by his angry exclamations of "Why do you listen to such stuff?" or "Why do you believe such trash? don't you know the niggers are all d—d liars?" etc., I do not know; but he desired me this morning to bring him no more complaints or requests of any sort, as the people had hitherto had no such advocate, and had done very well without, and I was only kept in an incessant state of excitement with all the falsehoods they "found they could make me believe." How well they have done without my advocacy, the conditions which I see with my own eyes, even more than their pitiful petitions, demonstrate; it is indeed true that the sufferings of those who come to me for redress, and, still more, the injustice done to the great majority who can not, have filled my heart with bitterness and indignation that have overflowed my lips, till, I suppose, —— is weary of hearing what he has never heard before, the voice of passionate expostulation and importunate pleading against wrongs that he will not even acknowledge, and for creatures whose common humanity with his own I half think he does not believe; but I must return to the North, for my condition would be almost worse than theirs—condemned to hear and see so much wretchedness, not only without the means of alleviating it, but without permission even to represent it for alleviation: this is no place for me, since I was not born among slaves, and can not bear to live among them.

Perhaps, after all, what he says is true: when I am gone they will fall back into the desperate uncomplaining habit of suffering, from which my coming among them, willing to hear and ready to help, has tempted them; he says that bringing their complaints to me, and the sight of my credulous commiseration, only tend to make them discontented and idle, and brings renewed chastisement upon them; and that so, instead of really befriending them, I am only preparing more suffering for them whenever I leave the place, and they can no more cry to me for help. And so I see nothing for it but to go and leave them to their fate; perhaps, too, he is afraid of the mere contagion of freedom which breathes from the very existence of those who are free; my way of speaking to the people, of treating them, of living with them, the appeals I make to their sense of truth, of duty, of self-respect, the infinite compassion and the human consideration I feel for them—all this, of course, makes my intercourse with them dangerously suggestive of relations far different from any thing they have ever known; and, as Mr. O—— once almost hinted to me, my existence among slaves was an element of danger to the "institution." If I should go away, the human sympathy that I have felt for them will certainly never come near them again.

I was too unhappy to write any more, my dear friend, and you have been spared the rest of my paroxysm, which hereabouts culminated in the blessed refuge of abundant tears. God will provide. He has not forgotten, nor will He forsake these His poor children; and if I may no longer minister to them, they yet are in His hand, who cares for them more and better than I can.

Toward the afternoon yesterday I rowed up the river to the rice-island by way of refreshment to my spirits, and came back to-day, Wednesday, the 27th, through rather a severe storm. Before going to bed last night I finished Mr. Clay's speech, and ground my teeth over it. Before starting this morning I received from head man Frank a lesson on the various qualities of the various sorts of rice, and should be (at any rate till I forget all he told me, which I "feel in my bones" will be soon) a competent judge and expert saleswoman. The dead white speck, which shows itself sometimes in rice as it does in teeth, is in the former, as in the latter, a sign of decay; the finest quality of rice is what may be called flinty, clear and unclouded, and a pretty, clean, sparkling-looking thing it is.

I will tell you something curious and pleasant about my row back. The wind was so high and the river so rough when I left the rice-island, that just as I was about to get into the boat I thought it might not be amiss to carry my life-preserver with me, and ran back to the house to fetch it. Having taken that much care for my life, I jumped into the boat, and we pushed off. The fifteen miles' row with a furious wind, and part of the time the tide against us, and the huge broad, turbid river broken into a foaming sea of angry waves, was a pretty severe task for the men. They pulled with a will, however, but I had to forego the usual accompaniment of their voices, for the labor was tremendous, especially toward the end of our voyage, where, of course, the nearness of the sea increased the roughness of the water terribly. The men were in great spirits, however (there were eight of them rowing, and one behind was steering); one of them said something which elicited an exclamation of general assent, and I asked what it was; the steerer said they were pleased because there was not another planter's lady in all Georgia who would have gone through the storm all alone with them in a boat; *i. e.*, without the protecting presence of a white man. "Why," said I, "my good fellows, if the boat capsized, or any thing happened, I am sure I should have nine chances for my life instead of one;" at this there was one shout of "So you would, missis; true for dat, missis;" and in great mutual good-humor we reached the landing at Hampton Point.

As I walked home I pondered over this compliment of Mr. ——'s slaves to me, and did not feel quite sure that the very absence of the fear which haunts the Southern women in their intercourse with these people, and prevents them from trusting themselves ever with them out of reach of white companionship and supervision, was not one of the circumstances which makes my intercourse with them unsafe and undesirable. The idea of apprehending any mischief from them never yet crossed my brain; and in the perfect confidence with which I go among them, they must perceive a curious difference between me and my lady neighbors in these parts; all have expressed unbounded astonishment at my doing so.

The spring is fast coming on, and we shall, I suppose, soon leave Georgia. How new and sad a chapter of my life this winter here has been!

DEAR E——,—I can not give way to the bitter impatience I feel at my present position, and come back to the North without leaving my babies; and though I suppose their stay will not in any case be much prolonged in these regions of swamp and slavery, I must, for their sakes, remain where they are, and learn this dreary lesson of human suffering to the end. The record, it seems to me, must be utterly wearisome to you, as the instances themselves, I suppose, in a given time (thanks to that dreadful reconciler to all that is evil—habit), would become to me.

This morning I had a visit from two of the women, Charlotte and Judy, who came to me for help and advice for a complaint, which it really seems to me every other woman on the estate is cursed with, and which is a direct result of the conditions of their existence; the practice of sending women to labor in the fields in the third week after their confinement is a specific for causing this infirmity, and I know no specific for curing it under these circumstances. As soon as these poor things had departed with such comfort as I could give them, and the bandages they especially begged for, three other sable graces introduced themselves, Edie, Louisa, and Diana; the former told me she had had a family of seven children, but had lost them all through "ill luck," as she denominated the ignorance and ill treatment which were answerable for the loss of these, as of so many other poor little creatures their fellows. Having dismissed her and Diana with the sugar and rice they came to beg, I detained Louisa, whom I had never seen but in the presence of her old grandmother, whose version of the poor child's escape to, and hiding in the woods, I had a desire to compare with the heroine's own story. She told it very simply, and it was most pathetic. She had not finished her task one day, when she said she felt ill, and unable to do so, and had been severely flogged by Driver Bran, in whose "gang" she then was. The next day, in spite of this encouragement to labor, she had again been unable to complete her appointed work; and Bran having told her that he'd tie her up and flog her if she did not get it done, she had left the field and run into the swamp. "Tie you up, Louisa!" said I; "what is that?" She then described to me that they were fastened up by their wrists to a beam or a branch of a tree, their feet barely touching the ground, so as to allow them no purchase for resistance or evasion of the lash, their clothes turned over their heads, and their backs scored with a leather thong, either by the driver himself, or, if he pleases to inflict their punishment by deputy, any of the men he may choose to summon to the office; it might be father, brother, husband, or lover, if the overseer so ordered it. I turned sick, and my blood curdled listening to these details from the slender young slip of a lassie, with her poor piteous face and murmuring, pleading voice. "Oh," said I, "Louisa; but the rattlesnakes—the dreadful rattlesnakes in the swamps; were you not afraid of those horrible creatures?" "Oh, missis," said the poor child, "me no tink of dem; me forget all 'bout dem for de fretting." "Why did you come home at last?" "Oh, missis, me starve with hunger, me most dead with hunger before me come back." "And were you flogged, Louisa?" said I, with a shudder at what the answer might be. "No, missis, me go to hospital; me almost dead and sick so long, 'spec Driver Bran him forgot 'bout de flogging." I am getting perfectly savage over all these doings, E——, and really think I should consider my own throat and those of my children well cut if some night the people were to take it into their heads to clear off scores in that fashion.

The Calibanish wonderment of all my visitors at the exceedingly coarse and simple furniture and rustic means

of comfort of my abode is very droll. I have never inhabited any apartment so perfectly devoid of what we
should consider the common decencies of life; but to them,
my rude chintz-covered sofa and common pine-wood table,
with its green baize cloth, seem the adornings of a palace;
and often in the evening, when my bairns are asleep, and
M—— up stairs keeping watch over them, and I sit writing this daily history for your edification, the door of the
great barn-like room is opened stealthily, and one after
another, men and women come trooping silently in, their
naked feet falling all but inaudibly on the bare boards as
they betake themselves to the hearth, where they squat
down on their hams in a circle, the bright blaze from the
huge pine logs, which is the only light of this half of the
room, shining on their sooty limbs and faces, and making
them look like a ring of ebony idols surrounding my domestic hearth. I have had as many as fourteen at a time
squatting silently there for nearly half an hour, watching
me writing at the other end of the room. The candles on
my table give only light enough for my own occupation,
the fire-light illuminates the rest of the apartment; and
you can not imagine any thing stranger than the effect of
all these glassy whites of eyes and grinning white teeth
turned toward me, and shining in the flickering light. I
very often take no notice of them at all, and they seem
perfectly absorbed in contemplating me. My evening
dress probably excites their wonder and admiration no
less than my rapid and continuous writing, for which they
have sometimes expressed compassion, as if they thought
it must be more laborious than hoeing; sometimes at the
end of my day's journal I look up and say suddenly, "Well,
what do you want?" when each black figure springs up
at once, as if moved by machinery; they all answer, "Me
come say ha do (how d'ye do), missis;" and then they
troop out as noiselessly as they entered, like a procession

of sable dreams, and I go off in search, if possible, of whiter ones.

Two days ago I had a visit of great interest to me from several lads from twelve to sixteen years old, who had come to beg me to give them work. To make you understand this, you must know that, wishing very much to cut some walks and drives through the very picturesque patches of woodland not far from the house, I announced, through Jack, my desire to give employment in the wood-cutting line to as many lads as chose, when their unpaid task was done, to come and do some work for me, for which I engaged to pay them. At the risk of producing a most dangerous process of reflection and calculation in their brains, I have persisted in paying what I considered wages to every slave that has been my servant; and these my laborers must, of course, be free to work or no, as they like, and if they work for me must be paid by me. The proposition met with unmingled approbation from my "gang;" but I think it might be considered dangerously suggestive of the rightful relation between work and wages; in short, very involuntarily no doubt, but, nevertheless, very effectually I am disseminating ideas among Mr. ——'s dependents, the like of which have certainly never before visited their wool-thatched brains.

*Friday, March* 1. Last night, after writing so much to you, I felt weary, and went out into the air to refresh my spirit. The scene just beyond the house was beautiful; the moonlight slept on the broad river, which here is almost the sea, and on the masses of foliage of the great Southern oaks; the golden stars of German poetry shone in the purple curtains of the night, and the measured rush of the Atlantic unfurling its huge skirts upon the white sands of the beach (the sweetest and most awful lullaby in nature) resounded through the silent air.

I have not felt well, and have been much depressed for

some days past. I think I should die if I had to live here.
This morning, in order not to die yet, I thought I had better take a ride, and accordingly mounted the horse which
I told you was one of the equestrian alternatives offered
me here; but no sooner did he feel my weight, which,
after all, is mere levity and frivolity to him, than he thought
proper to rebel, and find the grasshopper a burden, and
rear and otherwise demonstrate his disgust. I have not
ridden for a long time now; but Montreal's opposition
very presently aroused the Amazon which is both natural
and acquired in me, and I made him comprehend that,
though I object to slaves, I expect obedient servants;
which views of mine being imparted by a due administration of both spur and whip, attended with a judicious combination of coaxing pats on his great crested neck, and
endearing commendations of his beauty, produced the desired effect. Montreal accepted me as inevitable, and carried me very wisely and well up the island to another of
the slave settlements on the plantation, called Jones's
Creek.

On my way I passed some magnificent evergreen oaks,*
and some thickets of exquisite evergreen shrubs, and one
or two beautiful sites for a residence, which made me
gnash my teeth when I thought of the one we had chosen.
To be sure, these charming spots, instead of being con-
veniently in the middle of the plantation, are at an out of
the way end of it, and so hardly eligible for the one quality desired for the overseer's abode, viz., being central.

All the slaves' huts on St. Simon's are far less solid, comfortable, and habitable than those at the rice-island. I do

* The only ilex-trees which I have seen comparable in size and beauty with those of the sea-board of Georgia are some to be found in the
Roman Campagna, at Passerano, Lunghegna, Castel Fusano, and other of its great princely farms, but especially in the magnificent woody
wilderness of Valerano.

not know whether the laborer's habitation bespeaks the alteration in the present relative importance of the crops, but certainly the cultivators of the once far-famed long staple sea-island cotton of St. Simon's are far more miserably housed than the rice-raisers of the other plantation. These ruinous shielings, that hardly keep out wind or weather, are deplorable homes for young or aged people, and poor shelters for the hard-working men and women who cultivate the fields in which they stand. Riding home I passed some beautiful woodland, with charming pink and white blossoming peach and plum trees, which seemed to belong to some orchard that had been attempted, and afterward delivered over to wildness. On inquiry, I found that no fruit worth eating was ever gathered from them. What a pity it seems! for in this warm, delicious winter climate any and every species of fruit might be cultivated with little pains and to great perfection. As I was cantering along the side of one of the cotton-fields I suddenly heard some inarticulate vehement cries, and saw what seemed to be a heap of black limbs tumbling and leaping toward me, renewing the screams at intervals as it approached. I stopped my horse, and the black ball bounded almost into the road before me, and, suddenly straightening itself up into a haggard hag of a half-naked negress, exclaimed, with panting, eager breathlessness, "Oh, missis, missis, you no hear me cry, you no hear me call. Oh, missis, me call, me cry, and me run; make me a gown like dat. Do, for massy's sake, only make me a gown like dat." This modest request for a riding habit in which to hoe the cotton-fields served for an introduction to sundry other petitions for rice, and sugar, and flannel, all which I promised the petitioner, but not the "gown like dat;" whereupon I rode off, and she flung herself down in the middle of the road to get her wind and rest.

The passion for dress is curiously strong in these people, and seems as though it might be made an instrument in converting them, outwardly at any rate, to something like civilization; for, though their own native taste is decidedly both barbarous and ludicrous, it is astonishing how very soon they mitigate it in imitation of their white models. The fine figures of the mulatto women in Charleston and Savannah are frequently as elegantly and tastefully dressed as those of any of their female superiors; and here on St. Simon's, owing, I suppose, to the influence of the resident lady proprietors of the various plantations, and the propensity to imitate in their black dependents, the people that I see all seem to me much tidier, cleaner, and less fantastically dressed than those on the rice plantation, where no such influences reach them.

On my return from my ride I had a visit from Captain F——, the manager of a neighboring plantation, with whom I had a long conversation about the present and past condition of the estate, the species of feudal magnificence in which its original owner, Major ——, lived, the iron rule of old overseer K—— which succeeded to it, and the subsequent sovereignty of his son, Mr. R—— K——, the man for whom Mr. —— entertains such a cordial esteem, and of whom every account I receive from the negroes seems to me to indicate a merciless sternness of disposition that may be a virtue in a slave-driver, but is hardly a Christian grace. Captain F—— was one of our earliest visitors at the rice plantation on our arrival, and I think I told you of his mentioning, in speaking to me of the orange-trees which formerly grew all round the dikes there, that he had taken Basil Hall there once in their blossoming season, and that he had said the sight was as well worth crossing the Atlantic for as Niagara. To-day he referred to that again. He has resided for a great many years on a plantation here, and is connected with our neighbor, old Mr. C——, whose daughter, I believe, he married. He interested me extremely by his description of the house Major —— had many years ago on a part of the island called St. Clair. As far as I can understand, there must have been an indefinite number of "masters'" residences on this estate in the old major's time; for, what with the one we are building, and the ruined remains of those not quite improved off the face of the earth, and the tradition of those that have ceased to exist, even as ruins, I make out no fewer than seven. How gladly would I exchange all that remain and all that do not for the smallest tenement in your blessed Yankee mountain village!

Captain F—— told me that at St. Clair General Oglethorpe, the good and brave English governor of the State of Georgia in its colonial days, had his residence, and that among the magnificent live oaks which surround the site of the former settlement, there was one especially venerable and picturesque, which in his recollection always went by the name of General Oglethorpe's Oak. If you remember the history of the colony under his benevolent rule, you must recollect how absolutely he and his friend and counselor Wesley opposed the introduction of slavery in the colony. How wrathfully the old soldier's spirit ought to haunt these cotton-fields and rice-swamps of his old domain, with their population of wretched slaves! I will ride to St. Clair and see his oak; if I should see him, he can not have much to say to me on the subject that I should not cry amen to.

*Saturday, March* 2. I have made a gain, no doubt, in one respect in coming here, dear E——, for, not being afraid of a rearing stallion, I can ride; but, on the other hand, my aquatic diversions are all likely, I fear, to be much curtailed. Well may you, or any other Northern Abolitionist, consider this a heaven-forsaken region—why, I can not even get worms to fish with, and was solemnly assured by Jack this morning that the whole "Point," *i. e.*, neighborhood of the house, had been searched in vain for these useful and agreeable animals. I must take to some more sportsman-like species of bait; but, in my total ignorance of even the kind of fish that inhabit these waters, it is difficult for me to adapt my temptations to their taste.

Yesterday evening I had a visit that made me very sorrowful, if any thing connected with these poor people can be called more especially sorrowful than their whole condition; but Mr. ——'s declaration that he will receive no more statements of grievances or petitions for redress through me makes me as desirous now of shunning the vain appeals of these unfortunates as I used to be of receiving and listening to them. The imploring cry, "Oh missis!" that greets me whichever way I turn, makes me long to stop my ears now; for what can I say or do any more for them? The poor little favors—the rice, the sugar, the flannel—that they beg for with such eagerness, and receive with such exuberant gratitude, I can, it is true, supply, and words and looks of pity, and counsel of patience, and such instruction in womanly habits of decency and cleanliness as may enable them to better, in some degree, their own hard lot; but to the entreaty, "Oh, missis, you speak to massa for us! Oh, missis, you beg massa for us! Oh, missis, you tell massa for we, he sure do as you say!" I can not now answer as formerly, and I turn away choking and with eyes full of tears from the poor creatures, not even daring to promise any more the faithful transmission of their prayers.

The women who visited me yesterday evening were all in the family-way, and came to entreat of me to have the sentence (what else can I call it?) modified which condemns them to resume their labor of hoeing in the fields three weeks after their confinement. They knew, of course, that I can not interfere with their appointed labor, and therefore their sole entreaty was that I would use my influence with Mr. —— to obtain for them a month's respite from labor in the field after childbearing. Their principal spokeswoman, a woman with a bright sweet face, called Mary, and a very sweet voice, which is by no means an uncommon excellence among them, appealed to my own experience; and while she spoke of my babies, and my carefully tended, delicately nursed, and tenderly watched confinement and convalescence, and implored me to have a kind of labor given to them less exhausting during the month after their confinement, I held the table before me so hard in order not to cry that I think my fingers ought to have left a mark on it. At length I told them that Mr. —— had forbidden me to bring him any more complaints from them, for that he thought the ease with which I received and believed their stories only tended to make them discontented, and that, therefore, I feared I could not promise to take their petitions to him; but that he would be coming down to "the Point" soon, and that they had better come then some time when I was with him, and say what they had just been saying to me; and with this, and various small bounties, I was forced, with a heavy heart, to dismiss them; and when they were gone, with many exclamations of, "Oh yes, missis, you will, you will speak to massa for we; God bless you, missis, we sure you will!" I had my cry out for them, for myself, for us. All these women had had large families, and *all* of them had lost half their children, and several of them had lost more. How I do ponder upon the strange fate which has brought me here, from so far away, from surroundings so curiously different—how my own people in that blessed England of my birth would marvel if they could suddenly have a vision of me as I sit here, and how sorry some of them would be for me!

I am helped to bear all that is so very painful to me here by my constant enjoyment of the strange, wild scenery in the midst of which I live, and which my resumption of my equestrian habits gives me almost daily opportunity of observing. I rode to-day to some new-cleared and plowed ground that was being prepared for the precious cotton-crop. I crossed a salt marsh upon a raised causeway that was perfectly alive with land-crabs, whose desperately active endeavors to avoid my horse's hoofs were so ludicrous that I literally laughed alone and aloud at them. The sides of this road across the swamp were covered with a thick and close embroidery of creeping moss, or rather lichens of the most vivid green and red: the latter made my horse's path look as if it was edged with an exquisite pattern of coral; it was like a thing in a fairy tale, and delighted me extremely.

I suppose, E——, one secret of my being able to suffer as acutely as I do, without being made either ill or absolutely miserable, is the childish excitability of my temperament, and the sort of ecstasy which any beautiful thing gives me. No day, almost no hour, passes without some enjoyment of the sort this coral-bordered road gave me, which not only charms my senses completely at the time, but returns again and again before my memory, delighting my fancy, and stimulating my imagination. I sometimes despise myself for what seems to me an inconceivable rapidity of emotion, that almost makes me doubt whether any one who feels so many things can really be said to feel any thing; but I generally ⸗ecover from this perplexity by remembering whither invariably every impression of beauty leads my thoughts, and console myself for my contemptible facility of impression by the reflection that it is, upon the whole, a merciful system of compensation by which my whole nature, tortured as it was last night, can be absorbed this morning in a perfectly pleasurable contemplation of the capers of crabs and the color of mosses as if nothing else existed in creation. One thing, however, I think, is equally certain, and that is, that I need never expect much sympathy, and perhaps this special endowment will make me, to some degree, independent of it; but I have no doubt that to follow me through half a day with any species of lively participation in my feelings would be a severe breathless moral calisthenic to most of my friends — what Shakspeare calls "sweating labor." As far as I have hitherto had opportunities of observing, children and maniacs are the only creatures who would be capable of sufficiently rapid transitions of thought and feeling to keep pace with me.

And so I rode through the crabs and the coral. There is one thing, however, I beg to commend to your serious consideration as a trainer of youth, and that is, the expediency of cultivating in all the young minds you educate an equal love of the good, the beautiful, and the absurd (not an easy task, for the latter is apt in its development to interfere a little with the two others) : doing this, you command all the resources of existence. The love of the good and beautiful of course you are prepared to cultivate—that goes without saying, as the French say; the love of the ludicrous will not appear to you as important, and yet you will be wrong to undervalue it. In the first place, I might tell you that it was almost like cherishing the love of one's fellow-creatures — at which, no doubt, you shake your head reprovingly; but, leaving aside the enormous provision for the exercise of this natural faculty which we offer to each other, why should crabs scuttle from under my horse's feet in such a way as to make me laugh again every time I think of it, if there is not an inherent propriety in laughter, as the only emotion which certain objects challenge—an emotion wholesome for the soul and body of man? After all, *why* are we contrived to laugh at all, if laughter is not essentially befitting and beneficial? and most people's lives are too lead-colored to afford to lose one sparkle on them, even the smallest twinkle of light gathered from a flash of nonsense. Hereafter point out for the "appreciative" study of your pupils all that is absurd in themselves, others, and the universe in general; 'tis an element largely provided, of course, to meet a corresponding and grateful capacity for its enjoyment.

After my crab and coral causeway I came to the most exquisite thickets of evergreen shrubbery you can imagine. If I wanted to paint Paradise I would copy this undergrowth, passing through which I went on to the settlement at St. Annie's, traversing another swamp on another raised causeway. The thickets through which I next rode were perfectly draped with the beautiful wild jasmine of these woods. Of all the parasitical plants I ever saw, I do think it is the most exquisite in form and color, and its perfume is like the most delicate heliotrope.

I stopped for some time before a thicket of glittering evergreens, over which hung, in every direction, streaming garlands of these fragrant golden cups, fit for Oberon's banqueting service. These beautiful shrubberies were resounding with the songs of mocking-birds. I sat there on my horse in a sort of dream of enchantment, looking, listening, and inhaling the delicious atmosphere of those flowers; and suddenly my eyes opened, as if I had been asleep, on some bright red bunches of spring leaves on one of the winter-stripped trees, and I as suddenly thought of the cold Northern skies and earth, where the winter was still inflexibly tyrannizing over you all, and, in spite of the loveliness of all that was present, and the harshness of all that I seemed to see at that moment, no first tokens of the spring's return were ever more welcome to me than those bright leaves that reminded me how soon I should leave this scene of material beauty and moral degradation, where the beauty itself is of an appropriate character to the human existence it surrounds: above all, loveliness, brightness, and fragrance; but below! it gives one a sort of melusina feeling of horror—all swamp and poisonous stagnation, which the heat will presently make alive with venomous reptiles.

I rode on, and the next object that attracted my attention was a very startling and by no means agreeable one —an enormous cypress-tree which had been burnt stood charred and blackened, and leaning toward the road so as to threaten a speedy fall across it, and on one of the limbs of this great charcoal giant hung a dead rattlesnake. If I tell you that it looked to me at least six feet long, you will say you only wonder I did not say twelve; it was a hideous-looking creature, and some negroes I met soon after told me they had found it in the swamp, and hung it dead on the burning tree. Certainly the two together made a dreadful trophy, and a curious contrast to the lovely bowers of bloom I had just been contemplating with such delight.

This settlement at St. Annie's is the remotest on the whole plantation, and I found there the wretchedest huts, and most miserably squalid, filthy, and forlorn creatures I had yet seen here—certainly the condition of the slaves on this estate is infinitely more neglected and deplorable than that on the rice plantation. Perhaps it may be that the extremely unhealthy nature of the rice cultivation makes it absolutely necessary that the physical condition of the laborers should be maintained at its best to enable them to abide it; and yet it seems to me that even the process of soaking the rice can hardly create a more dangerous miasma than the poor creatures must inhale who live in the midst of these sweltering swamps, half sea, half river slime. Perhaps it has something to do with the fact that the climate on St. Simon's is generally considered peculiarly mild and favorable, and so less protection of clothes and shelter is thought necessary here for the poor residents; perhaps, too, it may be because the cotton crop is now, I believe, hardly as valuable as the rice crop, and the plantation here, which was once the chief source of its owner's wealth, is becoming a secondary one, and so not worth so much care or expense in repairing and constructing negro huts and feeding and clothing the slaves. More pitiable objects than some of those I saw at the St. Annie's settlement to-day I hope never to see: there was an old crone called Hannah, a sister, as well as I could understand what she said, of old House Molly, whose face and figure, seamed with wrinkles, and bowed and twisted with age and infirmity, really hardly retained the semblance of those of a human creature, and as she crawled to me almost half her naked body was exposed through the miserable tatters that she held on with one hand, while the other eagerly clutched my hand, and her poor blear eyes wandered all over me as if she was bewildered by the strange aspect of any human being but those whose sight was familiar to her. One or two forlorn creatures like herself, too old or too infirm to be compelled to work, and the half-starved and more than half-naked children apparently left here under their charge, were the only inmates I found in these wretched hovels.

I came home without stopping to look at any thing, for I had no heart any longer for what had so charmed me on my way to this place. Galloping along the road after leaving the marshes, I scared an ox who was feeding leisurely, and, to my great dismay, saw the foolish beast betake himself with lumbering speed into the "bush:" the slaves will have to hunt after him, and perhaps will discover more rattlesnakes six or twelve feet long.

After reaching home I went to the house of the over-

seer to see his wife, a tidy, decent, kind-hearted little woman, who seems to me to do her duty by the poor people
she lives among as well as her limited intelligence and still
more limited freedom allow. The house her husband lives
in is the former residence of Major ——, which was the
great mansion of the estate. It is now in a most ruinous
and tottering condition, and they inhabit but a few rooms
in it; the others are gradually mouldering to pieces, and
the whole edifice will, I should think, hardly stand long
enough to be carried away by the river, which in its yearly inroads on the bank on which it stands has already approached within a perilous proximity to the old dilapidated planter's palace. Old Molly, of whom I have often
before spoken to you, who lived here in the days of the
prosperity and grandeur of "Hampton," still clings to the
relics of her old master's former magnificence, and with a
pride worthy of old Caleb of Ravenswood showed me
through the dismantled decaying rooms and over the remains of the dairy, displaying a capacious fish-box or well,
where, in the good old days, the master's supply was kept
in fresh salt water till required for table. Her prideful
lamentations over the departure of all this quondam glory
were ludicrous and pathetic; but, while listening with
some amusement to the jumble of grotesque descriptions,
through which her impression of the immeasurable grandeur and nobility of the house she served was the predominant feature, I could not help contrasting the present
state of the estate with that which she described, and
wondering why it should have become, as it undoubtedly
must have done, so infinitely less productive a property
than in the old major's time.

Before closing this letter, I have a mind to transcribe
to you the entries for to-day recorded in a sort of day-
book, where I put down very succinctly the number of
people who visit me, their petitions and ailments, and also

such special particulars concerning them as seem to me worth recording. You will see how miserable the physical condition of many of these poor creatures is; and their physical condition, it is insisted by those who uphold this evil system, is the only part of it which is prosperous, happy, and compares well with that of Northern laborers. Judge from the details I now send you; and never forget, while reading them, that the people on this plantation are well off, and consider themselves well off, in comparison with the slaves on some of the neighboring estates.

*Fanny* has had six children; all dead but one. She came to beg to have her work in the field lightened.

*Nanny* has had three children; two of them are dead. She came to implore that the rule of sending them into the field three weeks after their confinement might be altered.

*Leah*, Cæsar's wife, has had six children; three are dead.

*Sophy*, Lewis's wife, came to beg for some old linen. She is suffering fearfully; has had ten children; five of them are dead. The principal favor she asked was a piece of meat, which I gave her.

*Sally*, Scipio's wife, has had two miscarriages and three children born, one of whom is dead. She came complaining of incessant pain and weakness in her back. This woman was a mulatto daughter of a slave called Sophy, by a white man of the name of Walker, who visited the plantation.

*Charlotte*, Renty's wife, had had two miscarriages, and was with child again. She was almost crippled with rheumatism, and showed me a pair of poor swollen knees that made my heart ache. I have promised her a pair of flannel trowsers, which I must forthwith set about making.

*Sarah*, Stephen's wife—this woman's case and history were alike deplorable. She had had four miscarriages, had brought seven children into the world, five of whom were dead, and was again with child. She complained of dreadful pains in the back, and an internal tumor which swells with the exertion of working in the fields; probably, I think, she is ruptured. She told me she had once been mad and had ran into the woods, where she contrived to elude discovery for some time, but was at last tracked and brought back, when she was tied up by the arms, and heavy logs fastened to her feet, and was severely flogged. After this she contrived to escape again, and lived for some time skulking in the woods, and she supposes mad, for when she was taken again she was entirely naked. She subsequently recovered from this derangement, and seems now just like all the other poor creatures who come to me for help and pity. I suppose her constant childbearing and hard labor in the fields at the same time may have produced the temporary insanity.

*Sukey*, Bush's wife, only came to pay her respects. She had had four miscarriages; had brought eleven children into the world, five of whom are dead.

*Molly*, Quambo's wife, also only came to see me. Hers was the best account I have yet received; she had had nine children, and six of them were still alive.

This is only the entry for to-day, in my diary, of the people's complaints and visits. Can you conceive a more wretched picture than that which it exhibits of the conditions under which these women live? Their cases are in no respect singular, and though they come with pitiful entreaties that I will help them with some alleviation of their pressing physical distresses, it seems to me marvelous with what desperate patience (I write it advisedly, patience of utter despair) they endure their sorrow-laden existence. Even .the poor wretch who told that miserable story of insanity, and lonely hiding in the swamps, and scourging when she was found, and of her renewed madness and flight, did so in a sort of low, plaintive, monotonous murmur of misery, as if such sufferings were all "in the day's work."

I ask these questions about their children because I think the number they bear as compared with the number they rear a fair gauge of the effect of the system on their own health and that of their offspring. There was hardly one of these women, as you will see by the details I have noted of their ailments, who might not have been a candidate for a bed in a hospital, and they had come to me after working all day in the fields.

---

Dearest E——,—When I told you in my last letter of the encroachments which the waters of the Altamaha are daily making on the bank at Hampton Point and immediately in front of the imposing-looking old dwelling of the former master, I had no idea how rapid this crumbling process has been of late years; but to-day, standing there with Mrs. G——, whom I had gone to consult about the assistance we might render to some of the poor creatures whose cases I sent you in my last letter, she told me that within the memory of many of the slaves now living on the plantation, a grove of orange-trees had spread its fragrance and beauty between the house and the river. Not a vestige remains of them. The earth that bore them was gradually undermined, slipped, and sank down into the devouring flood; and when she saw the astonished incredulity of my look, she led me to the ragged and broken bank, and there, immediately below it, and just covered by the turbid waters of the in-rushing tide, were the heads of the poor drowned orange-trees, swaying like black twigs in the briny flood, which had not yet dislodged all of them from their hold upon the soil which had gone down beneath the water wearing its garland of bridal blossom. As I looked at those trees a wild wish rose in my heart that the river and the sea would swallow up and melt in their salt waves the whole of this accursed property of ours. I am afraid the horror of slavery with which I came down to the South, the general theoretic abhorrence of an Englishwoman for it, has gained, through the intensity it has acquired, a morbid character of mere desire to be delivered from my own share in it. I think so much of these wretches that I see, that I can hardly remember any others; and my zeal for the general emancipation of the slave has almost narrowed itself to this most painful desire that I and mine were freed from the responsibility of our share in this huge misery; and so I thought, "Beat, beat, the crumbling banks and sliding shores, wild waves of the Atlantic and the Altamaha! Sweep down and carry hence this evil earth and these homes of tyranny, and roll above the soil of slavery, and wash my soul and the souls of those I love clean from the blood of our kind!" But I have no idea that Mr. —— and his brother would cry amen to any such prayer. Sometimes, as I stand and listen to the roll of the great ocean surges on the farther side of little St. Simon's Island, a small green screen of tangled wilderness that interposes between this point and the Atlantic, I think how near our West Indian Islands and freedom are to these unfortunate people, many of whom are expert and hardy boatmen, as far as the mere mechanical management of a boat goes; but, unless Providence were compass and steersman too, it avails nothing that they should know how near their freedom might be found, nor have I any right to tell them if they could find it, for the slaves are not mine, they are Mr. ——'s.

The mulatto woman, Sally, accosted me again to-day, and begged that she might be put to some other than field labor. Supposing she felt herself unequal to it, I asked her some questions, but the principal reason she urged for her promotion to some less laborious kind of work was, that hoeing in the field was so hard to her on *" account of her color,"* and she therefore petitions to be allowed to learn a trade. I was much puzzled at this reason for her petition, but was presently made to understand that, being a mulatto, she considered field labor a degradation; her white bastardy appearing to her a title to consideration in my eyes. The degradation of these people is very complete, for they have accepted the contempt of their masters to that degree that they profess, and really seem to feel it for themselves, and the faintest admixture of white blood in their black veins appears at once, by common consent of their own race, to raise them in the scale of humanity. I had not much sympathy for this petition. The woman's father had been a white man who was employed for some purpose on the estate. In speaking upon this subject to Mrs. G——, she said that, as far as her observation went, the lower class of white men in the South lived with colored women precisely as they would at the North with women of their own race; the outcry that one hears against amalgamation appears therefore to be something educated and acquired rather than intuitive. I can not perceive, in observing my children, that they exhibit the slightest repugnance or dislike to these swarthy dependents of theirs, which they surely would do if, as is so often pretended, there is an inherent, irreconcilable repulsion on the part of the white toward the negro race. All the Southern children that I have seen seem to have a special fondness for these good-natured, childish human beings, whose mental condition is kin in its simplicity and proneness to impulsive emotion to their own, and I can detect in them no trace of the abhorrence and contempt for their dusky skins which all questions of treating them with common justice is so apt to elicit from American men and women.

To-day, for the first time since I left the rice-island, I went out fishing, but had no manner of luck. Jack rowed me up Jones's Creek, a small stream which separates St. Simon's from the main, on the opposite side from the great waters of the Altamaha. The day was very warm. It is becoming almost too hot to remain here much longer, at least for me, who dread and suffer from heat so much. The whole summer, however, is passed by many members of the Georgia families on their estates by the sea. When the heat is intense, the breeze from the ocean and the salt air, I suppose, prevent it from being intolerable or hurtful. Our neighbor, Mr. C——, and his family reside entirely, the year round, on their plantations here without apparently suffering in their health from the effects of the climate. I suppose it is the intermediate region between the sea-board and the mountains that becomes so pestilential when once the warm weather sets in. I remember the Belgian minister, M. de ——, telling me that the mountain country of Georgia was as beautiful as Paradise, and that the climate, as far as his experience went, was perfectly delicious. He was, however, only there on an exploring expedition, and, of course, took the most favorable season of the year for the purpose.

I have had several women with me this afternoon more or less disabled by chronic rheumatism. Certainly, either their labor or the exposure it entails must be very severe, for this climate is the last that ought to engender rheumatism. This evening I had a visit from a bright young woman, calling herself Minda, who came to beg for a little rice or sugar. I inquired from which of the settlements she had come down, and found that she has to walk three miles every day to and from her work. She made no complaint whatever of this, and seemed to think her laborious tramp down to the Point after her day of labor on the field well rewarded by the pittance of rice and sug-

ar she obtained. Perhaps she consoled herself for the exertion by the reflection which occurred to me while talking to her, that many women who have borne children,
and many women with child, go the same distance to and
from their task-ground—that seems dreadful!

I have let my letter lie from a stress of small interrup-
tions. Yesterday, Sunday, 3d, old Auber, a stooping, halt-
ing hag, came to beg for flannel and rice. As usual, of
course, I asked various questions concerning her condition, family, etc.; she told me she had never been married, but had had five children, two of whom were dead.
She complained of flooding, of intolerable backache, and
said that with all these ailments she considered herself
quite recovered, having suffered horribly from an abscess
in her neck, which was now nearly well. I was surprised
to hear of her other complaints, for she seemed to me like
quite an old woman; but constant childbearing, and the
life of labor, exposure, and privation which they lead, ages
these poor creatures prematurely.

Dear E——, how I do defy you to guess the novel accomplishment I have developed within the last two days;
what do you say to my turning butcher's boy, and cutting
up the carcase of a sheep for the instruction of our butcher and cook, and benefit of our table? You know, I have
often written you word that we have mutton here—thanks
to the short salt grass on which it feeds—that compares
with the best South Down or *Prè salé;* but such is the
barbarous ignorance of the cook, or rather the butcher
who furnishes our kitchen supplies, that I defy the most
expert anatomist to pronounce on any piece (joints they
can not be called) of mutton brought to our table to what
part of the animal sheep it originally belonged. I have
often complained bitterly of this, and in vain implored
Abraham the cook to send me some dish of mutton to
which I might with safety apply the familiar name of leg,

shoulder, or haunch. These remonstrances and expostulations have produced no result whatever, however, but
an increase of eccentricity in the *chunks* of sheeps' flesh
placed upon the table; the squares, diamonds, cubes, and
rhomboids of mutton have been more ludicrously and
hopelessly unlike any thing we see in a Christian butcher's shop, with every fresh endeavor Abraham has made
to find out " zackly wot de missis do want;" so the day
before yesterday, while I was painfully dragging S——
through the early intellectual science of the alphabet and
first reading lesson, Abraham appeared at the door of the
room brandishing a very long thin knife, and with many
bows, grins, and apologies for disturbing me, begged that
I would go and cut up a sheep for him. My first impulse,
of course, was to decline the very unusual task offered me
with mingled horror and amusement. Abraham, however, insisted and besought, extolled the fineness of his sheep,
declared his misery at being unable to cut it as I wished,
and his readiness to conform for the future to whatever
*patterns* of mutton " de missis would only please to give
him." Upon reflection, I thought I might very well contrive to indicate upon the sheep the size and form of the
different joints of civilized mutton, and so, for the future,
save much waste of good meat; and, moreover, the lesson, once taught, would not require to be repeated, and I
have ever held it expedient to accept every opportunity
of learning to do any thing, no matter how unusual, which
presented itself to be done; and so I followed Abraham
to the kitchen, when, with a towel closely pinned over my
silk dress, and knife in hand, I stood for a minute or two
meditating profoundly before the rather unsightly object
which Abraham had pronounced " de beautifullest sheep
de missis eber saw." The sight and smell of raw meat
are especially odious to me, and I have often thought that
if I had had to be my own cook, I should inevitably be-

come a vegetarian, probably, indeed, return entirely to my green and salad days. Nathless, I screwed my courage to the sticking-point, and slowly and delicately traced out with the point of my long carving-knife two shoulders, two legs, a saddle, and a neck of mutton; not probably in the most thoroughly artistic and butcherly style, but as nearly as my memory and the unassisted light of nature would enable me; and having instructed Abraham in the various boundaries, sizes, shapes, and names of the several joints, I returned to S—— and her belles-lettres, rather elated, upon the whole, at the creditable mode in which I flattered myself I had accomplished my unusual task, and the hope of once more seeing roast mutton of my acquaintance. I will confess to you, dear E——, that the *neck* was not a satisfactory part of the performance, and I have spent some thoughts since in trying to adjust in my own mind its proper shape and proportions.

As an accompaniment to "de beautifullest mutton de missis eber see," we have just received from my neighbor Mr. C—— the most magnificent supply of fresh vegetables, green peas, salad, etc. He has a garden, and a Scotchman's real love for horticulture, and I profit by them in this very agreeable manner.

I have been interrupted by several visits, my dear E——, among other, one from a poor creature called Judy, whose sad story and condition affected me most painfully. She had been married, she said, some years ago to one of the men called Temba, who, however, now has another wife, having left her because she went mad. While out of her mind she escaped into the jungle, and contrived to secrete herself there for some time, but was finally tracked and caught, and brought back and punished by being made to sit, day after day, for hours in the stocks—a severe punishment for a man, but for a woman perfectly barbarous. She complained of chronic rheumatism, and other terrible ailments, and said she suffered such intolerable pain while laboring in the fields, that she had come to entreat me to have her work lightened. She could hardly crawl, and cried bitterly all the time she spoke to me.

She told me a miserable story of her former experience on the plantation under Mr. K——'s overseership. It seems that Jem Valiant (an extremely difficult subject, a mulatto lad, whose valor is sufficiently accounted for now by the influence of the mutinous white blood) was her first-born, the son of Mr. K——, who forced her, flogged her severely for having resisted him, and then sent her off, as a farther punishment, to Five Pound—a horrible swamp in a remote corner of the estate, to which the slaves are sometimes banished for such offenses as are not sufficiently atoned for by the lash. The dismal loneliness of the place to these poor people, who are as dependent as children upon companionship and sympathy, makes this solitary exile a much-dreaded infliction; and this poor creature said that, bad as the flogging was, she would sooner have taken that again than the dreadful lonely days and nights she spent on the penal swamp of Five Pound.

I make no comment on these terrible stories, my dear friend, and tell them to you as nearly as possible in the perfectly plain, unvarnished manner in which they are told to me. I do not wish to add to, or perhaps I ought to say take away from, the effect of such narrations by amplifying the simple horror and misery of their bare details.

———————

My dearest E——,—I have had an uninterrupted stream of women and children flowing in the whole morning to say " Ha de, missis ?" Among others, a poor woman called Mile, who could hardly stand for pain and swelling in her limbs; she had had fifteen children and two miscarriages; nine of her children had died; for the last

three years she had become almost a cripple with chronic
rheumatism, yet she is driven every day to work in the
field. She held my hands, and stroked them in the most
appealing way while she exclaimed, " Oh my missis! my
missis! me neber sleep till day for de pain," and with the
day her labor must again be resumed. I gave her flannel
and sal volatile to rub her poor swelled limbs with; rest
I could not give her—rest from her labor and her pain—
this mother of fifteen children.

Another of my visitors had a still more dismal story to
tell; her name was Die; she had had sixteen children,
fourteen of whom were dead; she had had four miscarriages: one had been caused with falling down with a
very heavy burden on her head, and one from having her
arms strained up to be lashed. I asked her what she
meant by having her arms tied up. She said their hands
were first tied together, sometimes by the wrists, and
sometimes, which was worse, by the thumbs, and they
were then drawn up to a tree or post, so as almost to
swing them off the ground, and then their clothes rolled
round their waist, and a man with a cowhide stands and
stripes them. I give you the woman's words. She did
not speak of this as of any thing strange, unusual, or especially horrid and abominable; and when I said, "Did
they do that to you when you were with child?" she simply replied, " Yes, missis." And to all this I listen—I, an
English woman, the wife of the man who owns these
wretches, and I can not say, "That thing shall not be
done again; that cruel shame and villainy shall never be
known here again." I gave the woman meat and flannel,
which were what she came to ask for, and remained choking with indignation and grief long after they had all left
me to my most bitter thoughts.

I went out to try and walk off some of the weight of
horror and depression which I am beginning to feel daily

more and more, surrounded by all this misery and degradation that I can neither help nor hinder. The blessed spring is coming very fast, the air is full of delicious wildwood fragrances, and the wonderful songs of Southern birds; the wood paths are as tempting as paths into Paradise, but Jack is in such deadly terror about the snakes, which are now beginning to glide about with a freedom and frequency certainly not pleasing, that he will not follow me off the open road, and twice to-day scared me back from charming wood paths I ventured to explore with his exclamations of terrified warning.

I gathered some exquisite pink blossoms, of a sort of waxen texture, off a small shrub which was strange to me, and for which Jack's only name was dye-bush; but I could not ascertain from him whether any dyeing substance was found in its leaves, bark, or blossoms.

I returned home along the river side, stopping to admire a line of noble live oaks beginning, alas! to be smothered with the treacherous white moss under whose pale trailing masses their verdure gradually succumbs, leaving them, like huge hoary ghosts, perfect mountains of parasitical vegetation, which, strangely enough, appears only to hang upon and swing from their boughs without adhering to them. The mixture of these streams of gray-white filaments with the dark foliage is extremely beautiful as long as the leaves of the tree survive in sufficient masses to produce the rich contrast of color; but when the moss has literally conquered the whole tree, and, after stripping its huge limbs bare, clothed them with its own wan masses, they always looked to me like so many gigantic Druid ghosts, with flowing robes and beards, and locks all of one ghastly gray, and I would not have broken a twig off them for the world, lest a sad voice, like that which reproached Dante, should have moaned out of it to me,

"Non hai tu spirto di pietade alcuno?"

A beautiful mass of various woodland skirted the edge
of the stream, and mingled in its foliage every shade of
green, from the pale, stiff spikes and fans of the dwarf palmetto to the dark canopy of the magnificent ilex—bowers
and brakes of the loveliest wildness, where one dare not
tread three steps for fear. What a tantalization! it is like
some wicked enchantment.

———

DEAREST E———,—I have found growing along the edge
of the dreary inclosure where the slaves are buried such
a lovely wild flower; it is a little like the euphrasia or
eyebright of the English meadows, but grows quite close
to the turf, almost into it, and consists of clusters of tiny
white flowers that look as if they were made of the finest
porcelain. I took up a root of it yesterday, with a sort
of vague idea that I could transplant it to the North;
though I can not say that I should care to transplant any
thing thither that could renew to me the associations of
this place—not even the delicious wild flowers, if I could.

The woods here are full of wild plum-trees, the delicate
white blossoms of which twinkle among the evergreen
copses, and, besides illuminating them with a faint starlight, suggest to my mind a possible liqueur like kirsch,
which I should think could quite as well be extracted from
wild plums as wild cherries, and the trees are so numerous
that there ought to be quite a harvest from them. You
may, and, doubtless, have seen palmetto plants in Northern green and hot houses, but you never saw palmetto
roots; and what curious things they are! huge, hard, yel-
lowish-brown stems, as thick as my arm, or thicker, ex-
tending and ramifying under the ground in masses that
seem hardly justified or accounted for by the elegant,
light, spiky fans of dusky green foliage with which they

fill the under part of the woods here. They look very tropical and picturesque, but both in shape and color suggest something metallic rather than vegetable; the bronze-green hue and lance-like form of their foliage has an arid, hard character, that makes one think they could be manufactured quite as well as cultivated. At first I was extremely delighted with the novelty of their appearance; but now I feel thirsty when I look at them, and the same with their kinsfolk, the yuccas and their intimate friends, if not relations, the prickly pears, with all of which once strange growth I have grown contemptuously familiar now.

Did it ever occur to you what a strange affinity there is between the texture and color of the wild vegetables of these sandy Southern soils, and the texture and color of shells? The prickly pear, and especially the round little cactus plants all covered with hairy spikes, are curiously suggestive of a family of round spiked shells, with which you, as well as myself, are doubtless familiar; and though the splendid flame-color of some cactus blossoms never suggests any nature but that of flowers, I have seen some of a peculiar shade of yellow-pink, that resembles the mingled tint on the inside of some elaborately colored shell, and the pale white and rose flowers of another kind have the coloring and almost texture of shell, much rather than of any vegetable substance.

To-day I walked out without Jack, and, in spite of the terror of snakes with which he has contrived slightly to inoculate me, I did make a short exploring journey into the woods. I wished to avoid a plowed field, to the edge of which my wanderings had brought me; but my dash into the woodland, though unpunished by an encounter with snakes, brought me only into a marsh as full of land-crabs as an ant-hill is of ants, and from which I had to retreat ingloriously, finding my way home at last by the beach.

I have had, as usual, a tribe of visitors and petitioners ever since I came home. I will give you an account of those cases which had any thing beyond the average of interest in their details. One poor woman, named Molly, came to beg that I would, if possible, get an extension of their exemption from work after childbearing. The close of her argument was concise and forcible. "Missis, we hab um pickanniny — tree weeks in de ospital, and den right out upon the hoe again — *can we strong* dat way, missis? No!" And truly I do not see that they can. This poor creature has had eight children and two miscarriages. All her children were dead but one. Another of my visitors was a divinely named but not otherwise divine Venus; it is a favorite name among these sable folk, but, of course, must have been given originally in derision. The Aphrodite in question was a dirt-colored (convenient color I should say for these parts) mulatto. I could not understand how she came on this property, for she was the daughter of a black woman and the overseer of an estate to which her mother formerly belonged, and from which I suppose she was sold, exchanged, or given, as the case may be, to the owners of this plantation. She was terribly crippled with rheumatism, and came to beg for some flannel. She had had eleven children, five of whom had died, and two miscarriages. As she took her departure, the vacant space she left on the other side of my writing-table was immediately filled by another black figure with a bowed back and piteous face, one of the thousand "Mollies" on the estate, where the bewildering redundancy of their name is avoided by adding that of their husband; so when the question, "Well, who are you?" was answered with the usual genuflexion, and "I'se Molly, missis!" I, of course, went on with "whose Molly," and she went on to refer herself to the ownership (under Mr. —— and heaven) of one Tony, but proceeded to say that he was not her *real* husband. This appeal to an element of reality in the universally accepted fiction which passes here by the title of marriage surprised me; and on asking her what she meant, she replied that her real husband had been sold from the estate for repeated attempts to run away. He had made his escape several times, and skulked starving in the woods and morasses, but had always been tracked and brought back, and flogged almost to death, and finally sold as an incorrigible runaway. What a spirit of indomitable energy the wretched man must have had, to have tried so often that hideously hopeless attempt to fly! I do not write you the poor woman's jargon, which was ludicrous; for I can not write you the sighs, and tears, and piteous looks, and gestures, that made it pathetic; of course she did not know whither or to whom her *real* husband had been sold; but in the mean time Mr. K——, that merciful Providence of the estate, had provided her with the above-named Tony, by whom she had had nine children, six of whom were dead; she, too, had miscarried twice. She came to ask me for some flannel for her legs, which were all swollen with constant rheumatism, and to beg me to give her something to cure some bad sores and ulcers, which seemed to me dreadful enough in their present condition, but which she said break out afresh and are twice as bad every summer.

I have let my letter lie since the day before yesterday, dear E——, having had no leisure to finish it. Yesterday morning I rode out to St. Clair's, where there used formerly to be another negro settlement, and another house of Major ——'s. I had been persuaded to try one of the mares I had formerly told you of, and to be sure a more " curst" quadruped, and one more worthy of a Petruchio for a rider I did never back. Her temper was furious, her gait intolerable, her mouth the most obdurate that ever tugged against bit and bridle. It is not wise any

where — here it is less wise than any where else in the
world—to say, "Jamais de cette eau je ne boirai;" but I
*think* I will never ride that delightful creature Miss Kate
again.

I wrote you of my having been to a part of the estate
called St. Clair's, where there was formerly another residence of Major ——'s; nothing remains now of it but a
ruined chimney of some of the offices, which is standing
yet in the middle of what has become a perfect wilderness.
At the best of times, with a large house, numerous household, and paths, and drives of approach, and the usual external conditions of civilization about it, a residence here
would have been the loneliest that can well be imagined;
now it is the shaggiest desert of beautiful wood that I
ever saw. The magnificent old oaks stand round the
place in silent solemn grandeur; and among them I had
no difficulty in recognizing, by the description Captain
F—— had given me of it, the crumbling, shattered relic
of a tree called Oglethorpe's oak. That worthy, valiant
old governor had a residence here himself in the early
days of the colony, when, under the influence of Wesley,
he vainly made such strenuous efforts to keep aloof from
his infant province the sore curse of slavery.

I rode almost the whole way through a grove of perfect
evergreen. I had with me one of the men of the name of
Hector, who has a good deal to do with the horses, and
so had volunteered to accompany me, being one of the
few negroes on the estate who can sit a horse. In the
course of our conversation, Hector divulged certain opinions relative to the comparative gentility of driving in a
carriage and the vulgarity of walking, which sent me into
fits of laughing; at which he grinned sympathetically, and
opened his eyes very wide, but certainly without attaining
the least insight into what must have appeared to him
my very unaccountable and unreasonable merriment.

Among various details of the condition of the people on the several estates in the island, he told me that a great number of the men on all the different plantations had *wives* on the neighboring estates as well as on that to which they properly belonged. "Oh, but," said I, "Hector, you know that can not be; a man has but one lawful wife." Hector knew this, he said, and yet seemed puzzled himself, and rather puzzled me to account for the fact, that this extensive practice of bigamy was perfectly well known to the masters and overseers, and never in any way found fault with or interfered with. Perhaps this promiscuous mode of keeping up the slave population finds favor with the owners of creatures who are valued in the market at so much per head. This was a solution which occurred to me, but which I left my Trojan hero to discover, by dint of the profound pondering into which he fell.

Not far from the house, as I was cantering home, I met S——, and took her up on the saddle before me, an operation which seemed to please her better than the vicious horse I was riding, whose various demonstrations of dislike to the arrangement afforded my small equestrian extreme delight and triumph. My whole afternoon was spent in shifting my bed and bedroom furniture from a room on the ground floor to one above; in the course of which operation a brisk discussion took place between M—— and my boy Jack, who was nailing on the vallence of the bed, and whom I suddenly heard exclaim, in answer to something she had said, "Well, den, I do tink so; and dat's the speech of a man, whether um bond or free." A very trifling incident, and insignificant speech; and yet it came back to my ears very often afterward — "the speech of a *man*, whether bond or free." They might be made conscious—some of them are evidently conscious— of an inherent element of manhood superior to the bitter accident of slavery, and to which, even in their degraded condition, they might be made to refer that vital self-respect which can survive all external pressure of mere circumstance, and give their souls to that service of God, which is perfect freedom, in spite of the ignoble and cruel bondage of their bodies.

My new apartment is what I should call decidedly airy; the window, unless when styled by courtesy shut, which means admitting of draught enough to blow a candle out, must be wide open, being incapable of any intermediate condition; the latch of the door, to speak the literal truth, does shut; but it is the only part of it that does—that is, the latch and the hinges; every where else its configuration is traced by a distinct line of light and air. If what old Dr. Physic used to say be true, that a draught which will not blow out a candle will blow out a man's life (a Spanish proverb originally I believe), my life is threatened with extinction in almost every part of this new room of mine, wherein, moreover, I now discover to my dismay, having transported every other article of bedroom furniture to it, it is impossible to introduce the wardrobe for my clothes. Well, our stay here is drawing to a close, and therefore these small items of discomfort can not afflict me much longer.

Among my visitors to-day was a poor woman named Oney, who told me her husband had gone away from her now for four years; it seems he was the property of Mr. K——, and when that gentleman went to slave-driving on his own account, and ceased to be the overseer of this estate, he carried her better half, who was his chattel, away with him, and she never expects to see him again. After her departure I had a most curious visitor, a young lad of the name of Renty, whose very decidedly mulatto tinge accounted, I suppose, for the peculiar disinvoltura of his carriage and manner; he was evidently, in his own opinion, a very superior creature, and yet, as his conversation with me testified, he was conscious of some flaw in the honor of his "yellow" complexion. "Who is your mother, Renty?" said I (I give you our exact dialogue). "Betty, head man Frank's wife." I was rather dismayed at the promptness of this reply, and hesitated a little at my next question, "Who is your father?" My sprightly young friend, however, answered, without an instant's pause, "Mr. K——." Here I came to a halt, and, willing to suggest some doubt to the lad, because for many peculiar reasons this statement seemed to me shocking, I said, "What, old Mr. K——?" "No, Massa R——." "Did your mother tell you so?" "No, missis, me ashamed to ask her; Mr. C——'s children told me so, and I 'spect they know it." Renty, you see, did not take Falconbridge's view of such matters; and as I was by no means sorry to find that he considered his relation to Mr. K—— a disgrace to his mother, which is an advance in moral perception not often met with here, I said no more upon the subject.

*Tuesday, March* 3. This morning, old House Molly, coming from Mr. G——'s upon some errand to me, I asked her if Renty's statement was true; she confirmed the whole story, and, moreover, added that this connection took place after Betty was married to head man Frank. Now he, you know, E——, is the chief man at the rice-island, second in authority to Mr. O——, and, indeed, for a considerable part of the year, absolute master and guardian during the night of all the people and property at the rice plantation; for, after the early spring, the white overseer himself is obliged to betake himself to the main land to sleep, out of the influence of the deadly malaria of the rice swamp, and Frank remains sole sovereign of the island from sunset to sunrise—in short, during the whole period of his absence. Mr. —— bestowed the highest commendations upon his fidelity and intelligence, and,

during the visit Mr. R—— K—— paid us at the island,
he was emphatic in his praise of both Frank and his wife,
the latter having, as he declared, by way of climax to his
eulogies, quite the principles of a white woman.   Perhaps
she imbibed them from his excellent influence over her.
Frank is a serious, sad, sober-looking, very intelligent
man; I should think he would not relish having his wife
borrowed from him even by the white gentleman who admired her principles so much; and it is quite clear, from
poor Renty's speech about his mother, that by some of
these people (and if by any, then very certainly by Frank)
the disgrace of such an injury is felt and appreciated much
after the fashion of white men.

This old woman Molly is a wonderfully intelligent,
active, energetic creature, though considerably over seventy years old; she was talking to me about her former
master, Major ——, and what she was pleased to call the
*revelation* war (*i. e.*, revolution war), during which that
gentleman, having embraced the side of the rebellious colonies in their struggle against England, was by no means
on a bed of roses.   He bore King George's commission,
and was a major in the British army; but having married
a great Carolina heiress, and become proprietor of these
plantations, sided with the country of his adoption, and
not that of his birth, in the war between them, and was a
special object of animosity on that account to the English
officers who attacked the sea-board of Georgia, and sent
troops on shore and up the Altamaha to fetch off the negroes, or incite them to rise against their owners.   " De
British," said Molly, " make old massa run about bery
much in de great revelation war."   He ran effectually,
however, and contrived to save both his life and property
from the invader.

Molly's account was full of interest, in spite of the grotesque lingo in which it was delivered, and which once or

twice nearly sent me into convulsions of laughing, where-upon she apologized with great gravity for her mispro-nunciation, modestly suggesting that *white words* were impossible to the organs of speech of black folks. It is curious how universally any theory, no matter how ab-surd, is accepted by these people; for any thing in which the contemptuous supremacy of the dominant race is ad-mitted, and their acquiescence in the theory of their own incorrigible baseness is so complete, that this, more than any other circumstance in their condition, makes me doubt-ful of their rising from it.

In order to set poor dear old Molly's notions straight with regard to the negro incapacity for speaking plain the noble white words, I called S—— to me and set her talk-ing; and having pointed out to Molly how very imperfect her mode of pronouncing many words was, convinced the worthy old negress that want of training, and not any ab-solute original impotence, was the reason why she disfig-ured the *white words*, for which she had such a profound respect. In this matter, as in every other, the slaves pay back to their masters the evil of their own dealings with usury, though unintentionally. No culture, however slight, simple, or elementary, is permitted to these poor creatures, and the utterance of many of them is more like what Prospero describes Caliban's to have been, than the speech of men and women in a Christian and civilized land: the children of their owners, brought up among them, acquire their negro mode of talking—slavish speech surely it is—and it is distinctly perceptible in the utterances of all Southerners, particularly of the women, whose avocations, taking them less from home, are less favorable to their throwing off this ignoble trick of pronunciation than the more varied occupation and the more extended and pro-miscuous business relations of men. The Yankee twang of the regular down Easter is not more easily detected by

any ear, nice in enunciation and accent, than the thick negro speech of the Southerners: neither is lovely or melodious; but, though the Puritan snuffle is the harsher of
the two, the slave *slobber* of the language is the more ignoble, in spite of the softer voices of the pretty Southern
women who utter it.

I rode out to-day upon Miss Kate again, with Jack for
my esquire. I made various vain attempts to ride through
the woods, following the cattle-tracks; they turned round
and round into each other, or led out into the sandy pine
barren, the eternal frame in which all nature is set here,
the inevitable limit to the prospect, turn landward which
way you will. The wood paths which I followed between
evergreen thickets, though little satisfactory in their ulti-
mate result, were really more beautiful than the most perfect arrangement of artificial planting that I ever saw in
an English park; and I thought, if I could transplant the
region which I was riding through bodily into the midst
of some great nobleman's possessions on the other side of
the water, how beautiful an accession it would be thought
to them. I was particularly struck with the elegant
growth of a profuse wild shrub I passed several times to-
day, the leaves of which were pale green underneath, and
a deep red, varnished brown above.

I must give you an idea of the sort of service one is liable to obtain from one's most intelligent and civilized
servants hereabouts, and the consequent comfort and luxury of one's daily existence. Yesterday Aleck, the youth
who fulfills the duties of what you call a waiter, and we
in England a footman, gave me a salad for dinner, mixed
with so large a portion of the soil in which it had grown
that I requested him to-day to be kind enough to wash
the lettuce before he brought it to table. M—— later in
the day told me that he had applied to her very urgently
for soap and a brush, " as missis wished de lettuce scrub-

bed," a fate from which my second salad was saved by her refusal of these desired articles, and farther instructions upon the subject.

---

DEAREST E——,—I have been long promising poor old House Molly to visit her in her own cabin, and so the day before yesterday I walked round the settlement to her dwelling, and a most wretched hovel I found it. She has often told me of the special directions left by her old master for the comfort and well-being of her old age, and certainly his charge has been but little heeded by his heirs, for the poor faithful old slave is most miserably off in her infirm years. She made no complaint, however, but seemed overjoyed at my coming to see her. She took me to the hut of her brother, old Jacob, where the same wretched absence of every decency and every comfort prevailed; but neither of them seemed to think the condition that appeared so wretched to me one of peculiar hardship—though Molly's former residence in her master's house might reasonably have made her discontented with the lot of absolute privation to which she was now turned over—but, for the moment, my visit seemed to compensate for all sublunary sorrows, and she and poor old Jacob kept up a duet of rejoicing at my advent, and that I had brought " de little missis among um people afore they die."

Leaving them, I went on to the house of Jacob's daughter Hannah, with whom Psyche, the heroine of the rice-island story, and wife of his son Joe, lives. I found their cabin as tidy and comfortable as it could be made, and their children, as usual, neat and clean; they are capital women, both of them, with an innate love of cleanliness and order most uncommon among these people. On my way home I overtook two of my daily suppliants, who were going to the house in search of me, and meat, flannel, rice, and sugar, as the case might be; they were both old and infirm-looking women, and one of them, called Scylla, was extremely lame, which she accounted for by an accident she had met with while carrying a heavy weight of rice on her head; she had fallen on a sharp stake, or snag, as she called it, and had never recovered the injury she had received. She complained also of falling of the womb. Her companion (who was not Charybdis, however, but Phœbe) was a cheery soul who complained of nothing, but begged for flannel. I asked her about her family and children; she had no children left, nothing but grandchildren; she had had nine children, and seven of them died quite young; the only two who grew up left her to join the British when they invaded Georgia in the last war, and their children, whom they left behind, were all her family now.

In the afternoon I made my first visit to the hospital of the estate, and found it, as indeed I find every thing else here, in a far worse state even than the wretched establishments on the rice-island, dignified by that name; so miserable a place for the purpose to which it was dedicated I could not have imagined on a property belonging to Christian owners. The floor (which was not boarded, but merely the damp hard earth itself) was strewn with wretched women, who, but for their moans of pain, and uneasy, restless motions, might very well each have been taken for a mere heap of filthy rags; the chimney refusing passage to the smoke from the pine-wood fire, it puffed out in clouds through the room, where it circled and hung, only gradually oozing away through the windows, which were so far well adapted to the purpose that there was not a single whole pane of glass in them. My eyes, unaccustomed to the turbid atmosphere, smarted and watered, and refused to distinguish at first the different dismal forms, from which cries and wails assailed me in every corner of the place. By degrees I was able to endure for a few minutes what they were condemned to live their hours and days of suffering and sickness through; and, having given what comfort kind words and promises of help in more substantial forms could convey, I went on to what seemed a yet more wretched abode of wretchedness. This was a room where there was no fire because there was no chimney, and where the holes made for windows had no panes or glasses in them. The shutters being closed, the place was so dark that, on first entering it, I was afraid to stir lest I should fall over some of the deplorable creatures extended upon the floor. As soon as they perceived me, one cry of "Oh missis!" rang through the darkness; and it really seemed to me as if I was never to exhaust the pity, and amazement, and disgust which this receptacle of suffering humanity was to excite in me. The poor dingy supplicating sleepers upraised themselves as I cautiously advanced among them; those who could not rear their bodies from the earth held up piteous beseeching hands, and as I passed from one to the other I felt more than one imploring clasp laid upon my dress, to solicit my attention to some new form of misery. One poor woman, called Tressa, who was unable to speak above a whisper from utter weakness and exhaustion, told me she had had nine children, was suffering from incessant flooding, and felt "as if her back would split open." There she lay, a mass of filthy tatters, without so much as a blanket under her or over her, on the bare earth in this chilly darkness. I promised them help and comfort, beds and blankets, and light and fire—that is, I promised to ask Mr. —— for all this for them; and, in the very act of doing so, I remembered with a sudden pang of anguish that I was to urge no more petitions for his slaves to their master. I groped my way out, and, emerging on the piazza, all the choking tears and sobs I had controlled broke forth, and I leaned there crying over the lot of these unfortunates till I heard a feeble voice of "Missis, you no cry; missis, what for you cry?" and, looking up, saw that I had not yet done with this intolerable infliction. A poor crippled old man, lying in the corner of the piazza, unable even to crawl toward me, had uttered this word of consolation, and by his side (apparently too idiotic, as he was too impotent, to move) sat a young woman, the expression of whose face was the most suffering, and, at the same time, the most horribly repulsive I ever saw. I found she was, as I supposed, half-witted; and, on coming nearer to inquire into her ailments and what I could do for her, found her suffering from that horrible disease—I believe some form of scrofula—to which the negroes are subject, which attacks and eats away the joints of their hands and fingers —a more hideous and loathsome object I never beheld; her name was Patty, and she was granddaughter to the old crippled creature by whose side she was squatting.

I wandered home, stumbling with crying as I went, and feeling so utterly miserable that I really hardly saw where I was going, for I as nearly as possible fell over a great heap of oyster-shells left in the middle of the path. This is a horrid nuisance, which results from an indulgence which the people here have and value highly; the waters round the island are prolific in shell-fish, oysters, and the most magnificent prawns I ever saw. The former are a considerable article of the people's diet, and the shells are allowed to accumulate, as they are used in the composition of which their huts are built, and which is a sort of combination of mud and broken oyster-shells, which forms an agglomeration of a kind very solid and durable for such building purposes; but, instead of being all carried to some specified place out of the way, these great heaps of oyster-shells are allowed to be piled up any where and every where, forming the most unsightly obstructions in every direction. Of course, the cultivation of order for the sake of its own seemliness and beauty is not likely to be an element of slave existence; and as masters have been scarce on this plantation for many years now, a mere unsightliness is not a matter likely to trouble any body much; but, after my imminent overthrow by one of these disorderly heaps of refuse, I think I may make bold to request that the paths along which I am likely to take my daily walks may be kept free from them.

On my arrival at home—at the house—I can not call any place here my home!—I found Renty waiting to exhibit to me an extremely neatly-made leather pouch, which he has made by my order, of fitting size and dimensions to receive Jack's hatchet and saw. Jack and I have set up a sort of Sir Walter and Tom Purdie companionship of clearing and cutting paths through the woods nearest to the house; thinning the overhanging branches, clearing the small evergreen thickets which here and there close over and across the grassy track. To me this occupation was especially delightful until quite lately, since the weather began to be rather warmer and the snakes to slide about. Jack has contrived to inoculate me with some portion of his terror of them; but I have still a daily hankering after the lovely green wood walks; perhaps, when once I have seen a live rattlesnake, my enthusiasm for them will be modified to the degree that his is.

DEAR E——,—This letter has remained unfinished, and my journal interrupted for more than a week. Mr. —— has been quite unwell, and I have been traveling to and fro daily between Hampton and the rice-island in the

long-boat to visit him; for the last three days I have remained at the latter place, and only returned here this
morning early. My daily voyages up and down the river
have introduced me to a great variety of new musical performances of our boatmen, who invariably, when the rowing is not too hard, moving up or down with the tide,
accompany the stroke of their oars with the sound of
their voices. I told you formerly that I thought I could
trace distinctly some popular national melody with which
I was familiar in almost all their songs; but I have been
quite at a loss to discover any such foundation for many
that I have heard lately, and which have appeared to me
extraordinarily wild and unaccountable. The way in
which the chorus strikes in with the burden, between
each phrase of the melody chanted by a single voice, is
very curious and effective, especially with the rhythm of
the rowlocks for accompaniment. The high voices all in
unison, and the admirable time and true accent with which
their responses are made, always make me wish that some
great musical composer could hear these semi-savage performances. With a very little skillful adaptation and in-
strumentation, I think one or two barbaric chants and
choruses might be evoked from them that would make
the fortune of an opera.

The only exception that I have met with yet among
our boat voices to the high tenor which they seem all to
possess is in the person of an individual named Isaac, a
basso profondo of the deepest dye, who nevertheless never
attempts to produce with his different register any different effects in the chorus by venturing a second, but sings
like the rest in unison, perfect unison, of both time and
tune. By-the-by, this individual *does* speak, and therefore I presume he is not an ape, orang-outang, chimpan-
zee, or gorilla; but I could not, I confess, have conceived
it possible that the presence of articulate sounds, and the

absence of an articulate tail, should make, externally at least, so completely the only appreciable difference between a man and a monkey, as they appear to do in this individual "black brother." Such stupendous long thin hands, and long flat feet, I did never see off a large quadruped of the ape species. But, as I said before, Isaac *speaks*, and I am much comforted thereby.

You can not think (to return to the songs of my boatmen) how strange some of their words are : in one, they repeatedly chanted the " sentiment" that " God made man, and man makes"—what do you think?—" money!" Is not that a peculiar poetical proposition? Another ditty to which they frequently treat me they call Cæsar's song; it is an extremely spirited war-song, beginning "The trumpets blow, the bugles sound—Oh, stand your ground!" It has puzzled me not a little to determine in my own mind whether this title of Cæsar's song has any reference to the great Julius, and, if so, what may be the negro notion of him, and whence and how derived. One of their songs displeased me not a little, for it embodied the opinion that "twenty-six black girls not make mulatto yellow girl;" and as I told them I did not like it, they have omitted it since. This desperate tendency to despise and undervalue their own race and color, which is one of the very worst results of their abject condition, is intolerable to me.

While rowing up and down the broad waters of the Altamaha to the music of these curious chants, I have been reading Mr. Moore's speech about the abolition of slavery in the District of Columbia, and I confess I think his the only defensible position yet taken, and the only consistent argument yet used in any of the speeches I have hitherto seen upon the subject.

I have now settled down at Hampton again; Mr. —— is quite recovered, and is coming down here in a day or two for change of air; it is getting too late for him to stay on the rice plantation even in the day, I think. You can not imagine any thing so exquisite as the perfect curtains of yellow jasmine with which this whole island is draped; and as the boat comes sweeping down toward the Point, the fragrance from the thickets hung with their golden garlands greets one before one can distinguish them; it is really enchanting.

I have now to tell you of my hallowing last Sunday by gathering a congregation of the people into my big sitting-room, and reading prayers to them. I had been wishing very much to do this for some time past, and obtained Mr. ——'s leave while I was with him at the rice-island, and it was a great pleasure to me. Some of the people are allowed to go up to Darien once a month to church; but, with that exception, they have no religious service on Sunday whatever for them. There is a church on the island of St. Simon, but they are forbidden to frequent it, as it leads them off their own through neighboring plantations, and gives opportunities for meetings between the negroes of the different estates, and very likely was made the occasion of abuses and objectionable practices of various kinds; at any rate, Mr. K—— forbade the Hampton slaves resorting to the St. Simon's church, and so for three Sundays in the month they are utterly without Christian worship or teaching, or any religious observance of God's day whatever.

I was very anxious that it should not be thought that I *ordered* any of the people to come to prayers, as I particularly desired to see if they themselves felt the want of any Sabbath service, and would of their own accord join in any such ceremony; I therefore merely told the house servants that if they would come to the sitting-room at eleven o'clock, I would read prayers to them, and that they might tell any of their friends or any of the people that I should be very glad to see them if they liked to come. Accordingly, most of those who live at the Point, *i. e.*, in the immediate neighborhood of the house, came, and it was encouraging to see the very decided efforts at cleanliness and decorum of attire which they had all made. I was very much affected and impressed myself by what I was doing, and I suppose must have communicated some of my own feeling to those who heard me. It is an extremely solemn thing to me to read the Scriptures aloud to any one, and there was something in my relation to the poor people by whom I was surrounded that touched me so deeply while thus attempting to share with them the best of my possessions, that I found it difficult to command my voice, and had to stop several times in order to do so. When I had done, they all with one accord uttered the simple words, "We thank you, missis," and instead of overwhelming me as usual with petitions and complaints, they rose silently and quietly, in a manner that would have become the most orderly of Christian congregations accustomed to all the impressive decorum of civilized church privileges. Poor people! They are said to have what a very irreligious young English clergyman once informed me I had—a "*turn*" for religion." They seem to me to have a "turn" for instinctive good manners too; and certainly their mode of withdrawing from my room after our prayers bespoke either a strong feeling of their own, or a keen appreciation of mine.

I have resumed my explorations in the woods with renewed enthusiasm, for during my week's absence they have become more lovely and enticing than ever: unluckily, however, Jack seems to think that fresh rattlesnakes have budded together with the tender spring foliage, and I see that I shall either have to give up my wood walks and rides, or go without a guide. Lovely blossoms are springing up every where—weeds, of course, wild·things, impertinently so called. Nothing is cultivated here but cotton; but in some of the cotton-fields beautiful creatures are peeping into blossom, which I suppose will all be duly hoed off the surface of the soil in proper season; meantime I rejoice in them, and in the splendid, magnificent thistles, which would be in flower-gardens in other parts of the world, and in the wonderful, strange, beautiful butterflies that seem to me almost as big as birds, that go zigzagging in the sun. I saw yesterday a lovely monster, who thought proper, for my greater delectation, to alight on a thistle I was admiring, and as the flower was purple, and he was all black velvet fringed with gold, I was exceedingly pleased with his good inspiration.

This morning I drove up to the settlement at St. Annie's, having various bundles of benefaction to carry in the only equipage my estate here affords — an exceedingly small, rough, and uncomfortable cart, called the sick-house wagon, inasmuch as it is used to convey to the hospital such of the poor people as are too ill to walk there. Its tender mercies must be terrible indeed for the sick, for I, who am sound, could very hardly abide them; however, I suppose Montreal's pace is moderated for them: to-day he went rollicking along with us behind him, shaking his fine head and mane, as if he thought the more we were jolted the better we should like it. We found, on trying to go on to Cartwright's Point, that the state of the tide would not admit of our getting thither, and so had to return, leaving it unvisited. It seems to me strange that, where the labor of so many hands might be commanded, piers, and wharves, and causeways are not thrown out (wooden ones, of course, I mean) wherever the common traffic to or from different parts of the plantation is thus impeded by the daily rise and fall of the river; the trouble and expense would be nothing, and the gain in conven-

ience very considerable. However, perhaps the nature of
the tides, and of the banks and shores themselves, may
not be propitious for such constructions, and I rather in-
cline, upon reflection, to think this may be so, because to
go from Hampton to our neighbor Mr. C——'s plantation,
it is necessary to consult the tide in order to land conven-
iently. Driving home to-day by Jones's Creek, we saw
an immovable row of white cranes, all standing with imperturbable gravity upon one leg. I thought of Boccac-
cio's cook, and had a mind to say Ha! at them, to try if
they had two. I have been over to Mr. C——'s, and was
very much pleased with my visit, but will tell you of it in
my next.

----

Dear E——,—I promised to tell you of my visit to my
neighbor Mr. C——, which pleased and interested me very
much. He is an old Glasgow man, who has been settled
here many years. It is curious how many of the people
round this neighborhood have Scotch names; it seems
strange to find them thus gathered in the vicinity of a
new Darien; but those in our immediate neighborhood
seem to have found it a far less fatal region than their
countrymen did its namesake of the Isthmus. Mr. C——'s
house is a roomy, comfortable, handsomely laid-out mansion, to which he received me with very cordial kindness,
and where I spent part of a very pleasant morning, talking with him, hearing all he could tell me of the former
history of Mr. ——'s plantation. His description of its
former master, old Major ——, and of his agent and overseer Mr. K——, and of that gentleman's worthy son and
successor the late overseer, interested me very much; of
the two latter functionaries his account was terrible, and
much what I had supposed any impartial account of them
would be; because, let the propensity to lying of the poor

wretched slaves be what it will, they could not invent, with a common consent, the things that they one and all tell me with reference to the manner in which they have been treated by the man who has just left the estate, and his father, who for the last nineteen years have been sole sovereigns of their bodies and souls. The crops have satisfied the demands of the owners, who, living in Philadelphia, have been perfectly contented to receive a large income from their estate without apparently caring how it was earned. The stories that the poor people tell me of the cruel tyranny under which they have lived are not complaints, for they are of things past and gone, and very often, horridly as they shock and affect me, they themselves seem hardly more than half conscious of the misery their condition exhibits to me, and they speak of things which I shudder to hear of almost as if they had been matters of course with them.

Old Mr. C—— spoke with extreme kindness of his own people, and had evidently bestowed much humane and benevolent pains upon endeavors to better their condition. I asked him if he did not think the soil and climate of this part of Georgia admirably suited to the cultivation of the mulberry and the rearing of the silkworm; for it has appeared to me that hereafter silk may be made one of the most profitable products of this whole region: he said that that had long been his opinion, and he had at one time had it much at heart to try the experiment, and had proposed to Major —— to join him in it, on a scale large enough to test it satisfactorily; but he said Mr. K—— opposed the scheme so persistently that of course it was impossible to carry it out, as his agency and co-operation were indispensable; and that in like manner he had suggested sowing turnip crops, and planting peach-trees for the benefit and use of the people on the Hampton estate, experiments which he had tried with excellent success on his own; but all these plans for the amelioration and progress of the people's physical condition had been obstructed and finally put entirely aside by old Mr. K—— and his son, who, as Mr. C—— said, appeared to give satisfaction to their employers, so it was not his business to find fault with them; he said, however, that the whole condition and treatment of the slaves had changed from the time of Major ——'s death, and that he thought it providential for the poor people that Mr. K—— should have left the estate, and the young gentleman, the present owner, come down to look after the people.

He showed me his garden, from whence come the beautiful vegetables he had more than once supplied me with; in the midst of it was a very fine and flourishing date-palm-tree, which he said bore its fruit as prosperously here as it would in Asia. After the garden we visited a charming, nicely-kept poultry-yard, and I returned home much delighted with my visit and the kind good-humor of my host.

In the afternoon I sat as usual at the receipt of custom, hearing of aches and pains till I ached myself sympathetically from head to foot.

Yesterday morning, dear E——, I went on horseback to St. Annie's, exploring on my way some beautiful woods, and in the afternoon I returned thither in a wood-wagon, with Jack to drive and a mule to draw me, Montreal being quite beyond his management; and then and there, the hatchet and saw being in company, I compelled my slave Jack, all the rattlesnakes in creation to the contrary notwithstanding, to cut and clear a way for my chariot through the charming copse.

My letter has been lying unfinished for the last three days. I have been extraordinarily busy, having emancipated myself from the trammels of Jack and all his terror, and as I fear no serpents on horseback, have been daily

riding through new patches of woodland without any
guide, taking my chance of what I might come to in the
shape of impediments. Last Tuesday I rode through a
whole wood of burned and charred trees, cypresses and
oaks, that looked as if they had been each of them blasted
by a special thunderbolt, and whole thickets of young
trees and shrubs perfectly black and brittle from the effect of fire, I suppose the result of some carelessness of
the slaves. As this charcoal woodland extended for some
distance, I turned out of it, and round the main road
through the plantation, as I could not ride through the
blackened boughs and branches without getting begrimed.
It had a strange, wild, desolate effect, not without a certain gloomy picturesqueness.

In the afternoon I made Israel drive me through Jack's
new-made path to break it down and open it still more,
and Montreal's powerful trampling did good service to
that effect, though he did not seem to relish the narrow
wood road with its grass path by any means as much as
the open way of what may be called the high road.   After this operation I went on to visit the people at the Busson Hill settlement.   I here found, among other noteworthy individuals, a female named Judy, whose two children
belong to an individual called (not Punch, but) Joe, who
has another wife, called Mary, at the rice-island.   In one
of the huts I went to leave some flannel, and rice, and sugar for a poor old creature called Nancy, to whom I had
promised such indulgences : she is exceedingly infirm and
miserable, suffering from sore limbs and an ulcerated leg
so cruelly that she can hardly find rest in any position
from the constant pain she endures, and is quite unable to
lie on her hard bed at night.   As I bent over her to-day,
trying to prop her into some posture where she might find
some ease, she took hold of my hand, and with the tears
streaming over her face, said, "I have worked every day

through dew and damp, and sand and heat, and done good work; but oh, missis, me old and broken now; no tongue can tell how much I suffer." In spite of their curious thick utterance and comical jargon, these people sometimes use wonderfully striking and pathetic forms of speech. In the next cabin, which consisted of an inclosure called by courtesy a room, certainly not ten feet square, and owned by a woman called Dice—that is, not owned, of course, but inhabited by her—three grown-up human beings and eight children stow themselves by day and night, which may be called close packing, I think. I presume that they must take turns to be inside and outside the house, but they did not make any complaint about it, though I should think the aspect of my countenance, as I surveyed their abode and heard their numbers, might have given them a hint to that effect; but I really do find these poor creatures patient of so much misery, that it inclines me the more to heed as well as hear their petitions and complaints when they bring them to me.

After my return home I had my usual evening reception, and, among other pleasant incidents of plantation life, heard the following agreeable anecdote from a woman named Sophy, who came to beg for some rice. In asking her about her husband and children, she said she had never had any husband; that she had had two children by a white man of the name of Walker, who was employed at the mill on the rice-island; she was in the hospital after the birth of the second child she bore this man, and at the same time two women, Judy and Sylla, of whose children Mr. K—— was the father, were recovering from their confinements. It was not a month since any of them had been delivered, when Mrs. K—— came to the hospital, had them all three severely flogged, a process which *she* personally superintended, and then sent them to Five Pound—the swamp Botany Bay of the plantation, of which I have told you—with farther orders to the drivers to flog them every day for a week. Now, E——, if I make you sick with these disgusting stories, I can not help it; they are the life itself here; hitherto I have thought these details intolerable enough, but this appari- tion of a female fiend in the middle of this hell I confess adds an element of cruelty which seems to me to surpass all the rest. Jealousy is not an uncommon quality in the feminine temperament; and just conceive the fate of these unfortunate women between the passions of their masters and mistresses, each alike armed with power to oppress and torture them. Sophy went on to say that Isaac was her son by Driver Morris, who had forced her while she was in her miserable exile at Five Pound. Almost be- yond my patience with this string of detestable details, I exclaimed—foolishly enough, heaven knows—" Ah! but don't you know—did nobody ever tell or teach any of you that it is a sin to live with men who are not your hus- bands?" Alas! E——, what could the poor creature an- swer but what she did, seizing me at the same time vehe- mently by the wrist: " Oh yes, missis, we know—we know all about dat well enough; but we do any thing to get our poor flesh some rest from de whip; when he made me follow him into de bush, what use me tell him no? he have strength to make me." I have written down the woman's words; I wish I could write down the voice and look of abject misery with which they were spoken. Now you will observe that the story was not told to me as a complaint; it was a thing long past and over, of which she only spoke in the natural course of accounting for her children to me. I make no comment; what need, or can I add, to such stories? But how is such a state of things to endure? and again, how is it to end? While I was pondering, as it seemed to me, at the very bottom of the Slough of Despond, on this miserable creature's story, another woman came in (Tema), carrying in her arms a child the image of the mulatto Bran; she came to beg for flannel. I asked her who was her husband. She said she was not married. Her child is the child of Bricklayer Temple, who has a wife at the rice-island. By this time, what do you think of the moralities, as well as the amenities, of slave life? These are the conditions which can only be known to one who lives among them; flagrant acts of cruelty may be rare, but this ineffable state of utter degradation, this really *beastly* existence, is the normal condition of these men and women, and of that no one seems to take heed, nor have I ever heard it described, so as to form any adequate conception of it, till I found myself plunged into it; where and how is one to begin the cleansing of this horrid pestilential immondezzio of an existence?

It is Wednesday, the 20th of March; we can not stay here much longer; I wonder if I shall come back again! and whether, when I do, I shall find the trace of one idea of a better life left in these poor people's minds by my sojourn among them.

One of my industries this morning has been cutting out another dress for one of our women, who had heard of my tailoring prowess at the rice-island. The material, as usual, was a miserable cotton, many-colored like the scarf of Iris. While shaping it for my client, I ventured to suggest the idea of the possibility of a change of the nethermost as well as the uppermost garment. This, I imagine, is a conception that has never dawned upon the female slave mind on this plantation. They receive twice a year a certain supply of clothing, and wear them (as I have heard some nasty fine ladies do their stays, for fear they should get out of shape), without washing, till they receive the next suit. Under these circumstances I think it is unphilosophical, to say the least of it, to speak of the negroes as a race whose unfragrance is heaven-ordained, and the result of special organization.

I must tell you that I have been delighted, surprised, and the very least perplexed, by the sudden petition on the part of our young waiter, Aleck, that I will teach him to read. He is a very intelligent lad of about sixteen, and preferred his request with an urgent humility that was very touching. I told him I would think about it. I mean to do it. I will do it; and yet, it is simply breaking the laws of the government under which I am living. Unrighteous laws are made to be broken—*perhaps*—but then, you see, I am a woman, and Mr. —— stands between me and the penalty. If I were a man, I would do that and many a thing besides, and doubtless should be shot some fine day from behind a tree by some good neighbor, who would do the community a service by quietly getting rid of a mischievous incendiary; and I promise you, in such a case, no questions would be asked, and my lessons would come to a speedy and silent end; but teaching slaves to read is a finable offense, and I am *feme couverte*, and my fines must be paid by my legal owner, and the first offense of the sort is heavily fined, and the second more heavily fined, and for the third, one is sent to prison. What a pity it is I can't begin with Aleck's third lesson, because going to prison can't be done by proxy, and that penalty would light upon the right shoulders! I certainly intend to teach Aleck to read. I certainly won't tell Mr. —— any thing about it. I'll leave him to find it out, as slaves, and servants, and children, and all oppressed, and ignorant, and uneducated and unprincipled people do; then, if he forbids me, I can stop—perhaps before then the lad may have learned his letters. I begin to perceive one most admirable circumstance in this slavery: you are absolute on your own plantation. No slaves' testimony avails against you, and no white testimony exists but such as you choose to admit. Some owners have a fancy for maiming their slaves, some brand them, some pull out their teeth, some shoot them a little here and there (all details gathered from advertisements of runaway slaves in Southern papers); now they do all this on their plantations, where nobody comes to see, and I'll teach Aleck to read, for nobody is here to see, at least nobody whose seeing I mind; and I'll teach every other creature that wants to learn. I haven't much more than a week to remain in this blessed purgatory; in that last week perhaps I may teach the boy enough to go on alone when I am gone.

*Thursday*, 21*st.* I took a long ride to-day all through some new woods and fields, and finally came upon a large space sown with corn for the people. Here I was accosted by such a shape as I never beheld in the worst of my dreams; it looked at first, as it came screaming toward me, like a live specimen of the arms of the Isle of Man, which, as you may or may not know, are three legs joined together, and kicking in different directions. This uncouth device is not an invention of the Manxmen, for it is found on some very ancient coins—Greek, I believe; but, at any rate, it is now the device of our subject Island of Man, and, like that set in motion, and nothing else, was the object that approached me, only it had a head where the three legs were joined, and a voice came out of the head to this effect: "Oh, missis, you hab to take me out of dis here bird-field; me no able to run after birds, and ebery night me lick because me no run after dem." When this apparition reached me and stood as still as it could, I perceived it consisted of a boy who said his name was "Jack de bird-driver." I suppose some vague idea of the fitness of things had induced them to send this living scarecrow into the cornfield, and if he had been set up in the midst of it, nobody, I am sure, would have imagined he was any thing else; but it seems he was expected to run after the

feathered fowl who alighted on the grain-field, and I do not
wonder that he did not fulfill this expectation. His feet,
legs, and knees were all maimed and distorted, his legs
were nowhere thicker than my wrist, his feet were a yard
apart from each other, and his knees swollen and knocking
together. What a creature to run after birds! He implored me to give him some meat, and have him sent back
to Little St. Simon's Island, from which he came, and
where he said his poor limbs were stronger and better.

Riding home, I passed some sassafras-trees, which are
putting forth deliciously fragrant tassels of small leaves
and blossoms, and other exquisite flowering shrubs, which
are new to me, and enchant me perhaps all the more for
their strangeness. Before reaching the house I was
stopped by one of our multitudinous Jennies with a request for some meat, and that I would help her with some
clothes for Ben and Daphne, of whom she had the sole
charge; these are two extremely pretty and interesting-
looking mulatto children, whose resemblance to Mr.
K—— had induced me to ask Mr. ——, when first I saw
them, if he did not think they must be his children. He
said they were certainly like him, but Mr. K—— did not
acknowledge the relationship. I asked Jenny who their
mother was. "Minda." "Who their father?" "Mr.
K——." "What! old Mr. K——?" "No, Mr. R——
K——." "Who told you so?" "Minda, who ought to
know." "Mr. K—— denies it." "That's because he
never has looked upon them, nor done a thing for them."
"Well, but he acknowledged Renty as his son, why should
he deny these?" "Because old master was here then
when Renty was born, and he made Betty tell all about
it, and Mr. K—— had to own it; but nobody knows any
thing about this, and so he denies it"—with which information I rode home. I always give you an exact report
of any conversation I may have with any of the people,

and you see from this that the people on the plantation themselves are much of my worthy neighbor Mr. C——'s mind, that the death of Major —— was a great misfortune for the slaves on his estate.

I went to the hospital this afternoon to see if the condition of the poor people was at all improved since I had been last there; but nothing had been done. I suppose Mr. G—— is waiting for Mr. —— to come down in order to speak to him about it. I found some miserable new cases of women disabled by hard work. One poor thing, called Priscilla, had come out of the fields to-day scarcely able to crawl; she has been losing blood for a whole fortnight without intermission, and, until to-day, was laboring in the fields. Leah, another new face since I visited the hospital last, is lying quite helpless from exhaustion; she is advanced in her pregnancy, and doing task-work in the fields at the same time. What piteous existences, to be sure! I do wonder, as I walk among them, well fed, well clothed, young, strong, idle, doing nothing but ride and drive about all day, a woman, a creature like themselves, who have borne children too, what sort of feeling they have toward me. I wonder it is not one of murderous hate—that they should lie here almost dying with unrepaid labor for me. I stand and look at them, and these thoughts work in my mind and heart, till I feel as if I must tell them how dreadful and how monstrous it seems to me myself, and how bitterly ashamed and grieved I feel for it all.

To-day I rode in the morning round poor Cripple Jack's bird-field again, through the sweet, spicy-smelling pine land, and home by my new road cut through Jones's wood, of which I am as proud as if I had made instead of found it—the grass, flowering shrubs, and all. In the afternoon I drove in the wood-wagon back to Jones's, and visited Busson Hill on the way, with performances of certain promises of flannel, quarters of dollars, etc., etc. At Jones's, the women to-day had all done their work at a quarter past three, and had swept their huts out very scrupulously for my reception. Their dwellings are shockingly dilapidated and overcrammed—poor creatures!—and it seems hard that, while exhorting them to spend labor in cleaning and making them tidy, I can not promise them that they shall be repaired and made habitable for them.

In driving home through my new wood cut, Jack gave me a terrible account of a flogging that a negro called Glasgow had received yesterday. He seemed awfully impressed with it, so I suppose it must have been an unusually severe punishment; but he either would not or could not tell me what the man had done. On my return to the house I found Mr. —— had come down from the rice plantation, whereat I was much delighted on all accounts. I am sure it is getting much too late for him to remain in that pestilential swampy atmosphere; besides, I want him to see my improvements in the new wood paths, and I want him to come and hear all these poor people's complaints and petitions himself. They have been flocking in to see him ever since it was known he had arrived. I met coming on that errand Dandy, the husband of the woman for whom I cut out the gown the other day; and asking him how it had answered, he gave a piteous account of its tearing all to pieces the first time she put it on; it had appeared to me perfectly rotten and good for nothing, and, upon questioning him as to where he bought it and what he paid for it, I had to hear a sad account of hardship and injustice. I have told you that the people collect moss from the trees and sell it to the shopkeepers in Darien for the purpose of stuffing furniture; they also raise poultry, and are allowed to dispose of the eggs in the same way. It seems that poor Dandy had taken the miserable material Edie's gown was made of as payment for a quantity of moss and eggs furnished by him at various times to one of the Darien storekeepers, who refused him payment in any other shape, and the poor fellow had no redress; and this, he tells me, is a frequent experience with all the slaves both here and at the rice-island. Of course, the rascally shopkeepers can cheat these poor wretches to any extent they please with perfect impunity.

Mr. —— told me of a visit Renty paid him, which was not a little curious in some of its particulars. You know none of the slaves are allowed the use of fire-arms; but Renty put up a petition to be allowed Mr. K——'s gun, which it seems that gentleman left behind him. Mr. —— refused this petition, saying at the same time to the lad that he knew very well that none of the people were allowed guns. Renty expostulated on the score of his *white blood*, and finding his master uninfluenced by that consideration, departed with some severe reflections on Mr. K——, his father, for not having left him his gun as a keepsake, in token of (paternal) affection, when he left the plantation.

It is quite late, and I am very tired, though I have not done much more than usual to-day, but the weather is beginning to be oppressive to me, who hate heat; but I find the people, and especially the sick in the hospital, speak of it as cold. I will tell you hereafter of a most comical account Mr. —— has given me of the prolonged and still protracted pseudo-pregnancy of a woman called Markie, who for many more months than are generally required for the process of continuing the human species, pretended to be what the Germans pathetically and poetically call "in good hope," and continued to reap increased rations as the reward of her expectation, till she finally had to disappoint the estate and receive a flogging.

He told me, too, what interested me very much, of a

conspiracy among Mr. C——'s slaves some years ago.
I can not tell you about it now; I will some other time.
It is wonderful to me that such attempts are not being
made the whole time among these people to regain their
liberty; probably because many are made ineffectually,
and never known beyond the limits of the plantation
where they take place.

————————

DEAR E——,—We have been having something like
Northern March weather—blinding sun, blinding wind,
and blinding dust, through all which, the day before yesterday, Mr. —— and I rode together round most of the
fields, and over the greater part of the plantation. It was
a detestable process, the more so that he rode Montreal
and I Miss Kate, and we had no small difficulty in managing them both. In the afternoon we had an equally detestable drive through the new wood paths to St. Annie's,
and having accomplished all my errands among the people there, we crossed over certain sounds, and seas, and
separating waters, to pay a neighborly visit to the wife
of one of our adjacent planters.

How impossible it would be for you to conceive, even
if I could describe, the careless desolation which pervaded
the whole place; the shaggy unkempt grounds we passed
through to approach the house; the ruinous, rackrent,
tumble-down house itself; the untidy, slatternly, all but
beggarly appearance of the mistress of the mansion herself. The smallest Yankee farmer has a tidier estate, a
tidier house, and a tidier wife than this member of the
proud Southern chivalry, who, however, inasmuch as he
has slaves, is undoubtedly a much greater personage in
his own estimation than those capital fellows W—— and
B——, who walk in glory and in joy behind their plows
upon your mountain sides. The Brunswick Canal project

was descanted upon, and pronounced, without a shadow of dissent, a scheme the impracticability of which all but convicted its projectors of insanity.  Certainly, if, as I hear, the moneyed men of Boston have gone largely into this speculation, their habitual sagacity must have been seriously at fault, for here on the spot nobody mentions the project but as a subject of utter derision.

While the men discussed about this matter, Mrs. B—— favored me with the congratulations I have heard so many times on the subject of my having a white nursery-maid for my children.  Of course, she went into the old subject of the utter incompetency of negro women to discharge such an office faithfully; but, in spite of her multiplied examples of their utter inefficiency, I believe the discussion ended by simply our both agreeing that ignorant negro girls of twelve years old are not as capable or trustworthy as well-trained white women of thirty.

Returning home, our route was changed, and Quash the boatman took us all the way round by water to Hampton. I should have told you that our exit was as wild as our entrance to this estate, and was made through a broken wooden fence, which we had to climb partly over and partly under, with some risk and some obloquy, in spite of our dexterity, as I tore my dress, and very nearly fell flat on my face in the process.  Our row home was perfectly enchanting; for, though the morning's wind and (I suppose) the state of the tide had roughened the waters of the great river, and our passage was not as smooth as it might have been, the wind had died away, the evening air was deliciously still, and mild, and soft.  A young slip of a moon glimmered just above the horizon, and "the stars climbed up the sapphire steps of heaven," while we made our way over the rolling, rushing, foaming waves, and saw to right and left the marsh fires burning in the swampy meadows, adding another colored light in the landscape to the amber-tinted lower sky and the violet arch above, and giving wild picturesqueness to the whole scene by throwing long flickering rays of flame upon the distant waters.

*Sunday, the* 14*th.* I read service again to-day to the people. You can not conceive any thing more impressive than the silent devotion of their whole demeanor while it lasted, nor more touching than the profound thanks with which they rewarded me when it was over, and they took their leave; and to-day they again left me with the utmost decorum of deportment, and without pressing a single petition or complaint such as they ordinarily thrust upon me on all other occasions, which seems to me an instinctive feeling of religious respect for the day and the business they have come upon, which does them infinite credit.

In the afternoon I took a long walk with the chicks in the woods—long at least for the little legs of S—— and M——, who carried baby. We came home by the shore, and I stopped to look at a jutting point, just below which a sort of bay would have afforded the most capital position for a bathing-house. If we staid here late in the season, such a refreshment would become almost a necessary of life, and any where along the bank just where I stopped to examine it to-day an establishment for that purpose might be prosperously founded.

I am amused, but by no means pleased, at an entirely new mode of pronouncing which S—— has adopted. Apparently the negro jargon has commended itself as euphonious to her infantile ears, and she is now treating me to the most ludicrous and accurate imitations of it every time she opens her mouth. Of course I shall not allow this, comical as it is, to become a habit. This is the way the Southern ladies acquire the thick and inelegant pronunciation which distinguishes their utterances from the Northern snuffle, and I have no desire that S—— should adorn her mother tongue with either peculiarity. It is a curious and sad enough thing to observe, as I have frequent opportunities of doing, the unbounded insolence and tyranny (of manner, of course it can go no farther) of the slaves toward each other. "Hi! you boy!" and "Hi! you girl!" shouted in an imperious scream, is the civilest mode of apostrophizing those at a distance from them; more frequently it is "You niggar, you hear? hi! you niggar!" And I assure you no contemptuous white intonation ever equaled the *prepotenza* of the despotic insolence of this address of these poor wretches to each other.

I have left my letter lying for a couple of days, dear E——. I have been busy and tired; my walking and riding is becoming rather more laborious to me, for, though nobody here appears to do so, I am beginning to feel the relaxing influence of the spring.

The day before yesterday I took a disagreeable ride, all through swampy fields, and charred, blackened thickets, to discover nothing either picturesque or beautiful; the woods in one part of the plantation have been on fire for three days, and a whole tract of exquisite evergreens has been burnt down to the ground. In the afternoon I drove in the wood-wagon to visit the people at St. Annie's. There has been rain these last two nights, and their wretched hovels do not keep out the weather; they are really miserable abodes for human beings. I think pigs who were at all particular might object to some of them. There is a woman at this settlement called Sophy, the wife of a driver, Morris, who is so pretty that I often wonder if it is only by contrast that I admire her so much, or if her gentle, sweet, refined face, in spite of its dusky color, would not approve itself any where to any one with an eye for beauty. Her manner and voice, too, are peculiarly soft and gentle; but, indeed, the voices of all these poor people, men as well as women, are much pleasanter and more melodious than the voices of white people in general. Most of the wretched hovels had been swept and tidied out in expectation of my visit, and many were the consequent petitions for rations of meat, flannel, osnaburgs, etc.; promising all which, in due proportion to the cleanliness of each separate dwelling, I came away. On my way home I called for a moment at Jones's settlement to leave money and presents promised to the people there for similar improvement in the condition of their huts. I had not time to stay and distribute my benefactions myself, and so appointed a particularly bright, intelligent-looking woman, called Jenny, paymistress in my stead, and her deputed authority was received with the utmost cheerfulness by them all.

I have been having a long talk with Mr. —— about Ben and Daphne, those two young mulatto children of Mr. K——'s, whom I mentioned to you lately. Poor pretty children ! they have refined and sensitive faces as well as straight, regular features; and the expression of the girl's countenance, as well as the sound of her voice, and the sad humility of her deportment, are indescribably touching. Mr. B—— expressed the strongest interest in and pity for them, *because of their color:* it seems unjust almost to the rest of their fellow-unfortunates that this should be so, and yet it is almost impossible to resist the impression of the unfitness of these two forlorn young creatures for the life of coarse labor and dreadful degradation to which they are destined. In any of the Southern cities the girl would be pretty sure to be reserved for a worse fate; but even here, death seems to me a thousand times preferable to the life that is before her.

In the afternoon I rode with Mr. —— to look at the fire in the woods. We did not approach it, but stood where the great volumes of smoke could be seen rising steadily above the pines, as they have now continued to

do for upward of a week; the destruction of the pine timber must be something enormous. We then went to visit
Dr. and Mrs. G——, and wound up these exercises of civilized life by a call on dear old Mr. C——, whose nursery
and kitchen garden are a real refreshment to my spirits.
How completely the national character of the worthy
canny old Scot is stamped on the care and thrift visible
in his whole property, the judicious, successful culture of
which has improved and adorned his dwelling in this remote corner of the earth! The comparison, or rather
contrast, between himself and his quondam neighbor, Major ——, is curious enough to contemplate. The Scotch
tendency of the one to turn every thing to good account,
the Irish propensity of the other to leave every thing to
ruin, to disorder, and neglect; the careful economy and
prudent management of the mercantile man, the reckless
profusion and careless extravagance of the soldier. The
one made a splendid fortune and spent it in Philadelphia,
where he built one of the finest houses that existed there
in the old-fashioned days, when fine old family mansions
were still to be seen breaking the monotonous uniformity
of the Quaker city. The other has resided here on his estate, ameliorating the condition of his slaves and his property, a benefactor to the people and the soil alike—a useful and a good existence, an obscure and tranquil one.

Last Wednesday we drove to Hamilton, by far the finest
estate on St. Simon's Island. The gentleman to whom it
belongs lives, I believe, habitually in Paris; but Captain
F—— resides on it, and, I suppose, is the real 'overseer of
the plantation. All the way along the road (we traversed
nearly the whole length of the island) we found great
tracts of wood all burnt or burning; the destruction had
spread in every direction, and against the sky we saw the
slow rising of the smoky clouds that showed the pine forest to be on. fire still. What an immense quantity of

property such a fire must destroy! The negro huts on several of the plantations that we passed through were the most miserable human habitations I ever beheld. The wretched hovels at St. Annie's, on the Hampton estate, that had seemed to me the *ne plus ultra* of misery, were really palaces to some of the dirty, desolate, dilapidated dog-kennels which we passed to-day, and out of which the negroes poured like black ants at our approach, and stood to gaze at us as we drove by.

The planters' residences we passed were only three. It makes one ponder seriously when one thinks of the mere handful of white people on this island. In the midst of this large population of slaves, how absolutely helpless they would be if the blacks were to become restive! They could be destroyed to a man before human help could reach them from the main, or the tidings even of what was going on be carried across the surrounding waters. As we approached the southern end of the island we began to discover the line of the white sea-sands beyond the bushes and fields, and presently, above the sparkling, dazzling line of snowy white—for the sands were as white as our English chalk cliffs—stretched the deep blue sea-line of the great Atlantic Ocean.

We found that there had been a most terrible fire in the Hamilton woods—more extensive than that on our own plantation. It seems as if the whole island had been burning at different points for more than a week. What a cruel pity and shame it does seem to have these beautiful masses of wood so destroyed! I suppose it is impossible to prevent it. The "field-hands" make fires to cook their midday food wherever they happen to be working, and sometimes through their careless neglect, but sometimes, too, undoubtedly on purpose, the woods are set fire to by these means. One benefit they consider that they derive from the process is the destruction of the dreaded rattlesnakes that infest the woodland all over the island; but really the funeral pyre of these hateful reptiles is too costly at this price.

Hamilton struck me very much—I mean the whole appearance of the place; the situation of the house, the noble water prospect it commanded, the magnificent old oaks near it, a luxuriant vine trellis, and a splendid hedge of yucca gloriosa, were all objects of great delight to me. The latter was most curious to me, who had never seen any but single specimens of the plant, and not many of these. I think our green-house at the North boasts but two; but here they were growing close together, and in such a manner as to form a compact and impenetrable hedge, their spiky leaves striking out on all sides like *chevaux de frise*, and the tall, slender stems, that bear those delicate ivory-colored bells of blossoms, springing up against the sky in a regular row. I wish I could see that hedge in blossom. It must be wonderfully strange and lovely, and must look by moonlight like a whole range of fairy Chinese pagodas carved in ivory.

At dinner we had some delicious green peas, so much in advance of you are we down here with the seasons. Don't you think one might accept the rattlesnakes, or perhaps indeed the slavery, for the sake of the green peas? 'Tis a world of compensations—a life of compromises, you know; and one should learn to set one thing against another if one means to thrive and fare well, *i. e.*, eat green peas on the twenty-eighth of March.

After dinner I walked up and down before the house for a long while with Mrs. F——, and had a most interesting conversation with her about the negroes and all the details of their condition. She is a kind-hearted, intelligent woman; but, though she seemed to me to acquiesce, as a matter of inevitable necessity, in the social system in the midst of which she was born and lives, she did not appear to me, by several things she said, to be by any means in love with it. She gave me a very sad character of Mr. K——, confirming by her general description of him the impression produced by all the details I have received from our own people. As for any care for the moral or religious training of the slaves, that, she said, was a matter that never troubled his thoughts; indeed, his only notion upon the subject of religion, she said, was that it was something *not bad* for white women and children.

We drove home by moonlight; and as we came toward the woods in the middle of the island, the fireflies glittered out from the dusky thickets as if some magical golden veil was every now and then shaken out into the darkness. The air was enchantingly mild and soft, and the whole way through the silvery night delightful.

My dear friend, I have at length made acquaintance with a live rattlesnake. Old Scylla had the pleasure of discovering it while hunting for some wood to burn. Israel captured it, and brought it to the house for my edification. I thought it an evil-looking beast, and could not help feeling rather nervous while contemplating it, though the poor thing had a noose round its neck, and could by no manner of means have extricated itself. The flat head, and vivid, vicious eye, and darting tongue, were none of them lovely to behold; but the sort of threatening whirr produced by its rattle, together with the deepening and fading of the marks on its skin, either with its respiration, or the emotions of fear and anger it was enduring, were peculiarly dreadful and fascinating. It was quite a young one, having only two or three rattles in its tail. These, as you probably know, increase in number by one annually, so that you can always tell the age of the amiable serpent you are examining—if it will let you count the number of joints of its rattle. Captain F—— gave me the rattle of one which had as many as twelve joints. He said it had belonged to a very large snake, which had crawled from under a fallen tree-trunk on which his children were playing. After exhibiting his interesting captive, Israel killed, stuffed, and presented it to me for preservation as a trophy, and made me extremely happy by informing me that there was a nest of them where this one was found. I think with terror of S—— running about with her little socks not reaching half way up her legs, and her little frocks not reaching half way down them. However, we shall probably not make acquaintance with many more of these natives of Georgia, as we are to return as soon as possible now to the North. We shall soon be free again.

This morning I rode to the burnt district, and attempted to go through it at St. Clair's, but unsuccessfully: it was impossible to penetrate through the charred and blackened thickets. In the afternoon I walked round the Point, and visited the houses of the people who are our nearest neighbors. I found poor Edie in sad tribulation at the prospect of resuming her field labor. It is really shameful treatment of a woman just after child-labor. She was confined exactly three weeks ago to-day, and she tells me she is ordered out to field-work on Monday. She seems to dread the approaching hardships of her task-labor extremely. Her baby was born dead, she thinks in consequence of a fall she had while carrying a heavy weight of water. She is suffering great pain in one of her legs and sides, and seems to me in a condition utterly unfit for any work, much less hoeing in the fields; but I dare not interfere to prevent this cruelty. She says she has already had to go out to work three weeks after her confinement with each of her other children, and does not complain of it as any thing special in her case. She says that is now the invariable rule of the whole plantation, though it used not to be so formerly.

I have let my letter lie since I wrote the above, dear E——; but as mine is a story without beginning, middle, or end, it matters extremely little where I leave it off or where I take it up; and if you have not, between my wood rides and sick slaves, come to Falstaff's conclusion that I have "damnable iteration," you are patient of sameness. But the days are like each other; and the rides and the people, and, alas! their conditions, do not vary.

To-day, however, my visit to the Infirmary was marked by an event which has not occurred before—the death of one of the poor slaves while I was there. I found, on entering the first ward—to use a most inapplicable term for the dark, filthy, forlorn room I have so christened—an old negro called Friday lying on the ground. I asked what ailed him, and was told he was dying. I approached him, and perceived, from the glazed eyes and the feeble rattling breath, that he was at the point of expiring. His tattered shirt and trowsers barely covered his poor body; his appearance was that of utter exhaustion from age and feebleness; he had nothing under him but a mere handful of straw that did not cover the earth he was stretched on; and under his head, by way of pillow for his dying agony, two or three rough sticks just raising his skull a few inches from the ground. The flies were all gathering around his mouth, and not a creature was near him. There he lay—the worn-out slave, whose life had been spent in unrequited labor for me and mine, without one physical alleviation, one Christian solace, one human sympathy, to cheer him in his extremity—panting out the last breath of his wretched existence like some forsaken, overworked, wearied-out beast of burden, rotting where it falls! I bent over the poor awful human creature in the supreme hour of his mortality; and while my eyes, blinded with tears of unavailing pity and horror, were fixed upon him, there was a sudden quivering of the eyelids and falling of the jaw—and he was free. I stood up, and remained long lost in the imagination of the change that creature had undergone, and in the tremendous overwhelming consciousness of the deliverance God had granted the soul whose cast-off vesture of decay lay at my feet. How I rejoiced for him; and how, as I turned to the wretches who were calling to me from the inner room, whence they could see me as I stood contemplating the piteous object, I wished they all were gone away with him, the delivered, the freed by death from bitter, bitter bondage. In the next room I found a miserable, decrepid old negress, called Charity, lying sick, and I should think near too to die; but she did not think her work was over, much as she looked unfit for farther work on earth; but with feeble voice and beseeching hands implored me to have her work lightened when she was sent back to it from the hospital. She is one of the oldest slaves on the plantation, and has to walk to her field labor, and back again at night, a distance of nearly four miles. There were an unusual number of sick women in the room to-day; among them quite a young girl, daughter of Boatman Quash's, with a sick baby, who has a father, though she has no husband. Poor thing! she looks like a mere child herself. I returned home so very sad and heart-sick that I could not rouse myself to the effort of going up to St. Annie's with the presents I had promised the people there. I sent M—— up in the wood-wagon with them, and remained in the house with my thoughts, which were none of the merriest.

———

DEAREST E——,—On Friday I rode to where the rattlesnake was found, and where I was informed by the negroes there was a *nest* of them—a pleasing domestic picture of home and infancy that word suggests, not altogether appropriate to rattlesnakes, I think. On horseback I felt bold to accomplish this adventure, which I certainly should not have attempted on foot; however, I could discover no sign of either snake or nest—(perhaps it is of the nature of a mare's nest, and undiscoverable) ; but, having done my duty by myself in endeavoring to find it, I rode off and coasted the estate by the side of the marsh till I came to the causeway. There I found a new cleared field, and stopped to admire the beautiful appearance of the stumps of the trees scattered all about it, and wreathed and garlanded with the most profuse and fantastic growth of various plants, wild roses being among the most abundant. What a lovely aspect one side of nature presents here, and how hideous is the other!

In the afternoon I drove to pay a visit to old Mrs. A——, the lady proprietress whose estate immediately adjoins ours. On my way thither I passed a woman called Margaret walking rapidly and powerfully along the road. She was returning home from the field, having done her task at three o'clock; and told me, with a merry, beaming black face, that she was going "to clean up de house, to please de missis." On driving through my neighbor's grounds, I was disgusted more than I can express with the miserable negro huts of her people; they were not fit to shelter cattle—they were not fit to shelter any thing, for they were literally in holes, and, as we used to say of our stockings at school, too bad to darn. To be sure, I will say, in excuse for their old mistress, her own habitation was but a very few degrees less ruinous and disgusting. What would one of your Yankee farmers say to such abodes? When I think of the white houses, the green blinds, and the flower-plots of the villages in New England, and look at these dwellings of lazy filth and inert degradation, it does seem amazing to think that physical and moral conditions so widely opposite should be found among people occupying a similar place in the social scale of the same country. The Northern farmer, however, thinks it no shame to work, the Southern planter does; and there begins and ends the difference. Industry, man's crown of honor elsewhere, is here his badge of utter degradation; and so comes all by which I am here surrounded—pride, profligacy, idleness, cruelty, cowardice, ignorance, squalor, dirt, and ineffable abasement.

When I returned home I found that Mrs. F—— had sent me some magnificent prawns. I think of having them served singly, and divided as one does a lobster—their size really suggests no less respect.

*Saturday*, 31*st*. I rode all through the burnt district and the bush to Mrs. W——'s field, in making my way out of which I was very nearly swamped, and, but for the valuable assistance of a certain sable Scipio who came up and extricated me, I might be floundering hopelessly there still. He got me out of my Slough of Despond, and put me in the way to a charming wood ride which runs between Mrs. W——'s and Colonel H——'s grounds. While going along this delightful boundary of these two neighboring estates, my mind not unnaturally dwelt upon the terms of deadly feud in which the two families owning them are living with each other. A horrible quarrel has occurred quite lately upon the subject of the ownership of this very ground I was skirting, between Dr. H—— and young Mr. W——; they have challenged each other, and what I am going to tell you is a good sample of the sort of spirit which grows up among slaveholders. So read it, for it is curious to people who have not lived habitually among savages. The terms of the challenge that has passed between them have appeared like a sort of advertisement in the local paper, and are to the effect that they are to fight at a certain distance with

certain weapons—fire-arms, of course; that there is to be
on the person of each a white paper, or mark, immediately
over the region of the heart, as a point for direct aim;
and whoever kills 'the other is to have the privilege of
*cutting off his head, and sticking it up on a pole on the
piece of land which was the origin of the debate ;* so that,
some fine day, I might have come hither as I did to-day,
and found myself riding under the shadow of the gory
locks of Dr. H—— or Mr. W——, my peaceful and pleasant neighbors.

I came home through our own pine woods, which are
actually a wilderness of black desolation. The scorched
and charred tree-trunks are still smoking and smouldering; the ground is a sort of charcoal pavement, and the
fire is still burning on all sides, for the smoke was rapidly
rising in several directions on each hand of the path I pursued. Across this dismal scene of strange destruction,
bright blue and red birds, like living jewels, darted in the
brilliant sunshine. I wonder if the fire has killed and
scared away many of these beautiful creatures. In the
afternoon I took Jack with me to clear some more of the
wood paths; but the weather is what I call hot, and what
the people here think warm, and the air was literally thick
with little black points of insects, which they call sand-
flies, and which settle upon one's head and face literally
like a black net; you hardly see them or feel them at the
time, but the irritation occasioned by them is intolerable,
and I had to relinquish my work and fly before this winged
plague as fast as I could from my new acquaintance the
rattlesnakes. Jack informed me, in the course of our expedition, that the woods on the island were sometimes
burnt away in order to leave the ground in grass for fod-
der for the cattle, and that the very beautiful ones he and
I had been clearing paths through were not unlikely to
be so doomed, which strikes me as a horrible idea.

In the evening poor Edie came up to the house to see me, with an old negress called Sackey, who has been one of the chief nurses on the island for many years. I suppose she has made some application to Mr. G—— for a respite for Edie, on finding how terribly unfit she is for work; or perhaps Mr. ——, to whom I represented her case, may have ordered her reprieve; but she came with much gratitude to me (who have, as far as I know, had nothing to do with it), to tell me that she is not to be sent into the field for another week. Old Sackey fully confirmed Edie's account of the terrible hardships the women underwent in being thus driven to labor before they had recovered from childbearing. She said that old Major —— allowed the women at the rice-island five weeks, and those here four weeks, to recover from a confinement, and then never permitted them for some time after they resumed their work to labor in the fields before sunrise or after sunset; but Mr. K—— had altered that arrangement, allowing the women at the rice-island only four weeks, and those here only three weeks, for their recovery; "and then, missis," continued the old woman, "out into the field again, through dew and dry, as if nothing had happened; that is why, missis, so many of the women have falling of the womb and weakness in the back; and if he had continued on the estate, he would have utterly destroyed all the breeding women." Sometimes, after sending them back into the field at the expiration of their three weeks, they would work for a day or two, she said, and then fall down in the field with exhaustion, and be brought to the hospital almost at the point of death.

Yesterday, Sunday, I had my last service at home with these poor people; nearly thirty of them came, all clean, neat, and decent, in their dress and appearance. S—— had begged very hard to join the congregation, and upon the most solemn promise of remaining still she was ad-

mitted; but, in spite of the perfect honor with which she
kept her promise, her presence disturbed my thoughts
not a little, and added much to the poignancy of the feeling with which I saw her father's poor slaves gathered
round me. The child's exquisite complexion, large gray
eyes, and solemn and at the same time eager countenance,
was such a wonderful piece of contrast to their sable
faces, so many of them so uncouth in their outlines and
proportions, and yet all of them so pathetic, and some so
sublime in their expression of patient suffering and religious fervor : their eyes never wandered from me and my
child, who sat close by my knee, their little mistress, their
future providence, my poor baby! Dear E——, bless
God that you have never reared a child with such an
awful expectation : and at the end of the prayers, the
tears were streaming over their faces, and one chorus of
blessings rose round me and the child—farewell blessings,
and prayers that we would return; and thanks so fervent
in their incoherency, it was more than I could bear, and
I begged them to go away and leave me to recover myself. And then I remained with S——, and for quite a
long while even her restless spirit was still in wondering
amazement at my bitter crying. I am to go next Sunday to the church on the island, where there is to be
service; and so this is my last Sunday with the people.

When I had recovered from the emotion of this scene,
I walked out with S—— a little way, but meeting M——
and the baby, she turned home with them, and I pursued
my walk alone up the road, and home by the shore. They
are threatening to burn down all my woods to make grass-
land for the cattle, and I have terrified them by telling
them that I will never come back if they destroy the
woods. I went and paid a visit to Mrs. G——; poor little, well-meaning, helpless woman, what can she do for
these poor people, where I, who am supposed to own

them, can do nothing? and yet how much may be done, is done, by the brain and heart of one human being in contact with another! We are answerable for incalculable opportunities of good and evil in our daily intercourse with every soul with whom we have to deal; every meeting, every parting, every chance greeting, and every appointed encounter, are occasions open to us for which we are to account. To our children, our servants, our friends, our acquaintances—to each and all every day, and all day long, we are distributing that which is best or worst in existence—influence: with every word, with every look, with every gesture, something is given or withheld of great importance it may be to the receiver, of inestimable importance to the giver.

Certainly the laws and enacted statutes on which this detestable system is built up are potent enough; the social prejudice that buttresses it is almost more potent still; and yet a few hearts and brains well bent to do the work would bring within this almost impenetrable dungeon of ignorance, misery, and degradation, in which so many millions of human souls lie buried, that freedom of God which would presently conquer for them their earthly liberty. With some such thoughts I commended the slaves on the plantation to the little overseer's wife; I did not tell my thoughts to her—they would have scared the poor little woman half out of her senses. To begin with, her bread, her husband's occupation, has its root in slavery; it would be difficult for her to think as I do of it. I am afraid her care, even of the bodily habits and sicknesses of the people left in Mrs. G——'s charge, will not be worth much, for nobody treats others better than they do themselves; and she is certainly doing her best to injure herself and her own poor baby, who is two and a half years old, and whom she is still suckling.

This is, I think, the worst case of this extraordinary

delusion so prevalent among your women that I have ever met with yet; but they all nurse their children much longer than is good for either baby or mother. The summer heat, particularly when a young baby is cutting teeth, is, I know, considered by young American mothers an exceedingly critical time, and therefore I always hear of babies being nursed till after the second summer; so that a child born in January would be suckled till it was eighteen or nineteen months old, in order that it might not be weaned till its second summer was over. I am sure that nothing can be worse than this system, and I attribute much of the wretched ill health of young American mothers to over-nursing; and of course a process that destroys their health and vigor completely must affect most unfavorably the child they are suckling. It is a grievous mistake. I remember my charming friend F—— D—— telling me that she had nursed her first child till her second was born—a miraculous statement, which I can only believe because she told it me herself. Whenever any thing seems absolutely impossible, the word of a true person is the only proof of it worth any thing.

---

DEAR E——,—I have been riding into the swamp behind the new house; I had a mind to survey the ground all round it before going away, to see what capabilities it afforded for the founding of a garden, but I confess it looked very unpromising. Trying to return by another way, I came to a morass, which, after contemplating, and making my horse try for a few paces, I thought it expedient not to attempt. A woman named Charlotte, who was working in the field, seeing my dilemma, and the inglorious retreat I was about to make, shouted to me at the top of her voice, " You no turn back, missis; if you want to go through, send, missis, send; you hab slave enough, nigger enough, let 'em come, let 'em fetch planks, and make de bridge; what you say dey must do—send, missis, send, missis!" It seemed to me, from the lady's imperative tone in my behalf, that if she had been in my place, she would presently have had a corduroy road through the swamp of prostrate "niggers," as she called her family in Ham, and have ridden over the sand dry-hoofed; and to be sure, if I pleased, so might I, for, as she very truly said, "what you say, missis, they must do." Instead of summoning her sooty tribe, however, I backed my horse out of the swamp, and betook myself to another pretty wood path, which only wants widening to be quite charming. At the end of this, however, I found swamp the second, and out of this having been helped by a grinning, facetious personage, most appropriately named Pun, I returned home in dudgeon, in spite of whât dear Miss M—— calls the "moral suitability" of finding a foul bog at the end of every charming wood path or forest ride in this region.

In the afternoon I drove to Busson Hill to visit the people there. I found that both the men and women had done their work at half past three. Saw Tema with her child, that ridiculous image of Driver Bran, in her arms, in spite of whose whity-brown skin she still maintains that its father is a man as black as herself—and she (to use a most extraordinary comparison I heard of a negro girl making with regard to her mother) is as black as "de hinges of hell." Query: Did she really mean hinges, or angels? The angels of hell is a polite and pretty paraphrase for devils, certainly. In complimenting a woman called Joan upon the tidy condition of her house, she answered, with that cruel humility that is so bad an element in their character, "Missis no 'spect to find colored folks' house clean as white folks'." The mode in which they have learned to accept the idea of their own degradation and unalterable inferiority is the most serious impediment that I see in the way of their progress, since assuredly "self-love is not so vile a sin as self-neglecting." In the same way yesterday, Abraham the cook, in speaking of his brother's theft at the rice-island, said "it was a shame even for a colored man to do such things." I labor hard, whenever any such observation is made, to explain to them that the question is one of moral and mental culture—not the color of an integument—and assure them, much to my own comfort, whatever it may be to theirs, that white people are as dirty and as dishonest as colored folks, when they have suffered the same lack of decent training. If I could but find one of these women on whose mind the idea had' dawned that she was neither more nor less than my equal, I think I should embrace her in an ecstasy of hopefulness.

In the evening, while I was inditing my journal for your edification, Tema made her appearance with her Bran-brown baby, having walked all the way down from Busson Hill to claim a little sugar I had promised her. She had made her child perfectly clean, and it looked quite pretty. When I asked her what I should give her the sugar in, she snatched her filthy handkerchief off her head; but I declined this sugar-basin, and gave it to her in some paper. Hannah came on the same errand.

After all, dear E——, we shall not leave Georgia so soon as I expected; we can not get off for at least another week. You know, our movements are apt to be both tardy and uncertain. I am getting sick in spirit of my stay here; but I think the spring heat is beginning to affect me miserably, and I long for a cooler atmosphere. Here, on St. Simon's, the climate is perfectly healthy, and our neighbors, many of them, never stir from their plantations within reach of the purifying sea influence. But a land that grows magnolias is not fit for me—I was going to say magnolias and rattlesnakes; but I remember K——'s adventure with her friend the rattlesnake of Monument Mountain, and the wild wood-covered hill half way between Lenox and Stockbridge, which your Berkshire farmers have christened Rattlesnake Mountain. These agreeable serpents seem, like the lovely little humming-birds which are found in your northernmost as well as southernmost states, to have an accommodating disposition with regard to climate.

Not only is the vicinity of the sea an element of salubrity here, but the great masses of pine wood growing in every direction indicate lightness of soil and purity of air. Wherever these fragrant, dry, aromatic fir forests extend, there can be no inherent malaria, I should think, in either atmosphere or soil. The beauty and profusion of the weeds and wild flowers in the fields now is something, too, enchanting. I wish I could spread one of these enameled tracts on the side of one of your snow-covered hills now, for I dare say they are snow-covered yet.

I must give you an account of Aleck's first reading lesson, which took place at the same time that I gave S—— hers this morning. It was the first time he had had leisure to come, and it went off most successfully. He seems to me by no means stupid. I am very sorry he did not ask me to do this before; however, if he can master his alphabet before I go, he may, if chance favor him with the occasional sight of a book, help himself on by degrees. Perhaps he will have the good inspiration to apply to Cooper London for assistance; I am much mistaken if that worthy does not contrive that Heaven shall help Aleck, as it formerly did him, in the matter of reading.

I rode with Jack afterward, showing him where I wish paths to be cut and brushwood removed. I passed the new house, and again circumvented it meditatingly to discover its available points of possible future comeliness, but remained as convinced as ever that there are absolute-

ly none. Within the last two days a perfect border of
the dark blue virginicum has burst into blossom on each
side of the road, fringing it with purple as far as one can
look along it; it is lovely. I must tell you of something
which has delighted me greatly. I told Jack yesterday
that, if any of the boys liked, when they had done their
tasks, to come and clear the paths that I want widened
and trimmed, I would pay them a certain small sum per
hour for their labor; and behold, three boys have come,
having done their tasks early in the afternoon, to apply
for *work* and *wages:* so much for a suggestion not barely
twenty-four hours old, and so much for a prospect of compensation!

In the evening I attempted to walk out when the air
was cool, but had to run precipitately back into the house
to escape from the clouds of sand-flies that had settled on
my neck and arms. The weather has suddenly become in-
tensely hot; at least that is what it appears to me. After I had come in I had a visit from Venus and her daughter, a young girl of ten years old, for whom she begged a
larger allowance of food, as, she said, what she received
for her was totally inadequate to the girl's proper nourishment. I was amazed, upon inquiry, to find that three
quarts of grits a week—that is not a pint a day—was considered a sufficient supply for children of her age. The
mother said her child was half-famished on it, and it seemed to me terribly little.

My little workmen have brought me in from the woods
three darling little rabbits which they have contrived to
catch. They seemed to me slightly different from our
English bunnies; and Captain F——, who called to-day,
gave me a long account of how they differed from the
same animal in the Northern states. I did not like to
mortify my small workmen by refusing their present; but
the poor little things must be left to run wild again, for

we have no conveniences for pets here, besides we are just weighing anchor ourselves. I hope these poor little fluffy things will not meet any rattlesnakes on their way back to the woods.

I had a visit for flannel from one of our Dianas to-day —who had done her task in the middle of the day, yet came to receive her flannel—the most horribly dirty human creature I ever beheld, unless, indeed, her child, whom she brought with her, may have been half a degree dirtier.

The other day, Psyche (you remember the pretty under nurse, the poor thing whose story I wrote you from the rice plantation) asked me if her mother and brothers might be allowed to come and see her when we are gone away. I asked her some questions about them, and she told me that one of her brothers, who belonged to Mr. K——, was hired by that gentleman to a Mr. G——, of Darien, and that, upon the latter desiring to purchase him, Mr. K—— had sold the man without apprising him or any one member of his family that he had done so—a humane proceeding that makes one's blood boil when one hears of it. He had owned the man ever since he was a boy. Psyche urged me very much to obtain an order permitting her to see her mother and brothers. I will try and obtain it for her; but there seems generally a great objection to the visits of slaves from neighboring plantations, and, I have no doubt, not without sufficient reason. The more I see of this frightful and perilous social system, the more I feel that those who live in the midst of it must make their whole existence one constant precaution against danger of some sort or other.

I have given Aleck a second reading lesson with S——, who takes an extreme interest in his newly-acquired alphabetical lore. He is a very quick and attentive scholar, and I should think a very short time would suffice to teach him to read; but, alas! I have not even that short time. When I had done with my class I rode off with Jack, who has become quite an expert horseman, and rejoices in being lifted out of the immediate region of snakes by the length of his horse's legs. I cantered through the new wood paths, and took a good sloping galop through the pine land to St. Annie's. The fire is actually still burning in the woods. I came home quite tired with the heat, though my ride was not a long one.

Just as I had taken off my habit and was preparing to start off with M—— and the chicks for Jones's in the wood-wagon, old Dorcas, one of the most decrepid, rheumatic, and miserable old negresses from the farther end of the plantation, called in to beg for some sugar. She had walked the whole way from her own settlement, and seemed absolutely exhausted then, and yet she had to walk all the way back. It was not otherwise than slightly meritorious in me, my dear E——, to take her up in the wagon and endure her abominable dirt and foulness in the closest proximity, rather than let her drag her poor old limbs all that way back; but I was glad when we gained her abode and lost her company. I am mightily reminded occasionally in these parts of Trinculo's soliloquy over Caliban. The people at Jones's had done their work at half past three. Most of the houses were tidy and clean, so were many of the babies. On visiting the cabin of an exceedingly decent woman called Peggy, I found her, to my surprise, possessed of a fine large Bible. She told me her husband, Carpenter John, can read, and that she means to make him teach her. The fame of Aleck's literature has evidently reached Jones's, and they are not afraid to tell me that they can read or wish to learn to do so. This poor woman's health is miserable; I never saw a more weakly, sickly-looking creature. She says she has been broken down ever since the birth of her last child. I asked her how soon after her confinement she went out into the field to work again. She answered very quietly, but with a deep sigh, "Three weeks, missis; de usual time." As I was going away, a man named Martin came up, and with great vehemence besought me to give him a Prayer-book. In the evening he came down to fetch it, and to show me that he can read. I was very much pleased to see that they had taken my hint about nailing wooden slats across the windows of their poor huts, to prevent the constant ingress of the poultry. This in it-self will produce an immense difference in the cleanliness and comfort of their wretched abodes. In one of the huts I found a broken looking-glass; it was the only piece of furniture of the sort that I had yet seen among them. The woman who owned it was, I am sorry to say, pecul-iarly untidy and dirty, and so were her children; so that I felt rather inclined to scoff at the piece of civilized van-ity, which I should otherwise have greeted as a promising sign.

I drove home, late in the afternoon, through the sweet-smelling woods, that are beginning to hum with the voice of thousands of insects. My troop of volunteer workmen is increased to five—five lads working for my wages after they have done their task-work; and this evening, to my no small amazement, Driver Bran came down to join them for an hour, after working all day at Five Pound, which certainly shows zeal and energy.

Dear E——, I have been riding through the woods all the morning with Jack, giving him directions about the clearings, which I have some faint hope may be allowed to continue after my departure. I went on an exploring expedition round some distant fields, and then home through the St. Annie's woods. They have almost strip-ped the trees and thickets along the swamp road since I first came here. I wonder what it is for; not fuel surely, nor to make grass-land of, or otherwise cultivate the swamp. I do deplore these pitiless clearings; and as to this once pretty road, it looks "forlorn," as a worthy Pennsylvania farmer's wife once said to me of a pretty hill-side from which her husband had ruthlessly felled a beautiful grove of trees.

I had another snake encounter in my ride this morning. Just as I had walked my horse through the swamp, and while contemplating ruefully its naked aspect, a huge black snake wriggled rapidly across the path, and I pulled my reins tight and opened my mouth wide with horror. These hideous-looking creatures are, I believe, not poisonous, but they grow to a monstrous size, and have tremendous *constrictive* power. I have heard stories that sound like the nightmare of their fighting desperately with those deadly creatures, rattlesnakes. I can not conceive, if the black snakes are not poisonous, what chance they have against such antagonists, let their squeezing powers be what they will. How horrid it did look, *slithering* over the road! Perhaps the swamp has been cleared on account of its harboring these dreadful worms.

I rode home very fast, in spite of the exquisite fragrance of the wild cherry blossoms, the carpets and curtains of wild flowers, among which a sort of glorified dandelion glowed conspicuously—dandelions such as I should think grew in the garden of Eden, if there were any at all there. I passed the finest magnolia that I have yet seen; it was magnificent, and I suppose had been spared for its beauty, for it grew in the very middle of a cotton-field; it was as large as a fine forest tree, and its huge glittering leaves shone like plates of metal in the sun; what a spectacle that tree must be in blossom, and I should think its perfume must be smelt from one end of the plantation to the other. What a glorious creature! Which do you think ought to weigh most in the scale, the delight of such a vegetable, or the disgust of the black animal I had just met a few minutes before? Would you take the one with the other? Neither would I.

I have spent the whole afternoon at home; my "gang" is busily at work again. Sawney, one of them, came to join it nearly at sundown, not having got through his day's task before. In watching and listening to these lads, I was constantly struck with the insolent tyranny of their demeanor toward each other. This is almost a universal characteristic of the manner of the negroes among themselves. They are diabolically cruel to animals too, and they seem to me, as a rule, hardly to know the difference between truth and falsehood. These detestable qualities, which I constantly hear attributed to them as innate and inherent in their race, appear to me the direct result of their condition. The individual exceptions among them are, I think, quite as many as would be found, under similar circumstances, among the same number of white people.

In considering the whole condition of the people on this plantation, it appears to me that the principal hardships fall to the lot of the women—that is, the principal physical hardships. The very young members of the community are of course idle and neglected; the very, very old, idle and neglected too; the middle-aged men do not appear to me overworked, and lead a mere animal existence, in itself not peculiarly cruel or distressing, but involving a constant element of fear and uncertainty, and the trifling evils of unrequited labor, ignorance the most profound (to which they are condemned by law), and the unutterable injustice which precludes them from all the merits and all the benefits of voluntary exertion, and the progress that results from it. If they are absolutely unconscious of these evils, then they are not very ill-off brutes, always barring the chance of being given or sold away from their mates or their young—processes which even brutes do

not always relish. I am very much struck with the vein
of melancholy, which assumes almost a poetical tone in
some of the things they say. Did I tell you of that poor
old decrepid creature Dorcas, who came to beg some sugar of me the other day? saying, as she took up my watch
from the table and looked at it, "Ah! I need not look at
this; I have almost done with time!" Was not that
striking from such a poor old ignorant crone?

---

DEAR E——,—This is the fourth day that I have had
a " gang" of lads working in the woods for me after their
task hours for pay; you can not think how zealous and
energetic they are; I dare say the novelty of the process
pleases them almost as much as the money they earn.    I
must say they quite deserve their small wages.

Last night I received a present from Mrs. F—— of a
drum-fish, which animal I had never beheld before, and
which seemed to me first cousin to the great Leviathan.
It is to be eaten, and is certainly the biggest fish food I
ever saw; however, every thing is in proportion, and the
prawns that came with it are upon a similarly extensive
scale; this magnificent piscatorial bounty was accompanied by a profusion of Hamilton green peas, really a
munificent supply.

I went out early after breakfast with Jack hunting for
new paths; we rode all along the road by Jones's Creek,
and most beautiful it was. We skirted the plantation
burial-ground, and a dismal place it looked; the cattle
trampling over it in every direction, except where Mr.
K—— had had an inclosure put up round the graves of
two white men who had worked on the estate. They
were strangers, and of course utterly indifferent to the
people here; but by virtue of their white skins, their resting-place was protected from the hoofs of the cattle, while

the parents and children, wives, husbands, brothers and sisters, of the poor slaves, sleeping beside them, might see the graves of those they loved trampled upon and browsed over, desecrated and defiled, from morning till night. There is something intolerably cruel in this disdainful denial of a common humanity pursuing these wretches even when they are hid beneath the earth.

The day was exquisitely beautiful, and I explored a new wood path, and found it all strewed with a lovely wild flower not much unlike a primrose. I spent the afternoon at home. I dread going out twice a day now, on account of the heat and the sand-flies. While I was sitting by the window, Abraham, our cook, went by with some most revolting-looking "raw material" (part, I think, of the interior of the monstrous drum-fish of which I have told you). I asked him, with considerable disgust, what he was going to do with it; he replied, "Oh! we colored people eat it, missis." Said I, "Why do you say we colored people?" "Because, missis, white people won't touch what we too glad of." "That," said I, "is because you are poor, and do not often have meat to eat, not because you are colored, Abraham; rich white folks will not touch what poor white folks are too glad of; it has nothing in the world to do with color; and if there were white people here worse off than you (amazing and inconceivable suggestion, I fear), they would be glad to eat what you perhaps would not touch." Profound pause of meditation on the part of Abraham, wound up by a considerate "Well, missis, I suppose so;" after which he departed with the horrid-looking offal.

To-day—Saturday—I took another ride of discovery round the fields by Jones's. I think I shall soon be able to survey this estate, I have ridden so carefully over it in every direction; but my rides are drawing to a close, and even were I to remain here this must be the case, unless

I got up and rode under the stars in the cool of the night. This afternoon I was obliged to drive up to St. Annie's : I had promised the people several times that I would do so. I went after dinner and as late as I could, and found very considerable improvement in the whole condition of the place; the houses had all been swept, and some of them actually scoured. The children were all quite tolerably clean; they had put slats across all their windows, and little chicken-gates to the doors to keep out the poultry. There was a poor woman lying in one of the cabins in a wretched condition. She begged for a bandage, but I do not see of what great use that can be to her, as long as she has to hoe in the fields so many hours a day, which I can not prevent.

Returning home, Israel undertook to pilot me across the cotton-fields into the pine land; and a more excruciating process than being dragged over that very uneven surface in that wood-wagon without springs I did never endure, mitigated and soothed though it was by the literally fascinating account my charioteer gave me of the rattlesnakes with which the place we drove through becomes infested as the heat increases. I can not say that his description of them, though more demonstrative as far as regarded his own horror of them, was really worse than that which Mr. G—— was giving me of them yesterday. He said they were very numerous, and were found in every direction all over the plantation, but that they did not become really vicious until quite late in the summer; until then, it appears that they generally endeavor to make off if one meets them, but during the intense heats of the latter part of July and August they never think of escaping, but at any sight or sound which they may consider inimical they instantly coil themselves for a spring. The most intolerable proceeding on their part, however, that he described, was their getting up into the trees, and either coiling themselves in or depending from the branches. There is something too revolting in the idea of serpents looking down upon one from the shade of the trees to which one may betake one's self for shelter in the dreadful heat of the Southern midsummer; decidedly I do not think the dog-days would be pleasant here. The moccasin snake, which is nearly as deadly as the rattlesnake, abounds all over the island.

In the evening I had a visit from Mr. C—— and Mr. B——, who officiates to-morrow at our small island church. The conversation I had with these gentlemen was sad enough. They seem good, and kind, and amiable men, and I have no doubt are conscientious in their capacity of slaveholders; but to one who has lived outside this dreadful atmosphere, the whole tone of their discourse has a morally muffled sound, which one must hear to be able to conceive. Mr. B—— told me that the people on this plantation not going to church was the result of a positive order from Mr. K——, who had peremptorily forbidden their doing so, and of course to have infringed that order would have been to incur severe corporal chastisement. Bishop B——, it seems, had advised that there should be periodical preaching on the plantations, which, said Mr. B——, would have obviated any necessity for the people of different estates congregating at any given point at stated times, which might perhaps be objectionable, and at the same time would meet the reproach which was now beginning to be directed toward Southern planters as a class, of neglecting the eternal interest of their dependents. But Mr. K—— had equally objected to this. He seems to have held religious teaching a mighty dangerous thing—and how right he was! I have met with conventional cowardice of various shades and shapes in various societies that I have lived in, but any thing like the pervading timidity of tone which I

find here on all subjects, but, above all, on that of the condition of the slaves, I have never dreamed of. Truly slavery begets slavery, and the perpetual state of suspicion
and apprehension of the slaveholders is a very handsome
offset, to say the least of it, against the fetters and the
lash of the slaves. Poor people, one and all, but especially
poor oppressors of the oppressed! The attitude of these
men is really pitiable; they profess (perhaps some of them
strive to do so indeed) to consult the best interests of their
slaves, and yet shrink back terrified from the approach of
the slightest intellectual or moral improvement which
might modify their degraded and miserable existence. I
do pity these deplorable servants of two masters more
than any human beings I have ever seen—more than their
own slaves a thousand times!

To-day is Sunday, and I have been to the little church
on the island. It is the second time since I came down
to the South that I have been to a place of worship. A
curious little incident prefaced my going thither this
morning. I had desired Israel to get my horse ready and
himself to accompany me, as I meant to ride to church;
and you can not imagine any thing droller than his horror and dismay when he at length comprehended that my
purpose was to attend divine service in my riding-habit.
I asked him what was the trouble; for, though I saw
something was creating a dreadful convulsion in his mind,
I had no idea what it was till he told me, adding that he
had never seen such a thing on St. Simon's in his life—as
who should say, such a thing was never seen in Hyde
Park or the Tuileries before. You may imagine my
amusement; but presently I was destined to shock something much more serious than poor Israel's sense of *les
convénances et bienséances*, and it was not without something of an effort that I made up my mind to do so. I
was standing at the open window speaking to him about

the horses, and telling him to get ready to ride with me, when George, another of the men, went by with a shade or visor to his cap exactly the shape of the one I left behind at the North, and for want of which I have been suffering severely from the intense heat and glare of the sun for the last week. I asked him to hand me his cap, saying, "I want to take the pattern of that shade." Israel exclaimed, "Oh, missis, not to-day; let him leave the cap with you to-morrow, but don't cut pattern on de Sabbath day!" It seemed to me a much more serious matter to offend this scruple than the prejudice with regard to praying in a riding-habit; still, it had to be done. "Do you think it wrong, Israel," said I, "to work on Sunday?" "Yes, missis, parson tell we so." "Then, Israel, be sure you never do it. Did your parson never tell you that your conscience was for yourself and not for your neighbors, Israel?" "Oh yes, missis, he tell we that too." "Then mind that too, Israel." The shade was cut out and stitched upon my cap, and protected my eyes from the fierce glare of the sun and sand as I rode to church.

On our way we came to a field where the young corn was coming up. The children were in the field—little living scarecrows—watching it, of course, as on a week-day, to keep off the birds. I made Israel observe this, who replied, "Oh, missis, if de people's corn left one whole day not watched, not one blade of it remain to-morrow; it must be watched, missis." "What, on the Sabbath-day, Israel?" "Yes, missis, or else we lose it all." I was not sorry to avail myself of this illustration of the nature of works of necessity, and proceeded to enlighten Israel with regard to what I conceive to be the genuine observance of the Sabbath.

You can not imagine any thing wilder or more beautiful than the situation of the little rustic temple in the woods where I went to worship to-day, with the magnificent live oaks standing round it and its picturesque burial-ground. The disgracefully neglected state of the latter, its broken and ruinous inclosure, and its shaggy, weed-grown graves, tell a strange story of the residents of this island, who are content to leave the resting-place of their dead in so shocking a condition. In the tiny little chamber of a church, the grand old Litany of the Episcopal Church of England was not a little shorn of its ceremonial stateliness; clerk there was none, nor choir, nor organ, and the clergyman did duty for all, giving out the hymn and then singing it himself, followed as best might be by the uncertain voices of his very small congregation, the smallest I think I ever saw gathered in a Christian place of worship, even counting a few of the negroes who had ventured to place themselves standing at the back of the church—an infringement on their part upon the privileges of their betters, as Mr. B—— generally preaches a second sermon to them after the *white* service, to which, as a rule, they are not admitted.

On leaving the church, I could not but smile at the quaint and original costumes with which Israel had so much dreaded a comparison for my irreproachable London riding-habit. However, the strangeness of it was what inspired him with terror; but, at that rate, I am afraid a Paris gown and bonnet might have been in equal danger of shocking his prejudices. There was quite as little affinity with the one as the other in the curious speci-mens of the "art of dressing" that gradually distributed themselves among the two or three indescribable ma-chines (to use the appropriate Scotch title) drawn up un-der the beautiful oak-trees, on which they departed in va-rious directions to the several plantations on the island.

I mounted my horse, and resumed my ride and my con-versation with Israel. He told me that Mr. K——'s great objection to the people going to church was their meeting with the slaves from the other plantations; and one reason, he added, that he did not wish them to do that was, that they trafficked and bartered away the cooper's wares, tubs, piggins, etc., made on the estate. I think, however, from every thing I hear of that gentleman, that the mere fact of the Hampton people coming in contact with the slaves of other plantations would be a thing he would have deprecated. As a severe disciplinarian, he was probably right.

In the course of our talk, a reference I made to the Bible, and Israel's answer that he could not read, made me ask him why his father had never taught any of his sons to read; old Jacob, I know, can read. What followed I shall never forget. He began by giving all sorts of childish unmeaning excuses and reasons for never having tried to learn—became confused and quite incoherent —and then, suddenly stopping, and pulling up his horse, said, with a look and manner that went to my very heart, "Missis, what for me learn to read? me have no prospect!" I rode on without venturing to speak to him again for a little while. When I had recovered from that remark of his, I explained to him that, though indeed "without prospect" in some respects, yet reading might avail him much to better his condition, moral, mental, and physical. He listened very attentively, and was silent for a minute; after which he said, "All you say very true, missis, and me sorry now me let de time pass; but you know what de white man dat goberns de estate him seem to like and favor, dat de people find out bery soon and do it; now Massa K——, him neber favor our reading, him not like it; likely as not he lick you if he find you reading; or, if you wish to teach your children, him always say, 'Pooh! teach 'em to read—teach 'em to work.' According to dat, we neber paid much attention to it; but

now it will be different; it was different in former times.
De old folks of my father and mother's time could read
more than we can, and I expect de people will dare to
give some thought to it again now." There's a precious
sample of what one man's influence may do in his own
sphere, dear E——! This man Israel is a remarkably fine
fellow in every way, with a frank, open, and most intelligent countenance, which rises before me with its look of
quiet sadness whenever I think of these words (and they
haunt me), "I have no prospect."

On my arrival at home I found that a number of the
people, not knowing I had gone to church, had come up
to the house, hoping that I would read prayers to them,
and had not gone back to their homes, but waited to see
me. I could not bear to disappoint them, for many of
them had come from the farthest settlements on the estate; and so, though my hot ride had tired me a good
deal, and my talk with Israel troubled me profoundly, I
took off my habit, and had them all in, and read the afternoon service to them. When it was over, two of the
women—Venus and Tressa—asked if they might be permitted to go to the nursery and see the children. Their
account of the former condition of the estate was a cor-
roboration of Israel's. They said that the older slaves on
the plantation had been far better off than the younger
ones of the present day; that Major —— was considerate
and humane to his people; and that the women were especially carefully treated. But they said Mr. K—— had
ruined all the young women with working them too soon
after their confinements; and as for the elder ones, he
would kick them, curse them, turn their clothes over their
heads, flog them unmercifully himself, and abuse them
shamefully, no matter what condition they were in. They
both ended with fervent thanks to God that he had left
the estate, and rejoicing that we had come, and, above all,

that we "had made young missis for them." Venus went down on her knees, exclaiming, "Oh, missis, I glad now; and when I am dead, I glad in my grave that you come to us and bring us little missis."

---

DEAR E——,—I still go on exploring, or rather surveying the estate, the aspect of which is changing every day with the unfolding of the leaves and the wonderful profusion of wild flowers. The cleared ground all round the new building is one sheet of blooming blue of various tints; it is perfectly exquisite. But in the midst of my delight at these new blossoms, I am most sorrowfully bidding adieu to that paragon of parasites, the yellow jasmine; I think I must have gathered the very last blossoms of it to-day. Nothing can be more lovely, nothing so exquisitely fragrant. I was surprised to recognize by their foliage to-day some fine mulberry-trees by Jones's Creek; perhaps they are the remains of the silk-worm experiment that Mr. C—— persuaded Major —— to try so ineffectually. While I was looking at some wild plum and cherry trees that were already swarming with blight in the shape of multitudinous caterpillars' nests, an ingenious darkie, by name Cudgie, asked me if I could explain to him why the trees blossomed out so fair, and then all "went off into a kind of dying." Having directed his vision and attention to the horrid white glistening webs, all lined with their brood of black devourers, I left him to draw his own conclusions.

The afternoon was rainy, in spite of which I drove to Busson Hill, and had a talk with Bran about the vile caterpillar blights on the wild plum-trees, and asked him if it would not be possible to get some sweet grafts from Mr. C—— for some of the wild fruit-trees, of which there are such quantities. Perhaps, however, they are not worth grafting. Bran promised me that the people should not be allowed to encumber the paths and the front of their houses with unsightly and untidy heaps of oyster-shells. He promised all sorts of things. I wonder how soon after I am gone they will all return into the condition of brutal filth and disorder in which I found them.

The men and women had done their work here by half past three. The chief labor in the cotton-fields, however, is both earlier and later in the season. At present they have little to do but let the crop grow. In the evening I had a visit from the son of a very remarkable man, who had been one of the chief drivers on the estate in Major ——'s time, and his son brought me a silver cup which Major —— had given his father as a testimonial of approbation, with an inscription on it recording his fidelity and trustworthiness at the time of the invasion of the coast of Georgia by the English troops. Was not that a curious reward for a slave who was supposed not to be able to read his own praises? And yet, from the honorable pride with which his son regarded this relic, I am sure the master did well so to reward his servant, though it seemed hard that the son of such a man should be a slave. Maurice himself came with his father's precious silver cup in his hand, to beg for a small pittance of sugar, and for a Prayer-book, and also to know if the privilege of a milch cow for the support of his family, which was among the favors Major —— allowed his father, might not be continued to him. He told me he had ten children "working for massa," and I promised to mention his petition to Mr. ——.

On Sunday last I rode round the woods near St. Annie's, and met with a monstrous snake, which Jack called a chicken-snake; but whether because it particularly affected poultry as its diet, or for what other reason, he could not tell me. Nearer home I encountered another gliding creature, that stopped a moment just in front of my horse's feet, as if it was too much afraid of being trampled upon to get out of the way: it was the only snake animal I ever saw that I did not think hideous. It was of a perfectly pure apple-green color, with a delicate line of black like a collar round its throat; it really was an exquisite worm, and Jack said it was harmless. I did not, however, think it expedient to bring it home in my bosom, though, if ever I have a pet snake, it shall be such a one.

In the afternoon I drove to Jones's with several supplies of flannel for the rheumatic women and old men. We have ridden over to Hamilton again, to pay another visit to the F——'s, and on our way passed an enormous rattlesnake hanging dead on the bough of a tree. Dead as it was, it turned me perfectly sick with horror, and I wished very much to come back to the North immediately, where these are not the sort of blackberries that grow on every bush. The evening air now, after the heat of the day, is exquisitely mild, and the nights dry and wholesome, the whole atmosphere indescribably fragrant with the perfume of flowers; and as I stood, before going to bed last night, watching the slow revolving light on Sapelo Island, that warns the ships from the dangerous bar at the river's mouth, and heard the measured pulse of the great Atlantic waters on the beach, I. thought no more of rattlesnakes—no more, for one short while, of slavery. How still, and sweet, and solemn it was!

We have been paying more friendly and neighborly visits, or rather returning them; and the recipients of these civilized courtesies on our last calling expedition were the family one member of which was a party concerned in that barbarous challenge I wrote you word about. Hitherto that very brutal and bloodthirsty cartel appears to have had no result. You must not, on that account, im-

agine that it will have none.  At the North, were it possible for a duel intended to be conducted on such savage
terms to be matter of notoriety, the very horror of the
thing would create a feeling of grotesqueness, and the antagonists in such a proposed encounter would simply incur an immense amount of ridicule and obloquy.  But
here nobody is astonished and nobody ashamed of such
preliminaries to a mortal combat between two gentlemen,
who propose firing at marks over each other's hearts, and
cutting off each other's heads; and though this agreeable
party of pleasure has not come off yet, there seems to be
no reason why it should not at the first convenient season.
Reflecting upon all which, I rode, not without trepidation,
through Colonel H——'s grounds, and up to his house.
Mr. W——'s head was not stuck upon a pole any where
within sight, however, and as soon as I became pretty
sure of this, I began to look about me, and saw instead a
trellis tapestried with the most beautiful roses I ever beheld, another of these exquisite Southern flowers — the
Cherokee rose.  The blossom is very large, composed of
four or five pure white petals, as white and as large as
those of the finest camellia, with a bright golden eye for
a focus; the buds and leaves are long and elegantly slender, like those of some tea-roses, and the green of the foliage is dark, and at the same time vivid and lustrous; it
grew in masses so as to form almost a hedge, all starred
with these wonderful white blossoms, which, unfortunately, have no perfume.

We rode home through the pine land to Jones's, looked at the new house which is coming on hideously, saw
two beautiful kinds of trumpet honeysuckle already lighting up the woods in every direction with gleams of scarlet, and when we reached home found a splendid donation
of vegetables, flowers, and mutton from our kind neighbor Mrs. F——, who is a perfect Lady Bountiful to us.

This same mutton, however—my heart bleeds to say it— disappeared the day after it was sent to us. Abraham the cook declares that he locked the door of the safe upon it, which I think may be true, but I also think he unlocked it again. I am sorry; but, after all, it is very natural these people should steal a little of our meat from us occasionally, who steal almost all their bread from them habitually.

I rode yesterday to St. Annie's with Mr. ——. We found a whole tract of marsh had been set on fire by the facetious negro called Pun, who had helped me out of it some time ago. As he was set to work in it, perhaps it was with a view of making it less damp; at any rate, it was crackling, blazing, and smoking cheerily, and I should think would be insupportable for the snakes. While stopping to look at the conflagration, Mr. —— was accosted by a three parts naked and one part tattered little she slave—black as ebony, where her skin was discoverable through its perfect incrustation of dirt—with a thick mat of frizzly wool upon her skull, which made the sole request she preferred to him irresistibly ludicrous: "Massa, massa, you please to buy me a comb to tick in my head?" Mr. —— promised her this necessary of life, and I promised myself to give her the luxury of one whole garment. Mrs. —— has sent me the best possible consolation for the lost mutton, some lovely flowers, and these will not be stolen.

---

*Saturday, the* 13*th*. DEAR E——,—I rode to-day through all my wood paths for the last time with Jack, and I think I should have felt quite melancholy at taking leave of them and him but for the apparition of a large black snake, which filled me with disgust and nipped my other sentiments in the bud. Not a day passes now that I do not encounter one or more of these hateful reptiles; it is curious how much more odious they are to me than the alligators that haunt the mud banks of the river round the rice plantation. It is true that there is something very dreadful in the thick shapeless mass, uniform in color almost to the black slime on which it lies basking, and which you hardly detect till it begins to move. But even those ungainly crocodiles never sickened me as those rapid, lithe, and sinuous serpents do. Did I ever tell you that the people at the rice plantation caught a young alligator and brought it to the house, and it was kept for some time in a tub of water? It was an ill-tempered little monster; it used to set up its back like a cat when it was angry, and open its long jaws in a most vicious manner.

After looking at my new path in the pine land, I crossed Pike Bluff, and, breaking my way all through the burnt district, returned home by Jones's. In the afternoon we paid a long visit to Mr. C——. It is extremely interesting to me to talk with him about the negroes; he has spent so much of his life among them, has managed them so humanely, and apparently so successfully, that his experience is worthy of all attention. And yet it seems to me that it is impossible, or rather, perhaps, for those very reasons it is impossible, for him ever to contemplate them in any condition but that of slavery. He thinks them very like the Irish, and instanced their subserviency, their flattering, their lying, and pilfering, as traits common to the characters of both peoples. But I can not persuade myself that in both cases, and certainly in that of the negroes, these qualities are not in great measure the result of their condition. He says that he considers the extremely low diet of the negroes one reason for the absence of crimes of a savage nature among them; most of them do not touch meat the year round. But in this respect they certainly do not resemble the Irish, who contrive, upon about as low a national diet as civilization is acquainted with, to commit the bloodiest and most frequent outrages with which civilization has to deal. His statement that it is impossible to bribe the negroes to work on their own account with any steadiness may be generally true, but admits of quite exceptions enough to throw doubt upon its being natural supineness in the race rather than the inevitable consequence of denying them the entire right to labor for their own profit. Their laziness seems to me the necessary result of their primary wants being supplied, and all progress denied them. Of course, if the natural spur to exertion, necessity, is removed, you do away with the will to work of a vast proportion of all who do work in the world. It is the law of progress that man's necessities grow with his exertions to satisfy them, and labor and improvement thus continually act and react upon each other to raise the scale of desire and achievement; and I do not believe that, in the majority of instances among any people on the face of the earth, the will to labor for small indulgences would survive the loss of freedom and the security of food enough to exist upon. Mr. —— said that he had offered a bribe of twenty dollars apiece, and the use of a pair of oxen, for the clearing of a certain piece of land, to the men on his estate, and found the offer quite ineffectual to procure the desired result; the land was subsequently cleared as usual task-work under the lash. Now, certainly, we have among Mr. ——'s people instances of men who have made very considerable sums of money by boat-building in their leisure hours, and the instances of almost life-long, persevering, stringent labor, by which slaves have at length purchased their own freedom and that of their wives and children, are on record in numbers sufficient to prove that they are capable of severe sustained effort of the most patient and heroic kind for that great object, liberty. For my own part, I know no people who dote upon labor for its own sake; and it seems to me quite natural to any absolutely ignorant and nearly brutish man, if you say to him, " No effort of your own can make you free, but no absence of effort shall starve you," to decline to work for any thing less than mastery over his whole life, and to take up with his mess of porridge as the alternative. One thing that Mr. —— said seemed to me to prove rather too much. He declared that his son, objecting to the folks on his plantation going about bareheaded, had at one time offered a reward of a dollar to those who should habitually wear hats without being able to induce them to do so, which he attributed to sheer careless indolence; but I think it was merely the force of habit of going uncovered rather than absolute laziness. The universal testimony of all present at this conversation was in favor of the sweetness of temper and natural gentleness of disposition of the negroes; but these characteristics they seemed to think less inherent than the result of diet and the other lowering influences of their condition; and it must not be forgotten that on the estate of this wise and kind master a formidable conspiracy was organized among his slaves.

We rowed home through a world of stars, the steadfast ones set in the still blue sky, and the flashing swathes of phosphoric light turned up by our oars and keel in the smooth blue water. It was lovely.

————————

*Sunday*, 14*th*. MY DEAR E——,—That horrid tragedy with which we have been threatened, and of which I was writing to you almost jestingly a few days ago, has been accomplished, and apparently without exciting any thing but the most passing and superficial sensation in this community. The duel between Dr. H—— and Mr. W——

did not take place, but an accidental encounter in the hotel at Brunswick did, and the former shot the latter dead on the spot. He has been brought home and buried here by the little church close to his mother's plantation; and the murderer, if he is even prosecuted, runs no risk of finding a jury in the whole length and breadth of Georgia who could convict him of any thing. It is horrible.

I drove to church to-day in the wood-wagon, with Jack and Aleck, Hector being our charioteer, in a gilt guard-chain and pair of slippers to match as the Sabbatic part of his attire. The love of dirty finery is not a trait of the Irish in Ireland, but I think it crops out strongly when they come out here; and the proportion of their high wages put upon their backs by the young Irish maidservants in the North indicates a strong addiction to the female passion for dress. Here the tendency seems to exist in men and women alike; but I think all savage men rejoice, even more than their women, in personal ornamentation. The negroes certainly show the same strong predilection for finery with their womenkind.

I stopped before going into church to look at the new grave that has taken its place among the defaced stones, all overgrown with briers, that lie round it. Poor young W——! poor widowed mother, of whom he was the only son! What a savage horror! And no one seems to think any thing of it, more than of a matter of course. My devotions were any thing but satisfactory or refreshing to me. My mind was dwelling incessantly upon the new grave under the great oaks outside, and the miserable mother in her home. The air of the church was perfectly thick with sand-flies; and the disgraceful carelessness of the congregation in responding and singing the hymns, and the entire neglect of the Prayer-book regulations for kneeling, disturbed and displeased me even more

than the last time I was at church; but I think that was
because of the total absence of excitement or feeling
among the whole population of St. Simon's upon the subject of the bloody outrage with which my mind was full,
which has given me a sensation of horror toward the
whole community. Just imagine—only it is impossible
to imagine—such a thing taking place in a New England
village; the dismay, the grief, the shame, the indignation,
that would fill the hearts of the whole population. I
thought we should surely have some reference to the
event from the pulpit, some lesson of Christian command
over furious passions. Nothing—nobody looked or spoke
as if any thing unusual had occurred; and I left the
church, rejoicing to think that I was going away from
such a dreadful state of society. Mr. B—— remained to
preach a second sermon to the negroes—the duty of submission to masters who intermurder each other.

I had service at home in the afternoon, and my congregation was much more crowded than usual; for I believe
there is no doubt at last that we shall leave Georgia this
week. Having given way so much before when I thought
I was praying with these poor people for the last time, I
suppose I had, so to speak, expended my emotion, and I
was much more composed and quiet than when I took
leave of them before. But, to tell you the truth, this
dreadful act of slaughter done in our neighborhood by
one man of our acquaintance upon another, impresses me
to such a degree that I can hardly turn my mind from it,
and Mrs. W—— and her poor young murdered son have
taken almost complete possession of my thoughts.

After prayers I gave my poor people a parting admonition, and many charges to remember me and all I had
tried to teach them during my stay. They promised with
one voice to mind and do all that "missis tell we;" and
with many a parting benediction, and entreaties to me to

return, they went their way. I think I have done what I could for them—I think I have done as well as I could by them; but when the time comes for ending any human relation, who can be without their misgivings? who can be bold to say, I could have done no more, I could have done no better?

In the afternoon I walked out, and passed many of the people, who are now beginning, whenever they see me, to say "Good-by, missis!" which is rather trying. Many of them were clean and tidy, and decent in their appearance to a degree that certainly bore strong witness to the temporary efficacy of my influence in this respect. There is, however, of course much individual difference even with reference to this, and some take much more kindly and readily to cleanliness, no doubt to godliness too, than some others. I met Abraham, and thought that, in a quiet tête-à-tête, and with the pathetic consideration of my near departure to assist me, I could get him to confess the truth about the disappearance of the mutton; but he persisted in the legend of its departure through the locked door; and as I was only heaping sins on his soul with every lie I caused him to add to the previous ones, I desisted from my inquiries. Dirt and lying are the natural tendencies of humanity, which are especially fostered by slavery. Slaves may be infinitely wrong, and yet it is very hard to blame them.

I returned home, finding the heat quite oppressive. Late in the evening, when the sun had gone down a long time, I thought I would try and breathe the fresh sea air, but the atmosphere was thick with sand-flies, which drove me in at last from standing listening to the roar of the Atlantic on Little St. Simon's Island, the wooded belt that fends off the ocean surges from the north side of Great St. Simon's. It is a wild little sand-heap, covered with thick forest growth, and belongs to Mr. ——. I have long had a great desire to visit it. I hope yet to be able to do so before our departure.

I have just finished reading, with the utmost interest and admiration, J—— C——'s narrative of his escape from the wreck of the Pulaski: what a brave, and gallant, and unselfish soul he must be! You never read any thing more thrilling, in spite of the perfect modesty of this account of his. If I can obtain his permission, and squeeze out the time, I will surely copy it for you. The quiet, unassuming character of his usual manners and deportment adds greatly to his prestige as a hero. What a fine thing it must be to be such a man!

---

DEAR E——,—We shall leave this place next Thursday or Friday, and there will be an end to this record; meantime I am fulfilling all sorts of last duties, and especially those of taking leave of my neighbors, by whom the neglect of a farewell visit would be taken much amiss.

On Sunday I rode to a place called Frederica to call on a Mrs. A——, who came to see me some time ago. I rode straight through the island by the main road that leads to the little church.

How can I describe to you the exquisite spring beauty that is now adorning these woods, the variety of the fresh, new-born foliage, the fragrance of the sweet, wild perfumes that fill the air? Honeysuckles twine round every tree; the ground is covered with a low, white-blossomed shrub more fragrant than lilies of the valley. The accacuas are swinging their silver censers under the green roof of these wood temples; every stump is like a classical altar to the sylvan gods, garlanded with flowers; every post, or stick, or slight stem, like a Bacchante's thyrsus, twined with wreaths of ivy and wild vine, waving in the tepid wind. Beautiful butterflies flicker like flying flowers among the bushes, and gorgeous birds, like winged jewels, dart from the boughs, and—and—a huge ground snake slid like a dark ribbon across the path while I was stopping to enjoy all this deliciousness, and so I became less enthusiastic, and cantered on past the little deserted church-yard, with the new-made grave beneath its grove of noble oaks, and a little farther on reached Mrs. A——'s cottage, half hidden in the midst of ruins and roses.

This Frederica is a very strange place; it was once a town—*the* town, the metropolis of the island. The English, when they landed on the coast of Georgia in the war, destroyed this tiny place, and it has never been built up again. Mrs. A——'s, and one other house, are the only dwellings that remain in this curious wilderness of dismantled crumbling gray walls compassionately cloaked with a thousand profuse and graceful creepers. These are the only ruins, properly so called, except those of Fort Putnam, that I have ever seen in this land of contemptuous youth. I hailed these picturesque groups and masses with the feelings of a European, to whom ruins are like a sort of relations. In my country, ruins are like a minor chord in music; here they are like a discord; they are not the relics of time, but the results of violence; they recall no valuable memories of a remote past, and are mere encumbrances to the busy present. Evidently they are out of place in America except on St. Simon's Island, between this savage selvage of civilization and the great Atlantic deep. These heaps of rubbish and roses would have made the fortune of a sketcher; but I imagine the snakes have it all to themselves here, and are undisturbed by camp-stools, white umbrellas, and ejaculatory young ladies.

I sat for a long time with Mrs. A——, and a friend of hers staying with her, a Mrs. A——, lately from Florida. The latter seemed to me a remarkable woman; her con-

versation was extremely interesting. She had been stopping at Brunswick, at the hotel where Dr. H—— murdered young W——, and said that the mingled ferocity
and blackguardism of the men who frequented the house
had induced her to cut short her stay there, and come on
to her friend Mrs. A——'s. We spoke of that terrible
crime which had occurred only the day after she left
Brunswick, and both ladies agreed that there was not the
slightest chance of Dr. H——'s being punished in any way
for the murder he had committed; that shooting down a
man who had offended you was part of the morals and
manners of the Southern gentry, and that the circumstance was one of quite too frequent occurrence to cause
any sensation, even in the small community where it ob-
literated one of the principal members of the society. If
the accounts given by these ladies of the character of the
planters in this part of the South may be believed, they
must be as idle, arrogant, ignorant, dissolute, and ferocious as that mediæval chivalry to which they are fond of
comparing themselves; and these are Southern women,
and should know the people among whom they live.

We had a long discussion on the subject of slavery, and
they took, as usual, the old ground of justifying the system, *where* it was administered with kindness and indulgence. It is not surprising that women should regard
the question from this point of view; they are very seldom *just*, and are generally treated with more indulgence
than justice by men. They were very patient of my
strong expressions of reprobation of the whole system,
and Mrs. A——, bidding me good-by, said that, for aught
she could tell, I might be right, and might have been led
down here by Providence to be the means of some great
change in the condition of the poor colored people.

I rode home pondering on the strange fate that has
brought me to this place so far from where I was born,

this existence so different in all its elements from that of my early years and former associations. If I believed Mrs. A——'s parting words, I might perhaps verify them; perhaps I may yet verify, although I do not believe them. On my return home I found a most enchanting bundle of flowers, sent to me by Mrs. G——; pomegranate blossoms, roses, honeysuckle, every thing that blooms two months later with us in Pennsylvania.

I told you I had a great desire to visit Little St. Simon's, and the day before yesterday I determined to make an exploring expedition thither. I took M—— and the children, little imagining what manner of day's work was before me. Six men rowed us in the "Lily," and Israel brought the wood-wagon after us in a flat. Our navigation was a very intricate one, all through sea swamps and marshes, mud-banks and sand-banks, with great white shells and bleaching bones stuck upon sticks to mark the channel. We landed on this forest in the sea by Quash's house, the only human residence on the island. It was larger and better, and more substantial than the negro huts in general, and he seemed proud and pleased to do the honors to us. Thence we set off, by my desire, in the wagon through the woods to the beach; road there was none, save the rough clearing that the men cut with their axes before us as we went slowly on. Presently we came to a deep dry ditch, over which there was no visible means of proceeding. Israel told me if we would sit still he would undertake to drive the wagon into and out of it; and so, indeed, he did, but how he did it is more than I can explain to you now, or could explain to myself then. A less powerful creature than Montreal could never have dragged us through; and when we presently came to a second rather worse edition of the same, I insisted upon getting out and crossing it on foot. I walked half a mile while the wagon was dragged up and down the deep gully, and lifted bodily over some huge trunks of fallen trees. The wood through which we now drove was all on fire, smoking, flaming, crackling, and burning round us. The sun glared upon us from the cloudless sky, and the air was one cloud of sand-flies and musquitoes. I covered both my children's faces with veils and handkerchiefs, and repented not a little in my own breast of the rashness of my undertaking. The back of Israel's coat was covered so thick with musquitoes that one could hardly see the cloth; and I felt as if we ‧ should be stifled if our way lay much longer through this terrible wood. Presently we came to another impassable place, and again got out of the wagon, leaving Israel to manage it as best he could. I walked with the baby in my arms a quarter of a mile, and then was so overcome with the heat that I sat down in the burning wood, on the floor of ashes, till the wagon came up again. I put the children and M—— into it, and continued to walk till we came to a ditch in a tract of salt marsh, over which Israel drove triumphantly, and I partly jumped and was partly hauled over, having declined the entreaties of several ·of the men to let them lie down and make a bridge with their bodies for me to walk over. At length we reached the skirt of that tremendous wood, to my unspeakable relief, and came upon the white sand-hillocks of the beach. The trees were all strained crooked, from the constant influence of the sea-blast. The coast was a fearful-looking stretch of dismal, trackless sand, and the ocean lay boundless and awful beyond the wild and desolate beach, from which we were now only divided by a patch of low, coarse-looking bush, growing as thick and tangled as heather, and so stiff and compact that it was hardly possible to drive through it. Yet in spite of this, several lads who had joined our train rushed off into it in search of rabbits, though Israel called repeatedly to them, warning them of the danger of rattlesnakes. We drove at last down to the smooth sea sand; and here, outstripping our guides, was barred farther progress by a deep gully, down which it was impossible to take the wagon. Israel, not knowing the beach well, was afraid to drive round the mouth of it; and so it was determined that from this point we should walk home under his guidance. I sat in the wagon while he constructed a rough foot-bridge of bits of wood and broken planks for us over the narrow chasm, and he then took Montreal out of the wagon and tied him behind it, leaving him for the other men to take charge of when they should arrive at this point. And so, having mightily desired to see the coast of Little St. Simon's Island, I did see it thoroughly; for I walked a mile and a half round it, over beds of sharp shells, through swamps half knee deep, poor little S—— stumping along with dogged heroism, and Israel carrying the baby, except at one deep *mal passo*, when I took the baby and he carried S——; and so, through the wood round Quash's house, where we arrived almost fainting with fatigue and heat, and where we rested but a short time, for we had to start almost immediately to save the tide home.

I called at Mr. C——'s on my way back, to return him his son's manuscript, which I had in the boat for that purpose. I sent Jack, who had come to meet me with the horses, home, being too tired to attempt riding; and, covered with mud literally up to my knees, I was obliged to lie down ignominiously all the afternoon to rest. And now I will give you a curious illustration of the utter subserviency of slaves. It seems that by taking the tide in proper season, and going by boat, all that horrible wood journey might have been avoided, and we could have reached the beach with perfect ease in half the time; but because, being of course absolutely ignorant of this, I had expressed a desire to go through the wood, not a syllable

of remonstrance was uttered by any one; and the men
not only underwent the labor of cutting a path for the
wagon and dragging it through and over all the impediments we encountered, but allowed me and the children
to traverse that burning wood, rather than tell me that by
waiting and taking another way I could get to the sea.
When I expressed my astonishment at their not having
remonstrated against my order, and explained how I could
best achieve the purpose I had in view, the sole answer I
got even from Israel was, " Missis say so, so me do; missis
say me go through the wood, me no tell missis go another
way." You see, my dear E——, one had need bethink
one's self what orders one gives, when one has the misfortune to be despotic.

How sorry I am that I have been obliged to return that
narrative of Mr. C——'s without asking permission to
copy it, which I did not do because I should not have been
able to find the time to do it! We go away the day after
to-morrow. All the main incidents of the disaster the
newspapers have made you familiar with—the sudden and
appalling loss of that fine vessel laden with the very flower
of the South. There seems hardly to be a family in Georgia and South Carolina that had not some of its members
on board that ill-fated ship. You know it was a sort of
party of pleasure more than any thing else; the usual an-
nual trip to the North for change of air and scene, for the
gayeties of Newport and Saratoga, that all the wealthy
Southern people invariably take every summer.

The weather had been calm and lovely; and dancing,
talking, and laughing, as if they were in their own drawing-rooms, they had passed the time away till they all separated for the night. At the first sound of the exploding
boiler Mr. C—— jumped up, and in his shirt and trowsers
ran on deck. The scene was one of horrible confusion;
women screaming, men swearing, the deck strewn with

broken fragments of all descriptions, the vessel leaning frightfully to one side, and every body running hither and thither in the darkness in horror and dismay. He had left Georgia with Mrs. F—— and Mrs. N——, the two children, and one of the female servants of these ladies under his charge. He went immediately to the door of the ladies' cabin and called Mrs. F——; they were all there half dressed; he bade them dress as quickly as possible, and be ready to follow and obey him. He returned almost instantly, and led them to the side of the vessel, where, into the boats, that had already been lowered, desperate men and women were beginning to swarm, throwing themselves out of the sinking ship. He bade Mrs. F—— jump down into one of these boats which was only in the possession of two sailors; she instantly obeyed him, and he threw her little boy to the men after her. He then ordered Mrs. N——, with the negro woman, to throw themselves off the vessel into the boat, and, with Mrs. N——'s baby in his arms, sprang after them. His foot touched the gunwale of the boat, and he fell into the water; but, recovering himself instantly, he clambered into the boat, which he then peremptorily ordered the men to set adrift, in spite of the shrieks, and cries, and commands, and entreaties of the frantic crowds who were endeavoring to get into it. The men obeyed him, and rowing while he steered, they presently fell astern of the ship, in the midst of the darkness, and tumult, and terror. Another boat laden with people was near them. For some time they saw the heart-rending spectacle of the sinking vessel, and the sea strewn with mattresses, seats, planks, etc., to which people were clinging, floating, and shrieking for succor, in the dark water all round them. But they gradually pulled farther and farther out of the horrible chaos of despair, and, with the other boat still consorting with them, rowed on. They watched from a distance the piteous sight of the ill-fated steamer settling down, the gray girdle of light that marked the line of her beautiful saloons and cabins gradually sinking nearer and nearer to the blackness, in which they were presently extinguished; and the ship, with all its precious human freight ingulfed —all but the handful left in those two open boats, to brave the dangers of that terrible coast!

They were somewhere off the North Carolina shore, which, when the daylight dawned, they could distinctly see, with its ominous line of breakers and inhospitable perilous coast. The men had continued rowing all night, and as the summer sun rose flaming over their heads, the task of pulling the boat became dreadfully severe; still they followed the coast, Mr. C—— looking out for any opening, creek, or small inlet that might give them a chance of landing in safety. The other boat rowed on at some little distance from them.

All the morning, and through the tremendous heat of the middle day, they toiled on without a mouthful of food —without a drop of water. At length, toward the afternoon, the men at the oars said they were utterly exhausted and could row no longer, and that Mr. C—— must steer the boat ashore. With wonderful power of command, he prevailed on them to continue their afflicting labor. The terrible blazing sun pouring on all their unsheltered heads had almost annihilated them; but still there lay between them and the land those fearful foaming ridges, and the women and children, if not the men themselves, seemed doomed to inevitable death in the attempt to surmount them. Suddenly they perceived that the boat that had kept them company was about to adventure itself in the perilous experiment of landing. Mr. C—— kept his boat's head steady, the men rested on their oars, and watched the result of the fearful risk they were themselves about to run. They saw the boat enter the breakers—they saw her whirled round and capsized, and then they watched, slowly emerging and dragging themselves out of the foaming sea, *some*, and only some, of the people that they knew the boat contained. Mr. C——, fortified with this terrible illustration of the peril that awaited them, again besought them to row yet for a little while farther along the coast, in search of some possible place to take the boat safely to the beach, promising at sunset to give up the search, and again the poor men resumed their toil; but the line of leaping breakers stretched along the coast as far as eye could see, and at length the men declared they could labor no longer, and insisted that Mr. C—— should steer them to shore. He then said that he would do so, but they must take some rest before encountering the peril which awaited them, and for which they might require whatever remaining strength they could command. He made the men leave the oars and lie down to sleep for a short time, and then, giving the helm to one of them, did the same himself. When they were thus a little refreshed with this short rest, he prepared to take the boat into the breakers.

He laid Mrs. N——'s baby on her breast, and wrapped a shawl round and round her body so as to secure the child to it, and said, in the event of the boat capsizing, he would endeavor to save her and her child. Mrs. F—— and her boy he gave in charge to one of the sailors, and the colored woman who was with her to the other, and they promised solemnly, in case of misadventure to the boat, to do their best to save these helpless creatures; and so they turned, as the sun was going down, the bows of the boat to the terrible shore. They rose two of the breakers safely, but then the oar of one of the men was struck from his hand, and in an instant the boat whirled round and turned over. Mr. C—— instantly struck out to seize Mrs. N——, but she had sunk, and, though he dived twice, he could not see her; at last he felt her hair floating loose with his foot, and seizing hold of it, grasped her securely and swam with her to shore. While in the act of doing so, he saw the man who had promised to save the colored woman making alone for the beach; and even then, in that extremity, he had power of command enough left to drive the fellow back to seek her, which he did, and brought her safe to land. The other man kept his word of taking care of Mrs. F——, and the latter never released her grasp of her child's wrist, which bore the mark of her agony for weeks after their escape. They reached the sands, and Mrs. N——'s shawl having been unwound, her child was found laughing on her bosom. But hardly had they had time to thank God for their deliverance when Mr. C—— fell fainting on the beach; and Mrs. F——, who told me this, said that for one dreadful moment they thought that the preserver of all their lives had lost his own in the terrible exertion and anxiety that he had undergone. He revived, however, and crawling a little farther up the beach, they burrowed for warmth and shelter as well as they could in the sand, and lay there till the next morning, when they sought and found succor.

You can not imagine, my dear E——, how strikingly throughout this whole narrative the extraordinary power of Mr. C——'s character makes itself felt—the immediate obedience that he obtained from women whose terror might have made them unmanageable, and men whose selfishness might have defied his control; the wise though painful firmness which enabled him to order the boat away from the side of the perishing vessel, in spite of the pity that he felt for the many, in attempting to succor whom he could only have jeopardized the few whom he was bound to save; the wonderful influence he exercised over the poor oarsmen, whose long protracted labor postponed to the last possible moment the terrible risk of their landing. The firmness, courage, humanity, wisdom, and presence of mind of all his preparations for their final tremendous risk, and the authority which he was able to exercise, while struggling in the foaming water for his own life and that of the woman and child he was saving, over the man who was proving false to a similar sacred charge — all these admirable traits are most miserably transmitted to you by my imperfect account; and when I assure you that his own narrative, full as it necessarily was of the details of his own heroism, was as simple, modest, and unpretending as it was interesting and touching, I am sure you will agree with me that he must be a very rare man. When I spoke with enthusiasm to his old father of his son's noble conduct, and asked him if he was not proud of it, his sole reply was, "I am glad, madam, my son was not selfish."

Now, E——, I have often spoken with you and written to you of the disastrous effect of slavery upon the character of the white men implicated in it; many among themselves feel and acknowledge it to the fullest extent, and no one more than myself can deplore that any human being I love should be subjected to such baneful influences; but the devil must have his due, and men brought up in habits of peremptory command over their fellow-men, and under the constant apprehension of danger, and awful necessity of immediate readiness to meet it, acquire qualities precious to themselves and others in hours of supreme peril such as this man passed through, saving by their exercise himself and all committed to his charge. I know that the Southern men are apt to deny the fact that they do live under an habitual sense of danger; but a slave population, coerced into obedience, though unarmed and half fed, *is* a threatening source of constant insecurity, and every Southern *woman* to whom I have spoken on the subject has admitted to me that they live in terror of their slaves. Happy are such of them as have protectors like J—— C——. Such men will best avoid and best encounter the perils that may assail them from the abject subject, human element, in the control of which their noble faculties are sadly and unworthily employed.

*Wednesday, 17th April.* I rode to-day, after breakfast, to Mrs. D——'s, another of my neighbors, who lives full twelve miles off. During the last two miles of my expedition I had the white sand hillocks and blue line of the Atlantic in view. The house at which I called was a tumble-down barrack of a dwelling in the woods, with a sort of poverty-stricken pretentious air about it, like sundry "proud planters'" dwellings that I have seen. I was received by the sons as well as the lady of the house, and could not but admire the lordly rather than manly indifference with which these young gentlemen, in gay guardchains and fine attire, played the gallants to me, while filthy, barefooted, half-naked negro women brought in refreshments, and stood all the while fanning the cake, and sweetmeats, and their young masters, as if they had been all the same sort of stuff. I felt ashamed for the lads. The conversation turned upon Dr. H——'s trial; for there has been a trial as a matter of form, and an acquittal as a matter of course; and the gentlemen said, upon my expressing some surprise at the latter event, that there could not be found in all Georgia a jury who would convict him, which says but little for the moral sense of "all Georgia." From this most painful subject we fell into the Brunswick Canal, and thereafter I took my leave and rode home. I met my babies in the wood-wagon, and took S—— up before me, and gave her a good gallop home. Having reached the house with the appetite of a twenty-four miles' ride, I found no preparation for dinner, and not so much as a boiled potato to eat, and the sole reply to my famished and disconsolate exclamations was, "Being that you order none, missis, I not know." I had forgotten to order my dinner, and my *slaves*, unauthorized, had not ventured to prepare any. Wouldn't a Yankee have said, "Wal, now, you went off so uncommon quick, I kinder guessed you forgot all about dinner," and have had it all ready for me? But my slaves durst not, and so I fasted till some tea could be got for me.

---

This was the last letter I wrote from the plantation, and I never returned there, nor ever saw again any of the poor people among whom I lived during this winter but Jack, once, under sad circumstances. The poor lad's health failed so completely that his owners humanely brought him to the North, to try what benefit he might derive from the change; but this was before the passing of the Fugitive Slave Bill, when, touching the soil of the Northern states, a slave became free; and such was the apprehension felt lest Jack should be enlightened as to this fact by some philanthropic Abolitionist, that he was kept shut up in a high upper room of a large empty house, where even I was not allowed to visit him. I heard at length of his being in Philadelphia; and upon my distinct statement that I considered freeing their slaves the business of the Messrs. —— themselves, and not mine, I was at length permitted to see him. Poor fellow! coming to the North did not prove to him the delight his eager desire had so often anticipated from it; nor, under such circumstances, is it perhaps much to be wondered at that he benefited but little by the change—he died not long after.

I once heard a conversation between Mr. O—— and Mr. K——, the two overseers of the plantation on which I was living, upon the question of taking slaves, servants, necessary attendants, into the Northern states; Mr. O—— urged the danger of their being "got hold of," *i. e.*, set

free by the Abolitionists, to which Mr. K—— very per-
tinently replied, "Oh, stuff and nonsense; I take care,
when my wife goes North with the children, to send Lucy
with her; *her children are down here, and I defy all the
Abolitionists in creation to get her to stay North.*"    Mr.
K—— was an extremely wise man.

# APPENDIX.

I WROTE the following letter after reading several leading articles in the *Times* newspaper, at the time of the
great sensation occasioned by Mrs. Beecher Stowe's novel
of "Uncle Tom's Cabin," and after the Anti-slavery Protest which that book induced the women of England to
address to those of America on the subject of the condition of the slaves in the Southern states.

MY DEAR E——,—I have read the articles in the *Times*
to which you refer on the subject of the inaccuracy of
Mrs. Beecher Stowe's book as a picture of slavery in
America, and have ascertained who they were written by.
Having done so, I do not think it worth while to send
my letter for insertion, because, as that is the tone deliberately taken upon the subject by that paper, my
counter statement would not, I imagine, be admitted into
its columns. I inclose it to you, as I should like you to
see how far from true, according to my experience, the
statements of the "*Times*' Correspondent" are. It is
impossible, of course, to know why it erects itself into an
advocate for slavery; and the most charitable conjecture
I can form upon the subject is, that the Stafford House
demonstration may have been thought likely to wound
the sensitive national views of America upon this subject;
and the statement put forward by the *Times*, contradicting Mrs. Stowe's picture, may be intended to soothe their
irritation at the philanthropic zeal of our lady Abolitionists. Believe me, dear E——, yours always truly,

F. A. K.

### Letter to the Editor of the "TIMES."

SIR,—As it is not to be supposed that you consciously afford the support of your great influence to misstatements, I request your attention to some remarks I wish to make on an article on a book called "Uncle Tom's Cabin as it is," contained in your paper of the 11th. In treating Mrs. Harriet Beecher Stowe's work as an exaggerated picture of the evils of slavery, I beg to assure you that you do her serious injustice: of the merits of her book as a work of art I have no desire to speak; to its power as a most interesting and pathetic story, all England and America can bear witness; but of its truth and moderation as a representation of the slave system in the United States, I can testify with the experience of an eye-witness, having been a resident in the Southern states, and had opportunities of observation such as no one who has not lived on a slave estate can have. It is very true that in reviving the altogether exploded fashion of making the hero of her novel "the perfect monster that the world ne'er saw," Mrs. Stowe has laid herself open to fair criticism, and must expect to meet with it from the very opposite taste of the present day; but the ideal excellence of her principal character is no argument at all against the general accuracy of her statements with regard to the evils of slavery; every thing else in her book is not only possible, but probable, and not only probable, but a very faithful representation of the existing facts: faithful, and not, as you accuse it of being, exaggerated; for, with the exception of the horrible catastrophe, the flogging to death of poor Tom, she has portrayed none of the most revolting instances of crime produced by the slave system, with which she might have darkened her picture, without detracting from its perfect truth. Even with respect to the incident of Tom's death, it must not be said that if such an event is possible, it is hardly probable; for this is unfortunately not true. It is not true that the value of the slave as property infallibly protects his life from the passions of his master. It is no new thing for a man's passions to blind him to his most obvious and immediate temporal interests, as well as to his higher and everlasting ones—in various parts of the world and stages of civilization, various human passions assume successive prominence, and become developed, to the partial exclusion or deadening of others. In savage existence, and those states of civilization least removed from it, the animal passions predominate. In highly cultivated modern society, where the complicated machinery of human existence is at once a perpetually renewed cause and effect of certain legal and moral restraints, which, in the shape of government and public opinion, protect the congregated lives and interests of men from the worst outrages of open violence, the natural selfishness of mankind assumes a different development, and the love of power, of pleasure, or of pelf, exhibits different phenomena from those elicited from a savage under the influence of the same passions. The channel in which the energy and activity of modern society inclines more and more to pour itself is the peaceful one of the pursuit of gain. This is preeminently the case with the two great commercial nations of the earth, England and America; and in either England or the Northern states of America, the prudential and practical views of life prevail so far, that instances of men sacrificing their money interests at the instigation of rage, revenge, and hatred will certainly not abound. But the Southern slaveholders are a very different race of men from either Manchester manufacturers or Massachusetts merchants; they are a remnant of barbarism and feudalism, maintaining itself with infinite difficulty and danger by the side of the latest and most powerful development of commercial civilization.

The inhabitants of Baltimore, Richmond, Charleston, Savannah, and New Orleans, whose estates lie, like the suburban retreats of our city magnates, in the near neighborhood of their respective cities, are not now the people I refer to. They are softened and enlightened by many influences — the action of city life itself, where human sympathy and human respect, stimulated by neighborhood, produce salutary social restraint as well as less salutary social cowardice. They travel to the Northern states and to Europe, and Europe and the Northern states travel to them, and, in spite of themselves, their peculiar conditions receive modifications from foreign intercourse. The influence, too, of commercial enterprise, which in these latter days is becoming the agent of civilization all over the earth, affects even the uncommercial residents of the Southern cities, and, however cordially they may dislike or despise the mercantile tendencies of Atlantic Americans or transatlantic Englishmen, their frequent contact with them breaks down some of the barriers of difference between them, and humanizes the slaveholder of the great cities into some relation with the spirit of his own times and country. But these men are but a most inconsiderable portion of the slaveholding population of the South—a nation, for as such they should be spoken of, of men whose organization and temperament is that of the southern European; living under the influence of a climate at once enervating and exciting; scattered over trackless wildernesses of arid sand and pestilential swamp; intrenched within their own boundaries; surrounded by creatures absolutely subject to their despotic will; delivered over by hard necessity to the lowest excitements of drinking, gambling, and debauchery for sole recreation; independent of all opinion; ignorant of all progress; isolated from all society—it is impossible to conceive a more savage existence within the pale of any modern civilization.

The South Carolinian gentry have been fond of styling themselves the chivalry of the South, and perhaps might not badly represent, in their relations with their dependents, the nobility of France before the purifying hurricane of the Revolution swept the rights of the suzerain and the wrongs of the serf together into one bloody abyss. The planters of the interior of the Southern and Southwestern states, with their furious feuds and slaughterous combats, their stabbings and pistolings, their gross sensuality, brutal ignorance, and despotic cruelty, resemble the chivalry of France before the horrors of the Jacquerie admonished them that there was a limit even to the endurance of slaves. With such men as these, human life, even when it can be bought or sold in the market for so many dollars, is but little protected by considerations of interest from the effects of any violent passion. There is yet, however, another aspect of the question, which is, that it is sometimes clearly *not* the interest of the owner to prolong the life of his slaves; as in the case of inferior or superannuated laborers, or the very notorious instance in which some of the owners of sugar plantations stated that they found it better worth their while to *work off* (*i. e.*, kill with labor) a certain proportion of their force, and replace them by new hands every seven years, than work them less severely and maintain them in diminished efficiency for an indefinite length of time. Here you will observe a precise estimate of the planter's material interest led to a result which you argue passion itself can never be so blind as to adopt. This was a deliberate economical calculation, openly avowed some years ago by a number of sugar planters in Louisiana. If, instead of accusing Mrs. Stowe of exaggeration, you had brought the same charge against the author of the "White Slave," I should not have been surprised; for his book presents some of the most revolting instances of atrocity and crime that the miserable

abuse of irresponsible power is capable of producing, and
it is by no means written in the spirit of universal humanity which pervades Mrs. Stowe's volumes; but it is not
liable to the charge of exaggeration any more than her
less disgusting delineation. The scenes described in the
" White Slave" *do* occur in the slave states of North
America; and in two of the most appalling incidents of
the book—the burning alive of the captured runaway, and
the hanging without trial of the Vicksburg gamblers—
the author of the " White Slave" has very simply related
positive facts of notorious occurrence. To which he might
have added, had he seen fit to do so, the instance of a slave
who perished in the sea-swamps, where he was left bound
and naked, a prey to the torture inflicted upon him by the
venomous musquito swarms. My purpos~, however, in
addressing you was not to enter into a disquisition on
either of these publications; but I am not sorry to take
this opportunity of bearing witness to the truth of Mrs.
Stowe's admirable book, and I have seen what few Englishmen can see—the working of the system in the midst
of it.

In reply to your " Dispassionate Observer," who went
to the South professedly with the purpose of seeing and
judging of the state of things for himself, let me tell you
that, little as he may be disposed to believe it, his testimony is worth less than nothing; for it is morally impossible for any Englishman going into the Southern states,
except as a *resident*, to know any thing whatever of the
real condition of the slave population. This was the case
some years ago, as I experienced, and it is now likely to
be more the case than ever; for the institution is not *yet*
approved divine to the perceptions of Englishmen, and
the Southerners are as anxious to hide its uglier features
from any note-making observer from this side of the water as to present to his admiration and approval such as

can by any possibility be made to wear the most distant approach to comeliness.

The gentry of the Southern states are pre-eminent in their own country for that species of manner which, contrasted with the breeding of the Northerners, would be emphatically pronounced " good" by Englishmen. Born to inhabit landed property, they are not inevitably made clerks and counting-house men of, but inherit with their estates some of the invariable characteristics of an aristocracy. The shop is not their element; and the eager spirit of speculation and the sordid spirit of gain do not infect their whole existence, even to their very demeanor and appearance, as they too manifestly do those of a large proportion of the inhabitants of the Northern states. Good manners have an undue value for Englishmen, generally speaking; and whatever departs from their peculiar standard of breeding is apt to prejudice them, as whatever approaches it prepossesses them, far more than is reasonable. The Southerners are infinitely better bred men, according to English notions, than the men of the Northern states. The habit of command gives them a certain self-possession, the enjoyment of leisure a certain ease. Their temperament is impulsive and enthusiastic, and their manners have the grace and spirit which seldom belong to the deportment of a Northern people; but, upon more familiar acquaintance, the vices of the social system to which they belong will be found to have infected them with their own peculiar taint; and haughty, overbearing irritability, effeminate indolence, reckless extravagance, and a union of profligacy and cruelty, which is the immediate result of their irresponsible power over their dependents, are some of the less pleasing traits which acquaintance develops in a Southern character. In spite of all this, there is no manner of doubt that the " candid English observer" will, for the season of his sojourning among them, greatly prefer their intercourse to that of their Northern brethren. Moreover, without in the least suspecting it, he will be bribed insidiously and incessantly by the extreme desire and endeavor to please and prepossess him which the whole white population of the slave states will exhibit—as long as he goes only as a "candid observer," with a mind not *yet* made up upon the subject of slavery, and open to conviction as to its virtues. Every conciliating demonstration of courtesy and hospitable kindness will be extended to him, and, as I said before, if his observation is permitted (and it may even appear to be courted), it will be to a fairly bound, purified edition of the black book of slavery, in which, though the inherent viciousness of the whole story can not be suppressed, the coarser and more offensive passages will be carefully expunged. And now permit me to observe that the remarks of your traveler must derive much of their value from the scene of his inquiry. In Maryland, Kentucky, and Virginia, the outward aspect of slavery has ceased to wear its most deplorable features. The remaining vitality of the system no longer resides in the interests, but in the pride and prejudices of the planters. Their soil and climate are alike favorable to the labors of a white peasantry: the slave cultivation has had time to prove itself there the destructive pest which, in time, it will prove itself wherever it prevails. The vast estates and large fortunes that once maintained, and were maintained by, the serfdom of hundreds of negroes, have dwindled in size and sunk in value, till the slaves have become so heavy a burden on the resources of the exhausted soil and impoverished owners of it, that they are made themselves objects of traffic in order to ward off the ruin that their increase would otherwise entail. Thus the plantations of the Northern slave states now present to the traveler very few of the darker and more oppressive peculiarities of the system; and, provided he does not stray too near the precincts where the negroes are sold, or come across gangs of them on their way to Georgia, Louisiana, or Alabama, he may, if he is a very superficial observer, conclude that the most prosperous slavery is not much worse than the most miserable freedom.

But of what value will be such conclusions applied to those numerous plantations where no white man ever sets foot without the express permission of the owner? not estates lying close to Baltimore and Charleston, or even Lexington and Savannah, but remote and savage wildernesses like Legree's estate in "Uncle Tom," like all the plantations in the interior of Tennessee and Alabama, like the cotton-fields and rice-swamps of the great muddy rivers of Louisiana and Georgia, like the dreary pine barrens and endless woody wastes of North Carolina. These, especially the islands, are like so many fortresses, approachable for "observers" only at the owners' will. On most of the rice plantations in these pestilential regions, no white man can pass the night at certain seasons of the year without running the risk of his life; and during the day, the master and overseer are as much alone and irresponsible in their dominion over their black cattle, as Robinson Crusoe was over his small family of animals on his desert habitation. Who, on such estates as these, shall witness to any act of tyranny or barbarity, however atrocious? No black man's testimony is allowed against a white, and who, on the dismal swampy rice-grounds of the Savannah, or the sugar-brakes of the Mississippi and its tributaries, or the up-country cotton-lands of the Ocmulgee, shall go to perform the task of candid observation and benevolent inquiry?

I passed some time on two such estates—plantations where the negroes esteemed themselves well off, and, compared with the slaves on several of the neighboring properties, might very well consider themselves so; and I will,

with your permission, contrast some of the items of my
observation with those of the traveler whose report you
find so satisfactory on the subject of the " consolations"
of slavery.

And, first, for the attachment which he affirms to sub-
sist between the slave and master. I do not deny that
certain manifestations on the part of the slave may suggest the idea of such a feeling; but whether, upon better
examination, it will be found to deserve the name, I very
much doubt. In the first place, on some of the great
Southern estates, the owners are habitual absentees, utterly unknown to their serfs, and enjoying the proceeds
of their labor in residences as far remote as possible from
the sands and swamps where their rice and cotton grow,
and their slaves bow themselves under the eye of the
white overseer, and the lash of the black driver. Some
of these Sybarites prefer living in Paris, that paradise of
American republicans, some in the capitals of the Middle
States of the Union, Philadelphia or New York.

The air of New England has a keen edge of liberty,
which suits few Southern constitutions; and unkindly as
abolition has found its native soil and native skies, that is
its birthplace, and there it flourishes, in spite of all attempts to root it out and trample it down, and within any
atmosphere poisoned by its influence no slaveholder can
willingly draw breath. Some travel in Europe, and few,
whose means permit the contrary, ever pass the entire
year on their plantations. Great intervals of many years
pass, and no master ever visits some of these properties:
what species of attachment do you think the slave entertains for him? In other cases, the visits made will be of
a few days in one of the winter months, the estate and its
cultivators remaining for the rest of the year under the
absolute control of the overseer, who, provided he con-
trives to get a good crop of rice or cotton into the mar-

ket for his employers, is left to the arbitrary exercise of a will seldom uninfluenced for evil by the combined effects of the grossest ignorance and habitual intemperance. The temptation to the latter vice is almost irresistible to a white man in such a climate, and leading an existence of brutal isolation, among a parcel of human beings as like brutes as they can be made. But the owner who at these distant intervals of months or years revisits his estates, is looked upon as a returning providence by the poor negroes. They have no experience of his character to destroy their hopes in his goodness, and all possible and impossible ameliorations of their condition are anticipated from his advent, less work, more food, fewer stripes, and some of that consideration which the slave hopes may spring from his positive money value to his owner—a fallacious dependence, as I have already attempted to show, but one which, if it has not always predominating weight with the master, never can have any with the overseer, who has not even the feeling of regard for his own property to mitigate his absolutism over the slaves of another man.

There is a very powerful cause which makes the prosperity and well-being (as far as life is concerned) of most masters a subject of solicitude with their slaves. The only stability of their condition, such as it is, hangs upon it. If the owner of a plantation dies, his estates may fall into the market, and his slaves be sold at public auction the next day; and whether this promises a better, or threatens a worse condition, the slaves can not know, and no human being cares. One thing it inevitably brings, the uprooting of all old associations; the disruption of all the ties of fellowship in misery; the tearing asunder of all relations of blood and affection; the sale into separate and far-distant districts of fathers, mothers, husbands, wives, and children. If the estate does not lie in the extreme South, there is the vague dread of being driven thither from Virginia to Georgia, from Carolina to Alabama, or Louisiana, a change which, for reasons I have shown above, implies the passing from a higher into a lower circle of the infernal pit of slavery.

I once heard a slave on the plantation of an absentee express the most lively distress at hearing that his master was ill. Before, however, I had recovered from my surprise at this warm "attachment" to a distant and all but unknown proprietor, the man added, "Massa die, what become of all him people?"

On my arrival on the plantation where I resided, I was hailed with the most extravagant demonstrations of delight, and all but lifted off my feet in the arms of people who had never seen me before, but who, knowing me to be connected with their owners, expected from me some of the multitudinous benefits which they always hope to derive from masters. These, until they come to reside among them, are always believed to be sources of beneficence and fountains of redress by the poor people, who have known no rule but the delegated tyranny of the overseer. In these expectations, however, they very soon find themselves cruelly mistaken. Of course, if the absentee planter has received a satisfactory income from his estate, he is inclined to be satisfied with the manager of it; and as subordination to the only white man among hundreds of blacks must be maintained at any and every cost, the overseer is justified and upheld in his whole administration. If the wretched slave ever dared to prefer a complaint of ill usage the most atrocious, the law which refuses the testimony of a black against a white is not only the law of the land, but of every man's private dealings; and lying being one of the natural results of slavery, and a tendency to shirk compelled and unrequited labor another, the overseer stands on excellent vantage-ground when he refers to these undoubted characteristics of the system, if called upon to rebut any charge of cruelty or injustice. But pray consider for a moment the probability of any such charge being preferred by a poor creature who has been for years left to the absolute disposal of this man, and who knows very well that in a few days, or months at farthest, the master will again depart, leaving him again for months, perhaps for years, utterly at the mercy of the man against whom he has dared to prefer a complaint. On the estates which I visited, the owners had been habitually absent, and the "attachment" of slaves to such masters as these, you will allow, can hardly come under the denomination of a strong personal feeling.

Your authority next states that the infirm and superannuated slaves no longer capable of ministering to their masters' luxuries, on the estate that he visited, were ending their lives among all the comforts of home, with kindred and friends around them, in a condition which he contrasts, at least by implication, very favorably with the work-house, the last refuge provided by the social humanity of England for the pauper laborer when he has reached that term when "unregarded age is in corners thrown." On the plantation where I lived the Infirmary was a large room, the walls of which were simply mud and laths; the floor, the soil itself, damp with perpetual drippings from the holes in the roof; and the open space which served for a window was protected only by a broken shutter, which, in order to exclude the cold, was drawn so near as almost to exclude the light at the same time. Upon this earthen floor, with nothing but its hard, damp surface beneath him, no covering but a tattered shirt and trowsers, and a few sticks under his head for a pillow, lay an old man of upward of seventy, dying. When I first looked at him I thought, by the glazed stare of his eyes, and the flies that had gathered round his half-open mouth,

that he was dead; but on stooping nearer, I perceived
that the last faint struggle of life was still going on, but
even while I bent over him it ceased; and so, like a worn-
out hound, with no creature to comfort or relieve his last
agony, with neither Christian solace or human succor near
him, with neither wife, nor child, nor even friendly fellow-
being to lift his head from the knotty sticks on which he
had rested it, or drive away the insects that buzzed round
his lips and nostrils like those of a fallen beast, died
this poor old slave, whose life had been exhausted in unrequited labor, the fruits of which had gone to pamper
the pride and feed the luxury of those who knew and
cared neither for his life or death, and to whom, if they
had heard of the latter, it would have been a matter of
absolute though small gain, the saving of a daily pittance
of meal, which served to prolong a life no longer available
to them.

I proceed to the next item in your observer's record.
All children below the age of twelve were unemployed,
he says, on the estate he visited: this is perhaps a questionable benefit, when, no process of mental cultivation
being permitted, the only employment for the leisure thus
allowed is that of rolling, like dogs or cats, in the sand
and the sun. On all the plantations I visited, and on
those where I resided, the infants in arms were committed
to the care of these juvenile slaves, who were denominated
nurses, and whose sole employment was what they call to
"mind baby." The poor little negro sucklings were cared
for (I leave to your own judgment how efficiently or how
tenderly) by these half-savage slips of slavery—carried by
them to the fields where their mothers were working under the lash, to receive their needful nourishment, and
then carried back again to the "settlement," or collection
of negro huts, where they wallowed unheeded in utter
filth and neglect until the time again returned for their

being carried to their mother's breast. Such was the employment of the children of eight or nine years old, and the only supervision exercised over either babies or "baby-minders" was that of the old woman left in charge of the Infirmary, where she made her abode all day long, and bestowed such samples of her care and skill upon its inmates as I shall have occasion to mention presently. The practice of thus driving the mothers afield, even while their infants were still dependent upon them for their daily nourishment, is one of which the evil as well as the cruelty is abundantly apparent without comment. The next note of admiration elicited from your "impartial observer" is bestowed upon the fact that the domestic servants (*i. e.*, house slaves) on the plantation he visited were *allowed* to live away from the owner's residence, and to marry. But I never was on a Southern plantation, and I never heard of one, where any of the slaves were *allowed* to sleep under the same roof with their owner. With the exception of the women to whose care the children of the planter, if he had any, might be confided, and perhaps a little boy or girl slave, kept as a sort of pet animal, and allowed to pass the night on the floor of the sleeping apartment of some member of the family, the residence of *any* slaves belonging to a plantation night and day in their master's house, like Northern or European servants, is a thing I believe unknown throughout the Southern states. Of course I except the cities, and speak only of the estates, where the house-servants are neither better housed or accommodated than the field-hands. Their intolerably dirty habits and offensive persons would indeed render it a severe trial to any family accustomed to habits of decent cleanliness; and, moreover, considerations of safety, and that cautious vigilance which is a hard necessity of the planter's existence, in spite of the supposed attachment of his slaves, would never permit the near proximity, during the unprotected hours of the night, of those whose intimacy with the daily habits and knowledge of the nightly securities resorted to might prove terrible auxiliaries to any attack from without. The city guards, patrols, and night-watches, together with their stringent rules about about negroes being abroad after night, and their well-fortified lock-up houses for all detected without a pass, afford some security against these attached dependents; but on remote plantations, where the owner and his family, and perhaps a white overseer are alone, surrounded by slaves and separated from all succor against them, they do not sleep under the white man's roof, and for politic reasons, pass the night away from their master's abode. The house-servants have no other or better allowance of food than the field-laborers, but have the advantage of eking it out by what is left from the master's table—if possible, with even less comfort in one respect, inasmuch as no time whatever is set apart for their meals, which they snatch at any hour and in any way that they can—generally, however, standing or squatting on their hams round the kitchen fire; the kitchen being a mere out-house or barn with a fire in it. On the estate where I lived, as I have mentioned, they had no sleeping-rooms in the house; but when their work was over, they retired like the rest to their hovels, the discomfort of which had to them all the additional disadvantage of comparison with their owner's mode of living. In all establishments whatever, of course some disparity exists between the accommodation of the drawing-rooms and best bedrooms and the servants' kitchen and attics; but on a plantation it is no longer a matter of degree. The young women who performed the offices of waiting and house-maids, and the lads who attended upon the service of their master's table where I lived, had neither table to feed at nor chair to sit down upon themselves; the "boys" lay all night on the hearth by the kitchen fire, and the women upon the usual slave's bed—a frame of rough boards, strewed with a little moss off the trees, with the addition perhaps of a tattered and filthy blanket. As for the so-called privilege of marrying—surely it is gross mockery to apply such a word to a bond which may be holy in God's sight, but which did not prevent the owner of a plantation where my observations were made from selling and buying men and their so-called wives and children into divided bondage, nor the white overseer from compelling the wife of one of the most excellent and exemplary of his master's slaves to live with him; nor the white wife of another overseer, in her husband's temporary absence from the estate, from barbarously flogging three *married* slaves within a month of their confinement, their condition being the result of the profligacy of the said overseer, and probably compelled by the very same lash by which it was punished. This is a very disgusting picture of married life on slave estates; but I have undertaken to reply to the statements of your informant, and I regret to be obliged to record the facts by which alone I can do so. "Work," continues your authority, "began at six in the morning; at nine an hour's rest was allowed for breakfast, and by two or three o'clock the day's work was done." Certainly this was a pattern plantation, and I can only lament that my experience lay amid such far less favorable circumstances. The negroes among whom I lived went to the fields at daybreak, carrying with them their allowance of food, which toward noon, and not till then, they ate, cooking it over a fire which they kindled as best they could where they were working; their *second* meal in the day was at night, after their labor was over, having worked at the *very least* six hours without rest or refreshment since their noonday meal—properly so called, indeed, for it was meal and nothing else, or a preparation something thicker than porridge, which they call hominy. Perhaps the candid observer, whose report of the estate he visited appeared to you so consolatory, would think that this diet contrasted favorably with that of potato and buttermilk fed Irish laborers. But a more just comparison surely would be with the mode of living of the laboring population of the United States, the peasantry of Ohio, Pennsylvania, and Massachusetts, or indeed with the condition of those very potato and buttermilk fed Irishmen when they have exchanged their native soil for the fields of the Northern and North-western states, and when, as one of them once was heard to say, it was of no use writing home that he got meat three times a day, for nobody in Ireland would believe it. The next item in the list of commendation is the hospital, which your informant also visited, and of which he gives the following account: "It consisted of three separate wards, all clean and well ventilated: one was for lying-in women, who were invariably allowed a month's rest after their confinement." Permit me to place beside this picture that of a Southern Infirmary, such as I saw it, and taken on the spot. In the first room that I entered I found only half of the windows, of which there were six, glazed; these were almost as much obscured with dirt as the other windowless ones were darkened by the dingy shutters which the shivering inmates had closed in order to protect themselves from the cold. In the enormous chimney glimmered the powerless embers of a few chips of wood, round which as many of the sick women as had strength to approach were cowering, some on wooden settles (there was not such a thing as a chair with a back in the whole establishment), most of them on the ground, excluding those who were too ill to rise; and these poor wretches lay prostrate on the earth, without bedstead, bed, mattress, or pillow, with no

covering but the clothes they had on and some filthy rags
of blanket in which they endeavored to wrap themselves
as they lay literally strewing the floor, so that there was
hardly room to pass between them. Here, in their hour of
sickness and suffering, lay those whose health and strength
had given way under unrequited labor—some of them, no
later than the previous day, had been urged with the lash
to their accustomed tasks—and their husbands, fathers,
brothers, and sons were even at that hour sweating over
the earth whose increase was to procure for others all the
luxuries which health can enjoy, all the comforts which can
alleviate sickness. Here lay women expecting every hour
the terror and agonies of childbirth, others who had just
brought their doomed offspring into the world, others
who were groaning under the anguish and bitter disappointment of miscarriages—here lay some burning with
fever, others chilled with cold and aching with rheumatism, upon the hard cold ground, the draughts and damp
of the atmosphere increasing their sufferings, and dirt,
noise, stench, and every aggravation of which sickness is
capable combined in their condition. There had been
among them one or two cases of prolonged and terribly
hard labor; and the method adopted by the ignorant old
negress, who was the sole matron, midwife, nurse, physician, surgeon, and servant of the Infirmary, to assist them
in their extremity, was to tie a cloth tight round the throats
of the agonized women, and by drawing it till she almost
suffocated them she produced violent and spasmodic struggles, which she assured me she thought materially assisted the progress of the labor. This was one of the Southern Infirmaries with which I was acquainted; and I beg to
conclude this chapter of contrasts to your informant's consolatory views of slavery by assuring you once more very
emphatically that they have been one and all drawn from
estates where the slaves esteemed themselves well treat-

ed, were reputed generally to be so, and undoubtedly, as
far as my observation went, were so, compared with those
on several of the adjoining plantations.

With regard to the statement respecting the sums of
money earned by industrious negroes, there is no doubt
that it is perfectly correct. I know of some slaves on a
plantation in the extreme South who had received, at various times, large sums of money from a shopkeeper in the
small town near their estate for the gray moss or lichen
collected from the evergreen oaks of Carolina and Georgia, upon which it hangs in vast masses, and after some
cleaning process becomes an excellent substitute for horse-
hair, for bed, chair, and sofa-stuffing.  On another estate,
some of the slaves were expert boat-makers, and had been
allowed by their masters to retain the price (no inconsiderable one) for some that they had found time to manu-
facture after their day's labor was accomplished.  These
were undoubtedly privileges ; but I confess it appears to
me that the juster view of the matter would be this : if
these men were industrious enough, out of their scanty
leisure, to earn these sums of money, which a mere exercise of arbitrary will on the part of the master allowed
them to keep, how much more of remuneration, of comfort, of improvement, physical and mental, might they not
have achieved, had the due price of their daily labor merely been paid to them?  It seems to me that this is the
mode of putting the case to Englishmen, and all who have
not agreed to consider uncertain favor an equivalent for
common justice in the dealings of man with man.  As the
slaves are well known to toil for years sometimes to amass
the means of rescuing themselves from bondage, the fact
of their being able and sometimes allowed to earn considerable sums of money is notorious.  But now that I have
answered one by one the instances you have produced,
with others—I am sure as accurate, and I believe as com-

mon—of an entirely opposite description, permit me to
ask you what this sort of testimony amounts to. I allow
you full credit for yours, allow me full credit for mine,
and the result is very simply a nullification of the one by
the other statement, and a proof that there is as much
good as evil in the details of slavery; but now, be pleased
to throw into the scale this consideration, that the principle of the whole is unmitigated abominable evil, as by
your own acknowledgment you hold it to be, and add,
moreover, that the principle being invariably bad beyond
the power of the best man acting under it to alter its ex-
ecrable injustice, the goodness of the detail is a matter absolutely dependent upon the will of each individual slaveholder, so that though the best can not make the system
in the smallest particular better, the bad can make every
practical detail of it as atrocious as the principle itself;
and then tell me upon what ground you palliate a monstrous iniquity, which is the rule, because of the accidental exceptions which go to prove it. Moreover, if, as you
have asserted, good preponderates over evil in the practice, though not in the theory of slavery, or it would not
maintain its existence, why do you uphold to us, with so
much complacency, the hope that it is surely, if not rapidly approaching its abolishment? Why is the preponderating good, which has, as you say, proved sufficient to uphold the institution hitherto, to become (in spite of the
spread of civilization and national progress, and the gradual improvement of the slaves themselves) inadequate to
its perpetuation henceforward? Or why, if good really
has prevailed in it, do you rejoice that it is speedily to
pass away? You say the emancipation of the slaves is
inevitable, and that through progressive culture the negro
of the Southern states daily approaches more nearly to
the recovery of the rights of which he has been robbed.
But whence do you draw this happy augury, except from

the hope, which all Christian souls must cherish, that God
will not permit much longer so great a wickedness to
darken the face of the earth? Surely the increased stringency of the Southern slave-laws, the more than ever vig-
ilant precautions against all attempts to enlighten or educate the negroes, the severer restrictions on manumission,
the thrusting forth out of certain states of all free persons
of color, the atrocious Fugitive Slave Bill, one of the latest
achievements of Congress, and the piratical attempt upon
Cuba, avowedly, on the part of all Southerners, abetting
or justifying it because it will add slave territory and
600,000 slaves to their possessions—surely these do not
seem indications of the better state of things you antici-
pate, except, indeed, as the straining of the chain beyond
all endurable tightness significantly suggests the probability of its giving way.

I do not believe the planters have any disposition to
put an end to slavery, nor is it perhaps much to be wondered at that they have not. To do so is, in the opinion
of the majority of them, to run the risk of losing their
property, perhaps their lives, for a benefit which they profess to think doubtful to the slaves themselves. How far
they are right in anticipating ruin from the manumission
of their slaves I think questionable, but that they do so is
certain, and self-impoverishment for the sake of abstract
principle is not a thing to be reasonably expected from
any large class of men. But, besides the natural fact that
the slaveholders wish to retain their property, emancipation is, in their view of it, not only a risk of enormous pe-
cuniary loss, and of their entire social status, but involves
elements of personal danger, and, above all, disgust to inveterate prejudices, which they will assuredly never encounter. The question is not alone one of foregoing great
wealth or the mere means of subsistence (in either case
almost equally hard); it is not alone the unbinding the

hands of those who have many a bloody debt of hatred and revenge to settle; it is not alone the consenting suddenly to see by their side, upon a footing of free social equality, creatures toward whom their predominant feeling is one of mingled terror and abhorrence, and who, during the whole of their national existence, have been, as the earth, trampled beneath their feet, yet ever threatening to gape and swallow them alive. It is not all this alone which makes it unlikely that the Southern planter should desire to free his slaves: freedom in America is not merely a personal right; it involves a political privilege. Freemen there are legislators. The rulers of the land are the majority of the people, and in many parts of the Southern states the black free citizens would become, if not at once, yet in process of time, inevitably voters, landholders, delegates to state Legislatures, members of Assembly—who knows?—senators, judges, aspirants to the presidency of the United States. You must be an American, or have lived long among them, to conceive the shout of derisive execration with which such an idea would be hailed from one end of the land to the other.

That the emancipation of the negroes need not necessarily put them in possession of the franchise is of course obvious; but, as a general consequence, the one would follow from the other; and at present certainly the slaveholders are no more ready to grant the political privilege than the natural right of freedom. Under these circumstances, though the utmost commiseration is naturally excited by the slaves, I agree with you that some forbearance is due to the masters. It is difficult to conceive a more awful position than theirs: fettered by laws which impede every movement toward right and justice, and utterly without the desire to repeal them—dogged by the apprehension of nameless retributions—bound beneath a burden of responsibility for which, whether they acknowledge it or not, they are held accountable by God and men —goaded by the keen consciousness of the growing reprobation of all civilized Christian communities, their existence presents the miserable moral counterpart of the physical condition of their slaves; and it is one compared with which that of the wretchedest slave is, in my judgment, worthy of envy.

---

## Letter to C. G., Esq.

BEFORE entering upon my answer to your questions, let me state that I have no claim to be ranked as an Abolitionist in the American acceptation of the word, for I have hitherto held the emancipation of the slaves to be exclusively the business and duty of their owners, whose highest moral interest I thought it was to rid themselves of such a responsibility, in spite of the manifold worldly interests almost inextricably bound up with it.

This has been my feeling hitherto with regard to the views of the Abolitionists, which I now, however, heartily embrace, inasmuch as I think that from the moment the United States government assumed an attitude of coercion and supremacy toward the Southern states, it was bound, with its fleets and armies, to introduce its polity with respect to slavery, and wherever it planted the standard of the Union, to proclaim the universal freedom which is the recognized law of the Northern United States. That they have not done so has been partly owing to a superstitious but honorable veneration for the letter of their great charter, the Constitution, and still more to the hope they have never ceased to entertain of bringing back the South to its allegiance under the former conditions of the Union, an event which will be rendered impossible by any attempt to interfere with the existence of slavery.

The North, with the exception of an inconsiderable minority of its inhabitants, has never been at all desirous of the emancipation of the slaves. The Democratic party, which has ruled the United States for many years past, has always been friendly to the slaveholders, who have, with few exceptions, been all members of it (for, by a strange perversion both of words and ideas, some of the most democratic states in the Union are Southern slave states, and in the part of Georgia where the slave population is denser than in any other part of the South, a county exists bearing the satirical title of *Liberty County*). And the support of the South has been given to the Northern Democratic politicians upon the distinct understanding that their "domestic institution" was to be guaranteed to them.

The condition of the free blacks in the Northern states has of course been affected most unfavorably by the slavery of their race throughout the other half of the Union; and, indeed, it would have been a difficult matter for Northern citizens to maintain toward the blacks an attitude of social and political equality as far as the borders of Delaware, while immediately beyond they were pledged to consider them as the "chattels" of their owners, animals no more noble or human than the cattle in their masters' fields.

How could peace have been maintained if the Southern slaveholders had been compelled to endure the sight of negroes rising to wealth and eminence in the Northern cities, or entering as fellow-members with themselves the halls of that Legislature to which all free-born citizens are eligible? They would very certainly have declined with fierce scorn, not the fellowship of the blacks alone, but of those white men who admitted the despised race of their serfs to a footing of such impartial equality. It therefore was the instinctive, and became the deliberate policy of the Northern people, once pledged to maintain slavery in the South, to make their task easy by degrading the blacks in the Northern states to a condition contrasting as little as possible with that of the Southern slaves. The Northern politicians struck hands with the Southern slaveholders, and the great majority of the most enlightened citizens of the Northern states, absorbed in the pursuit of wealth and the extension and consolidation of their admirable and wonderful national prosperity, abandoned the government of their noble country and the preservation of its nobler institutions to the slaveholding aristocracy of the South—to a mob of politicians by trade, the vilest and most venal class of men that ever disgraced and endangered a country—to foreign emigrants, whose brutish ignorance did not prevent the Democratic party from seizing upon them as voters, and bestowing on the Irish and German boors just landed on their shores the same political privileges as those possessed and intelligently exercised by the farmers and mechanics of New England, the most enlightened men of their class to be found in the world.

The gradual encroachment of the Southern politicians upon the liberties of the North, by their unrelaxing influence in Congress and over successive cabinets and presidents, was not without its effect in stimulating some resistance on the part of Northern statesmen of sufficient intelligence to perceive the inevitable results toward which this preponderance in the national councils was steadily tending; and I need not remind you of the rapidity and force with which General Jackson quelled an incipient rebellion in South Carolina, when Mr. Calhoun made the tariff question the pretext for a threatened secession in 1832, of the life-long opposition to Southern pretensions by John Quincy Adams, of the endeavor of Mr. Clay to stem the growing evil by the conditions of the Missouri Compromise, and all the occasional attempts of individuals of more conscientious convictions than their fellow-citizens on the subject of the sin of slavery, from Dr. Channing's eloquent protest on the annexation of Texas, to Mr. Charles Sumner's philippic against Mr. Brooks, of South Carolina.

The disorganization of the Democratic party, after a cohesion of so many years, at length changed the aspect of affairs, and the North appeared to be about to arouse itself from its apathetic consent to Southern domination. The Republican party, headed by Colonel Fremont, who was known to be an anti-slavery man, nearly carried the presidential election six years ago, and then every preparation had been made in the South for the process of secession, which was only averted by the election of Mr. Buchanan, a pro-slavery Southern sympathizer, though born in Pennsylvania. Under his presidency, the Southern statesmen, resuming their attitude of apparent friendliness with the North, kept in abeyance, maturing and perfecting by every treasonable practice, for which their preponderating share in the cabinet afforded them facilities, the plan of the violent disruption of the Union, upon which they had determined whenever the Republican party should have acquired sufficient strength to elect a president with Northern views. Before, however, this event occurred, the war in Kansas rang a prophetic peal of warning through the land; and the struggle there begun between New England emigrants bent on founding a free state, and Missouri border ruffians determined to make the new territory a slaveholding addition to the South, might have roused the whole North and West to the imminence of the peril by which the safety of the Union was threatened.

But neither the struggle in Kansas, nor the strange and piteous episode which grew out of it, of John Brown's attempt to excite an insurrection in Virginia, and his exe-

cution by the government of that state, did more than
startle the North with a nine days' wonder out of its
apathetic indifference. The Republican party, it is true,
gained adherents, and acquired strength by degrees; and
Mr. Buchanan's term of office approaching its expiration,
it became apparent that the Democratic party was about
to lose its supremacy, and the slaveholders their dominion; and no sooner was this evident than the latter threw
off the mask, and renounced their allegiance to the Union.
In a day—in an hour almost—those stood face to face as
mortal enemies who were citizens of the same country,
subjects of the same government, children of the same
soil; and the North, incredulous and amazed, found itself suddenly summoned to retrieve its lost power and
influence, and assert the dignity of the insulted Union
against the rebellious attempt of the South to overthrow
it.

But it was late for them to take that task in hand.
For years the conduct of the government of the United
States had been becoming a more desperate and degraded
*jobbery*, one from which day by day the Northern gentlemen of intelligence, influence, and education withdrew
themselves in greater disgust, devoting their energies to
schemes of mere personal advantage, and leaving the
commonweal with selfish and contemptuous indifference
to the guidance of any hands less nice and less busy than
their own.

Nor would the Southern planters—a prouder and more
aristocratic race than the Northern merchants—have rel-
ished the companionship of their fellow-politicians more
than the latter, but *their* personal interests were at stake,
and immediately concerned in their maintaining their predominant influence over the government; and while the
Boston men wrote and talked transcendentalism, and became the most accomplished of *æstetische* cotton-spinners

and railroad speculators, and made the shoes and cowhides of the Southerners, the latter made their laws (I believe New Jersey is really the great cowhide factory);
and the New York men, owners of the fastest horses and
finest houses in the land, having made a sort of Brum-
magem Paris of their city, were the bankers and brokers
of the Southerners, while the latter were the legislators.

The grip the slaveholders had fastened on the helm of
the state had been tightening for nearly half a century,
till the government of the nation had become literally
theirs, and the idea of their relinquishing it was one
which the North did not contemplate, and they would
not tolerate.

If I have said nothing of the grievances which the South
has alleged against the North—its tariff, made chiefly in
the interest of the Northeastern manufacturing states,
or its inconsiderable but enthusiastic Massachusetts and
Pennsylvania Abolition party, it is because I do not believe these causes of complaint would have had the same
effect upon any but a community of slaveholders, men
made impatient (by the life-long habit of despotism) not
only of all control, but of any opposition.  Thirty years
ago Andrew Jackson—a man of keen sagacity as well as
determined energy—wrote of them that they were bent
upon destroying the Union, and that, whatever was the
pretext of their discontent, that was their aim and purpose.  "To-day," he wrote, "it is the tariff, by-and-by it
will be slavery."  The event has proved how true a
prophet he was.  My own conviction is that the national
character produced and fostered by slaveholding is incompatible with free institutions, and that the Southern aristocracy, thanks to the pernicious influences by which
they are surrounded, are unfit to be members of a Christian republic.  It is slavery that has made the Southerners rebels to their government, traitors to their country,

and the originators of the bloodiest civil war that ever disgraced humanity and civilization. It is for their sinful complicity in slavery, and their shameful abandonment of all their duties as citizens, that the Northerners are paying in the blood of their men, the tears of their women, and the treasure which they have till now held more precious than their birthright. They must now not merely impose a wise restriction upon slavery, they must be prepared to extinguish it. They neglected and despised the task of moderating its conditions and checking its growth; they must now suddenly, in the midst of unparalleled difficulties and dangers, be ready to deal summarily with its entire existence. They have loved the pursuit of personal prosperity and pleasure more than their country; and now they must spend life and living to reconquer their great inheritance, and win back at the sword's point what Heaven had forbidden them to lose. Nor are we, here in England, without part in this tremendous sin and sorrow; we have persisted in feeding our looms, and the huge wealth they coin, with the produce of slavery. In vain our vast Indian territory has solicited the advantage of becoming our free cotton plantation; neither our manufacturers nor our government would venture, would wait, would spend or lose, for that purpose; the slave-grown harvest was ready, was abundant, was cheap—and now the thousand arms of our great national industry are folded in deplorable inactivity; the countless hands that wrought from morn till night the wealth that was a world's wonder are stretched unwillingly to beg their bread; and England has never seen a sadder sight than the enforced idleness of her poor operatives, or a nobler one than their patient and heroic endurance.

And now you ask me what plan, what scheme, what project the government of the United States has formed for the safe and successful emancipation of four millions of slaves, in the midst of a country distracted with all the horrors of war, and the male population of which is engaged in military service at a distance from their homes? Most assuredly none. Precipitated headlong from a state of apparent profound security and prosperity into a series of calamitous events which have brought the country to the verge of ruin, neither the nation or its governors have had leisure to prepare themselves for any of the disastrous circumstances they have had to encounter, least of all for the momentous change which the President's proclamation announces as imminent: a measure of supreme importance, not deliberately adopted as the result of philanthropic conviction or far-sighted policy, but (if not a mere feint of party politics) the last effort of the incensed spirit of endurance in the North — a punishment threatened against rebels, whom they can not otherwise subdue, and which a year ago half the Northern population would have condemned upon principle, and more than half revolted from on instinct.

The country being in a state of war necessarily complicates every thing, and renders the most plausible suggestions for the settlement of the question of emancipation futile, because from first to last now it will be one tremendous chapter of accidents, instead of a carefully considered and wisely prepared measure of government. But, supposing the war to have ceased, either by the success of the Northern arms or by the consent of both belligerents, the question of manumission in the Southern states when reduced to the condition of territories or restored to the sway of their own elected governors and Legislatures, though difficult, is by no means one of insuperable difficulty; and I do not believe that a great nation of Englishmen, having once the will to rid itself of a danger and a disgrace, will fail to find a way. The thing, therefore, most to be desired now is, that Americans may unanimously embrace the purpose of emancipation, and, though they have been reluctantly driven by the irresistible force of circumstances to contemplate the measure, may henceforward never avert their eyes from it till it is accomplished.

When I was in the South many years ago I conversed frequently with two highly intelligent men, both of whom agreed in saying that the immense value of the slaves as property was the only real obstacle to their manumission, and that whenever the Southerners became convinced that it was their interest to free them they would very soon find the means to do it. In some respects the conditions are more favorable than those we had to encounter in freeing our West India slaves. Though the soil and climate of the Southern states are fertile and favorable, they are not tropical, and there is no profuse natural growth of fruits or vegetables to render subsistence possible without labor; the winter temperature is like that of the Roman States; and even as far south as Georgia and the borders of Florida, frosts severe enough to kill the orange-trees are sometimes experienced. The inhabitants of the Southern states, throughout by far the largest portion of their extent, must labor to live, and will undoubtedly obey the beneficent law of necessity whenever they are made to feel that their existence depends upon their own exertions. The plan of a gradual emancipation, preceded by a limited apprenticeship of the negroes to white masters, is of course often suggested as less dangerous than their entire and immediate enfranchisement. But when years ago I lived on a Southern plantation, and had opportunities of observing the miserable results of the system on every thing connected with it—the souls, minds, bodies, and estates of both races of men, and the very soil on which they existed together—I came to the conclusion that immediate and entire emancipation was not only an act of imperative right, but would be the safest and most profitable course for the interests of both parties. The gradual and inevitable process of ruin which exhibits itself in the long run on every property involving slavery, naturally suggests some element of decay inherent in the system; the reckless habits of extravagance and prodigality in the masters, the ruinous wastefulness and ignorant incapacity of the slaves, the deterioration of the land under the exhausting and thriftless cultivation to which it is subjected, made it evident to me that there were but two means of maintaining a prosperous ownership in Southern plantations : either the possession of considerable capital wherewith to recruit the gradual waste of the energies of the soil, and supply by all the improved and costly methods of modern agriculture the means of profitable cultivation (a process demanding, as English farmers know, an enormous and incessant outlay of both money and skill), or an unlimited command of fresh soil, to which the slaves might be transferred as soon as that already under culture exhibited signs of exhaustion. Now the Southerners are for the most part men whose only wealth is in their land and laborers—a large force of slaves is their most profitable investment. The great capitalists and moneyed men of the country are Northern men; the planters are men of large estates but restricted means : many of them are deeply involved in debt, and there are very few who do not depend from year to year for their subsistence on the harvest of their fields and the chances of the cotton and rice crops of each season.

This makes it of vital importance to them to command an unrestricted extent of territory. The man who can move a " gang" of able-bodied negroes to a tract of virgin soil is sure of an immense return of wealth; as sure as that he who is circumscribed in this respect, and limited to the cultivation of certain lands with cotton or tobacco by slaves, will in the course of a few years see his estate gradually exhausted and unproductive, refusing its increase, while its black population, propagating and multiplying, will compel him eventually, under penalty of starvation, to make *them* his crop, and substitute, as the Virginians have been constrained to do, a traffic in human cattle for the cultivation of vegetable harvests.

The steady decrease of the value of the cotton-crop, even on the famous sea-island plantations of Georgia, often suggested to me the inevitable ruin of the owners within a certain calculable space of time, as the land became worn out, and the negroes continued to increase in number; and had the estate on which I lived been mine, and the laws of Georgia not made such an experiment impossible, I would have emancipated the slaves on it immediately, and turned them into a free tenantry, as the first means of saving my property from impending destruction. I would have paid them wages, and they should have paid me rent. I would have relinquished the charge of feeding and clothing them, and the burden of their old, young, and infirm; in short, I would have put them at once upon the footing of free hired laborers. Of course such a process would have involved temporary loss, and for a year or two the income of the estate would, I dare say, have suffered considerably; but, in all such diversions of labor or capital from old into new channels and modes of operation, there must be an immediate sacrifice of present to future profit, and I do not doubt that the estate would have recovered from the momentary necessary interruption of its productiveness, to resume it with an upward instead of a downward tendency, and a vigorous impulse toward progress and improvement substituted for the present slow but sure drifting to stagnation and decay.

As I have told you, the land affords no spontaneous produce which will sustain life without labor. The negroes, therefore, must work to eat; they are used to the soil and climate, and accustomed to the agriculture, and there is no reason at all to apprehend—as has been suggested—that a race of people singularly attached to the place of their birth and residence would abandon in any large numbers their own country, just as the conditions of their existence in it were made more favorable, to try the unknown and (to absolute ignorance) forbidding risks of emigration to the sterner climate and harder soil of the Northern states.

Of course, in freeing the slaves, it would be necessary to contemplate the possibility of their becoming eventual proprietors of the soil to some extent themselves. There is as little doubt that many of them would soon acquire the means of doing so (men who amass, during hours of daily extra labor, through years of unpaid toil, the means of buying themselves from their masters, would soon justify their freedom by the intelligent improvement of their condition), as that many of the present landholders would be ready and glad to alienate their impoverished estates by parcels, and sell the land which has become comparatively unprofitable to them, to its enfranchised cultivators. This, the future ownership of land by negroes, as well as their admission to those rights of citizenship which every where in America such ownership involves, would necessarily be future subjects of legislation; and either or both privileges might be withheld temporarily, indefinitely, or permanently, as might seem expedient, and the progress in civilization which might justify such an extension of rights. These, and any other modifications of the state of the black population in the South, would require great wisdom to deal with, but their immediate transformation from bondsmen to free might, I think, be accomplished with little danger or difficulty, and with certain increase of prosperity to the Southern states.

On the other hand, it is not impossible that, left to the unimpeded action of the natural laws that govern the existence of various races, the black population, no longer directly preserved and propagated for the purposes of slavery, might gradually decrease and dwindle, as it does at the North, where, besides the unfavorable influence of a cold climate on a race originally African, it suffers from its admixture with the whites, and the amalgamation of the two races, as far as it goes, tends evidently to the destruction of the weaker. The Northern mulattoes are an unhealthy, feeble population, and it might yet appear that even under the more favorable influence of a Southern climate, whenever the direct stimulus afforded by slavery to the increase of the negroes was removed, their gradual extinction or absorption by the predominant white race would follow in the course of time.

But the daily course of events appears to be rendering more and more unlikely the immediate effectual enfranchisement of the slaves: the President's proclamation will reach with but little efficacy beyond the mere borders of the Southern states. The war is assuming an aspect of indefinite duration; and it is difficult to conceive what will be the condition of the blacks, freed *de jure* but by no means *de facto*, in the vast interior regions of the Southern states, as long as the struggle raging all round their confines does not penetrate within them. Each of the combatants is far too busily absorbed in the furious strife to afford thought, leisure, or means either effectually to free the slaves or effectually to replace them in bondage; and, in the mean time, their condition is the worst possible for the future success of either operation. If the North succeeds in subjugating the South, its earliest business will be to make the freedom of the slaves real as well as nominal, and as little injurious to themselves as possible. If, on the other hand, the South makes good its pre-

tensions to a separate national existence, no sooner will
the disseverment of the Union be an established fact than
the slaveholders will have to consolidate once more the
system of their "peculiar institution," to reconstruct the
prison which has half crumbled to the ground, and rivet
afresh the chains which have been all but struck off.
This will be difficult: the determination of the North to
restrict the area of slavery by forbidding its ingress into
future territories and states has been considered by the
slaveholders a wrong, and a danger justifying a bloody
civil war; inasmuch as, if under those circumstances
they did not abolish slavery themselves in a given number of years, it would infallibly abolish them by the increase of the negro population, hemmed with them into
a restricted space by this *cordon sanitaire* drawn round
them. But, bad as this prospect has seemed to slaveholders (determined to continue such), and justifying—
as it may be conceded that it does from their point of
view—not a ferocious civil war, but a peaceable separation from states whose interests were declared absolutely irreconcilable with theirs, the position in which they
will find themselves if the contest terminates in favor of
secession will be undoubtedly more difficult and terrible
than the one the mere anticipation of which has driven
them to the dire resort of civil war. All round the Southern coast, and all along the course of the great Mississippi,
and all across the northern frontier of the slave states, the
negroes have already thrown off the trammels of slavery.
Whatever their condition may be—and doubtless, in many
respects, it is miserable enough—they are to all intents
and purposes free. Vast numbers of them have joined the
Northern invading armies, and considerable bodies of
them have become organized as soldiers and laborers, under the supervision of Northern officers and employers;
most of them have learned the use of arms, and possess

them; all of them have exchanged the insufficient slave diet of grits and rice for the abundant supplies of animal food, which the poorest laborer in that favored land of cheap provisions and high wages indulges in to an extent unknown in any other country. None of these slaves of yesterday will be the same slaves to-morrow. Little essential difference as may yet have been effected by the President's proclamation in the interior of the South in the condition of the blacks, it is undoubtedly known to them, and they are waiting in ominous suspense its accomplishment or defeat by the fortune of the war; they are watching the issue of the contest of which they well know themselves to be the theme, and at its conclusion, end how it will, they must be emancipated or exterminated. With the North not only not friendly to slavery, but henceforward bitterly hostile to slaveholders, and no more to be reckoned upon as heretofore, it might have been infallibly by the Southern white population in any difficulty with the blacks (a fact of which the negroes will be as well aware as their former masters)—with an invisible boundary stretching from ocean to ocean, over which they may fly without fear of a master's claim following them a single inch—with the hope and expectation of liberty suddenly snatched from them at the moment it seemed within their grasp—with the door of their dungeon once more barred between them and the light into which they were in the act of emerging, is it to be conceived that these four millions of people, many thousands of whom are already free and armed, will submit without a struggle to be again thrust down into the hell of slavery? Hitherto there has been no insurrection among the negroes, and observers friendly and inimical to them have alike drawn from that fact conclusions unfavorable to their appreciation of the freedom apparently within their grasp; but they are waiting to see what the North will really achieve for them. The liberty offered them is hitherto anomalous, and uncertain enough in its conditions; they probably trust it as little as they know it; but slavery they *do* know; and when once they find themselves again delivered over to *that* experience, there will not be ONE insurrection in the South—there will be an insurrection in every state, in every county, on every plantation—a struggle as fierce as it will be futile—a hopeless effort of hopeless men, which will baptize in blood the new American nation, and inaugurate its birth among the civilized societies of the earth, not by the manumission, but the massacre of every slave within its borders.

Perhaps, however, Mr. Jefferson Davis means to free the negroes. Whenever that consummation is attained, the root of bitterness will have perished from the land; and when a few years shall have passed, blunting the hatred which has been excited by this fratricidal strife, the Americans of both the Northern and Southern states will perceive that the selfish policy of other nations would not have so rejoiced over their division, had it not seemed, to those who loved them not, the proof of past failure and the prophecy of future weakness.

Admonished by its terrible experiences, I believe the nation will reunite itself under one government, remodel its Constitution, and again address itself to fulfill its glorious destiny. I believe that the country sprung from ours—of all our just subjects of national pride the greatest—will resume its career of prosperity and power, and become the noblest as well as the mightiest that has existed among the nations of the earth.

THE END.

# TEN YEARS

## ON A

# GEORGIA PLANTATION

*SINCE THE WAR*

BY

FRANCES BUTLER LEIGH

'Come from the four winds, O breath, and breathe upon these slain, that they may live'—*Ezekiel* xxxvii–9

      'O wheresoever these may be
      Betwixt the slumber of the poles
      To-day they count as kindred souls'—*In Memoriam*

# *BROTHERS AGAIN:*

SUGGESTED BY DECORATION DAY, 1877.

———◆◇◆———

## I.

Great Land! of all thy children 'tis the part
To give themselves to thee, to shelter thee,
To live for thee, and love with their whole heart,
Or die for thy fair fame, if needs must be :
And of thy children, both from South and North,
Some went to battle called in thousands forth
By thy dear voice, and conquered, though they
     died ;
And some, who heard indeed that solemn call,
But wrongly heard, fell on a vanquished side,
Yet well contented for that side to fall ;
Brothers with brothers fought, and in that fight
Let all rejoice who fell, still thinking they were
     right.

## II.

I wandered slowly through a far off-town,
Where the white winter comes not, nor the storm
Lashes with icy scourge fair flowers down
To early graves ; where balmy winds disarm
The wrathful tempest's rage ; and as I went,
Sudden I came upon a monument.
Inscribed was this : *To the Confederate Dead :*
And underneath, the period of the strife,—
Those four dire years that dashed away the life,
The life of priceless thousands, and o'erspread
Our land with mourning ;—on the other side
Only these words : ' *Come from the four winds, O*
 *Breath,*
*And breathe upon these slain that they may live :* '
No bitterness, no anger, naught beside
A sigh of silence, unexpressed, that saith
Of sorrow more than tears could weep, loud grief
 could give.

## III.

Then the whole story of the war, methought,
Passed in its dreary length from first to last,—
By those great words into my memory brought,
Summoned from out the pages of the past.
An April dawn, near ninety years before,
Had seen a horseman in the shadowy night

Flit through New England's towns announcing war,
Calling the stout old patriots out to fight :—
An April dawn saw that first crashing shell
Rush through the startled air, and thundering
    burst
On Sumter's head ; and as it shattering fell,
The herald sound shrieked discord.   This the last
Alarm of strife, and then in dark array
Battle on battle followed, fray on fray :
Name after name, in stern succession falling,
Bears with it countless tales of blood and woe ;
What countless others, mournful, sad, appalling,
Must silent rest, with voices silent too !
What multitudes of heroes now are resting
Unknown beneath the sod where first they fell !
And slander's tongue their name has ceased molest-
    ing,—
Has let them lie untroubled where they fell ;
While through the country each name with it bears
A memory of triumph or of tears.
Sadly to hearts bereaved they now must sound,
Beginning with themselves a life-long grief,
Recalling as each separate year comes round
Some sorrow borne alone beyond relief.
See quiet Williamsburg, where swaying shade
O'erspreads the tree-girt college ; fire and blood
In all their ghastly shapes her halls invade,
While flames resistless scar the scorching wood.
High soars the blaze, nor deigns on earth to tread,

But flies remorseless o'er the silent dead.
Above that fitful glare the leaden sky
Grows lurid at the sight of agony,
Till darker ever as the cloud descends
Heaven pours the flood, and night the horror ends.
Then followed seasons when the deadly heat
Fell in its fury on the parching earth,
And on the springing crops resistless beat,
Bearing a time of drought, a time of dearth :
Then gloomy Autumn, dismal with its rains,
A weary time, when our fair nation's brow
Was racked with sorrow, while on marshy plains
Still poured her life-blood, still increased her woe ;
Huge swamps extended o'er the tedious track,
And rivers rose, and pestilence was shed
On saddened ranks, and as report came back
Of some new fight, of some new hero dead,
Our land was forced to weep upon the graves
Of sons unnatural, of erring braves.
Still the grim trump of war, whose thrilling blast
Shaketh the battlements of peace, whose shock
Has made our country reel, its summons cast
Forth to the skies, and to the battle smoke
Marshalled both young and old, and wider through
Both North and South the desolation grew.
Up to the Northern gates the contest surges,
And three long days at Gettysburg runs high :
Out went both young and old ; the funeral dirges
Blend with the glorious chant of victory.

Three fearful days beneath the burning sun!
What hopes soared up, and fell, ere they were done!
And when the twilight bless'd came gently creep-
    ing,
For the third time over that bloody scene,
Where their last slumber gallant forms were sleep-
    ing
On hills that once, alas! were fair and green—
When in that night of stillness, sad, serene,
Fond mothers sought their voiceless sons with
    weeping,
And sounds of nature sang a solemn song
Through the deep woods, and rushing brooks
    along—
Then was the land in the abysm of war,
Yet still, how long a time ere it was o'er!


IV.

Here the grim picture on my sight
Crowded too swift to see each fight,
But in the darkness of the night,
    The Wilderness I saw;
And fighting forms and charging lines—
Or in the dusk the beacon signs
As through the wood the watch-fire shines,
    And skulking foes withdraw:—
Swift and more swift the pageant moves,
Now climbing hills, and now in groves,

Now on some blasted heath,
While still the lurid smoke and glare
Cover the sky and choke the air,
    Leaving their work beneath ;
For all along that weary way
The dead and dying scattered lay.
And so proceeding to the close,
    They fight, and fall, and die,
Until no more the watch-fire glows,
    Nor swells the battle cry :
'Tis done ;—the dead are now at rest
Upon their country's rugged breast.


## V.

The wild bird builds her nest in branches tall,
Amid the sheltering foliage of the tree
Whose life was shattered by the deadly ball
That crashed its green boughs once so ruthlessly :
The wild bird sings his carol o'er the graves
Of many fallen heroes where the grass
Has grown, or where the ceaseless murmuring
        waves
The site of some past conflict scarce can trace :
If Nature thus, with all her healing arts,
Hath striven to smooth the furrows from the breast
Of our dear land, should we not do our best
To smooth all furrows from our wounded hearts ?
Then let us pray that as the sun and showers

Have charmed with their soft spell the dreary
    scenes,
Till scarce they know themselves through all the
    flowers
Strewn in their brakes and on their sloping greens,
So we may let the showers of Lethe flow
Upon the memory of that time of woe.

## VI.

Shade-wrapped Savannah!   By thy monument
A lesson hath been taught to great and small,
O may thy prayers be heard, its answer sent,
Granted by Heaven's grace unto us all!
And when th' Eternal breath shall come at last,
Breathing upon the land and summoning
From all the battle-field an army vast,
And by its power from every region bring
Both young and old, from every sepulchre
On mountain side, by stream and forest brake,
And shall along the moaning ocean stir,
Causing our dead from their long sleep to wake—
The soldiers shall arise, mingled in death,
And come together to the throne all bright,
Each to be judged according to his light,
Made perfect by that Great All-healing Breath ;
No strife, no rancour, nothing bitter then,
But they shall join their hands Brothers again.

                        O. W.

# TEN YEARS

## ON

# A GEORGIA PLANTATION.

---

## CHAPTER I.

### CHAOS.

THE year after the war between the North and the South, I went to the South with my father to look after our property in Georgia and see what could be done with it.

The whole country had of course undergone a complete revolution. The changes that a four years' war must bring about in any country would alone have been enough to give a different aspect to everything ; but at the South, besides the changes brought about by the war, our slaves had been freed ; the

white population was conquered, ruined, and
disheartened, unable for the moment to see
anything but ruin before as well as behind,
too wedded to the fancied prosperity of the
old system to believe in any possible success
under the new. And even had the people
desired to begin at once to rebuild their
fortunes, it would have been in most cases
impossible, for in many families the young
men had perished in the war, and the old
men, if not too old for the labour and effort
it required to set the machinery of peace
going again, were beggared, and had not even
money enough to buy food for themselves
and their families, let alone their negroes, to
whom they now had to pay wages as well as
feed them.

Besides this, the South was still treated
as a conquered country. The white people
were disfranchised, the local government in
the hands of either military men or Northern
adventurers, the latter of whom, with no
desire to promote either the good of the

country or people, but only to advance their own private ends, encouraged the negroes in all their foolish and extravagant ideas of freedom, set them against their old masters, filled their minds with false hopes, and pandered to their worst passions, in order to secure for themselves some political office which they hoped to obtain through the negro vote.

Into this state of things we came from the North, and I was often asked at the time, and have been since, to write some account of my own personal experience of the condition of the South immediately after the war, and during the following five years. But I never felt inclined to do so until now, when, in reading over a quantity of old letters written at the time, I find so much in them that is interesting, illustrative of the times and people, that I have determined to copy some of my accounts and descriptions, which may interest some persons now, and my children hereafter. Soon everything will be so changed, and the old traits of the negro slave have so entirely vanished, as to make stories about them sound like tales of a lost race ; and also because even now, so little is really known of the state of things politically at the South.

The accounts which have been written from time to time have been written either by travellers, who with every desire to get at the truth, could but see things superficially, or by persons whose feelings were too strong either on one side or the other to be perfectly just in their representations. I copy my impressions of things as they struck me then, although in many cases later events proved how false these impressions were, and how often mistaken I was in the opinions I formed. Indeed, we very often found ourselves taking entirely opposite views of things from day to day, which will explain apparent inconsistencies and contradictions in my statements ; but the new and unsettled condition of everything could not fail to produce this result, as well as the excited state we were all in.

I mention many rumours that reached us, which at the time we believed to be true, and which sometimes turned out to be so, but as often, not, as well as the things I know to be facts from my own personal experience, for rumours and exaggerations of all kinds made in a great measure the interest and excitement of our lives, although the reality was strange and painful enough.

On March 22, 1866, my father and myself left the North. The Southern railroads were many of them destroyed for miles, not having been rebuilt since the war, and it was very questionable how we were to get as far as Savannah, a matter we did accomplish however, in a week's time, after the following adventures, of which I find an account in my letters written at the time. We stopped one day in Washington, and went all over the new Capitol, which had been finished since I was there five years ago.

On Saturday we left, reaching Richmond at
four o'clock on Sunday morning. I notice
that it is a peculiarity of Southern railroads
that they always either arrive, or start, at four
o'clock in the morning. That day we spent
quietly there, and sad enough it was, for
besides all the associations with the place
which crowded thick and fast upon one's
memory, half the town was a heap of burnt
ruins, showing how heavily the desolation of
war had fallen upon it. And in the afternoon
I went out to the cemetery, and after some
search found the grave I was looking for.
There he lay, with hundreds of others who
had sacrificed their lives in vain, their resting
place marked merely by small wooden head-
boards, bearing their names, regiments, and
the battles in which they fell. The grief
and excitement made me quite ill, so that I
was glad to leave the town before daylight
the next morning, and I hope I may never
be there again.

We travelled all that day in the train,

reaching Greensborough that night at eight
o'clock. Not having been able to get any
information about our route further on, we
thought it best to stop where we were until
we did find out. This difficulty was one
that met us at every fresh stopping place
along the whole journey; no one could tell
us whether the road ahead were open or not,
and, if open, whether there were any means of
getting over it. So we crawled on, dreading
at each fresh stage to find ourselves stranded
in the middle of the pine woods, with no
means of progressing further.

That night in Greensborough is one
never to be forgotten. The hotel was a miserable tumble-down old frame house, and the
room we were shown into more fit for a
stable than a human habitation; a dirty bare
floor, the panes more than half broken out of
the windows, with two ragged, dirty calico
curtains over them that waved and blew
about in the wind. The furniture consisted
of a bed, the clothes of which looked as if

they had not been changed since the war, but had been slept in, in the meanwhile, constantly, two rickety old chairs, and a table with three legs. The bed being entirely out of the question, and I very tired, I took my bundle of shawls, put them under my head against the wall, tilted my chair back, and prepared to go to sleep if I could. I was just dozing off when I heard my maid, whom I had kept in the room for protection, give a start and exclamation which roused me. I asked her what was the matter, to which she replied, a huge rat had just run across the floor. This woke me quite up, and we spent the rest of the night shivering and shaking with the cold, and knocking on the floor with our umbrellas to frighten away the rats, which from time to time came out to look at us.

At four in the morning my father came for us, and we started for the train, driving two miles in an old army ambulance. From that time until eight in the evening we did not leave the cars, and then only left them to get into an old broken-down stage coach, which was originally intended to hold six people, but into which on this occasion they put nine, and, thus cramped and crowded, we drove for five hours over as rough a road as can well be imagined, reaching Columbia at three o'clock A.M., by which time I could hardly move. Our next train started at six, but I was so stiff and exhausted that I begged my father to wait over one day to rest, to which he consented. At this place we struck General Sherman's track, and here the ruin and desolation was complete. Hardly any of the town remained; street after street was merely one long line of blackened ruins, which showed from their size and beautifully laid-out gardens, how handsome some of the houses had been. It was too horrible!

On Thursday, at six A.M., we again set off, going about thirty miles in a cattle van which brought us to the Columbia River, the bridge over which Sherman had destroyed. This we crossed on a pontoon bridge, after

which we walked a mile, sat two hours in
the woods, and were then picked up by a
rickety old car which was backed down to
where we were, and where the rails began
again, having been torn up behind us. In
this, at the rate of about five miles an
hour, we travelled until four in the afternoon, when we were again deposited in the
woods, the line this time being torn up in
front of us. Here, after another wait, we
were packed into a rough army waggon,
with loose boards put across for seats, and in
which we were jolted and banged about over
a road composed entirely of ruts and roots
for four more hours, until I thought I should
not have a whole bone left in my body.

It was a lovely evening however, and the
moon rose full and clear. The air, delicious
and balmy, was filled with the resinous scent
of the pine and perfume of yellow jessamine,
and we were a very jolly party, four gentlemen,
with ourselves, making up our number, so I
thought it good fun on the whole. In fact,

rough as the journey was, I rather enjoyed it all; it was so new a chapter in my book of travels.

Between nine and ten in the evening we arrived at a log cabin, where, until three A.M. we sat on the floor round a huge wood fire. The train then arrived and we started again, and did not stop for twenty-four hours; at least, when I say did not stop, I mean, did not leave the cars, for we really seemed to do little else but stop every few minutes. This brought us, at three A.M., to Augusta, where we were allowed to go to bed for three hours, starting again at six and travelling all day, until at seven in the evening we at last reached Savannah. Fortunately we started from the North with a large basket of pro-visions, that being our only luggage, the trunks having been sent by sea; and had it not been for this, I think we certainly should have starved, as we were not able to get anything to eat on the road, except at Columbia and Augusta.

The morning after our arrival in Savannah, my father came into my room to say he was off to the plantation at once, having seen some gentlemen the evening before, who told him if he wished to do anything at all in the way of planting this season, that he must not lose an hour, as it was very doubtful even now if a crop could be got in. So off he went, promising to return as soon as possible, and report what state of things he found on the island. I consoled myself by going off to church to hear Bishop Elliott, who preached one of the most beautiful sermons I ever heard, on the Resurrection, the one thought that can bring hope and comfort to these poor heart-broken people. There was hardly anyone at church out of deep mourning, and it was piteous to see so many mere girls' faces, shaded by deep crape veils and widows' caps.

I can hardly give a true idea of how crushed and sad the people are. You hear no bitterness towards the North ; they are too sad to be bitter ; their grief is overwhelming. Nothing can make any difference to them now ; the women live in the past, and the men only in the daily present, trying, in a listless sort of way, to repair their ruined fortunes. They are like so many foreigners, whose only interest in the country is their own individual business. Politics are never mentioned, and they know and care less about what is going on in Washington than in London. They received us with open arms, my room was filled with flowers, and crowds of people called upon me every day, and overwhelmed me with thanks for what I did for their soldiers during the war, which really did amount to but very little. I say this, and the answer invariably is, 'Oh yes, but your heart was with us,' which it certainly was.

We had, before leaving the North, re-ceived two letters from Georgia, one from an agent of the Freedmen's Bureau, and the other from one of our neighbours, both

stating very much the same thing, which was
that our former slaves had all returned to the
island and were willing and ready to work
for us, but refused to engage themselves to
anyone else, even to their liberators, the
Yankees ; but that they were very badly off,
short of provisions, and would starve if something were not done for them at once, and,
unless my father came directly (so wrote the
agent of the Freedmen's Bureau), the negroes
would be removed and made to work elsewhere.

On Wednesday, when my father returned,
he reported that he had found the negroes all
on the place, not only those who were there
five years ago, but many who were sold
three years before that.  Seven had worked
their way back from the up country.   They
received him very affectionately, and made
an agreement with him to work for one half
the crop, which agreement it remained to
be seen if they would keep.  Owing to our
coming so late, only a small crop could be

planted, enough to make seed for another
year and clear expenses. I was sorry we
could do no more, but too thankful that
things were as promising as they were.
Most of the finest plantations were lying idle
for want of hands to work them, so many of
the negroes had died; 17,000 deaths were
recorded by the Freedmen's Bureau alone.
Many had been taken to the South-west, and
others preferred hanging about the towns,
making a few dollars now and then, to working regularly on the plantations ; so most
people found it impossible to get any labourers, but we had as many as we wanted, and
nothing could induce our people to go anywhere else. My father also reported that
the house was bare, not a bed nor chair left,
and that he had been sleeping on the floor,
with a piece of wood for a pillow and a few
negro blankets for his covering. This I
could hardly do, and as he could attend to
nothing but the planting, we agreed that he
should devote himself to that, while I looked

after some furniture. So the day after, armed with five hundred bushels of seed rice, corn, bacon, a straw mattress, and a tub, he started off again for the plantation, leaving me to buy tables and chairs, pots and pans.

We heard that our overseer had removed many of the things to the interior with the negroes for safety on the approach of the Yankees, so I wrote to him about them, waiting to know what he had saved of our old furniture, before buying anything new. This done, I decided to proceed with my household goods to the plantation, arrange things as comfortably as possible, and then return to the North.

I cannot give a better idea of the condition of things I found on the Island than by copying the following letter written at the time.

April 12, 1866.

Dearest S——, I have relapsed into barbarism total! How I do wish you could see me ; you would be so disgusted. Well, I know now what the necessaries of life mean, and am surprised to find how few they are, and how many things we consider absolutely necessary which are really luxuries.

When I wrote last I was waiting in Savannah for the arrival of some things the overseer had taken from the Island, which I wished to look over before I made any further purchases for the house. When they came, however, they looked more like the possessions of an Irish emigrant than anything else; the house linen fortunately was in pretty good order, but the rest I fancy had furnished the overseer's house in the country ever since the war; the silver never reappeared. So I began my purchases with twelve common wooden chairs, four washstands, four bedsteads, four large tubs, two bureaux, two large tables and four smaller ones, some china, and one common lounge, my one luxury—and this finished the list.

Thus supplied, my maid and I started last Saturday morning for the Island; half-way down we stuck fast on a sand-bar in the river, where we remained six hours, very hot, and devoured by sand-flies, till the tide came in again and floated us off, which pleasant little episode brought us to Darien at 1 A.M. My father was there, however, to meet us with our own boat, and as it was bright moonlight we got off with all our things, and were rowed across to the island by four of our old negroes.

I wish I could give you any idea of the house. The floors were bare, of course, many of the panes were out of the windows, and the plaster in many places was off the walls, while one table and two old chairs constituted the furniture. It was pretty desolate, and my father looked at me in some anxiety to see how it would affect me, and seemed greatly relieved when I burst out laughing. My bed was soon unpacked and made, my tub filled, my basin and pitcher mounted on a barrel, and I settled for the rest of the night.

The next morning I and my little German maid, who fortunately takes everything very cheerily, went to work, and together we made things quite comfortable ; unpacked our tables and chairs, put up some curtains (made out of some white muslin I had brought down for petticoats) edged with pink calico, covered the tables with two bright-coloured covers I found in the trunk of house linen, had the windows mended, hung up my picture of General Lee (which had been sent to me the day before I left Philadelphia) over the mantelpiece, and put my writing things and nicknacks on the table, so that when my father and Mr. J—— came in they looked round in perfect astonishment, and quite rewarded me by their praise.

Our kitchen arrangements would amuse you. I have one large pot, one frying-pan, one tin saucepan, and this is all ; and yet you would be astonished to see how much our cook accomplishes with these three utensils, and the things don't taste *very* much alike.

Yesterday one of the negroes shot and gave me a magnificent wild turkey, which we roasted on one stick set up between two others before the fire, and capital it was. The broiling is done on two old pieces of iron laid over the ashes. Our food consists of corn and rice bread, rice, and fish caught fresh every morning out of the river, oysters, turtle soup, and occasionally a wild turkey or duck. Other meat, as yet, it is impossible to get.

Is it not all strange and funny ? I feel like Robinson Crusoe with three hundred men Fridays. Then my desert really blooms like the rose. On the acre of ground enclosed about the house are a superb magnolia tree, covered with its queenly flowers, roses running wild in every direction ; orange, fig, and peach trees now in blossom, give promise of fruit later on, while every tree and bush is alive with red-birds, mocking-birds, black-birds, and jays, so as I sit on the piazza the air comes to me laden with sweet smells and sweet sounds of all descriptions.

There are some drawbacks; fleas, sand-flies, and mosquitoes remind us that we are not quite in Heaven, and I agree with my laundry woman, Phillis, who upon my maid's remonstrating with her for taking all day to wash a few towels, replied, ' Dat's true, Miss Louisa, but de fleas jist have no principle, and dey bites me so all de time, I jist have to stop to scratch.'

The negroes seem perfectly happy at getting back to the old place and having us there, and I have been deeply touched by many instances of devotion on their part. On Sunday morning, after their church, having nothing to do, they all came to see me, and I must have shaken hands with nearly four hundred. They were full of their troubles and sufferings up the country during the war, and the invariable winding up was, ' Tank the Lord, missus, we's back, and sees you and massa again.' I said to about twenty strong men, ' Well, you know you are free and your own masters now,' when they broke out

with, ' No, missus, we belong to you ; we be
yours as long as we lib.'

Nearly all who have lived through the
terrible suffering of these past four years
have come back, as well as many of those
who were sold seven years ago. Their good
character was so well known throughout the
State that people were very anxious to hire
them and induce them to remain in the ' up
country,' and told them all sorts of stories to
keep them, among others that my father
was dead, but all in vain. One old man said,
' If massa be dead den, I'll go back to the old
place and mourn for him.' So they not only
refused good wages, but in many cases spent
all they had to get back, a fact that speaks
louder than words as to their feeling for their
old master and former treatment.

Our overseer, who was responsible for all
our property, has little or nothing to give us
back, while everything that was left in charge
of the negroes has been taken care of and
given back to us without the hope or wish of

reward. One old man has guarded the stock so well from both Southern and Northern marauders, that he has now ninety odd sheep and thirty cows under his care. Unfortunately they are on a pine tract some twelve miles away up the river, and as we have no means of transporting them we cannot get them until next year.

One old couple came up yesterday from St. Simon's, Uncle John and Mum Peggy, with five dollars in silver half-dollars tied up in a bag, which they said a Yankee captain had given them the second year of the war for some chickens, and this money these two old people had kept through all their want and suffering for three years because it had been paid for fowls belonging to us. I wonder whether white servants would be so faithful or honest! My father was much moved at this act of faithfulness, and intends to have something made out of the silver to commemorate the event, having returned them the same amount in other money.

One of the great difficulties of this new state of things is, what is to be done with the old people who are too old, and the children who are too young, to work ?   One Northern General said to a planter, in answer to this question, 'Well, I suppose they must die,' which, indeed, seems the only thing for them to do.   To-day Mr. J—— tells me my father has agreed to support the children for three years, and the old people till they die, that is, feed and clothe them.   Fortunately, as we have some property at the North we are able to do this, but most of the planters are utterly ruined and have no money to buy food for their own families, so on their plantations I do not see what else is to become of the negroes who cannot work except to die.

Yours affectionately,

F.——.

The prospect of getting in the crop did not grow more promising as time went on. The negroes talked a great deal about their desire and intention to work for us, but their idea of work, unaided by the stern law of necessity, is very vague, some of them working only half a day and some even less. I don't think one does a really honest full day's work, and so of course not half the necessary amount is done and I am afraid never will be again, and so our properties will soon be utterly worthless, for no crop can be raised by such labour as this, and no negro will work if he can help it, and is quite satisfied just to scrape along doing an odd job here and there to earn money enough to buy a little food.[1] They are affectionate and often trustworthy and honest, but so hopelessly lazy as to be almost worthless as labourers.

My father was quite encouraged at first, the people seemed so willing to work and said so much about their intention of doing so ; but not many days after they started he came in quite disheartened, saying that half

[1] N.B. I was mistaken. In the years 1877 and 1880 upwards of thirty thousand bushels of rice was raised on the place by these same negroes.

the hands had left the fields at one o'clock
and the rest by three o'clock, and this just at
our busiest time. Half a day's work will
keep them from starving, but won't raise a
crop. Our contract with them is for half
the crop ; that is, one half to be divided
among them, according to each man's rate of
work, we letting them have in the meantime
necessary food, clothing, and money for their
present wants (as they have not a penny)
which is to be deducted from whatever is due
to them at the end of the year.

This we found the best arrangement to
make with them, for if we paid them wages,
the first five dollars they made would have
seemed like so large a sum to them, that they
would have imagined their fortunes made
and refused to work any more. But even this
arrangement had its objections, for they told
us, when they missed working two or three
days a week, that they were losers by it as
well as ourselves, half the crop being theirs.
But they could not see that this sort of work

would not raise any crop at all, and that such should be the result was quite beyond their comprehension. They were quite convinced that if six days' work would raise a whole crop, three days' work would raise half a one, with which they as partners were satisfied, and so it seemed as if we should have to be too.

The rice plantation becoming unhealthy early in May, we removed to St. Simon's, a sea island on the coast, about fifteen miles from Butler's Island, where the famous Sea Island cotton had formerly been raised. This place had been twice in possession of the Northern troops during the war, and the negroes had consequently been brought under the influence of Northerners, some of whom had filled the poor people's minds with all sorts of vain hopes and ideas, among others that their former masters would not be allowed to return, and the land was theirs, a thing many of them believed, and they had planted both corn and cotton to a considerable extent. To disabuse their minds of this notion my father determined to put in a few acres of cotton, although the lateness of the season and work at Butler's Island prevented planting of any extent being done this season.

Our departure from one place and arrival at another was very characteristic. The house on St. Simon's being entirely stripped of furniture, we had to take our scanty provision of household goods down with us from Butler's Island by raft, our only means of transportation. Having learned from the negroes that the tide turned at six A.M., and to reach St. Simon's that day it would be necessary to start on the first of the ebb, we went to bed the night before, all agreeing to get up at four the next morning, so as to have our beds &c. on board and ready to start by six. By five, Mr. J——, my maid, and I were ready and our things on board, but nothing would induce my father to get up until eight o'clock, when he appeared on the wharf in his dressing-gown, clapped his hands to his head, exclaiming, ' My gracious ! that flat should be off; just look at the tide,' which indeed had then been running down two good hours. Without a word I had his bedroom furniture put on, and ordered the men to push off, which they did just as my father reappeared, calling out that half his things had been left behind, a remark which was fortunately useless as far as the flat was concerned, as it was rapidly disappearing on the swift current down the river.

At three o'clock we started in a large six-oared boat, with all the things forgotten in the morning piled in. The day was cloudless, the air soft and balmy ; the wild semi-tropical vegetation that edged the river on both sides beautiful beyond description ; the tender new spring green of the deciduous trees and shrubs, mingling with the dark green of the evergreen cypress, magnolia, and bay, all wreathed and bound together with the yellow jessamine and fringed with the soft delicate

grey moss which floated from every branch
and twig. Not a sound broke the stillness but
the dip of our oars in the water, accompanied
by the wild minor chant of the negro boatmen, who sang nearly the whole way down,
keeping time with the stroke of the oar.

Half-way down we passed the unfortunate
raft stuck in the mud, caught by the turning
tide. Unable to help it, we left it to wait
the return of the ebb, not however without
painful reflections, as we had had no dinner
before starting, and our cook with his frying-
pan and saucepan, was perched on a bag of
rice on the raft.

Shortly after five o'clock we reached St.
Simon's, and found the house a fair-sized
comfortable building, with a wide piazza
running all round it, but without so much as a
stool or bench in it. So, hungry and tired, we
sat down on the floor, to await the arrival of
the things. Night came on, but we had no
candles, and so sat on in darkness till after
ten o'clock, when the raft arrived with almost

everything soaked through, the result of a heavy thunder shower which had come on while it was stuck fast. This I confess was more than I could bear, and I burst out crying. A little cold meat and some bread consoled me somewhat, and finding the blankets had fortunately escaped the wetting, we spread these on the floor over the wet mattresses, and, all dressed, slowly and sadly laid us down to sleep.

The next morning the sun was shining as it only can shine in a southern sky, and the birds were singing as they only can sing in such sunlight. The soft sea air blew in at the window, mingled with the aromatic fragrance of the pines, and I forgot all my miseries, and was enchanted and happy. After breakfast, which was a repetition of last night's supper, with the addition of milk-less tea, I set about seeing how the house could be made comfortable. There were four good-sized rooms down and two upstairs, with a hall ten feet wide running through the house, and a wide verandah shut in from the sun by Venetian shades running round it; the kitchen, with the servants' quarters, was as usual detached. A nice enough house, capable of being made both pretty and comfortable, which in time I hope to do.

My father spent the time in talking to the negroes, of whom there were about fifty on the place, making arrangements with them for work, more to establish his right to the place than from any real good we expect to do this year. We found them in a very different frame of mind from the negroes on Butler's Island, who having been removed the first year of the war, had never been brought into contact with either army, and remained the same demonstrative and noisy childish people they had always been. The negroes on St. Simon's had always been the most intelligent, having belonged to an older estate, and a picked lot, but besides, they had tasted of the tree of knowledge. They were perfectly respectful, but quiet, and evidently disappointed to find they were not the masters of the soil and that their new friends the Yankees had deceived them. Many of them had planted a considerable quantity of corn and cotton, and this my father told them they might have, but that they must put in twenty acres for him, for which he would give them food and clothing, and another year, when he hoped to put in several hundred acres, they should share the crop. They consented without any show of either pleasure or the reverse, and went to work almost immediately under the old negro foreman or driver, who had managed the place before the war.

They still showed that they had confidence in my father, for when a miserable creature, an agent of the Freedmen's Bureau, who was our ruler then, and regulated all our contracts with our negroes, told them that they would be fools to believe that my father would really let them have all the crops they had planted before he came, and they would see that he would claim at least half, they replied, ' No, sir, our master is a just man; he has never lied to us, and we believe him.'    Rather taken aback by this, he turned to an old driver who was the principal person present, and said, ' Why, Bram, how can you care so much for your master—he sold you a few years ago ?'  ' Yes, sir,' replied the old man, ' he sold me and I was very unhappy, but he came to me and said, " Bram, I am in great trouble ; I have no money and I have to sell some of the people, but I know where you are all going to, and will buy you back again as soon as I can." And, sir, he told me, Juba, my old wife, must go with me, for though she was not strong, and the gentleman who bought me would not buy her, master said he could not let man and wife be separated ; and so, sir, I said, " Master, if you will keep me I will work for you as long as I live, but if you in trouble and it help you to sell me, sell me, master, I am willing."    And now that we free, I come back to my old home and my old master, and stay here till I die." ' This story the agent told a Northern friend of ours in utter astonishment.

To show what perfect confidence my father had on his side in his old slaves, the day after starting the work here, he returned to Butler's Island, leaving me and my maid entirely alone, with no white person within eight miles of us, and in a house on no door of which was there more than a latch, and neither then nor afterwards, when I was alone on the plantation with the negroes for weeks at a time, had I the slightest feeling of fear, except one night, when I had a fright which made me quite ill for two days, although it turned out to be a most absurd cause of terror. The quiet and solitude of the plantation was absolute, and at night there was not a movement, the negro settlement being two miles away from the house.

I was awaked one night about two o'clock by a noise at the river landing, which was not the eighth of a mile from the house, and on listening, heard talking, shouting, and apparently struggling. I got up and called my little German maid, who after listening a moment said, ' It is a fight, and I think the men are drunk.' Knowing that it could not be our own men, I made up my mind that a party of strange and drunken negroes were trying to land, and that my people were trying to prevent them. Knowing how few my people were, I felt for one moment utterly terrified and helpless, as indeed I was. Then I took two small pistols my father had left with me, and putting them full cock, and followed by my maid, who I must say was wonderfully brave, I proceeded out of the house to the nearest hut, where my man servant lived. I was a little reassured to hear his voice in answer when I called, and I sent him down to the river to see what was the matter. It turned out to be a raft full of mules from Butler's Island, which I had not expected, and who objected to being landed, hence the struggling and shouting. I had been too terrified to laugh, and suddenly becoming aware of the two pistols at full cock in my hands, was then seized with my natural terror of firearms. So I laid them, full cocked as they were, in a drawer, where they remained for several days, until my father came and uncocked them. This was my only real fright, although for the next two or three years we were constantly hearing wild rumours of intended negro insurrections, which however, as I never quite believed, did not frighten me.

I had a pretty hard time of it that first year, owing to my wretched servants, and to the scarcity of provisions of all sorts. The country was absolutely swept ; not a chicken, not an egg was left, and for weeks I lived on hominy, rice, and fish, with an occasional bit of venison. The negroes said the Yankees had eaten up everything, and one old woman told me they had refused to pay her for the eggs, but after they had eaten them said they were addled; but I think the people generally had not much to complain of. The only two good servants we had remained with my father at Butler's Island, and mine were all raw field hands, to whom everything was new and strange, and who were really savages. My white maid, watching my sable housemaid one morning through the door, saw her dip my toothbrush in the tub in which I had just bathed, and with my small hand-glass in the other hand, in which she was attentively regarding the operation, proceed to scrub her teeth with the brush. It is needless to say I presented her with that one, and locked my new one up as soon as I had finished using it.

My cook made all the flour and sugar I gave him (my own allowance of which was very small) into sweet cakes, most of which he ate himself, and when I scolded him, cried. The young man who was with us, dying of consumption, was my chief anxiety, for he was terribly ill, and could not eat the fare I did, and to get anything else was an impossibility. I scoured the island one day in search of chickens, but only succeeded in getting one old cock, of which my wretched cook made such a mess that Mr. J—— could not touch it after it was done. I tried my own hand at cooking, but without much success, not knowing really how to cook a potato, besides which the roof of the kitchen leaked badly, and as we had frequent showers, I often had to cook, holding up an umbrella in one hand and stirring with the other.

I remained on St. Simon's Island until the end of July, my father coming down from Butler's Island from Saturday till Monday every week for rest, which he sorely needed, for although he had got the negroes into something like working order, they required constant personal supervision, which on the rice fields in midsummer was frightfully trying, particularly as, after the day's work was over, he had to row a mile across

the river, and then drive out six miles to the
hut in the pine woods where he slept.    The
salt air, quiet, and peace of St. Simon's was
therefore a delightful rest and change, and
he refused to give an order when he came
down, referring all the negroes to me.    One
man whom he had put off in this way
several times, revenged himself one day
when my father told him to get a mule cart
ready, by saying, ' Does missus say so ? '
which, however, was more fun than impudence.

I will finish my account of this year by
copying a letter written on the spot at the
time.

Hampton Point : July 9, 1866.

Dearest S——, I did not expect to write
to you again from my desert island.    Aber ich
bin als noch hier, rapidly approaching the
pulpy gelatinous state.    Three times have I
settled upon a day for leaving, and three
times have I put it off ; the truth is, I am
very busy, very useful, and very happy.

Then I am anxious about leaving my father, for fear the unusual exposure to this Southern sun may make him ill ; and with no doctor, no nurse, no medicine, and no proper food nearer than Savannah, it would be a serious thing to be ill here.

I am just learning to be an experienced cook and doctress, for the negroes come to me with every sort of complaint to be treated, and I prescribe for all, pills and poultices being my favourite remedies. I was rather nervous about it at first, but have grown bolder since I find what good results always follow my doses. Faith certainly has a great deal to do with it, and that is unbounded on the part of my patients, who would swallow a red-hot poker if I ordered it.

The other day an old woman of over eighty came for a dose, so I prescribed a small one of castor oil, which pleased her so much she returned the next day to have it repeated, and again a third time, on which I remonstrated and said, ' No, Mum Charlotte, you are too old to be dosing yourself so.' To which she replied, ' Den, dear missus, do give me some for put on outside, for ain't you me mudder ? '

We are living directly on the Point, in the house formerly occupied by the overseer, a much pleasanter and prettier situation, I think, than the Hill House, in which you lived when you were here. Of course it is all very rough and overgrown now, but with the pretty water view across which you look to the wide stretch of broad green salt marsh, which at sunset turns the most wonderful gold bronze colour, and the magnolia, orange, and superb live oak trees around and near the house, it might, by a little judicious clearing and pruning, be made quite lovely, and if I am here next winter, as I suppose I shall be, I shall try my hand at a little landscape-gardening.

The fishing is grand, and we have fresh fish for breakfast, dinner, and tea. Our fisher-man, one of our old slaves, is a great character, and quite as enthusiastic about fishing as I am. I have been out once or twice with him, but not for deep-sea fishing yet, which however I hope to do soon, as he brings in the most magnificent bass, and blue fish weighing twenty and thirty pounds. The other day when we were out it began to thunder, and he said, ' Dere missus, go home. No use to fish more. De fish mind de voice of de Lord better dan we poor mortals, and when it tunders dey go right down to de bottom of de sea.'

I have two little pet bears, the funniest, jolliest little beasts imaginable. They have no teeth, being only six weeks old, and have to be fed on milk, which they will drink out of a dish if I hold it very quietly, but if I make the least noise they rush off, get up on their hind legs, and hiss and spit at me like cats. One spends his time turning summersets, and the other lies flat on his back, with his two little paws over his nose. They are too delightful.

I have been very fortunate in my weather, for although the days are terribly hot, there is always a pleasant sea-breeze, and the evenings and nights are delightfully cool. In fact I have suffered much less from the heat here than I usually do near Philadelphia in summer. The great trouble is that I cannot walk at all on account of the snakes, of which I live in terror. The daytime is too hot for them, and they take their walks abroad in the cool of the eveniug.

Last evening I was sauntering up the road, when about a quarter of a mile from the house I saw something moving very slowly across the path. At first I thought it was a cat, crouching as they do just before they spring, but in a moment more I saw it was a huge rattlesnake, as large round as my arm and quite six feet long. Two little birds were hovering over him, fluttering lower and lower every moment, fascinated by his evil eye and forked tongue which kept darting in and out. He was much too busy to notice me, so after looking at him for one moment I flew back to the house, shrieking with all my might, 'Pierce! John! Alex! William!' Hearing my voice they all rushed out, and, armed with sticks, axes, and spades, we proceeded to look for the monster, who however had crawled into the thick bushes when we had reached the spot, and although we could hear him rattle violently when we struck the bushes, the negroes could not see him, and were afraid to go into the thick undergrowth after him, so he still lives to walk abroad, and I—to stay at home.

Mr. James Hamilton Cooper died last week, and was buried at the little church on the island here yesterday. The whole thing was sad in the extreme, and a fit illustration of this people and country. Three years ago he was smitten with paralysis, the result of grief at the loss of his son, loss of his property, and the ruin of all his hopes and prospects; since which his life has been one of great suffering, until a few days ago, when death released him. Hearing from his son of his death, and the time fixed for his funeral, my father and I drove down in the old mule cart, our only conveyance, nine miles to the church. Here a most terrible scene of desolation met us. The steps of the church were broken down, so we had to walk up a plank to get in ; the roof was fallen in, so that the sun streamed down on our heads ; while the seats were all cut up and marked with the names of Northern soldiers, who had been quartered there during the war. The graveyard was so overgrown with weeds and bushes, and tangled with cobweb like grey moss, that we had difficulty in making our way through to the freshly dug grave.

In about half an hour the funeral party arrived. The coffin was in a cart drawn by one miserable horse, and was followed by the Cooper family on foot, having come this way from the landing, two miles off. From the cart to the grave the coffin was carried by four old family negroes, faithful to the end. Standing there I said to myself, ' Some day justice will be done, and the Truth shall be heard above the political din of slander and lies, and the Northern people shall see things as they are, and not through the dark veil of envy, hatred, and malice.' Good-bye. I sail on the 21st for the North.

Yours affectionately,

F——

## CHAPTER II.

### A FRESH START.

My return to the South in 1867 was much
later than I had expected it would be when
I left the previous summer, but my father
was repairing the house on Butler's Island,
and put off my coming, hoping to have things
more comfortable for me.  When, however,
March came, and it was still unfinished, I
determined to wait no longer, but if necessary
to go direct to St. Simon's, and not to Butler's
Island at all.  Wishing to make our habitation
more comfortable than it was last year, I
took from the North six large boxes, containing carpets, curtains, books, and various household articles, and accompanied by my maid, a
negro lad I had taken up with me, named

Pierce, and a little girl of ten, whom I was taking South for companionship, I started again for Georgia on March 10.

Owing to a mistake about my ticket I took the wrong route, went two hundred miles out of my way, and found myself one night, or rather morning at 2 A.M., landed in Augusta, where I was forced to remain until six the next morning, and where I had never been before and did not know anyone even by name. I felt rather nervous, but picking out the most respectable-looking man among my fellow-travellers, I asked him to recommend me to the best hotel in Augusta, which he did, and on my arriving at it found to my great joy that it was kept by Mr. Nickleson, formerly of the Mills House, Charleston, who knew who I was perfectly, received me most courteously, and after giving me first a comfortable bed, and then a good breakfast, sent me off the following morning with a nice little luncheon put up, a most necessary consideration, for it was impossible to get anything to eat on the road, and the day before we had nothing but some biscuits and an orange which we happened to have brought with us. We reached Savannah that evening, having been exactly ninety-four hours on the road, with no longer rest than the one at Augusta of four hours.

In Savannah I remained a week, and the following Saturday started for St. Simon's Island, sticking fast in the mud as usual, and being delayed in consequence six hours. The K——'s were on board with us, returning to their home for the first time since the war, bringing with them all their household goods and chattels; and a funnier sight than our disembarkation was never seen, as we looked like a genuine party of emigrants. The little wharf was covered with beds, tables, chairs, ploughs, pots, pans, boxes, and trunks, for we also had quantities of things of all kinds. A mule cart awaited us and an ox cart them, into which elegant conveyance we clambered, surrounded by our beds and pots and pans, and solemnly took our departure, each in a separate direction, for the opposite ends of the island.

I had not gone far when I met Major D ——, a young Philadelphian, who with his brother had rented a plantation next ours, and who is the proud possessor of a horse and waggon, in which he kindly offered to drive me to Hampton Point, an offer I very gladly accepted, thereby reaching my destination sooner than I should otherwise have done. I thought things would be better this year, but notwithstanding my Northern luxuries, I found it much harder to get along, My father, finding it impossible to manage the rice plantation on Butler's Island and the cotton one here, gladly agreed to the Misses D——'s offer to plant on shares, they undertaking the management here, which allowed him to devote all his time to the other place. The consequence is that 'the crop,' being the only thing thought of, every able-bodied man, woman, and child is engaged on it, and I find

my household staff reduced to two. I inquired after my friend Fisherman George,
' oh, he was ploughing,' so I could have no fish,
my cook and his wife have departed altogether, and my washerwoman and semp-
stress 'are picking cotton seed,' so Major
D—— smilingly informed me, leaving me
Daphne, who is expecting her eleventh confinement in less than a month, and Alex her
husband, who invariably is taken ill just as he
ought to get dinner, and Pierce, who since his
winter at the North is too fine to do anything
but wait at table. So I cook, and my maid
does the housework, and as it has rained hard
for three days and the kitchen roof is half off,
I cook in the dining-room or parlour. Fortunately, my provisions are so limited that I have
not much to cook ; for five days my food has
consisted of hard pilot biscuits, grits cooked
in different ways, oysters, and twice, as a great
treat, ham and eggs. I brought a box of
preserves from the North with me, but half
of them upset, and the rest were spoilt.

One window is entirely without a sash, so I have to keep the shutters closed all the time, and over the other I have pasted three pieces of paper where panes should be. My bed stood under a hole in the roof, through which the rain came, and I think if it rains much more there will not be a dry spot left in the house. However, as I would not wait at the North till the house on Butler's Island was finished, I have no one to blame for my present sufferings but myself, and when I get some servants and food from there, I shall be better off.

The people seem to me working fairly well, but Major D——, used only to Northern labour, is in despair, and says they don't do more than half a day's work, and that he has often to go from house to house to drive them out to work, and then has to sit under a tree in the field to see they don't run away.

A Mr. G—— from New York has bought Canon's Point, and is going to the greatest

expense to stock it with mules and farming
implements of all sorts, insisting upon it that
we Southerners don't know how to manage
our own places or negroes, and he will show
us, but I think he will find out his mistake.[1]
My father reported the negroes on Butler's

---

[1] The history of Canon's Point is as follows. Mr. G——
having started by putting the negroes on regular wages
expecting them to do regular work in return, and not being
at all prepared to go through the lengthy conversations and
explanations which they required, utterly failed in his attempts
either to manage the negroes or to get any work out of them.
Some ran off, some turned sulky, and some stayed and did
about half the work. So that at the end of two years he gave
the place up in perfect disgust, a little to our amusement, as
he had been so sure, like many another Northern man, that
all the negroes wanted was regular work and regular wages,
overlooking entirely the character of the people he was
dealing with, who required a different treatment every day
almost ; sometimes coaxing, sometimes scolding, sometimes
punishing, sometimes indulging, and always—unlimited
patience. After Mr. G—— failed in his management of the
negroes he gave the place up, leaving an agent there merely
to keep possession of the property. This man in turn moved
off, leaving about fifty negro families in undisputed possession, who two years later were driven off by a new tenant
who undertook to charge them high rent for their land ; and
it is now finally in the hands of a Western farmer and his
son, who told my husband last winter that they were delighted
with the place and climate, but had not learned to manage
the negroes yet, as when he scolded them they got scared
and ran off, and when he did not they would not work.

Island as working very well, although requir
ing constant supervision. That they should
be working well is a favourable sign of their
improved steadiness, for, as last year's crop
is not yet sold, no division has been possible.
So they have begun a second year, not having yet been paid for the first, and meanwhile
they are allowed to draw what food, clothing,
and money they want, all of which I fear
will make trouble when the day of settlement
comes, but it is pleasant to see how completely
they trust us.

On both places the work is done on the
old system, by task. We tried working by the
day, indeed I think we were obliged to do so
by the agent of the Freedmen's Bureau, to
whom all our contracts had to be submitted,
but we found it did not answer at all, the
negroes themselves begging to be allowed to
go back to the old task system. One man
indignantly asked Major D—— what the use
of being free was, if he had to work harder
than when he was a slave. To which Major

D——, exasperated by their laziness, replied that they would find being free meant harder work than they had ever done before, or starvation.

In all other ways the work went on just as it did in the old times. The force, of about three hundred, was divided into gangs, each working under a head man—the old negro drivers, who are now called captains, out of compliment to the changed times. These men make a return of the work each night, and it is very amusing to hear them say, as each man's name is called, ' He done him work ; ' ' He done half him task ; ' or 'Ain't sh'um' (have not seen him). They often did overwork when urged, and were of course credited for the same on the books. To make them do odd jobs was hopeless, as I found when I got some hands from Butler's Island, and tried to make them clear up the grounds about the house, cut the undergrowth and make a garden, &c. Unless I stayed on the spot all the time, the instant I disappeared they disappeared as well. On one occasion, having succeeded in getting a couple of cows, I set a man to churn some butter. After leaving him for a few moments, I returned to find him sitting on the floor with the churn between his legs, turning the handle slowly, about once a minute. 'Cato,' I exclaimed, 'that will never do. You must turn just as fast as ever you can to make butter!' Looking up very gravely, he replied, 'Missus, in dis country de butter must be coaxed; der no good to hurry.' And I generally found that if I wanted a thing done I first had to tell the negroes to do it, then show them how, and finally do it myself. Their way of managing not to do it was very ingenious, for they always were perfectly good-tempered, and received my orders with, 'Dat's so, missus; just as missus says,' and then always somehow or other left the thing undone.

The old people were up to all sorts of tricks to impose upon my charity, and get some favour out of me. They were far too old

and infirm to work for me, but once let them
get a bit of ground of their own given to them,
and they became quite young and strong
again. One old woman, called Charity, who
represented herself as unable to move, and
entirely dependent on my goodness for food
&c., I found was in the habit of walking
six miles almost every day to take eggs to
Major D—— to sell. I was complaining
once to him of my want of provisions, and
said, ' I can't even get eggs ; in old times all the
old women had eggs and chickens to sell, but
they none of them seem to have any left.'
' Why,' said he, ' we get eggs regularly from
one of your old women, who walks down
every day or two to us ; Charity her name is.'
' Charity ! impossible,' I exclaimed ; ' she can
hardly crawl round here from her hut.' ' It is
true though, nevertheless,' said he. So the
next time Mistress Charity presented herself,
almost on all fours, and said, ' Do, dear
missus, give me something for eat,' I said,
' No, you old humbug, I won't give you one

thing more. You know how much I want eggs, and yet you never told me you had any, and take them off to Major D—— to sell, because you think if I know you have eggs to sell I won't give you things.' For one moment the old wretch was taken aback at being found out, and then her ready negro wit came to her aid, and she exclaimed with a horrified and indignant air, 'Me sell eggs to me dear missus. Neber *sell* her eggs; gib dem to her.' I need hardly say she had never given me one, but after that did sell them to me.

I spent my birthday at the South, and my maid telling the people that it was my birthday, they came up in the evening to 'shout for me.' A negro must dance and sing, and as their religion, which is very strict in such matters, forbids secular dancing, they take it out in religious exercise, call it 'shouting,' and explained to me that the difference between the two was, that in their religious dancing they did not 'lift the heel.' All day they were bringing me little presents of honey, eggs, flowers, &c., and in the evening about fifty of them, of all sizes and ages and of both sexes, headed by old Uncle John, the preacher, collected in front of the house to 'shout.' First they lit two huge fires of blazing pine logs, around which they began to move with a slow shuffling step, singing a hymn beginning ' I wants to climb up Jacob's ladder.' Getting warmed up by degrees, they went faster and faster, shouting louder and louder, until they looked like a parcel of mad fiends. The children, finding themselves kicked over in the general *mêlée*, formed a circle on their own account, and went round like small catherine wheels.

When, after nearly an hour's performance, I went down to thank them, and to stop them —for it was getting dreadful, and I thought some of them would have fits—I found it no easy matter to do so, they were so excited. One of them, rushing up to my father, seized him by the hand, exclaiming, ' Massa, when

your birthday? We must "shout" for you.'
'Oh, Tony,' said my father, 'my birthday is
long passed.' Upon which the excited Tony
turned to Major D——, who with Mr. G——
had been dining with us, and said, 'Well den,
Massa Charlie, when yours?' I told him finally
it was Miss Sarah's birthday as well as mine.
On hearing this he turned to the people, saying, 'Children, hear de'y (hear do you), dis
Miss Sarah's birthday too. You must shout
so loud Miss Sarah hear you all de way to de
North!' At which off they went again, harder
than ever. Dear old Uncle John came up to
me, and taking my hands in his, said, 'God
bless you, missus, my dear missus.' My father,
who was standing near, put his arm round
the old man's shoulders, and said, 'You have
seen five generations of us now, John, haven't
you?' 'Yes, massa,' said John, 'Miss Sarah's
little boy be de fifth; bless de Lord.' Both
Major D—— and Mr. G—— spoke of this
afterwards, saying 'How fond your father is of
the people.' 'Yes,' said I, 'this is a relation-

ship you Northern people can't understand, and will soon destroy.'

I remained on St. Simon's Island this summer until the end of July, enjoying every moment of my time. The climate was perfect, and I had a delightful Southern-bred mare, on which I used to take long rides every day. My father had seen her running about the streets of Darien, and thought her so handsome he had bought her from the man who professed to own her. She was afterwards claimed by a gentleman from Virginia, who said she was a sister of Planet's, and had been raised on his brother's plantation. When the war ended he had gone to Texas, leaving her with a friend out of whose stable she had been stolen by a deserter from the 12th Maine Regiment, who sold her to the man from whom my father bought her. The story, which was proved to be quite true, nearly cost me my mare, who was the dearest and most intelligent horse I ever had, and who grew to know me so well that she would follow me about like a dog, and come from the furthest end of her pasture when she heard my voice, but fortunately the owner at last agreed to a compromise, and I kept my beauty.

Twice a week I rode nine miles to Frederika, our post town, to get and take our letters, and often, with a little bundle of clothes strapped on behind my saddle, I rode down twelve miles to the south end of the island, and spent the night with my dear friends the K——'s, returning the next morning before the heat of the day. There was a good shell road the whole twelve miles, and six of it at least ran through a beautiful wood of pines and live oak, with an undergrowth of the picturesque dwarf palmetto and sweet-smelling bay. In many places the trees met overhead, through which the sun broke in showers of gold, lighting up the red trunks of the pines and soft green underneath, while the grey moss floated silently overhead like a gossamer veil, covering the whole. I never met a human being, nor heard a sound save the notes of the different birds, and the soft murmur of the wind through the tall pines, which came to me laden with their fragrant aroma, mingled with the sweet salt breeze from the sea.

I have often thought since, that it was really hardly safe for me to ride about alone, or indeed live alone, as I did half the week; but I believe there was less danger in doing so then, than there would be now. The serpent had not entered into my paradise.

One day I went on a deer hunt with some of the gentlemen, quite as much in hopes of getting some venison as of seeing any real sport. My diet of ham, eggs, fish, rice, hominy, to which latterly, endless water-melons had been added, had become almost intolerable to me, and I absolutely longed for animal food. The morning was perfect and I was very much excited, although I did not see any deer. They shot one, however, and generously gave me half. We were to have gone again, but the weather got warm and the rattlesnakes came out, so it was not safe.

My neighbours the H——'s were great sportsmen, and had before the war a famous pack of hounds, of which a story is told that, after chasing a deer all one day and across two rivers, the gentlemen returned home worn out, and without either deer or hounds. After waiting for two weeks for the return of the dogs, they went out to look for them, and on a neighbouring island found the skeletons of their hounds, in a circle round the skeleton of a deer. Fortunately, one or two of this breed had been left behind, and they were still hunting with them, and after our first hunt often sent me presents of venison, which were most acceptable.

But while my summer was gliding away in such peace and happiness, things outside were growing more and more disturbed, and my father from time to time brought me news of political disturbances, and a general growing restlessness among the negroes, which he feared would end in great trouble and destroy their usefulness as labourers. Our properties

in such a case would have become worthless.
White labour could be used on these sea
islands, but never on the rice fields, which
if we lost our negro labourers would have
to be abandoned.  A letter written at that
time shows how different reports reached and
affected us then, and also the condition our
part of the South was in, the truth of which
never has been known.

St. Simon's Island : June 23, 1867.

Dearest S——, We are, I am afraid, going
to  have  terrible  trouble  by-and-by with
the negroes, and I see nothing but gloomy
prospects for us ahead.  The unlimited power
that the war has put into the hands of the
present Government at Washington seems to
have turned the heads of the party now in
office, and they don't know where to stop.
The whole South is settled and quiet, and
the people too ruined and crushed to do anything against the Government, even if they
felt so inclined, and all are returning to their

former peaceful pursuits, trying to rebuild their fortunes, and thinking of nothing else. Yet the treatment we receive from the Government becomes more and more severe every day, the last act being to divide the whole South into five military districts, putting each under the command of a United States General, doing away with all civil courts and law. Even D——, who you know is a Northern republican, says it is most unjustifiable, not being in any way authorised by the existing state of things, which he confesses he finds very different from what he expected before he came. If they would frankly say they intend to keep us down, it would be fairer than making a pretence of readmitting us to equal rights, and then trumping up stories of violence to give a show of justice to treating us as the conquered foes of the most despotic Government on earth, and by exciting the negroes to every kind of insolent lawlessness, to goad the people into acts of rebellion and resistance.

The other day in Charleston, which is under the command of that respectable creature General S——, they had a fire-men's parade, and took the occasion to hoist a United States flag, to which this modern Gesler insisted on everyone raising his cap as he passed underneath. And by a hundred other such petty tyrannies are the people, bruised and sore, being roused to despera-tion ; and had this been done directly after the war it would have been bad enough, but it was done the other day, three years after the close of the war.

The true reason is the desire and inten-tion of the Government to control the elections of the South, which under the constitution of the country they could not legally do. So they have determined to make an excuse for set-ting aside the laws, and in order to accomplish this more fully, each commander in his separate district has issued an order declaring that unless a man can take an oath that he had not voluntarily borne arms against the

United States Government, nor in any way aided or abetted the rebellion, he cannot vote. This simply disqualifies every white man at the South from voting, disfranchising the whole white population, while the negroes are allowed to vote *en masse*.

This is particularly unjust, as the question of negro voting was introduced and passed in Congress as an amendment to the constitution, but in order to become a law a majority of two-thirds of the State Legislatures must ratify it, and so to them it was submitted, and rejected by all the Northern States with two exceptions, where the number of negro voters would be so small as to be harmless. Our Legislatures are not allowed to meet, but this law, which the North has rejected, is to be forced upon us, whose very heart it pierces and prosperity it kills. Meanwhile, in order to prepare the negroes to vote properly, stump speakers from the North are going all through the South, holding political meetings for the negroes, saying things like this to them : ' My

friends, you will have your rights, won't you ? '
(' Yes,' from the negroes.)    ' Shall I not go
back to Massachusetts and tell your brothers
there that you are going to ride in the street
cars with white ladies if you please ? '  (' Yes,
yes,' from the crowd.)   ' That if you pay your
money to go to the theatre you will sit where
you please, in the best boxes if you like ? '
(' Yes,' and applause.)   This I copy verbatim
from a speech made at Richmond the other
day, since which there have been two serious
negro riots there, and the General commanding had to call out the military to suppress
them.

These men are making a tour through
the South, speaking in the same way to the
negroes everywhere.  Do you wonder we
are frightened ?   I have been so forcibly
struck lately while reading Baker's ' Travels
in Africa,' and some of Du Chaillu's lectures,
at finding how exactly the same characteristics
show themselves among the negroes there, in
their own native country, where no outside

influences have ever affected them, as with ours here. Forced to work, they improve and are useful ; left to themselves they become idle and useless, and never improve. Hard ethnological facts for the abolitionists to swallow, but facts nevertheless.

It seems foolish to fill my letter to you with such matters, but all this comes home to us with such vital force that it is hard to write, or speak, or think of anything else, and the one subject that Southerners discuss whenever they meet is, 'What is to become of us ?'

Affectionately yours,

F——

I left the South for the North late in July, after a severe attack of fever brought on by my own imprudence. Just before I left an old negro died, named Carolina, one hundred years old. He had been my great grand-father's body servant, and my father was much attached to him, and sat up with him the night before he died, giving him extract of beef-tea every hour. My sister had sent us down two little jars as an experiment, and although it did not save poor old Carolina's life, I am sure it did mine, as it was the only nourishment I could get in the shape of animal food after my fever. When Carolina was buried in the beautiful and picturesque bit of land set apart for the negro burying-ground on the island, my father had a tombstone with the following inscription on it erected over him.

CAROLINA,

DIED JUNE 26, 1866,

AGED 100 YEARS.

A long life, marked by devotion to his Heavenly Father and
fidelity to his earthly masters.

# CHAPTER III.

1867–1868.

ALONE.

In August of 1867 my father died, and as soon after as I was able I went down to the South to carry on his work, and to look after the negroes, who loved him so dearly and to whom he was so much attached. My brother-in-law went with me, and we reached Butler's Island in November. The people were indeed like sheep without a shepherd, and seemed dazed.

We had engaged a gentleman as overseer in Savannah, and appointed another our financial agent for the coming year, and besides this all my father's affairs were in the hands of an executor appointed by the Court to settle his estate, but before anything else could be done the negroes had to be settled with for the past two years, and their share of the crops divided according to the amount due to each man. My father had given each negro a little pass-book, in which had been entered from time to time the food, clothing, and money which each had received from him on account. Of these little books there were over three hundred, which represented their debits ; then there was the large planta-tion ledger, in which an account of the work each man had, or had not, done every day for nearly two years, had been entered, which represented their credits. To the task of balancing these two accounts I set myself, wishing to feel sure that it was fairly done, and also because I knew the negroes would be more satisfied with my settle-ment.

Night after night, when the day's work was over, I sat up till two and three o'clock in the morning, going over and over the long line of figures, and by degrees got them pretty straight. I might have saved myself the trouble. Not one negro understood it a bit, but all were quite convinced they had been cheated, most of them thinking that each man was entitled to half the crop. I was so anxious they should understand and see they had been fairly dealt with, that I went over and over again each man's account with him, and would begin, 'Well, Jack (or Quash, or Nero, as the case might be), you got on such a date ten yards of homespun from your master.' 'Yes, missus, massa gave me dat.' 'Then on such and such a day you had ten dollars.' 'Yes, missus, dat so.' And so on to the end of their debits, all of which they acknowledged as just at once. (I have thought since they were not clever enough to conceive the idea of disputing that part of the business.) When all these items were named and agreed to, I read the total amount, and then turned to the work account. And here the trouble began, every man insist-

ing upon it that he had not missed one day
in the whole two years, and had done full
work each day. So after endless discussions,
which always ended just where they began, I
paid them the money due to them, which
was always received with the same remark,
' Well, well, work for massa two whole years,
and only get dis much.' Finding that their
faith in my father's justice never wavered, I
repeated and repeated and repeated, ' But I
am paying you from your master's own books
and accounts.' But the answer was always
the same, ' No, no, missus, massa not treat
us so.' Neither, oddly enough, did they seem
to think I wished to cheat them, but that I
was powerless to help matters, one man saying to me one day, ' You see, missus, a woman
ain't much 'count.' I learnt very soon how
useless all attempts at ' making them sensible'
(as they themselves express it) were, and
after a time, used to pay them their wages
and tell them to be off, without allowing any
of the lengthy arguments and discourses over

their payments they wished to indulge in, often more, I think, with an idea of asserting their independence and dignity, than from any real belief that they were not properly paid.

Their love for, and belief in my father, was beyond expression, and made me love them more than I can say. They never spoke of him without some touching and affection- ate expression that comforted me far more than words uttered by educated lips could have done. One old woman said, ' Missus, dey tell me dat at de North people have to pay to get buried. Massa pay no money here; his own people nurse him, his own people bury him, and his own people grieve for him.' Another put some flowers in a tumbler by the grave; and another basin, water, and towels, saying, ' If massa's spirit come, I want him see dat old Nanny not forget how he call every morning for water for wash his hands ;' and several of them used the expression in speaking of his death, ' Oh,

missus, our back jest broke.' No wonder I
loved them.

Their religion, although so mixed up
with superstition, was very real, and many
were the words of comfort I got from them.
One day, when I was crying, an old woman
put her arms round me and said, ' Missus,
don't cry; it vex de Lord. I had tirteen
children, and I ain't got one left to put
even a coal in my pipe, and if I did not
trust de Lord Jesus, what would become of
me ?'

I am sorry to say, however, that finding
my intention was to alter nothing that my
father had arranged, some of them tried to
take advantage of it, one man assuring me
his master had given him a grove of orange
trees, another several acres of land, and so
on, always embellished with a story of his
own long and useful services, for which ' Massa
say, Boy, I gib you dis for your own.'

Notwithstanding their dissatisfaction at
the settlement, six thousand dollars was paid

out among them, many getting as much as
two or three hundred apiece. The result
was that a number of them left me and
bought land of their own, and at one time
it seemed doubtful if I should have hands
at all left to work. The land they bought,
and paid forty, fifty dollars and even more
for an acre, was either within the town limits,
for which they got no titles, and from which
they were soon turned off, or out in the pine
woods, where the land was so poor they could
not raise a peck of corn to the acre. These
lands were sold to them by a common class
of men, principally small shopkeepers and
Jews (the gentlemen refusing to sell their
land to the negroes, although they occasionally rented it to them), and most frightfully
cheated the poor people were. But they had
got their land, and were building their little
log cabins on it, fully believing that they
were to live on their property and incomes
the rest of their lives, like gentlemen.

The baneful leaven of politics had begun

working among them, brought to the South
by the lowest set of blackguards who ever
undertook the trade, making patriotism in
truth the 'last refuge of a scoundrel,' as Dr.
Johnson facetiously defines it, and themselves
'factious disturbers of the Government,'
according to his equally pleasant definition
of a patriot. Only in this case they came
accredited from the Government, and the
agent of the Freedmen's Bureau was our
master, one always ready to believe the
wildest complaints from negroes, and to call
the whites to account for the same.

A negro carpenter complained that a
gentleman owed him fifty dollars for work
done, so without further inquiry or any trial,
the agent sent the gentleman word to pay at
once, *or* he would have him arrested, the
sheriff at that time being one of his own
former slaves. My brother-in-law, who was
with me this year, for a short time was a
Northern man and a strong Republican in his
feelings, this being the first visit he had ever

paid to the South. But such a high-handed proceeding as this astonished him, and he expressed much indignation at it, and declared he would send an account of it to a Republican paper in Philadelphia, as the people at the North had no idea of the real state of things at the South. He had also expressed himself surprised and pleased at the courteous reception he had received, although known to be a Northerner, and also at the quietness of the country generally. I told him they would not publish his letter in the Philadelphia paper, and I was right, they did not.

A rather amusing incident occurred while he was with me. Having been in quiet possession of our property on St. Simon's Island for two years, we were suddenly notified one day, I never quite knew by whom, and in those days it was not easy always to know who our lawgivers were, that St. Simon's Island came under the head of abandoned property, being occupied by former owners, who, through contempt of the Government and President's authority, had refused to make application for its restoration under the law. 'Therefore,' so ran the order, 'such property shall be confiscated on the first day of January next, unless before that date the owners present themselves before the authorities (?), take the required oath of allegiance to the Government, and ask for its restoration.' This nothing would induce me to do, the whole thing was so preposterous, but my brother-in-law decided that under the circumstances it was better to obey. So he, a strong Republican, who had first voted for Lincoln and then for Grant, had never been at the South before in his life, and during the war had done all in his power to aid and support the Northern Government, even gallantly offering his services to his country when Pennsylvania was threatened by General Lee before the battle of Gettysburgh, had to go and take the oath of allegiance to the United States Government on behalf of his wife's property, she also having always sympathised with the Northern cause, and having been so bitter in her feelings at first as to refuse to receive a Southerner in her house.

What a farce it was! My brother-in-law could not help being amused, it was such an absurd position to find himself in, and he declared it all came of ever putting his foot in this miserable Southern country at all, and he had no doubt the result would be that on his return to the North he would find all his Northern property confiscated, and be hung as a rebel. He soon after left me, and then my real troubles began. It seemed quite hopeless ever to get the negroes to settle down to steady work, and although they still professed the greatest affection for and faith in me, it certainly did not show itself in works. My new agent assured me that there must be a contract made and signed with the negroes, binding them for a year, in order to have any hold upon them at all, and

I am not sure that the Freedmen's Bureau
agent did not require such an agreement to
be drawn up and submitted to him for
approval before having it signed. Whether
they were right or not as regarded the hold
it gave us over the labourers I cannot say.
I think possibly it impressed them a little
more with the sense of their obligations, but
after having two of them run off in spite of
the solemnity of the contract, and having to
pay something like twenty dollars to the
authorities to fetch them back, we didn't
trouble ourselves much about enforcing it
after that. At first the negroes flatly refused
to sign any contract at all, having been
advised by some of their Northern friends
not to do so, as it would put them back to
their former condition of slavery, and my
agents were quite powerless to make them
come to any terms. So I determined to try
what my personal influence would accomplish.

The day before I was to have my inter-

view with the Butler's Island people, I
received a most cheerful note from Major
D——, saying that he had paid off all the
hands at St. Simon's, who seemed perfectly
satisfied, and were quite willing to contract
again for another year. I felt a little surprised at this, as it is not the negro's nature
to be satisfied with anything but plenty to
eat and idleness, but was rejoicing over the
news, when I was summoned to the office
to see six of the Hampton Point people who
had just arrived from St. Simon's. There they
were, one and all with exactly the same story
as the people here, reserved for my benefit as
their proper mistress and protector ; ' that
they had not received full credit for their
day's work, had been underpaid and over-
charged,' &c. &c., winding up with, ' Missus,
de people wait to see you down dere, and dey
won't sign de contract till you come.' ' But,'
said I, in despair, ' I can't possibly leave here
for a week at least, and the work must
begin there at once, or we shall get in no crop

this year.' But in vain; they merely said,
'We wait, missus, till you come.' 'Very well,'
I said, 'I'll go to-morrow. Only, mind you
are all there, for I must be back here the next
day to have this contract signed.'

The next morning, at a little after seven,
I started for St. Simon's in my small boat,
rowed by my two favourite men, reaching
there about ten, and taking Major D——
utterly by surprise, as he knew nothing of
what had happened. From the way the
negroes spoke the day before, one would
have supposed the mere sight of my face
would have done; but not one signed the
contract without a long argument on the
subject, most of them refusing to sign at all,
though they all assured me they wished to
work for me as long 'as de Lord spared
dem.' I knew, however, too well, that this
simply meant that they were willing to continue to live on St. Simon's as long as the
Lord spared them, but not to work, so I was
firm, and said, 'No, you must sign or go

away.' So one by one, with groans and sighs, they put their marks down opposite to their names, and by five I had them all in. At nine o'clock, on the first of the flood tide, I started back, reaching Butler's Island at midnight, nearly frozen, but found my maid, who really was everything to me that year, waiting for me with a blazing fire and hot tea ready to warm me.

The next morning at ten, I had the big mill bell rung to summon the people here to sign the contract, and then my work began in earnest. For six mortal hours I sat in the office without once leaving my chair, while the people poured in and poured out, each one with long explanations, objections, and demonstrations. I saw that even those who came fully intending to sign would have their say, so after interrupting one man and having him say gravely, ' 'Top, missus, don't cut my discourse,' I sat in a state of dogged patience and let everyone have his talk out, reading the contract over and over again as each one asked for it, answering their many questions and meeting their many objections as best I could. One wanted this altered in the contract, and another that. One was willing to work in the mill but not in the field. Several would not agree to sign unless I promised to give them the whole of Saturday for a holiday. Others, like the St. Simon's people, would ' work for me till they died,' but would put their hand to no paper. And so it went on all day, each one ' making me sensible,' as he called it.

But I was immovable. ' No, they must sign the contract as it stood.' ' No, I could not have anyone work without signing.' ' No, they must work six days and rest on Sunday,' &c., &c. Till at last, six o'clock in the evening came and I closed the books with sixty-two names down, which was a good deal of a triumph, as my agent told me he feared none would sign the contract, they were so dissatisfied with last year's settlement. Even old Henry, one of the captains, and my chief friend and supporter, said in the morning, ' Missus, I bery sorriful, for half de people is going to leave.' ' Oh no, they won't, Henry,' said I. But I thought sixty-two the first day, good work, though I had a violent attack of hysterics afterwards, from fatigue and excitement. Only once did I lose my temper and self-control, and that was when one man, after showing decided signs of insolence, said, ' Well, you sign my paper first, and then I'll sign yours.' ' No,' I replied in a rage, ' I'll neither sign yours nor you mine. Go out of the room and off the place instantly.' But I soon saw how foolish I was, for looking up five minutes after, I beheld the same man standing against the door with a broad grin on his face, who, when I looked at him in perfect astonishment, said with the most perfect good nature, ' I'se come back to sign, missus.'

The next day, Sunday, I tried to keep clear of the people, both for rest and because I wanted to make some arrangements for my school, the young teacher having arrived on Friday.

Monday morning the bell again rang, and though I did not see more than twenty-five people, I was again in the office from ten A.M. to six P.M., and found it far more unpleasant than on Saturday, as I had several trouble-some, bad fellows to deal with. One man, who proposed leaving the place without pay-ing his debts, informed me, when I told him he must pay first, ' he'd see if he hadn't a law as well as I ; ' and another positively refused to work or leave the place, so he had to be informed that if he was not gone in three days he would be put off, which had such an effect that he came the next day and signed, and worked well afterwards.

Tuesday and Wednesday my stragglers came dropping in, the last man arriving under a large cotton umbrella, very defiant that he would not sign unless he could have Satur-day for a holiday. ' Five days I'll work, but (with a flourish of the umbrella) I works for no man on Saturday.' 'Then,' said I, 'William, I am sorry, but you can't work for me, for any man who works for me *must* work on Saturday.' 'Good morning, den, missus,' says my man, with another flourish of the umbrella, and departs. About an hour afterwards he returned, much subdued, with the umbrella shut, which I thought a good sign, and informed me that after 'much consideration wid himself,' he had returned to sign. So that ended it, and only two men really went—one from imagined ill-health, and one I dismissed for insubordination. The gentlemen seemed to think I had done wonders, and I was rather astonished at myself, but nothing would ever induce me to do such a thing again.

The backbone of the opposition thus broken, and the work started more or less steadily, I turned my thoughts to what I considered my principal work, and belonging more to my sphere than what I had been engaged in up to that time. I was anxious to have the negroes' houses, which were terribly dilapidated, repaired and white-washed, a school opened, and the old hospital building repaired and put in order for the following purposes. One of the four big rooms the people had taken possession of for a church, the old one being some three miles distant, at one of the upper settlements, and this I determined to let them keep, and to use one of the others for the school ; one for the old women who couldn't work, and the other for the young married women to be confined in, as, since the war, they bring their children into the world anyhow and anywhere, in their little cabins, where men, women, and children run in and out indis-criminately, so that it is both wretched and improper.

The people did not seem to like either of my proposals too much ; especially the old plantation midwife, who is indignant at her work being taken away from her. But as I find she now makes the charge of five dollars for each case, the negroes naturally decline employing her on their own account. I hoped by degrees to bring them to approve of my arrangements, by showing them how much more comfortable they would be in my hospital, and by presenting the babies born there with some clothes, and the old women who lived there with blankets, to make them like it. (I never did succeed, however, and after several attempts, had to give it up.)

I had one or two pupils at the same time, and found the greatest difference between the genuine full-blooded African and the mulattoes. The first, although learning to repeat quickly, like a clever parrot, did not really take in an idea, while the other was as intelligent as possible. I felt sure then, and still think, the pure negro incapable of advancement to any degree that would enable him to cope with the white race, intellectually, morally, or even physically. My white maid took infinite pains to show them

the best, quickest, as well as simplest way of
doing the house-work, absolutely taking their
breath away by the way she worked herself,
but without much effect, as the instant her
back was turned they went back to their old
lazy, slipshod ways of doing things. Her
efforts to make them tidy in their dress were
very amusing, and one morning, finding my
young housemaid working with her sun-
bonnet on, I said, 'Why do you keep your
bonnet on, Christine?' Upon which, without
any reply, she pulled the said bonnet down
over her eyes, and my maid informed me
she had come to work in the morning without brushing her hair, so for punishment had
to wear her sun-bonnet. The women showed
a strong inclination to give up wearing their
pretty, picturesque head handkerchiefs, 'because white people didn't,' but I was very
strict about the house servants never coming
without one on, for their black woolly heads
did look too ugly without their usual covering, which in itself was so handsome, and

gave them so much style, and in some cases beauty.

A few days after the contract was signed I started the school, which I hoped would be a success. The teacher was a young country lad just fresh from college ; clever enough, but very conceited, with no more manners than a young bear, which, however, I hoped he might learn in time from the negroes in return for some book learning, as they generally are singularly gentle and courteous in their manners. I had school in the morning for the children, and in the evening for the young people who worked in the fields. This is decidedly the most popular, and we have over fifty scholars, some of them quite old men—much too old to learn, and much in the way of the younger ones, but so zealous that I could not bear to turn them away.

Besides teaching school, my young man was to take charge of the store, which I found too much for me. My father's object in

opening the store was to give the negroes
good things at cost price, in order to save
them from paying three times the price
for most inferior goods in Darien, where a
number of small shops had been opened.
But we did not take into consideration the
heavy loss it must entail upon us not to put
even profit enough on the things to cover
our own expenses, and we sold them to the
negroes at exactly what we paid for them in
Philadelphia, bearing all the cost of transportation and spoilt goods, so that at the end of
the following year I found the store just three
thousand dollars out of pocket, and so decided
to shut it up, especially as I found that, notwithstanding our giving the negroes the very
best things at cost price, they much preferred
going to Darien to spend their money on
inferior goods and at greatly increased rates.
I suppose, poor people, it was natural they
should like to swagger a little, and spend
their newly, but certainly not hardly-earned
money freely, and it was an immense relief

to my pocket and labours to give up shop-keeping, although we only had it open for about two hours every afternoon.

But all this time, while we were getting things more and more settled on the place, the troubles from outside were drawing nearer and nearer as the day for voting approached, and in March burst upon us in the shape of political meetings and excitement of all kinds. Two or three Northern political agents arrived in Darien, and summoned all the negroes to attend meetings, threatening them with various punishments if they stayed away. I in vain reasoned with the negroes, and did all in my power to prevent their attending these meetings, and told them no one could punish them for not going : not because I cared in the least which way they voted, but because it interfered so terribly with their work. I doubled the watchmen at night, and did all I could to prevent strangers land-ing on the Island ; but one morning found that during the night a notice had been put

up on the wharf, calling upon all the people
to attend a political meeting on pain of being
fined five hundred dollars, or exiled to a
foreign land. As the meeting was some way
off, and the election followed in a few days,
I knew that if the people once broke off, no
more work would be done for at least a week,
and this was just the time one of our plant-
ings had to be put in, which, as we can only
do it on the spring tides, would have cost
me just two hundred acres of rice. So I
argued and threatened, and told them it was
all rubbish—no one could either exile or
fine them, and that they must not go to the
meeting at all, and when the day for voting
came must do all their day's work first and
vote afterwards; which they easily could
have done, having always finished their day's
work by three o'clock, and the voting place
not being half a mile off.

It was useless, however. My words were
powerless, the negroes naturally thinking
that the people who had freed them could

do anything they liked, and must be obeyed ;
so they not only prepared to go to the meeting, but, I knew, would not do a stroke of
work on the voting days.   At last, in despair,
I wrote to General Meade, who was then
the military commander of our district, and
a personal acquaintance of mine, to tell him
what was going on, and ask him if it was
impossible that the planters should be protected from these political disturbers and
agitators.   I received the following answer
and order from him almost immediately :—

Head-quarters, Third Military District.
(Department of Georgia, Florida, and Alabama.)
Atlanta, Georgia :  April 11, 1868.

My  dear  Miss  B——,—I  have  to  acknowledge the receipt of your letter, reporting
that certain persons are ordering the labourers
under your employment to attend political
meetings, and  threatening, in case of refusal,
to punish them  with  fines or exile them  to  a
foreign country ; and  have  to  state in reply,
that  no  interference  of  any  kind  with  the

just rights of employers is authorised by existing laws or orders, and that, on the contrary, you will see, from the enclosed order, which was being prepared at the time your letter was received, that such interference is positively prohibited, and is punishable on conviction before a military tribunal with fine and imprisonment. If you will furnish these Head-quarters with the names of parties thus attempting to interfere with your rights as an employer, together with the names of reliable witnesses, I shall not hesitate to investigate the case, and bring the offenders to trial and punishment.

Very respectfully yours,

GEORGE G. MEADE,

Major-General.

The order was as follows :—

Head-quarters, Third Military District.
(Department of Georgia, Florida, and Alabama.)

General Orders, No. 58.—The uncertainty which seems to exist in regard to holding municipal elections on the 20th inst., and the frequent inquiries addressed to these Head-quarters, renders it necessary for the commanding General to announce that said elections are not authorised by any orders from these Head-quarters. Managers of elections are hereby prohibited from receiving any votes, except such State and county offices as are provided for in the constitution, to be submitted for ratification, the voting for which offices is authorised by General Orders, Nos. 51 and 52.

No. 2. Complaints having been made to these Head-quarters, by planters and others, that improper means are being used to compel labourers to leave their work to attend political meetings, and threats being made that in case of refusal penalties will be attached to said refusal, the Major-General Commanding announces that all such attempts to control the movements of labourers and interfere with the rights of employers are strictly forbidden and will be considered, and, on conviction, will be punished, the same as any attempt to dissuade voters from going to the polls, as referred to in paragraph 11, General Orders, No. 57.

No. 3. The Major-General Commanding also makes known that, while he acknowledges, and will require to be respected, the right of labourers to peacefully assemble at night to discuss political questions, yet he discountenances and forbids the assembling of armed bodies, and requires that all such assemblages shall notify either the civil or military authorities of these proposed meetings, and said military and civil authorities are enjoined to see that the right of electors to peaceably assemble for legitimate purposes is not disturbed.

No. 4. The wearing or carrying of arms, either concealed or otherwise, by persons not connected with the military service of the Government, or such civil officers whose duties under the laws and orders is to preserve the public peace, at or in the vicinity of the polling places, on the days set apart for holding the election in the State of Georgia, is positively forbidden. Civil and military officers will see that this order, as well as all others relative to the preservation of the peace and quiet of the counties in which they are acting, is strictly observed.

By order of Major-General MEADE,

R. C. DRUM, A.A.G.

These orders were accompanied by a private letter, which was as follows :—

Easter Sunday : April 11, 1868.

My dear Miss B——,—You will see by my writing you to-day how much I feel flattered by your appeal to me, and how ready I am to respond to it. I regret very much to learn the state of affairs as described by you ; they are certainly un-authorised by any laws or orders from these Head-quarters, and, since the receipt of your letter I have had prepared an order to cover such case, and forbidding the interference of political agents with the rights of employers. I will have a copy sent to you officially, which you can make use of to correct this evil in future.

I have been twice in Savannah, on my way to Florida; have both times thought of you and inquired after you. If you had been a little more accessible, and had I not feared to compromise you by a visit from the awful military satrap and despot who rules so tyrannically over you, Miss W——— will tell you that I, as well as the Colonel (my son), were both desirous of visiting you. I am very much gratified to learn that you acknowledge being my subject, and beg you to remember the acknowledgment is reciprocal, as I acknowledge my allegiance to you—an allegiance founded on respect, kindly regard, and many pleasant recollections of former times.

Let me assure you I shall be ready at all times to aid and encourage you in your labours, and that you must not hesitate to appeal to me ; for, though many people will not believe it, I am trying to act impartially, and to do justice to all.

Very truly and sincerely yours,

GEORGE G. MEADE.

P.S.—Your letter being marked private, I have not deemed myself justified in acting on it, but you will see from my official letter that, if you will send me evidence and names of witnesses in Mr. Campbell's case, I will attend to that gentleman. Official letter goes by to-day's mail with this. Let me know if it does not reach you.

I was, of course, much pleased and very triumphant when I received these letters, although it was impossible to comply with General Meade's request that we would report the offenders, as the notices served on the negroes were never signed—which convinced us of their illegality, but did not in the least take away from their importance

to the negroes.   Still, I not only read my
order to them, but had it posted up in
Darien, and, on the strength of it, repeated
my previous orders to my negroes that, if
one of them neglected his work to attend
political meetings or to vote, I would dismiss
him from the place; adding, at the same
time, 'there is no difficulty about your
voting after your work is over.'   My surprise
and disgust were therefore extreme when I
received the following day a second letter
from General Meade, as follows :—

Atlanta : April 13, 1868.

My dear Miss B——,—I wrote you
very hastily yesterday on my return from
church, not wishing to lose a mail, advising
you of my views and action.   I find to-day,
on a careful re-perusal of your letter, that you
are in error in one particular.   You seem to
think you have the right to decide when your
people shall vote, and that as there is time
for them after three o'clock, the end of their
day's work, that you are authorised to pro-

hibit their leaving at an earlier hour. This is not so, and I would advise you not to insist on it. The theory of my order is that no restraint is to be put on the labourer to prevent his voting.

Now as it is sometimes difficult for a person to vote as soon as he reaches the polls, some having to wait days for their turn, and as, often, examination has to be made of the registration books, and the voter in addition to the delay of awaiting his turn after getting up to the polls, may find some error in the spelling of his name or omission to put his name on the list, and in consequence of these obstacles lose his turn to have the error corrected and then again take his chance, more time must be allowed than your rule would admit. I think you will have to make up your mind that the election will be a great nuisance, and that you will not get much out of your people during its continuance. If they are reasonable and the facilities good at Darien, they should not require any more time than is absolutely necessary, but as I know that voting is a work of time, for which reason we give *four days*, I fear these plausible, and perhaps actual obstacles, will be taken advantage of to spend the time in idleness and frolicking, on the plea that ' they could not get a chance to vote.'

I take the liberty of writing this to you because my letter of yesterday might lead you astray. Again assuring you of my warm regard,

I remain,

Yours very truly,

George G. Meade.

I naturally felt indignant at this letter, for I had told General Meade that I did not intend to interfere with my negroes voting, but only to save myself from loss, and in my case no difficulty existed about their reaching the polls, which were not a mile from the house. And this second letter undid all the good of the first, besides which I could not help feeling the gross injustice of coolly telling me that for four whole days I must not expect any work, for it would really just in that week have entailed a loss of two hundred acres, as I told General Meade in my letter. And what Northern farmer or manufacturer would have submitted for one moment to an order from the Government, directing him to give his employés four whole days for voting, just at the busiest season?

I was both hurt and angry, and never have to this day understood this afterthought of General Meade. He was always so kind and courteous, and had been a personal friend of my father, and could not really have dis-believed my statements. I suppose that he thought in fact I was not my own mistress, but acting under orders and advice from my Southern neighbours. But I can solemnly assert that neither then nor since, to my knowledge, have my negroes been influenced in their way of voting by the planters, beyond a mere joking remark as to whether they felt sure that they had the right ticket, or some such thing. I think most of the gentlemen felt as I did, that the negroes voting at all was such a wicked farce that it only deserved our contempt. I do not say that no outside influence was ever used afterwards, although I do not know of any personally, and certainly, no intimidation, as I think I can most clearly and satisfactorily prove by a statement as to how matters stand with us politically at present. From first to last all our political disturbances arose from agents belonging to the Republican party, mostly Northern adventurers, of whom, thank God, we are now rid.

After thinking the matter over I determined to pay no attention to General Meade's second letter, as I felt I was justified in doing by the facts of the case. So I put the letter in my pocket, and repeated my orders that the negroes were to do their work first, and vote afterwards.

The election day came, and my agent, who was not very judicious and was very excitable, had me awaked at six o'clock in the morning to tell me that there was not a negro in the field, all having announced their intention of going over to Darien to vote. By ten o'clock there was not a man left on the place, even the old half-idiot, who took care of the cows, having gone to vote with the rest; and my agent, who was much excited over it all, said, ' Now, Miss B——, what will you do ? You can't dismiss the whole plantation.' I confess for a moment I felt checkmated, and did not know what to do, but as I had intended to go down to St. Simon's that day I determined to carry out my intention, which would give me time to think quietly and coolly over the situation. So I sent word to my two boat hands that they must cast their votes as soon as possible and return to take me down, an order they promptly obeyed. The next day I received a note from my agent, saying that the hands had all returned to their work early in the day after voting, and had all finished the entire task with the exception of two or three, who promised to do double work the next day. Here was an unexpected triumph, and I truly believe that my plantation was almost the only one in the whole State of Georgia where any work was done during those four days, and apart from the actual loss of labour, four days of idleness would have made it doubly difficult to get the people in hand again. Down on St. Simon's their ardour about voting was considerably cooled by the fact that they had twelve miles to walk to the polls, and besides had not been visited by any political agents to stir them up. So only a few out of the whole number went, and we had no trouble about it. This ended our political troubles for this year, but the work was still anything but steady or satisfactory, and hardly a day passed without difficulty in some shape or other.

In a letter written at the end of April I say :—

All winter I have had a sort of feeling that before long I should get through and have things settled ; but I am beginning to find out that there is no getting through here, for just as you are about getting through, you have to begin all over again. I have had a good deal of trouble this last week with my people— not serious, but desperately wearisome. They are the most extraordinary creatures, and the mixture of leniency and severity which it is requisite to exercise in order to manage them is beyond belief. Each thing is explained satisfactorily to them and they go to work. Suddenly some one, usually the most stupid, starts an idea that perhaps by-and-by they may be expected to do a little more work, or be deprived of some privilege ; upon which the whole field gets in the most excited state, they put down their hoes and come up to the house for another explanation, which lasts till the same thing happens again.

They are the most effervescent people in the world, and to see them in one of their excitements, gesticulating wildly, talking so violently that no one on earth can understand one word they say, you would suppose they never could be brought under control again. But go into the field the next morning, and there they are, as quiet, peaceable, and cheerful as if nothing had happened. At first I used to talk too, but now I just stand perfectly quiet until they have talked themselves out, and then I ask some simple question which shows them how foolish they have been, and they cool down in a moment.

The other day, while I was at dinner, I heard tramp, tramp, outside, and a gang of fifty arrived, the idea having occurred to them that, while I was gone in harvest time, they might be overworked. They talked and they raved 'that they had contracted to do two tasks and no more,' going from one imaginary grievance to another, until one man suddenly broke out with, 'And, missus, when we work night and day, we ought to be paid extra.' Upon which they all took it up,

' Yes, missus, when we tired with working hard all day, den to work all night for nothing is too much.' Not having spoken before, I then said very quietly, ' Have you ever been asked to work at night ? ' There was a dead pause for a moment, and then one man said rather sheepishly, ' No.' ' Well,' said I, ' when you are, you will certainly be paid extra, and now, as you seem to have forgotten the contract, I will read it to you over again.'

So I brought it out and read it slowly and solemnly, dwelling particularly on the part in which it said, ' The undersigned freed men and women agree to obey all orders and to do the work required of them in a satisfactory manner, and in event of any violation of this contract, they are to be dismissed the place and to forfeit all wages due to them.' This cooled them considerably, and when I added, ' Now understand, your work is just what you are told to do, and if one bushel of rice is lost through your disobedience or carelessness, you shall pay for it,' this quenched them utterly, and they went to work the next morning with the greatest possible good-will, and all will go on well until the next time, whenever that may be. But what with troubles without and troubles within, life is a burden and rice a difficult crop to raise.

As for Mr. D——'s and Mr. W——'s opinions about the glorious future of our Sea Island cotton plantations, they are worth just as much as the paper on which their calculations are made, and are theoretical entirely.

Mr. G——, another rich New York man, who figured it all out on paper there, came here two years ago to make his fortune, and he told me the other day that he was perfectly convinced that Sea Island cotton never would pay again. Rice, he said, might, but this fine cotton, never. The expense and risk of raising it was too great, and the price too much lowered by foreign competition. The labour is too uncertain, and anyone who knows, as I do, that after all my hard work the crop may be lost at any moment by the negroes going off or refusing to work, knows how useless it is to count on any returns with certainty. Wherever white labour can be introduced, other crops will be cultivated, and wherever it can't, the land will remain uncultivated.

Rice lands now rent at ten dollars an acre, and cotton from two to three, so you can judge what the people here think about it; and, after all, I suppose they must know best. The orange trees are all in full bloom now, and smell most deliciously sweet, and the little place looks its prettiest, which is not say-ing much for it, it is true. Another year I hope to improve it by removing the negro houses away from where they now are, close to this house, to where I can neither see, hear, nor smell them. I shall then run my own fence out a little further, taking in a magnifi-cent magnolia and some large orange trees, which, with the quantities of flowers I have

set out everywhere, will at any rate make
the garden round the house pretty.

A little later on, the Island being sub-
merged by a sudden overflow and rise of the
river, I accepted an invitation from some
friends in South Carolina, also rice-planters,
to visit them. From there I write as
follows :—

Mrs. P.'s family consists of a very nice
girl about my own age, clever and well-
educated, and two sons, one about twenty-
seven and the other about twenty-four, both
of whom were educated abroad, and are well-
informed and intelligent. So altogether it is
a pleasant family to be in, and as we are all
trying to make our fortunes as rice-planters,
we have everything in common, and talk
' rice' all day.

I have ridden every day since I have
been here, and on Friday went deer-hunting,
which, of course, I enjoyed very much. We
started at eight o'clock in the morning, and

did not return till five o'clock in the afternoon, having seen six deer and killed two, one of which we lost, after a short run, in the river.

This part of the country has suffered more heavily than any other from the war. Hundreds of acres of rice land, which yielded millions before the war, are fast returning to the original swamp from which they were reclaimed with infinite pains and expense, simply because their owners are ruined, their houses burnt to the ground, and their negroes made worthless as labourers. It is very sad to see such wide-spread ruin, and to hear of girls well-educated, and brought up with every luxury, turned adrift as dressmakers, school-teachers, and even shop girls, in order to keep themselves and their families from starvation. One of Mrs. F——'s nieces paddles her old father over to the plantation every morning herself, and while he is giving his orders in the fields, sits on a heap of straw, making under-clothes to sell in Charleston. It is wonderful to me to see how bravely and cheerfully they do work, knowing as I do how they lived before the war.

I was agreeably surprised with the beauty of this place, for I thought all rice plantations, like Butler's Island, were ugly and uninteresting. Here the rice fields are quite out of sight. The garden, which is very large, is enclosed by a lovely hedge of some sweet-smelling shrub and roses ; in it are clematis and sweet olea bushes thirty feet high, with quantities of violets and all sorts of sweet things besides. Then there are three superb live oak trees, from under which we look out on the river, which runs clear and deep in front of the house. The house itself is a good-sized building, with remains of great elegance about it, and with some nice old family pictures and china in it. Mrs. P—— is very proud of having saved these things, which she did by remaining with her daughter in the house during a raid, when all her neighbours fled, leaving their houses to be literally emptied of their contents by the soldiers of the Northern army who visited this section of the country.

M—— told me a funny story of a visit she received from a tipsy Yankee captain, to whom she and her mother were, from interested motives, most civil, and who became so affected by her charms that he presented her with a silver pitcher to which he had just helped himself from a neighbouring house, which she gratefully accepted, and returned as soon as possible to its rightful owner.

I leave here this evening, as my agent writes me the waters have subsided from the face of the earth. So I must get back to my work and to my new planting machine, which I am very anxious to try, being the first step towards freeing ourselves from negro labourers.

On my return, the season being well advanced and the rice place no longer healthy, I went down at once to the cotton plantation, of which my final letter written from the South this year gives this account :——

Hampton Point : May 5, 1868.

I came down here last Tuesday, as, before
I return to the North I want to get a little
sea air, as well as to have the house re-
shingled, the rain now coming through the
old roof in plentiful showers.   The main
body of the house, I am glad to find, is perfectly good, so that repairing the roof and
piazzas will put it in thorough order ; and as
I have brought my whole force of eight
carpenters down, the work is going briskly
forward.   This place, always lovely, is now
looking its best, with all the young spring
greens and flowers lighting up the woods, and
I long to cut and trim, lay out and take up,
making the place as beautiful as it is capable of
being made.   It is a great contrast in every
way to Butler's Island, the place as well as
people.

The proximity of the other place to
Darien has a very demoralising effect upon
the negroes there.   Here everything moves
on steadily and quietly, as it used to do in old

times. Bram still has charge, and with his three nice grown sons, gives the tone to the place. We have planted about a hundred and twenty-five acres of cotton, all of which are coming up well and healthy. But this time last year it looked well too, and then, alas! alas! was totally destroyed by the army-worm, so who can tell if it may not again be swept from off the face of the earth in a single night, as it was last year.

Your notion, and Miss F——'s, that the negroes ought at once to be made to realise their new condition and position, is an impossibility, and you might just as well expect children of ten and eleven to suddenly realise their full responsibilities as men and women, as these people. That they will come to it in time I hope and believe, and for that purpose I am having them educated, trying to increase their desire for comforts, and excite their ambition to furnish their houses and make them neat and pretty. But the change was too great to expect them to adopt

the new state of things at once, and they
must come to it by degrees, during which
time my personal influence is necessary to
keep them up in their work, and to prevent
them falling into habits of utter worthlessness,
from which they can never be reclaimed.

From the first, the fixed notion in their
minds has been that liberty meant idleness,
and they must be forced to work until they
become intelligent enough to know the value
of labour. As for starving them into this,
that is impossible too, for it is a well-known
fact that you can't starve a negro. At this
moment there are about a dozen on Butler's
Island who do no work, consequently get no
wages and no food, and I see no difference
whatever in their condition and those who
get twelve dollars a month and full rations.
They all raise a little corn and sweet potatoes,
and with their facilities for catching fish and
oysters, and shooting wild game, they have
as much to eat as they want, and now are
quite satisfied with that, not yet having

learned to want things that money alone can give.

The proof that my theory about personal influence is the only means at present by which the people can be managed, is that my father, by his strong influence over them last year, made the best crop that was raised in the country, and this year our people are working far better than others in the neigh-bourhood, and we have again the prospect of a large crop, while our neighbours are in despair, their hands running off, refusing to work, and even in some places raising riots in the place. Not that their masters are not paying them their wages, for in some cases they are giving them more than we do ; but because they just pay them off so much a month and trouble their heads no more about them, just as if they were white labourers. Now, my desire and object is to put them on this footing as soon as possible, but they must be kept in leading-strings until they are able to stand alone.

# CHAPTER IV.

## 1868–1869.

### RECONSTRUCTION.

In November of the same year I again visited the South, having received during the summer one or two sensational telegrams from my agent, who was apt to lose his head, and although they sounded very alarming, they proved to be the creation of a vivid imagination or unfounded reports, and on the whole the people had done very well, and we had a large crop for the acreage planted. This year I took a friend with me, and my maid. Christmas, politics, and paying-off had again upset all the negroes, and many of them said they intended to leave the place, and some did. We were now giving 12 dollars a month, with rations, half the money being paid at the end of every month, and the rest, at the end of the year. Knowing that it was quite use- less to try and get them to settle down until after the first of the year, I let them alone and devoted myself to the children, for whom I had a beautiful Christmas tree. I wrote on Christmas evening an account of it all.

Christmas 1868.

Dearest M——, You have heard of our safe arrival, and how much more comfortable the travelling was than last year. We arrived about a month ago, and I have been hard at work ever since. The negroes do not seem to be in a very satisfactory condition, but it is owing in a great measure, I think, to its being Christmas time. They are all prepared again to make their own, and different, terms for next year, but except for the bother and trouble I don't feel very anxious about it, for we have a gang of Irishmen doing the

banking and ditching, which the negroes
utterly refuse to do any more at all, and
therefore, until the planting begins, we can
do without the negro labour.

Last year they humbugged me completely
by their expressions of affection and desire to
work for me, but now that the novelty of
their getting back once more to their old
home has entirely worn off and they have
lost their old habits of work, the effects of
freedom are beginning to tell, and everywhere
sullen unwillingness to work is visible, and all
round us people are discussing how to get
other labourers in the place of negroes. But
alas! on the rice lands white labour is impossible, so that I really don't know what we shall
do, and I think things look very gloomy for
the planters. Our Northern neighbours on St.
Simon's, the D——s, who were most hopeful
last year, are now perfectly discouraged with
the difficulties they have to encounter with
their labour, and of course having to lose two
or three months every year while the negroes

are making up their minds whether they will work or not, obliges us to plant much less ground than we should otherwise do. However, there is no use taking evil on account, and when we are ruined will be time enough to say free labour here is a failure, and I still hope that when their Christmas excitement is over, the people will settle down to work.

My Christmas tree this afternoon was a great success ; it was really very pretty. I had three rooms packed full of people, the women begging me to give them dolls and the toys, which I had brought of course for the children alone. The orange trees are a miracle of beauty ; many of the branches touch the ground from the weight of the fruit, and you cannot walk under them without knocking the oranges with your head. Several of the trees have yielded two thousand, and the whole crop is estimated at sixteen thousand.

We had a small excitement about this

time, owing to a report which went the
round of the plantations, that there was to be
a general negro insurrection on the 1st of the
year. I did not much believe it, but as I had
promised my friends at the North, who were
very anxious about me, to run no risks and
to take every precaution against danger, I
thought it best to seek some means of protection. I first asked my friend whether
she felt nervous and would rather leave
the Island, but she, being a true soldier's
daughter, said no, she would stay and take
her chance with me. We then agreed to say
nothing about it to my maid, who was a new
English maid, thinking that if we did not
mind having *our* throats cut, neither need
she—particularly as she now spent most of
her time weeping at the horrors which surrounded her.

I wrote therefore to our nearest military
station and asked that a guard of soldiers
might be sent over for a day or two, which
was done. But as they came without any

officer, and conducted themselves generally disagreeably, stealing the oranges, worrying the negroes, and making themselves entirely at home even to the point of demanding to be fed by me, I packed them off, preferring to take my chance with my negroes than with my protectors. I don't believe that there was the least foundation for the report of the insurrection, but we had trouble enough the whole winter in one form or other.

The negroes this year and the following seemed to reach the climax of lawless in-dependence, and I never slept without a loaded pistol by my bed. Their whole manner was changed ; they took to calling their former owners by their last name with-out any title before it, constantly spoke of my agent as old R——, dropped the pleasant term of ' Mistress,' took to calling me ' Miss Fanny,' walked about with guns upon their shoulders, worked just as much and when they pleased, and tried speaking to me with their hats on, or not touching them to me when they passed me on the banks. This last rudeness I never permitted for a moment, and always said sharply, ' Take your hat off instantly,' and was obliged to take a tone to them generally which I had never done before. One or two, who seemed rather more inclined to be insolent than the rest, I dismissed, always saying, ' You are free to leave the place, but not to stay here and behave as you please, for I am free too, and moreover own the place, and so have a right to give my orders on it, and have them obeyed.'

I felt sure that if I relaxed my discipline for one moment all was up, and I never could control the negroes or plant the place again ; and to this unerring rule I am sure I owe my success, although for that year, and the two following, I felt the whole time that it was touch-and-go whether I or the negroes got the upper hand.

A new trouble came upon us too, or

rather an old trouble in a new shape. Negro adventurers from the North, finding that politics was such a paying trade at the South, began pouring in, and were really worse than the whites, for their Southern brethren looked upon their advent quite as a proof of a new order of things, in which the negroes were to rule and possess the land.

We had a fine specimen in one Mr. Tunis Campbell, whose history is rather peculiar. Massachusetts had the honour of giving him birth, and on his first arrival in Georgia he established himself, whether with or without permission I know not, on St. Catherine's Island, a large island midway between Savannah and Darien, which was at that time deserted. The owner, without returning, rented it to a Northern party, who on coming to take possession found Mr. Campbell established there, who declined to move, on some pretended permission he had from the Government to occupy it, and it was necessary to apply to the authorities at Darien to

remove him, which was done by sending a
small armed force.   He then came to Darien,
and very soon became a leader of the negroes,
over whom he acquired the most absolute
control, and managed exactly as he pleased,
so that when the first vote for State and
county authorities was cast, he had no difficulty in having himself elected a magistrate,
and for several years administered justice
with a high hand and happy disregard of law,
there being no one to oppose him.

Happily, he at last went a little too far,
and arrested the captain of a British vessel,
which had come to Darien for timber, for
assault and battery, because he pushed
Campbell's son out of the way on the deck
of his own ship.   The captain was brought
before Campbell, tried, and sentenced to pay
a heavy fine, from which he very naturally
appealed to the English Consul in Savannah,
who of course ordered his release at once.
This and some other equally lawless acts
by which Mr. Campbell was in the habit of

filling his own pockets, drew the attention of the authorities to him, and a very good young judge having just been put on our circuit, he was tried for false imprisonment, and sentenced to one year's imprisonment himself, which not only freed us from his iniquitous rule, against which we had had no appeal, but broke the spell which he held over the negroes, who up till the time of his downfall, had believed his powers omnipotent, and at his instigation had defied all other authority ; which state of things had driven the planters to despair, for there seemed to be no remedy for this evil, the negroes throwing all our authority to the wind, and following Campbell wherever he chose to lead them.

So desperate were some of the gentlemen, that at one time they entertained the idea of seeing if they could not buy Campbell over, and induce him by heavy bribes to work for us, or rather to use his influence over our negroes to make them work for us. And this proposition was made to me, but I could not consent to such a plan. In the first place it was utterly opposed to my notions of what was right, and my pride revolted from the idea of making any such bargain with a creature like Campbell ; besides which I felt sure it was bad policy, that if we bought him one day he would sell us the next. So I refused to have anything to do with the project, and it was fortunately never carried out, for although during the next three or four years Campbell gave us infinite trouble, he would have given us far more had we put ourselves in his power by offering him a bribe.

My agent unfortunately was not much assistance to me, being nervous, timid, and irresolute. Naturally his first thought was to raise the crops by any means that he could, but feeling himself powerless to enforce his orders, owing to the fact that we had no proper authorities to appeal to, should our negroes misbehave themselves, these representatives of the Government pandering to the negroes in every way, in order to secure their votes for themselves, he was obliged to resort to any means he could, to get any work out of the negroes at all, often changing his tactics and giving different orders from day to day. In vain I implored him to be firm, and if he gave an order to stand to it ; but the invariable answer was, ' It's of no use, Miss B——, I should only get myself into trouble, and have the negro sheriff sent over by Campbell to arrest me.' And everyone went on the same principle. One of the negroes committed a brutal murder, but no notice was taken of it by any of the authorities, until, with much personal trouble, I had him arrested and shut up. Shortly afterwards, greatly to my astonishment and indignation, I met him walking about the place, and on inquiring how he had got out, was coolly informed that 'a gentleman had hired him, from the agent of the Freedmen's Bureau, to work on his plantation.' I went at once to the agent, and told him that if the man was not re-arrested at once and kept confined, I would report him to the higher authorities.

A few days afterwards I visited the same negro in his prison (!) which turned out to be a deserted warehouse, with no fastening upon the door, and here I found him playing the fiddle to a party who were dancing. He did meet his fate however, poor fellow, at last, but not for three years, when our own courts were re-established, and he was tried, sentenced, and hanged.

On another occasion I had to insist upon two of my own negroes being sent off the place, as they had been caught stealing rice. No one would try them, and my agent proposed to let them off for the present, as he needed their labour just then.

Finding things so unsettled and unsatisfactory, I determined to remain at the South during the summer, fearing that we might after all lose the crops we had with so much difficulty got planted; and part of the hot weather I passed at St. Simon's, and part in

South Carolina, with the same friends I had been with the winter before.

On St. Simon's I found as usual a very different state of things from that on Butler's Island. The people were working like machinery, and gave no trouble at all, which was owing perhaps somewhat to the fact that there were only fifty, instead of three hundred, and at the head of the fifty was Bram, with eight of his family at work under him. He was really a remarkable man, and gave the tone to the whole place. And oh! the place was so beautiful; each day it seemed to me to grow more so. All the cattle had come down, and it was a pretty sight to see first the thirty cows, then the sheep, of which there were over a hundred, with their lambs, come in for the night, and then the horses led out to water before going to bed. I used to go round every evening to visit them in their different pens and places, where they were all put up for the night. The stable I visited several times a day, as I

had not much faith in my groom, and once
when I was telling him how to rub one of
the horses down with a wisp of straw when
he came in hot, he said, 'Yis, so my ole
missus (my mother) taught me, and stand
dere to see it done.' To which I could only
say, 'You seem to have forgotten the lesson
pretty thoroughly.'

In July I went to South Carolina, and
found my friends moved from the rice plantation to a settlement about fifteen miles
distant in the pine woods, which formerly
had been occupied entirely by the overseers,
when the gentlemen and their families could
afford to spend their summer at the North, a
thing they no longer could afford, nor wished
to do. The place and the way of living
were altogether queerer than anything I
had ever imagined. The village consisted of
about a dozen houses, set down here and
there among the tall pine trees, which grew
up to the very doors, almost hiding one
house from another. The place was very

healthy and the sanitary laws very strict. No two houses were allowed to be built in a line, no one was allowed to turn up the soil, even for a garden, and no one, on pain of death, to cut down a pine tree ; in which way they succeeded in keeping it perfectly free from malaria, and the air one breathed was full of the delicious fragrance of the pines, which in itself is considered a cure for most ills. In front of each house was a high mound of sand, on which at night a blazing pine fire was lit to drive away malaria that might come from the dampness of the night. These fires had the most picturesque effect, throwing their glare upon the red trunks of the pines and lighting the woods for some distance around.

The houses were built in the roughest possible manner, many of them being mere log-houses. The one we were in was neither plastered nor lined inside, one thickness of boards doing for both inside and outside walls. M—— and I slept literally under the shingles, between which and the walls of the house, we could lie and watch the stars ; but I liked feeling the soft air on my face, and to hear it sigh softly through the tall pines outside, as I lay in bed. Occasionally bats came in, which was not so pleasant, and there was not one room in the house from which you could not freely discourse with anyone in any other part of the building. Hampton Point, which I had always regarded as the roughest specimen of a house anyone could live in, was a palace compared with this. We were nevertheless perfectly comfortable, and it was really pretty, with numbers of easy-chairs and comfortable sofas about, and the pretty bright chintz curtains and covers, which looked very well against the fresh whitewashed boards ; and there was an amusing incongruity between a grand piano and fine embroidered sheets and pillow cases, relics of past days of wealth and luxury, and our bare floors and walls.

Most of the people were very poor, which

created a sort of commonwealth, as there was
a friendly feeling among them all, and desire
to share anything good which one got with
his neighbours; so that, constantly through
the day, negro servants would be seen going
about from one house to another, carrying
a neatly covered tray, which contained presents of cakes or fruit, or even fresh bread
that some one had been baking. There was
a meat club, which everyone belonged
to, and to which everyone contributed in
turn, either an ox or a sheep a week, which
was then divided equally, each house receiving in turn a different part, so that all
fared alike, and one week we feasted sump-
tuously off the sirloin, and the next, not so
well, from the brisket.

Mrs. P—— was most energetic, directing the affairs of the estate with a masterly
hand, and at the same time devoting herself to the comfort and happiness of her
children; reading French or German, or
practising music with her daughter in the

mornings, and being always ready to receive her boys on their return from their
hard day's work on the plantation. to which
they rode fifteen miles every morning, and
back the same distance in the evening, with
interest and sympathy in the day's work, and
a capital good dinner, which especially excited my admiration, as half the time there
really seemed nothing to make it of. But
they were better off than most of the people,
who were very wretched. Many of them had
their fine plantation houses, with everything
in them, burnt to the ground during the war,
and had no money and very little idea of
how to help themselves. In the next house
to us was Mrs. M——, an elegant, refined,
and cultivated old lady, with soft silver
grey hair and delicate features that made
her look like a picture on Sèvres china,
and as unable as a Sèvres cup to bear any
rough handling, but who lived without many
of the ordinary necessaries of life, and was
really starving to death because she could

not eat the coarse food which was all she could get.

Poor people! they were little used to such hardships, and seemed as helpless as children, but nevertheless were patient and never complained.

The woods around were full of deer, and the gentlemen hunted very often—not for sport so much as for food. They generally started about five o'clock in the morning and were aroused by a horn which was sounded in the centre of the village by the huntsman. As soon as it was heard, the hounds began to bay from the different houses, at each of which two or three were kept, no one being rich enough to keep the whole pack ; but being always used to hunt together, they did very well, and made altogether a very respectable pack. One day they brought home three deer, having started ten ; so for the next few days we had a grand feast of venison.

Among other subjects connected with

our rice plantations was one which interested
us all very much at that time—the question of introducing Chinese labour on our
plantations in the place of negro labour,
which just then seemed to have become
hopelessly unmanageable.    There seemed
to be a general move in this direction all
through the Southern States, and I have
no doubt was only prevented by the want
of means of the planters, which, as far as
I personally am concerned, I am glad was the
case.  Just then, however, we were all very
keen about it, and it sounded very easy,
the Pacific Railway having opened a way for
them to reach us.   One agent actually came
for orders, and I, with the others, engaged
some seventy to try the experiment with,
first on General's Island.   I confess I felt a
little nervous about the result, but agreed
with my neighbours in not being willing to
see half my property uncultivated and going
to ruin for want of labour.   It was not only
that negro labour could no longer be de-

pended upon, but they seemed to be dying out so fast, that soon there would be but few left to work. This new labour would of course have sealed their doom, and in a few years none would have been left. I wrote about it at the time :—

'Poor people ! it seems impossible to arouse them to any good ambition, their one idea and desire being—not to work. Their newspaper in Charlestown, edited by a negro, published an article the other day on the prospect, and said it would be the best thing that could happen to the negroes if the Chinese did come, as then they too could get them as servants, and no longer have to work even for themselves. I confess I am utterly unable to understand them, and what God's will is concerning them, unless He intended they should be slaves. This may shock you ; but why in their own country have they no past history, no monuments, no literature, never advance or improve, and here, now that they are free, are going

steadily backwards, morally, intellectually,
and physically. I see it on my own place,
where, in spite of school and ministers, and
every inducement offered them to improve
their condition, they are steadily going down-
wards, working less and worse every year,
until, from having come to them with my
heart full of affection and pity for them, I
am fast growing weary and disgusted.

' Mrs. P——, who when she first married
and came to the South was a strong abolitionist, an intimate friend of Charles Sumners
and believer in Mrs. Stowe, says that she firmly
believes them incapable of being raised now ;
and a few days ago I had a long talk with
Mrs. W——, the cousin of an Englishwoman
who married and came out here with all the
English horror of, and ideas about, slavery.
Her husband dying shortly after, left her independent and very rich, so she determined
to devote her life and means to the people
who were thus thrown on her for help and
protection. She first sent out to England for

a young English clergyman, whom she established on the place; she then built a beautiful little church of stone, with coloured glass windows, at great expense; and their own houses, Mrs. W—— told me, were far better than English labourers' cottages.

'Well, for forty years she and her clergyman worked together among them. She never allowed one to be sold from the estate, and devoted herself to them as if they were her children. Then came the war, and in no part of the country did the negroes behave so badly as hers. They murdered the overseer, tore down the church, set up as a goddess a negro woman whom they called 'Jane Christ,' and now are in all respects as entire heathens as if they had never heard God's name mentioned, worshipping Obi, preaching every sort of heathen superstition, and a terror to the neighbourhood.[1] Mrs. W——, broken-hearted, returned to England, where she had property, and the clergyman, a Mr. G——,

[1] I now doubt a good deal of this story (1881).

her fellow-worker, on being asked some time ago to go to some gentleman's plantations to preach to the negroes, shook his head, and with his eyes full of tears said he would never preach again, his whole work and preaching for forty years having proved such a failure.    And our own clergyman at Darien told me he had been working among the negroes all his life to the best of his powers, but felt now that not one seed sown among them had borne any good fruit.

'I confess thinking of these things makes me heartsick.    I don't understand why really good men doing God's work should have failed so utterly, because although, intellectually, I feel sure the negroes are incapable of any high degree of improvement, morally, I have always thought their standard wonderfully high, considering their ignorance.'

I remained at the South until the harvest was well under way, my own interest being intensified by my friends, and we lived in a perpetual state of excitement, fearing from day to day that something would happen to destroy our hardly-made crops. First it blew hard and we feared a gale, and then the rice birds appeared in such swarms we feared the crops would be eaten up. Then it rained, and we feared the cut rice would be wetted and sprout. And so on, until one day Mrs. P—— exclaimed, 'What a state of excitement and alternate hope and fear we live in ! Why, the life of a gambler is nothing to it.' The news that reached me of the rice from Butler's Island was sufficiently good to re-assure me, but from St. Simon's it was terrible. Major D—— wrote me that the caterpillars had again attacked the cotton, and that for the third time we should probably see the entire crop eaten up before our eyes, within three weeks of perfection. Such beautiful crops as they were, too ! This gave the deathblow to the Sea Island cotton, at least as far as I was concerned, for I had not capital enough to plant again after losing three crops, and the place has never been planted since, but is rented out to the negroes for a mere nominal rent, and they keep the weeds down and that is about all. Some day I hope to see it turned into a stock farm, for which it is admirably suited, and would pay well.

Before leaving the history of the South for this year, I cannot help saying a few words upon a subject which did not strike me as strange then, but does now, in looking back, as very significant of the way politics were regarded and treated by Southerners at the time. There I was, in South Carolina, 'the hot-bed of Secession,' among some of the oldest South Carolina families, considered by most Northern people as the deepest-dyed rebels, whose time was still spent in devising schemes to overthrow the Government, who therefore could not be trusted with the rights of free citizens, and whose negroes it was necessary to protect in their rights by Northern troops, and yet neither in my letters nor in my memory can I find one single instance of political discussion, or attempts to rebel against the new state of things, or desire to interfere with the new rights of the negroes. Night after night gentlemen met at one house or another, and talked and discussed one, and only one subject, and that was rice, rice, rice.

Farmers are supposed never to exhaust the two subjects of weather and the crops, and we certainly never did, until one evening the daughter of the lady with whom I was staying burst out with, ' Do—do talk of something else ; I am so tired of rice, rice, from morning till night, and day after day.' We might all have been aliens and foreigners, so little interest did we any of us take in any public questions, and I never heard it suggested to prevent the negroes voting, but only to get rid of them and get reliable labour in their place. The war was over, the negroes free, and voters, and the South conquered ; and never by the smallest word did I hear any suggestions made to try to alter the new condition of things, or to wish to do so, each man's motto being 'Sauve qui peut.'

# CHAPTER V.

## 1870.

LATE in the winter of 1869 I returned to the South, having quite made up my mind that I must change my agent. The expenses were enormous; so large, that even remarkably good crops could not make the two ends meet, while there were no improvements made and no work done to justify such heavy expenditure, and not even accounts to show on what the money had been spent. The negroes were almost in a state of mutiny, and work for another year under existing circumstances was impossible. So I got rid of one agent and engaged another, the son of a former neighbouring planter, whom I liked personally and with whom the negroes professed themselves content. But owing to the mismanagement and want of firmness on the part of his predecessor, they were in an utterly demoralised and disorganised condition. Many of them left, not to work for anyone else, but to settle on their own properties in the pine woods ; and the others seemed inclined to be very troublesome. So for a time, until the effects of being paid, and Christmas, had worn off, I left them pretty much to themselves, giving the children another pretty tea and feast, which put the older ones somewhat in a good humour.

Mr. N—— certainly did not want either courage or firmness, and I was rather startled one day to have a young man named Liverpool, who had always been a troublesome subject, burst into the room in which I was sitting, and pointing to a wound in his forehead which was bleeding pretty freely, say, ' Missus, do you allow this kind of treatment ? '

I smothered my exclamation of horror and
indignant denial, and said, 'How did it
happen?' 'Why,' replied the lad, 'Mr. N——
knocked me down and cut my head like this.'
'Well,' I said, 'before I decide, I must know
what you have done.' 'Very well,' he said,
'very well;' and turning on his heel, left the
room. I was horribly frightened for fear, in
his anger, he would shoot my agent, and
throwing on my shawl, I ran out to find him
and put him on his guard. He told me that
Liverpool had been very insolent and in-
subordinate to both the negro captain, who
reported him, and to himself, and he had
simply knocked him down, and cut his head·
slightly. My fears were, I believe, needless,
for Liverpool's revenge was to try to sue
Mr. N—— for damages, which however
never came to anything, and so the trouble
ended, although the man was of course
dismissed from the place, being a really
troublesome, bad fellow.

One of my captains also had his head cut

open by another lad who was drunk, and who was flourishing a rice-hook about, which the old man tried to get from him, and was cut badly across the forehead. He came to me to have it plastered up, and was very anxious to know 'whether de brain was cut,' which I assured him was not the case, and being only a flesh wound it soon healed.

By degrees things settled down, and the work began. My school seemed flourishing under a new teacher I had got from the North (the other young man having left). This was a young negro, who had been at a Theological Seminary near Philadelphia, preparing himself for the ministry; but his old father, a Massachusetts Baptist preacher, not wishing his son to become an episcopal minister, refused to give him any more money to continue his studies, and so he was obliged to leave, and was anxious to get some employment by which he could earn enough money to finish his studies. This story the Bishop told me, adding that if I could get him some theological books, and let him read with some clergyman in the village, he would lose no time and could take up the course at the school again just where he had been obliged to leave off. Much interested, I at once got him several theological standard works which he asked for, and made arrangements with our Darien clergyman to let him read with him. How it ended belongs to next year's history. He certainly got the children on in a wonderful way ; but seeing how soon they forgot all he taught them, I doubt its having been more than a quick parrot-like manner of repeating what they had heard once or twice, which the negroes all have. But it sounded very startling to hear them rattle off the names of countries, lengths of rivers, and heights of mountains, as well as complicated answers in arithmetic. The little ones he taught to sing everything they learned, and they always began with a little song, that amused me very much, about the necessity

of coming to school and learning, the chorus
of which ran :—

> For we must get an education
> Befitting to our station
> In the rising generation
> Of the old Georg—ī—ā :

a thing I fear, however, they failed to do.
One day I heard one boy say to another,
' Carolina, can you spell " going in " ? ' ' Gwine
in,' promptly replied Carolina, that being
their negro way of pronouncing it.   On one
point I and this teacher never agreed, and
that was about the head handkerchiefs and
bead necklaces of the girls.   About the last
perhaps he was right, although their love of
coloured beads was a very harmless little bit
of vanity, and I always used to give them the
handsomest I could find for their Christmas
presents ; but the head handkerchief was not
only pretty and becoming, but made them
look far neater than either their uncovered
woolly heads, or the absurd little hats they
bought and stuck on in order to follow the

fashions of their white sisters. Now that ladies everywhere have taken to wearing silk handkerchiefs made into turban-shaped caps, I suppose the negro women may become reconciled to their gay bandanas.

We had a great many marriages this winter, and wishing to encourage the girls to become moral and chaste, we made the cere mony as important as possible, that is, if a grand cake and white wreath and veil could make it so, for the ceremony, as performed by our old black minister, could hardly be said to be imposing, and I think I have gone through more painful agonies to keep from laughing at some of these weddings than from any physical suffering I ever experienced. The girls were always dressed in white, with our present of the wreath and veil to finish the costume, and the bridesmaids in white or light dresses, while the bridegroom and groomsmen wore black frock coats, with white waistcoats and white gloves, all looking as nice as possible. The parson,

old John, received them at the reading-desk
of the little church, and after much arranging
of the candles, his book, and his big-rimmed
specs, would proceed and read the marriage
service of the Episcopal Church, part of which
he knew by heart, part of which he guessed
at, and the rest of which he spelt out with
much difficulty and many absurd mistakes.
Not satisfied with the usual text appointed
for the minister to read, he usually went
through all the directions too, explaining
them as he went along thus : ' " Here the man
shall take the woman by the right hand," ' at
which he would pause, look up over his
spectacles and say, ' Take her, child, by de
right hand and hold her,' and would then
proceed.    On one occasion, after he had read
the sentence, ' " Whereof this ring is given
and received as a token and pledge," ' he
said with much emphasis, ' Yes, children, it
is a *plague*, but you must have patience.'
When it was all over he would say to the
bridegroom with great solemnity and a wave

of his hand, 'Salute de bride,' upon which the happy man would give her a kiss that could be heard all over the room. The worst of John's readings and explanations was that they differed every time, so we never could be prepared for what was coming, which made it all the more difficult not to laugh.

On one occasion something happened which made the people titter,—not what he said, for that was always received most reverently, but some mistake on the part of the bridegroom, upon which he closed the book and in a severe tone said, 'What you larf for? dis not trifling, dis business;' which admonition effectually sobered us all. Poor old John Bull—he was a good old man, and had an excellent influence over the people, who obeyed him implicitly, and I was really sorry when he was no longer allowed to perform the service. The Government passed a law that no unlicensed minister or magistrate could perform the marriage service, which, of course, was quite right; but not wishing to lose my parson, or to have my people go off the place to be married, I sent him up to Savannah to have him licensed. But they found him too ignorant, and refused to do so, which I dare say was quite right too ; but it spoilt all my weddings and obliged John to retire into private life.

The negroes had their own ideas of morality, and held to them very strictly ; they did not consider it wrong for a girl to have a child before she married, but afterwards were extremely severe upon anything like infidelity on her part. Indeed, the good old law of female submission to the husband's will on all points held good, and I once found a woman sitting on the church steps, rocking herself backwards and forwards in great distress, and on inquiring the cause I was told she had been turned out of church because she refused to obey her husband in a small matter. So I had to intercede for her, and on making a public apology before the whole congregation she was re-admitted.

To raise the tone among our young un-
married women was our great object, and my
friend and I dwelt much on this in teaching
them, and encouraged their marrying young,
in which, indeed, they did not need much
encouragement, for they both marry very
young, and as often as they are left widows.
The funeral service was generally performed
about three weeks after the person was buried,
in order to have a larger gathering than was
possible to get together on a short notice,
and on one occasion I was rather startled to
hear a man's second engagement announced
on the day of his first wife's funeral. The
following morning he came to me, and with
many blushes and much stammering said,
' Missus, I'se come to tell you something.'
Not choosing to acknowledge that I had
heard the gossip, I said, ' Well, Quash, what
is it ? ' After a very long pause and much
hesitation, he informed me he was going to be
married again. ' Don't you think it is rather
soon after Betsy's death, Quash ? ' I asked ;

upon which he replied, 'Well, yes, missus, it is, but I thought if I waited, maybe I not get a gal suit me so well as Lizzie.' This was so unanswerable a reason that after consulting with my friend as to whether Quash's conduct could be countenanced under our code of morality, we agreed to allow it'; and a very gay, fine wedding it was, for he being a good-looking carpenter and she a pretty house-servant and a great favourite of ours, we exerted ourselves especially to give them a grand wedding.

I had visits from several friends that year, and among others three Englishmen, one of whom was Mr. Leigh. I mention this because of rather a curious circumstance connected with his visit. The first Sunday after his arrival we sent him up to preach to the negroes, and he took for his text, 'And Philip said to the eunuch, Understandest thou what thou readest?' telling them that the eunuch was some Ethiopian, and was the first individual conversion to Christianity

mentioned in the Bible. After church, one of
the negroes came up to him and, after thank-
ing him, said Philip was come again to the
Ethiopians ; and another, called Commodore
Bob, told him he had been expecting him
for three weeks. And when Mr. Leigh
said, ' You never saw me before, how did you
know I was coming ? ' replied, ' Oh yes, sir, I
saw you in de spirit. A milk-white gentleman rise out of the wild rushes and came
and preached to us, and I said to my wife,
" Katie, der will be a great movement in our
church on dis Island." So I knew you in the
spirit.' Of course when I told the negroes
afterwards I was going to marry Mr. Leigh,
old Commodore Bob was more convinced
than ever that the mantle of prophecy had
fallen upon his shoulders, and that the
' great movement ' was my marriage to their
preacher.

While I was receiving guests, and marrying and giving in marriage, the work on the
plantation was going on pretty smoothly.

After the first of the year, when about twenty
of the hands left, and frightened me with the
idea that all were going, then the exodus
stopped, and after several attempts to get the
upper hand of Mr. N——, my new agent,
they gave in and settled down to work.    But,
of course, the loss of time and hands obliged
us to cut down the quantity of land planted
about one-third, and the idea that each year
was to begin in this way was not encouraging.  So we still talked of Chinese labour and
machinery (my dream just then was a steam
plough which was to accomplish everything),
the want of capital being our only difficulty.
I adopted a new plan with the negroes this
year too, and would see and speak to no one
but the head men, and if anyone still insisted
on coming to me directly with complaints, I
simply told him he might leave the place,
finding that this silenced them, but did not
make them leave one whit more than when I
tried to persuade them to stay.

Just before we left we had a narrow

escape from drowning, and I have always
believed that I owed my life to the presence
of mind and coolness of the negroes. We had
gone down to the cotton place to pay a farewell visit, and in coming back, crossing the
Sound, which one is obliged to do for about
five miles, we were caught in a furious gale
and cross sea. Our boat, being cut out of one
log—a regular 'dug out'—did not rise the
least to the waves, and was made doubly
heavy by having all our trunks piled in the
bow. Then, besides the four carsmen, there
was my maid, my friend, and her sister, a
little girl of fourteen, and lastly, in the stern
steering, myself. The sea was running so high
that the boat would hardly mind the rudder
at all, and suddenly the tiller rope broke,
and I was just in time to catch the rudder
with my hand to keep it from swinging round,
and holding it so I had to steer the rest of
the way.

Not being used to steering in a rough
sea, I did not understand that the right thing

to do was to head the boat right at the
waves, and could not help instinctively trying
to dodge them, so that they struck us on the
side and deluged us with wet besides very
nearly capsizing us, and we were soon ankle
deep in water. The negroes rowed with
might and main, but seemed to make no progress, and the wind was blowing such a gale
they could not hear me when I shouted to
them at the top of my voice. About half-way
across the Sound some large piles or booms
had been driven during the war to prevent
the Northern gunboats entering, and on
these we were rapidly being driven, and I,
powerless to steer against the furious wind,
felt sure a few moments more would dash us
against them, and we should be drowned. I
in vain shouted to the men, who of course,
sitting with their backs to the bow, did not
see what was before them, but my voice could
not reach them, so I shut my eyes and held
my breath, expecting each moment to feel the
blow that would send us into eternity. Just as

we were literally on the piles, a huge wave
struck us and drove the boat a little to one
side, so that instead of striking the booms
with our bow we slid between two of them,
scraping each side of the boat as we did so—
but were safe! Utterly exhausted, I felt
I could hold on to my helm no longer, and I
told my friend, who was sitting directly in
front of me, to pass the order on to the men
to let us drift into the marsh, where we would
lie until sunset, when perhaps the wind
would go down. So we beat across and
reached the marsh, where we rested for a few
moments, holding on by the tall rushes, but
found even there the wind and waves so
violent we could not remain.

The stroke oar, a man I was particularly
fond of, though he was rather morose and
suspicious, stood up, and holding on to the
land by burying his oar in the mud, said,
' Missus, we can't stay here, the boat will be
overturned. Trust me, and I will take you
home safely. Only keep the head of the boat

right at the waves, and don't let them strike us sideways.' So bracing myself up I took hold of my helm again, to do which I was obliged to stretch my arm as far back as possible, having no tiller rope, and we turned our head to the waves once more. The men started a favourite hymn of mine as they began to row, but the wind of heaven soon knocked the wind out of them, and they were not only obliged to stop singing, but before long were absolutely groaning at each stroke they made with the oars. Peter's speech and the attempt at a song had, however, quieted me, and enabled me to recover my presence of mind, so I kept the boat headed steadily straight at the waves, and after four hours' more hard work we landed safe on Butler's Island, the river even there being lashed into such fury by the gale that we found it difficult to get out of the boat.

The agent and negroes were terrified at the mere idea of our having attempted to cross the Sound in such weather, and advised

me, as I valued my life, not to do it again,
which was certainly a needless piece of advice.
We afterwards compared notes, my friend
saying, like a true soldier's daughter, that she
felt sure we should be drowned, and had
made up her mind to it; the little sister had
only thought it very disagreeable, and had
not known there was any danger. And my
maid said that when the first wave came she
thought of her new bonnet, and put up her
arm to save it (a very hopeless protection);
that then, when she had seen we were rushing
on the pilings, she had felt sure we should
be drowned and was very much frightened.
Still she thought of us, and said to herself,
'Well, if we are drowned, there will be far
more to mourn them than me,' which we
thought rather touching. On one point we
all agreed, and that was that the effort the
men had made to sing was done to reassure
me; and as a proof of how exhausted they were
with their work, when I sent up for them,
not an hour after our arrival on the Island, to

give them some whisky, they were all lying on the floor before the fire, sound asleep. My arm, with which I had held the helm, ached and trembled so for four days afterwards that I could not use it; but thank God we were safe, and in less than a week afterwards on our way to the North.

A month later I went to England with my sister, hoping things would work smoothly enough at the South to enable me to stay abroad all winter. . . . Vain hope!

# CHAPTER VI.

### FRESH DIFFICULTIES—NEGRO TRAITS—
### ABDICATION.

In December I returned to the United States
and the South, the reports I had received
of the condition of things during my absence
not being satisfactory, and they certainly did
not improve on closer examination. There
were no accounts at all at this time, but much
money spent, and what my agent had done
to set things so by the ears I never could
make out, but by the ears they undeniably
were. He had been very injudicious, and
was far too hot-tempered to manage any
people. The whole plantation was up in
arms; half the people had gone and the other
half were ready to go when I arrived, and it
was desperately hard work to restore any-

thing like order.    Even as late as the end of
January I thought I should have to give up
all idea of planting the larger Island.  I merely
put in about two hundred acres on General's
Island, but by dint of bullying, scolding, and
a little judicious compromising, I kept those
who were going and brought back some who
had left.    One man, who had been a favourite
of mine, tried to get off without seeing me ;
but, hearing he was going, I went up to his
house and asked him what he was about, to
which he replied, ' Moving, missus, but I did
not mean to let you catch me ; ' to which I
said, ' Well, I have caught you, and you can
just stop moving, for I don't intend you to
leave the place,' which settled him, and he
has been ploughing now steadily for three
days.    To-night the last man came in, and
told me he would go to work in the morning.
So now the machine is fairly started again,
and will run for the year, the getting off being
the only difficulty.

I was very unhappy about my stroke oar,

Peter Mack, who behaved so splendidly last spring in that gale on the Sound, and who had also made up his mind to leave. I did not say one word to him, thinking that the best course to pursue in his case ; but when yesterday he came in to report himself ready for work, I said, ' Well, Peter, I am glad you are going to stay. I was sorry to hear you were so anxious to leave me.' ' No, missus,' he said, ' I not so anxious to leave you, else I done gone, but if you had not come I should have gone.' This being obliged to use personal influence in every individual case was rather troublesome, and yet it was very pleasant to have them affectionate in their manner to me, and influenced by my presence into doing what I wanted.

Not being able at once to find anyone in Mr. N——'s place, I determined to try working with the negro captains alone, and endeavoured to excite their ambition and pride by telling them that everything depended upon them now, and I expected them to show me how well they could manage, and what a fine crop they would raise for me. My friend Major D——, who, after six years of failure at cotton-planting had determined to give it up, but was anxious to remain at the South, consented to take charge of the financial part of the work for me, which was a great relief to my mind, and things seemed really for a time as if they would work smoothly.

My school arrangements were not going well at all, and I soon found that the teacher I had was a very different person from what I had hoped and believed him to be. He also had got bitten with the political mania, and asked my permission to accept some small office in Darien, assessor of taxes I think it was, which would not in any way interfere with his work for me, but greatly increase his income. So I could not well refuse, although I did not like it, and it was on my first return that he asked me, before I had found out other things about him. I afterwards found that he had entirely given up teaching Sunday school, or holding any services for the people on Sunday, and when I asked him why, merely said the people and children would not attend ; then, that he had quite given up all attempts at carrying on his own studies, and was no longer reading divinity with our Darien clergyman, but instead, was mixing himself up with all the local Darien politics ; and, lastly, bore but a very indifferent character there for morality, which at first I was inclined to disbelieve, until a disastrous affair proved the correctness of the reports. But this did not happen till the following year.

Either I am right in believing the negro incapable of any high degree of intellectual training, or of being raised to a position of equality with the white race without deteriorating morally, or my experience has been very unfortunate. This man was one proof of it, another was a negro clergyman, born in one of the British Colonies, educated in an

English college, and ordained deacon by an
English Colonial bishop, so that never at any
period of his life was he affected by having
been a slave or held an inferior position. He
had a church in Savannah, and conducted
the service as he had been used to hearing it
done, which was chorally; he had a fine
voice, and chanted and intoned very well
himself, and had trained a choir of little
negroes, whom he put in surplices, extremely
well. I was much interested in all the
accounts I had heard of him, and when I
reached Savannah I went to his church, believing that at last my question of whether
a full-blooded negro was capable of moral
and intellectual elevation, was affirmatively
answered. A full-blooded African he certainly was, and was so black you could hardly
see him. The service was beautifully done,
and his part of it was well and effectively
rendered, so that I was wrought up to the
highest pitch of excitement and enthusiasm
when the sermon came, for which I had been

anxiously waiting. It was on a religious life, and from beginning to end was highflown, and mere fine talk ; and when he mentioned the 'infidel Voltaire and the licentious Earl of Rochester ' (his audience being composed, with the exception of my friend and myself, of the most ignorant and simple negroes), my enthusiasm and excitement collapsed with a crash, and I could have cried with grief and disappointment. Here were just the same old predominating negro traits—vanity, conceit, and love of showing off. About that man, too, there were stories told very unbecoming a clergyman, and though I believe none of them were ever directly proved, he lost caste generally, and later on left Savannah.

Another instance of disappointment was the son of one of our own head men, whom my sister and myself tried to have educated at the North, hoping he might become a teacher on the Island. His father is one of the best, most intelligent, and trustworthy

men I ever knew, and with much more firmness of character than the negroes generally
possess, so much so that being now our head
man he controls everything, and the gang of
Irishmen who come to us regularly every
winter obey his orders and work under him
with perfect good temper and willingness—the
only case of the sort I know ; and this man
can neither read nor write, and is totally
ignorant about everything but his work.
He comes of a good stock ; his great-grandfather was my great-grandfather's foreman,
and of his uncle, who died in 1866, my
father, then alive, writes as follows : ' It is
with very sad feelings that I write to tell
you of the death of Morris, the head man
of General's Island ; he was attacked with
fever, and died in four days. Dr. Kenan
attended him and I nursed him, but his
disease was malignant in its character, and
the medicines produced no effect. To me
his loss is irreparable ; he was by far the
most intellectual negro I have ever known

among our slaves. His sense and judgment
were those of the white race rather than the
black, and the view he took of the present
position of his race was sensible and correct.
He knew that freedom entailed self-depend-
ence and labour, not idleness, and he set an
example to those whose labours he directed
by never sparing himself in any way where
work was to be done. These qualities were
inherited; his grandfather, likewise named
Morris, was my grandfather's driver, and on
one occasion was working on that exposed
cotton tract situated on the small island
opposite St. Simon's, and in consequence of
the situation being so much exposed to the
autumn gales, which are often tropical in
their fury, no settlement was ever made on
this tract, the negroes who worked it going
over daily in boats from their houses on St.
Simon's. The only building was the hurricane house, which was constructed of sufficient strength to withstand the force of the
gales, and in one of the years—1804 I think

it was—when a terrific gale visited the coast
and the negroes were at work on this place,
old Morris, seeing signs of an approaching storm, ordered the people into that hurricane house.    They, not wishing to take
refuge there, preferred to make the attempt
of reaching St. Simon's before the storm
burst ; but old Morris, knowing that there
was no time for this, drove them with the
lash into the house, where they were hardly
secured when the storm broke, and turned
out to be one of the most terrible ever known
on the southern coast.    Of our negroes not
a life was lost, though upwards of a hundred
were drowned from a neighbouring island,
who had rushed into their boats and tried to
reach the mainland.    My grandfather, wishing to reward Morris for his praiseworthy
conduct, offered him his freedom, which,
however, he declined, as he had a wife and
family on the island, and preferred remaining.
My grandfather then presented him with a
considerable sum of money and a silver

goblet, on which was engraved the following inscription :—

TO MORRIS,

FROM

P. BUTLER,

For his faithful, judicious, and spirited conduct in
the hurricane of September 8, 1804, whereby
the lives of more than 100 persons were,
by Divine permission, saved.

'This passed to his son, also a superior man, and from him to his grandson, Morris, who possessed it at the time of his death. He left no son to succeed him, but his nephew, Sey, I think, promises to turn out a worthy descendant.'

This man, Sey, quite fulfilled my father's expectations, and was soon placed in a position of trust, from which he rose to be my foreman, the post he now holds. My sister and myself thought, therefore, that we could not do better than choose his son to be educated as a teacher, hoping that he would inherit his father's good qualities, moral and intellectual, and being glad to show our appreciation of his father in this way. We accordingly sent him to a large negro school or college in Philadelphia, which was under the direction of the Quakers, and in every way admirably managed, except that unless all the students were instructed for teachers, the course of education, which comprised Greek and Latin, algebra and trigonometry, was rather unsuited to fit them for any manual labour by which they might have to earn their bread. But this fault would apply to all American schools, I think, of this order. We made arrangements that little Abraham should lodge with the lady superintendent of the school, and nothing could have been more promising or more satisfactory than his start.

For the first six months or year everything went well, and he learnt fast. Then the reports became less and less satisfactory, until, at the end of the second year, we were requested to remove him, as he was incorrigibly bad—had broken open the teacher's

desk, and climbed over the wall and in at
the window of the school-house to steal, and
otherwise so misbehaved himself as to make
it impossible for them to keep him. I was
dreadfully sorry to have to break this news
to Sey, and I told him as gently as I could,
but he felt the disgrace of having his son
returned to him under such circumstances
most keenly.

The lad returned to the plantation, and
his father at once set him to work in the
field; but time after time he ran off, twice
stealing his father's money, until at last Sey
begged that his name might be struck from
off the books, as he himself would no longer
have anything to do with him. Of course I
don't pretend to say that having him educated
was the entire cause of his turning out so
badly, but I do believe that, had we never
taken him from the South, and he had
grown up under his father's severe and high
standard of right, he would probably have
turned out very differently. I think most likely

that he was taught and encouraged in his bad ways by the town boys, who, finding him on his first arrival a simple and easy tool to manage, made a cat's-paw of him ; for, as I told his teacher, he certainly did not learn to climb walls and break in windows on the plantation, for there were no walls to climb or windows to break open there.

Last winter, when my husband returned to the South for a short time, he found Abraham there again, at work under his father once more, having been to the North and elsewhere to look for work, but without success. I fear, however, that he was not much improved, from a story my husband told me of him. He said he was standing near the mill one day, where all the people were at work, when he saw several of the negroes running towards him, crying out, 'Crazy man !' 'crazy man !' and perceived that Abraham—now grown into a powerful, large man—was rushing after them, brandishing an axe. He was followed by his father, who was trying to disarm him, but whenever he approached near, Abraham threatened to brain him, so Sey could not get at him. He rushed past Mr. Leigh and into the mill, where the terrified women and children at work scattered in all directions ; then, going out on the wharf and throwing his arms up, made a tragical speech and prepared to jump into the river. This my husband at once called to his father and the others to let him do, and when he had taken the wild plunge, had him pulled into a boat, brought in, rubbed down, put to bed, and left to recover, which he did after a long sleep, being apparently quite well the next day. Sey's explanation was that he had trouble in his head, and had been like this before ; but whether he really did not know, or was ashamed to confess, that his son had been drinking, I do not know, but I believe that was undoubtedly the case.

There was another half-descendant of old Morris—a son of a daughter of his by a white man whom she had met while in the interior during the war. Whatever became of the father is not known, as is usually the case in such instances, and the mother dying before the end of the war, old Morris took the little boy and his sister (whose father had undoubtedly been black, for she was as black as a little coal, while Dan, the boy, showed his white blood very plainly, and was extremely pretty), and it was with Morris's widow, old Cinda, that I found the two children living when I first took charge of the place, my father having allowed all three rations. My husband, who opened a night school the first year of our return after our marriage, soon picked Dan out as a favourite and begged me to give him employment about the house, which I did. I then took him to the North for the summer, and finally brought him to England. Having when I first married brought over a negro servant who gave me a good deal of trouble, although perhaps he was hardly to be blamed for having his head turned, considering how much all the English maid-servants preferred him to a white man, and that my lady's maid finally preferred to marry him—a penchant I could neither understand nor sympathise with—I had declared I would never bring another negro over; but the desire to have one of my own people about me, Dan's youth, and my fondness for the boy, prevailed, and I brought him. He was made the greatest pet by everyone—his pretty face, gentle voice, and extreme civility making everyone his friend. The butlers at all the large houses I took him to said he was worth a dozen white boys. My own cook, who was old enough to be his mother, kept all the tit-bits and nice morsels for him, all the women servants spoilt and petted him, and I foresaw that very soon he would be utterly ruined, as no one kept him up to his work, and everyone let him do pretty much as he pleased.

I was therefore greatly surprised to have

him come to me one day and say he wished
to be sent home, as he did not like his life in
England ; the work was too hard.   I had been
scolding him for some neglect of duty the
day before, and supposed he was a little put
out and would soon get over it, as his work
was certainly not hard, although it was of
course regular, a thing I am sure a negro
finds more irksome than anything else, as
they seem to require at least half the day to
lounge.    Dan, however, never altered his
desire, although I spoke to him several times
about it, and after being over two years in
England, not only well fed and clothed, but
petted and spoilt, he returned to the plantation last winter.  The boy had so much good
in him and was so clever, besides having had
such advantages, that I could not bear to let
him go back to the South just to run wild
and go to the bad, so I had a serious talk
with him before he left, and made him promise
that he would really take up some regular
trade, and as he chose carpentering, my

husband, who took him out, apprenticed him to our head carpenter, and I have hopes of his turning out well yet. But why he preferred returning to his rough and uncomfortable plantation life after having lived on the fat of the land in England, I never have understood, unless it be that the restraints of civilised life and regular habits were irksome and disagreeable to him.

Meanwhile the winter wore on, the last I was ever to spend on the place as mistress, or rather supreme dictator, whose acts had hitherto been controlled by neither master nor partner. My last letter written before leaving is as follows :—

Butler's Island : March 1871.

Dearest M——, My little place never looked so lovely, and the negroes are behaving like angels, so that my heart is very sad at the thought of leaving ; for although I suppose I shall come back some day, it will not be for some time, and no one knows what changes may take place meanwhile, and notwithstand-

ing all the trouble I have had I do love my
home and work here so dearly. I never
worked so hard as I have this winter, but never
has my work been so satisfactory. I wrote you
in my last how well my negroes were doing
under my management, and I find the news of
my success has spread far and wide. Everyone on the river started before I did, yet now
I am far ahead of them all, being the only
planter on the river who was ready to plant
on the first tides. I began to feel a little
anxious, however, at the idea of leaving the
place entirely in charge of the negro captains
as the time for my departure drew near, and
so was greatly relieved when they came to me
a few weeks ago, and begged that I would
leave some one over them in my place when
I left, saying, ' Missus, we must have a white
man to back us when you gone ; de people
not mind what we say ; ' which is one of the
many proofs of how incapable of self government these people are, and how dependent
upon the white race for support. I therefore

looked out for an overseer to take charge of
the planting (Major D—— acting only as
my financial manager), and have engaged a
Mr. S——, formerly an overseer at Altama, of
whom both Mr. C—— and the other gentlemen on the river who know him speak very
highly in every way. He has been here
about a week now, and so far has got on very
well with the negroes, who usually try all
sorts of pranks with a new-comer to see how
much they can make out of him. He told
Major D—— yesterday that he was utterly
surprised at the condition of the place, as
never since the war had he seen one in such
good order, work so well done, and so orderly,
obedient, and civil a set of negroes.

Dear M——, don't laugh at my boasting.
I have worked so hard and cared so much
about it, that it is more to me than I can
express to know that I have succeeded.
Major D—— too has straightened out all the
accounts, so far as he can, of the past three
years, so that I now see exactly what money

has been made and what spent, and although I am not quite prepared to say that anyone has cheated me, the reckless expenditure and extravagance that has been going on, with the absolute want of conscientious responsibility shown by my agents, makes me ill to think of. However, it is all over now, thank goodness! and I can not only hope to at last make something out of the place, but leave it with a feeling of perfect security.

My people had done so well that, feeling inclined for a little amusement myself, I thought I would reward them, and so gave them a holiday one day last week, and got up a boat race between my hands and Mr. C——'s, which was great fun. The river was crowded with boats of all sizes and shapes, in the midst of which lay the two elegant little race boats, manned by six of my men and six of the Altama negroes. Splendid fellows all of them, wild with excitement and showing every tooth in their heads, they were on such a broad grin.

Major W——, who was staying with me,
steered my boat, and Mr. C—— the other,
Major D—— acting as starting judge, and at
the crack of his pistol off they started, working like men, perfectly cool and steady, rowing down the river like the wind side by side,
until they were within a few hundred feet
of the wharf which was to be the goal, and
on which Mr. C——, his son, Mrs. C——,
Admiral T——, and F—— and I were all
assembled. Then my men made a mighty
effort and shot ahead, winning by about four
seconds. We had two races afterwards, one
of which we beat, so that out of the three
we won two. It was such fun, and I wish you
could have heard the negroes afterwards,
' explaining matters.'

To-day, a poor blind woman, whose eyes
F—— and S—— sometimes bathe, said to me,
' Missus, when we meet in heaven, and dey
say to me, Tina, der's your missus, I not look
for your face, missus, for I not know dat, but
I shall look for your works, as I shall know

dem.'    I was very much touched, indeed my heart is altogether very sad, and full of love for my poor people here, and I can't bear to think that in two weeks I shall have left them for so long.    Good-bye.

Yours affectionately,

F——.

# CHAPTER VII.

## 1871, 1872, AND 1873.

ABSENTEES—A NEW MASTER—WHITE LABOURERS
—'MASSA'—'LITTLE MISSUS'—NORTHERN
IDEAS—CHURCH WORK—GOOD-BYE.

IN May of the same year I sailed for Europe,
and in June was married. I remained in
England until the autumn of 1873, when we
returned to the United States. During the
interval the accounts that reached us from the
South were not satisfactory. The expenses,
it is true, were cut down to nearly one-half
what they had been before, and the negroes
gave but little trouble, but one overseer
turned out to be very incapable and entirely
wanting in energy, making no fresh improvements and planting the same fields each
year that had been under cultivation since the

war, letting all the rest of the place grow into a complete wilderness. We also had a terrible loss during our absence in the destruction by fire of our mills and principal buildings. They were undoubtedly set on fire by one of the negroes to whom we had shown many and special favours, which had only had the effect of spoiling him to such an extent that he would not bear the slightest contradiction or fault found with his work. He had been reprimanded by the overseer and a dollar deducted from his wages for some neglect in his work, and this put him into such a passion that he refused to take his wages at all and went off, saying that it should cost us more than a dollar. This, and the fact that he was seen about the mill the morning of the fire, where he had no business to be, made us feel pretty sure that he was the incendiary, and although we never could prove it, it was a generally accepted idea that he was the man.

By this fire about fifteen thousand dollars'

worth of property was destroyed, including all our seed rice for the coming planting, and had it not been for the efforts of the Irishmen who were at work on the place, the dwelling-houses and other buildings would have gone too. The sight of a large fire seems to arouse the savage nature of the negroes ; they shout and yell and dance about like fiends, and often become possessed by an incendiary mania which results in a series of fires. They never attempt to put it out, even if it is their own property burning.

Soon after this came the news that the teacher I had left on the Island to train and educate the people, not only intellectually but morally, had turned out very badly, and had led one of my nicest young servant girls astray, which, with the other disaster, so disheartened me as to make me feel unable to struggle any longer against the fate which seemed to frustrate all my efforts either to improve the property or the condition of the people, and I said I would do no more. My husband, however, took a more practical view of the matter, and decided that as we could not abandon the property altogether we must go on working it, so he telegraphed the agent to get estimates for a new mill and to buy seed, and in fact to go on, which he did, and in course of time a new mill was built and a fresh crop planted.

In the autumn of 1873 we determined to return to America, and the agitation among the agricultural labourers in England being then at its height, I thought we might advantageously avail ourselves of the rage among them for emigration, to induce a few to go out to Butler's Island and take the place of our Irish labourers there. It seemed a capital plan, but I did not know then what poor stuff the English agricultural labourer is made of as a general rule. Eight agreed to go, and a contract was made with them for three years, by which we bound ourselves to send them back at the end of the time should they desire to come, and have in the meantime fulfilled their part of the agreement; the wages we agreed to give them were the highest given in the United States, and about three times higher than what they had received at home. As we intended to stop some little time at the North we shipped them direct to the South, where they arrived about a month before we did. On November 1 we followed, and I was most warmly greeted by all the negroes, who at once accepted my husband as 'massa.'

Our own people seemed pretty well settled, and Major D—— said gave but little trouble, the greatest improvement being in their acceptance of their wages every Saturday night without the endless disputes and arguments in which they used formerly to indulge whenever they were paid. But there were still a great many idle worthless ones hanging about Darien, and when we arrived the wharf was crowded with as dirty and demoralised a looking lot of negroes as I ever saw, and these gave the town a bad name.

Our Englishmen we found settled in the old hospital building which I had assigned to them, and which had been unoccupied since the school had been broken up, with the exception of one room which the people still used as their church. Besides this there were three others, about twenty feet square, nicely ceiled and plastered, into which I had directed the Englishmen should be put, and in *one* of these we found them all, eight men sleeping, eating, and living in the same room, from preference. They had not made the least effort to make themselves decently comfortable, and were lying upon the floor like dogs, although Major D—— had advised them to put up some bedsteads, offering the carpenter of the party lumber for the purpose, and an old negro woman to make them some straw mattresses, giving them a week to get things straight before they began their work. Two of them fell ill soon after, and then we insisted upon their dividing, half the number using one sleeping room and the rest the other, keeping the third for a general living room, kitchen, &c. At first they seemed in good spirits and well satisfied, but nothing can describe their helplessness and want of adaptability to the new and different circumstances in which they found themselves. They were like so many troublesome children, and bothered me extremely by coming to the house the whole time to ask for something or other, until at last, one Saturday evening when they came to know if I would let them have a little coffee for Sunday, as they had forgotten to buy any, the shop being only half a mile distant across the river, I flatly refused, and said they must learn to take care of themselves. One was afterwards very ill, and I really thought he would die from want of heart, as from the first moment he was taken ill he made up his mind he should not recover, and I had to nurse him like a baby, giving him his medicine and food with my own hands, and finally when he was really well, only weak, we had to insist upon his getting up and trying to move about a little, or I think he would have spent the rest of his life in bed.

To make a long story short, they soon began to get troublesome and discontented, were constantly drunk, and shirked their work so abominably, that our negro foreman Sey begged that they might not be allowed to work in the same fields with his negroes, to whom they set so bad an example, by leaving before their day's work was finished, that they demoralised his gang completely, and made them grumble at being obliged to go on with their work after the ' white men ' had left. So when the end of their second year came we were most thankful to pay their way back to England and get rid of them. All left except one, who after starting rather badly settled down and became a useful hard-working man, and is still with us as head ploughman, in which capacity he works for about eight months of the year, spending the other three or four on our

deserted cotton place, as the unhealthiness of
the rice plantation prevents his remaining
there during the summer months. During
this time he plants a good vegetable garden
for himself, spends most of his time fishing,
and is taken care of by an old negro woman,
who he assured my husband worked harder
and was worth more than any white woman
he had ever seen. But I am afraid his
experience had been unfortunate, for he was
the only married man in the party we brought
out, and his being the only one who did not
wish to return made us suspect domestic
troubles might have had something to do
with his willingness to stay.

We had for several years employed a
gang of Irish labourers to do the banking
and ditching on the Island, and although we
made no agreement with them about returning in the spring when we dismissed them,
they came down each succeeding autumn,
taking the risk of either being engaged again
by us or by some of our neighbours, and

hitherto we had always been ready to do so. But the winter we first had our Englishmen we decided not to have the additional heavy expense of the Irishmen, and so told them we did not want them. The result was that they were very indignant with the English- men, whom they regarded as usurpers and interlopers, and whose heads they threatened to break in consequence.

Major D——, half in fun, said to them, ' Why, you shouldn't hate them ; you all come from the same country.' To which Pat indig- nantly replied, ' The same country, is it ? Ah, thin, jist you put them in the ditch along wid us, and ye'll soon see if it's the same country we come from.' A test they were quite safe in proposing, for the Englishmen certainly could not hold a spade to them, and after trying the latter in the ditch we were glad enough to engage our Irishmen again, which quite satisfied them, so that after that they got on very well with their 'fellow country- men,' only occasionally indulging in a little

Irish wit at their expense. They certainly were a very different lot of men, and while the Englishmen were endless in their complaints, wants, and need of assistance, the Irishmen turned into a big barn at the upper end of the plantation, got an old negro woman to cook for them, worked well and faithfully, were perfectly satisfied, and with the exception of occasionally meeting them going home from their work of an evening when I was walking, I never should have known they were on the place.

I must record one act to their honour, for which I shall ever feel grateful. Two years after the one of which I am now writing I was very ill on the plantation, and the white woman I had taken from the North as cook was lying dangerously ill at the same time, so that the management and direction of everything fell upon my nurse, an excellent Scotchwoman, who found some difficulty in providing for all the various wants of such a sick household. The Irishmen hearing her say one day that she did not know where she should get anything that I could eat, brought her down some game they had shot for themselves, and, being told that I liked it, every Monday morning regularly, for the rest of the winter, sent me in either hares, snipe, or ducks by one of the servants, without even waiting to be thanked, the game they shot being what they themselves depended upon for helping out their scanty larder.

I felt a little anxious at first about the effect such a new life and strange surroundings might have upon my husband, for although he had seen it before, it was a very different matter merely looking at it from a visitor's point of view, and returning to live there as owner, when all the differences between it and his life and home in England would be so apparent. However, I soon found that I need not be uneasy upon that score, as he at once became deeply interested in it, and set about learning all the details of the work and peculiarities of both place and people, which he mastered in a wonderfully short time, showing a quick appreciation of the faults and mistakes in the previous system of planting which he had followed since the war, and which he very soon tried on an entirely different plan. This was so successful that in a year the yield from the place was doubled and the whole plantation bore a different aspect, much to the astonishment of our neighbours, who could not understand how an Englishman, and English parson at that, who had never seen a rice field before in his life, should suddenly become such a good planter. The negroes, after trying what sort of stuff he was made of, became very devoted to him, and one of the old men, after informing my sister some little time afterwards how much they liked him and how much good he had done them all, wound up with 'Miss Fanny (me) made a good bargain dat time.'

My husband wrote a number of letters to England from the plantation during the time we remained there, which were published in a little village magazine for the amusement of the parishioners who knew him, and which I think I cannot do better than add to this account of mine, as they will show how everything at the South struck the fresh and unbiassed mind of a foreigner who had no traditions, no old associations, and no prejudices, unless indeed unfavourable ones, to influence him.

After having spent the summer at the North, we again returned to the plantation in November, taking with us this time an addition to the family in the shape of a little three-months-old baby, who was received most warmly by the negroes, and christened at once 'Little Missus,' many of them telling me, with grins of delight, how they remembered me 'just so big.' I very soon found that the arrival of 'young missus' had advanced me to the questionable position of 'old missus,' to which however I soon became reconciled when I found how tenderly 'Little

Missus' was treated by all her devoted subjects. Oddly enough, the black faces never
seemed to frighten her, and from the first she
willingly went to the sable arms stretched
out to take her. It was a pretty sight to see
the black nurse, with her shining ebony face,
surmounted by her bright-coloured turban,
holding the little delicate white figure up
among the branches of the orange trees to
let her catch the golden fruit in her tiny
hands ; and the house was kept supplied
almost the whole winter with eggs and
chickens, brought as presents to ' Little
Missus.'

Another summer at the North and back
again to the South, from whence nothing but
good reports had reached us of both harvest
and people. Indeed our troubles of all sorts
seemed to be at an end, at least such as arose
from ' reconstruction.' It came in another
shape, however, and in January 1876 I was
taken very ill, and for five days lay at the
point of death, during which time the anxiety

and affection shown by my negroes was most profound, all work stopped, and the house was besieged day and night by anxious inquirers. My negro nurse lay on the floor outside my door all night, and the morning I was pronounced out of danger she rushed out, and throwing up her arms, exclaimed, ' My missus'll get well ; my missus'll get well ! I don't care what happens to me now.' And when at last I was able to get about once more, the expressions of thankfulness that greeted me on all sides were most touching. One woman, meeting me on the bank, flung herself full length on the ground, and catching me round the knees, exclaimed, ' Oh, tank de Lord, he spared my missus.' A man to whom something was owing for some chickens he had furnished to the house during my illness refused to take any money for them, saying when I wished to pay him, ' No, dey tell me de chickens was for my missus, and I'se so glad she's got well I don't want no money for dem.' My dear people !

Our poor old housekeeper, less fortunate than myself, did not recover, but died just as I was getting better, and in looking over her letters after her death, in order to find out where her friends lived, so as to let them know of her death, I found to my astonishment that she had been in terror of the negroes from the first, and had a perfect horror of them. Being so fond of them myself, and feeling such entire confidence in them as not even to lock the doors of the house at night, it never occurred to me that perhaps a New England woman, who had never seen more than half-a-dozen negroes together in her life, might be frightened at finding herself surrounded by two or three hundred, and it was only after her death that I found from the letters written to her by different friends at the North, in answer to hers, what her state of mind had been. There were such expressions as these : ' I don't wonder you are frightened and think you hear stealthy steps going about the house at

night.' ' How horrible to be on the Island
with all those dreadful blacks.' ' The idea of
there being only you three white people on
the Island with two hundred blacks!' &c.
She had apparently forgotten, in making her
statement, the eight Irish and six English
labourers who were living on the Island, but
still the negroes certainly did greatly outnumber the whites, and could easily have
murdered us all had they been so inclined.
But there was not the least danger then,
whatever there might have been the first year
or two after the war, and even at that time I
never felt afraid, for had there been a general
negro insurrection, although my own negroes
would of course have joined it, there were
at least a dozen, I am sure, who would have
warned me to leave the place in time.

My sister paid me a visit this winter—her
first to the South since the war, except in
1867, when she spent a month with us, but
on St. Simon's Island, where she saw little or
nothing of the negroes—and she was greatly

struck with their whole condition and demeanour, in which she said she could not perceive that freedom had made any difference. In answer to this I could only say that if she had been at the South the first three years after the war, she would have seen a great change in their deportment, but that since that they had gradually been coming back to their senses and 'their manners.'

This winter we had the pleasure of seeing a very nice church started in Darien for the negroes. For three years my husband had been holding services for them regularly on the Island in a large unoccupied room which we had fitted as a chapel; but we found this hardly large enough to accommodate outsiders, and as many wished to attend who were not our own people, we thought Darien the best place for the church. While it was being built, service was held in a large barn or warehouse, which was kindly lent for the purpose by a coloured man of considerable property and good standing in the community, who although a staunch supporter of the Presbyterian Church himself, was liberal-minded enough to lend a helping hand to his brethren of a different persuasion.

The following extract from the report of our Bishop came to me somewhat later :—

*April* 9.—Held evening service, assisted by the Rev. J. W. Leigh, of England, and the Rev. Dr. Clute. Confirmed twenty-one coloured persons, and addressed the candidates in St. Philip's Mission Chapel, Butler's Island. I desire publicly to express my thanks to the Rev. Mr. Leigh, for the faithful and efficient service he has rendered the Church in Georgia during his stay in America. He has trained the coloured people on Butler's Island in the doctrines, and has brought to bear upon them the elevating influence, of the Church, with a thoroughness and kindness which must, under God, be fraught with good to those poor people who for so many years

have been the victims of so-called religious excitements and fancied religious experiences.

*April* 11.—Held morning service, assisted
by the Rev. Dr. Clute. Preached, and confirmed six in St. Andrew's, Darien. In the
afternoon I held service for coloured people
in Darien, assisted by the Rev. Dr. Clute,
who presented seven coloured candidates for
confirmation, and the Rev. Mr. Leigh, who
presented one. After confirmation I addressed the candidates. In the evening I
held service in the Methodist Church,
assisted by the same brethren. Preached, and
confirmed three coloured persons in Darien.
The Church is taking a strong hold upon
the coloured people in Darien, as also upon
Butler's Island. The Rev. Dr. Clute had
twenty-eight candidates whom he expected
to present, but they were prevented from
coming by a storm.

Also in the appendix is added the following paragraph :—

The Rev. the Hon. J. W. Leigh, M.A., reports from Butler's Island that he has had fourteen baptisms, twenty-two candidates confirmed, twenty-nine communicants, and three marriages. It is also announced that the frame of the Chapel (St. Athanasius) for the coloured mission in Darien has been erected, and will be enclosed as soon as money can be obtained for the expense. The confirmed, as well as many candidates who were absent from the rite because of a rain-storm and change of the day of appointment, have had no opportunity to communicate.

This winter was destined to be the last I was to spend at the South, as my husband had made up his mind finally to return to his own country to live. Before leaving I had broken up my little plantation establishment, selling the principal part of the furniture, carpets, and so forth, and I consider it a significant proof of the well-to-do condition of the negroes, that the best and most expensive things were bought and paid for on the spot by negroes. The drawing-room carpet, a handsome Brussels one, was bought by a rich coloured man in Darien, the owner of a large timber mill there, a man universally respected by everyone, and, if I am not mistaken, who has for years held an official position of some importance in Darien. He was not a slave before the war, but owned slaves himself.

The following November my husband returned to the plantation for a couple of months alone, in order to settle up everything finally, before we sailed in January for England. This was the winter of the Presidential election, when our part of the country was, like every other section, violently agitated and excited by politics. But with us, while of course everyone did the best he could for his party, there was not the least ill-feeling between the blacks and the whites, and the election passed off without any trouble of any sort, which is a noteworthy fact in itself, as our county is one of the two in Georgia where the negroes outnumber the whites ten to one, and in more than one instance a negro was elected to office by the white democratic votes.

# CHAPTER VIII.

## 1877, 1878, 1879.

### OVER THE WATER.

AND now I have come to these last three years of my history, which are so much the same, and marked by so few incidents, that a few pages will suffice for them.

In the autumn of 1877, not a year after our return to England, our old friend and agent Major D—— died, and in many ways his loss was an irreparable one to us, but nothing showed the changed and improved condition of the negroes more than the fact that his death did not in the least unsettle them, and that the work went steadily on just the same. A few years before, a sort of panic would have seized them, and the idea taken possession of them that a new man would not pay them, or would work them too hard, or make new rules, &c. &c., and it would have been months before we got them quieted and settled down again. But now, although Major D—— was much liked and respected by them, as indeed he was by the whole community, Northern man though he was, and Northern soldier though he had been, they knew that whoever was put in his place would carry out the old rules, and pay them their wages as regularly as before.

In September of the year 1878 a terrible storm visited the Southern coast. The hurricane swept over the Island just in the middle of the harvest, and quite half the crop was entirely destroyed, and the rest injured. What was saved was only rescued by the most energetic and laborious efforts on the part of the negroes, who did their utmost. Day after day they did almost double their usual task, several times working right through the night, and twice all Sunday ; cheerfully and willingly, not as men who were working for wages, but as men whose heart was in their work, and who felt their interests to be the same as their employer's.

Later on in the same year my husband returned to the United States and revisited the property, but finding everything working well and satisfactorily, only remained about six weeks.

Our present manager is the son of a former neighbour of ours, whom the negroes have known from childhood, and to whose control they willingly submit. In engaging a person to manage such a property two things are necessary : first, that he should be a Southern man, because no one not brought up with the negroes can understand their peculiarities, and a Northern man, with every desire to be just and kind, invariably fails from not understanding their character. Even Major D—— felt this, although he had been so long among them, and latterly never

would take charge of any but the financial
part of the business. And secondly, the
person put over them must be a gentleman
born and bred, for they have the most
comical contempt for anyone they do not
consider ' quite the thing,' and they perceive
instinctively the difference. This I suppose
is a remnant of slave times, when there were
the masters, the slaves, and the poor white
class, regarded with utter contempt by the
negroes, who called them ' poor white trash.'
To a gentleman's rule they will submit, but
to no other, and it is useless to put a person
holding an inferior social position over them.

The only plantations near us which are
well and successfully worked, are managed
either by their old masters, or gentlemen
from the neighbourhood. We all pay wages
either weekly or monthly, finding that the
best plan now. It is far the easiest for ourselves, as well as satisfactory to the negroes,
who can't think they are cheated when everything is paid in full every Saturday night,

nor can they forget in that short time what days they have been absent or missed work. I do not believe they put by one penny out of their good wages, but they like to have a little money always in hand to spend, and much prefer this system of payments to a share in the crop or to being paid in a lump at the end of the year. I have tried all three plans, and do not hesitate to say this is the best. And so, with good management, good wages paid regularly, and no outside inter- ference, there need be no trouble whatever with Southern labour. But of the three I con- sider outside interference by far the worst evil Southern planters have to contend against.

The negroes are so like children, so un- reasoning and easily influenced, that they are led away by any promise that sounds fair, or inducement which is offered. And although I confidently assert that nowhere in the world are agricultural labourers in a better condi- tion, or better paid, than our negroes, and that though for twelve years they have been well paid, and never have known us to break our promises to them, yet I am perfectly sure that if anyone should visit Butler's Island to-morrow, absolute stranger though he might be, and promise the negroes houses, or land, or riches in Kansas or in Timbuctoo, they would leave us without a moment's hesitation, or doubt in their new friend's trustworthiness, just as my child might be tempted away from me by any stranger who promised her a new toy.    Children they are in their nature and character, and children they will remain until the end of the chapter.

> Oh, bruders, let us leave
> Dis buckra land for Hayti,
> Dah we be receive
> Grand as Lafayetty.
> Make a mighty show
> When we land from steamship,
> You'll be like Monro,
> Me like Lewis Philip.
>
> O dat equal sod,
> Who not want to go-y,
> Dah we feel no rod,
> Dah we hab no foe-y,

Dah we lib so fine,
Dah hab coach and horsey,
Ebbry day we dine,
We hab tree, four coursey.

No more our son cry sweep,
No more he play de lackey,
No more our daughters weep,
'Kase dey call dem blacky.
No more dey servants be,
No more dey scrub and cook-y,
But ebbry day we'll see
Dem read de novel book-y.

Dah we sure to make
Our daughter de fine lady,
Dat dey husbands take
'Bove de common grady ;
And perhaps our son
He rise in glory splendour,
Be like Washington,
His country's brave defender.' [1]

Put Kansas for Hayti, and 1879 for 1840, and haven't we exactly the same story ?

[1] This delightful song was composed somewhere about 1840, at the time of one of the Haytian revolutions, when the negroes, imagining that they would have no more work to do, but all be ladies and gentlemen, took the most absurd airs, and went about calling themselves by all the different distinguished names they had ever heard.

# ADDENDA.

HAVING written the foregoing pages some years ago, and having just returned from another visit to the South, after an absence of six years, I cannot refrain from adding a few words with regard to the condition of the negroes now and formerly, and their own manner of speaking of their condition as slaves. The question whether slavery is or is not a moral wrong I do not wish or intend to discuss ; but in urging the injustice of requiring labour from people to whom no wages were paid, which was formerly one of the charges brought against the masters, it seems strange that wages were always thought of as mere money payments, and the fact that the negroes were fed, clothed, and housed at their masters' expense was never taken into account as wages, although often taking more money out of the owner's pocket than if the ordinary labourers' wages had been paid in hard money. Besides these items, a doctor's services were furnished, one being paid a certain yearly salary for visiting the plantation, three times a week I think it was, and of course all medicines were given to them free of charge. They were, besides, allowed to raise poultry to sell, and chickens, eggs, and the pretty baskets they used to make often brought the industrious ones in a nice little income of their own. At Christmas all the head men received a present of money, some being as high as ten pounds, and every deserving negro was similarly rewarded.

These facts I learned accidentally in looking over the old plantation books which fell into my hands about a year ago. I also found from old letters how particular the owners

always were to have the best goods furnished for the people's clothing. The winter
material was a heavy woollen cloth called
Welsh plains, which was imported from
England, and many of the letters contained
apologies and explanations from the Liverpool firm who furnished the goods about the
quality, which had evidently been found fault
with. The character of the goods was also
confirmed by the testimony of the negroes
themselves, my housemaid saying one day
*à propos* of the heavy blankets on my bed,
' Ah, in de old time we hab blankets like dese
gib to us, but now we can only buy such poor
ones dey no good at all ; ' and another, not
one of our people, meeting us in a shop in
Darien, turned from the rather flimsy cloth
he was bargaining for, and taking hold of the
dark blue tweed of my husband's coat, said,
' Sar, ware you git dis stuff ? We used to git
dis kind before the war, but now we neber
sees it.'

Two extracts from letters written by

former agents to my great-uncle about the
negroes bear such strong testimony to the
way in which the slaves were thought of,
spoken of, and treated ' in de old time,' that
I cannot resist copying them, especially
as it was with a feeling of real pleasure
that I read them myself. One was written in
1827 and the other in 1828.

In the first the overseer writes : ' I killed
twenty-eight head of beef for the people's
Christmas dinner. I can do more with them in
this way than if all the hides of the cattle were
made into lashes !' In the other he says, ' You
justly observe that if punishment is in one
hand, reward should be in the other. There
is but one way of managing negroes, particularly with so large a gang as I have to do
with, and many of them in point of intellect
far superior to the mass of common whites
about us. A faithful distribution of rewards
and punishments, and different modes of
punishment ; not always resorting to the lash,
but confinement at home, cutting short some

privilege, and never inflicting punishment without regular trial. We save many tons of rice by giving one to each driver; it makes them active and watchful.'

So much for their treatment as slaves, and surely food, clothing, medicine and medical attendance, to say nothing of the twenty-eight head of beef killed for their Christmas dinner, might justly be regarded as wages or an equivalent for their labour. It is quite true they were not free to leave the place or choose their masters, but, until a very few years ago, were the majority of English labourers able to change their places or better their condition? Far less well off in point of food, clothing, and houses, the low wages and large families of the English labourer tied him to the soil as effectually as ever slavery did the negroes; and I doubt our slaves being willing to change places with the free English labourer of those days, had the change been offered him.

Now with regard to their own views

regarding their condition. They were always represented, and supposed to be by the Abolitionists, as pining for freedom, thirsting for education, and breaking their hearts over ill-treatment, separation from their children, and so on. Now in answer to this, which still stands as a reproach against those who ever owned slaves, I give one or two stories from the lips of the negroes themselves, and also a few facts of the present state of things *twenty* years after the emancipation of the slaves.

One of our former drivers was robbed by one of the other negroes of two hundred dollars he had laid by, and in speaking of it he said with a sigh, ' Ah, missus, in de ole time de people work all day and sleep all night, and hab no time for 'teal ; ' evidently thinking that state better than the present condition of freedom to be idle, and its natural consequence, dishonesty. Another poor old man, who had had his house burnt down and lost all his little savings, chickens,

and pigs, happened to mention that his wife
had died shortly before. I had not heard it,
and told him so, expressing my sorrow at the
same time. 'You didn't know it, missus!'
said the old man, in a tone of indignant surprise. 'Ah, tings different now from de ole
times; den if any of de people die, de ober-
seer hab to write to Massa John or Massa
Peirce, and tell 'em so-and-so's dead, but now
de people die and dey buried, and nobody
know noting about it.' Another amused
me very much by regretting that he was no
longer allowed to correct the young people
indiscriminately, and said that formerly if you
'flogged de children de parents much obliged
to you, but now de young people 'lowed to
grow up wid no principle.'

One old man, who had been sold many
years ago, had found his way back after all
this time to the old home, and was full of affectionate gratitude at being allowed once more
to see us. When I said, 'I hope you found
some of your own people left, Bristol,' he said,

' I not come to see dem, missus, I come to see my ole massa's family, and it rejoiced my heart to see you and dear little missus.'

These it may be said are the old people, but I found the young ones had just the same feeling of belonging to the same place and family as their fathers, constantly saying, when I met them off the place and did not recognise them, 'We your people, missus;' and these, many of them, were not even born in slavery, and were not working for us now.

So much for their own feeling as regards their past condition of servitude. I don't for one moment pretend that they would willingly return to slavery, any more than we would have them slaves again, but I merely give these instances to show that they did not suffer under the system or regard it with the horror they were supposed to do by all the advocates of abolition.

Now for their present moral, physical, and intellectual condition, their own people will tell you of each other, that they will not only steal money when they get the chance, but their neighbours' poultry, and in fact nearly all they can lay their hands on. Yet before the war absolute confidence was placed in their trustworthiness, and that we were justified in so doing will be seen by some stories I have told in the foregoing pages, of their faithful guardianship of our property, and even money, during the trying war times.

Formerly, the race was a most prolific one, and ten or fifteen children a common number to a family ; now two or three seem to be the usual allowance, and many of the young women at whose weddings I had assisted ten years or so ago, in answer to my question, ' Have you any children ?' would answer, ' I had ' one, two, or three, as the case might be, ' but dey all dead.' Always inclined to be immoral, they have now thrown all semblance of chastity to the winds, and when I said to my old nurse how shocked and grieved I was to find how ill-conducted the young girls were, so much worse than they used to be, she said, ' Missus, dere not one decent gal left in de place.' Their thirst for knowledge, which made young and old go to school as soon as the war was over, seems to have been quenched entirely, for, with one or two laudable exceptions, no one sends even their children to school now, and soon we shall have to introduce compulsory education. The only two negroes on the place who can write and add up accounts are the one we had educated at the North, and the one we had in England for three years. And yet it is twenty years since they were freed, and have been their own masters.

What has become of their longing for better things, and what is to become of them, poor people, ignorant and degraded as they are, and, so far as one can see, becoming more and more so ? As far as the masters are concerned, they are far better off—relieved from the terrible load of responsi-

bility which slavery entailed, and I have
always been thankful that before the property came into my hands, the slaves were
freed. But for the negroes, I cannot help
thinking things are worse than when they
were disciplined and controlled by a superior
race, notwithstanding the drawbacks to the
system, and, in some cases, grave abuses
attending it. If slavery made a Legree, it
also made an Uncle Tom.